MASTERPIECES OF THE MODERN THEATRE

A NINE VOLUME SET EDITED BY ROBERT W. CORRIGAN

CENTRAL EUROPEAN THEATRE / *The Game of Love* and *La Ronde* Schnitzler / *Electra* Hofmannsthal / *R.U.R.* Čapek / *The Play's the Thing* Molnár

ENGLISH THEATRE / *The Importance of Being Earnest* Wilde / *Major Barbara* Shaw / *Loyalties* Galsworthy / *Dear Brutus* Barrie / *Enter Solly Gold* Kops

FRENCH THEATRE / *The Parisian Woman* Becque / *Christopher Columbus* de Ghelderode / *Electra* Giraudoux / *Eurydice* (*Legend of Lovers*) Anouilh / *Queen After Death* Montherlant / *Improvisation or The Shepherd's Chameleon* Ionesco

GERMAN THEATRE / *Woyzeck* Buechner / *Maria Magdalena* Hebbel / *The Weavers* Hauptmann / *The Marquis of Keith* Wedekind / *The Caucasian Chalk Circle* Brecht

IRISH THEATRE / *The Countess Cathleen* Yeats / *The Playboy of the Western World* and *Riders to the Sea* Synge / *The Silver Tassie* and *Cock-a-Doodle Dandy* O'Casey

ITALIAN THEATRE / *Six Characters in Search of an Author* and *The Pleasure of Honesty* Pirandello / *Crime on Goat Island* Betti / *Filumena Marturano* Filippo / *The Academy* and *The Return* Fratti

RUSSIAN THEATRE / *A Month in the Country* Turgenev / *Uncle Vanya* and *The Cherry Orchard* Chekhov / *The Lower Depths* Gorky / *The Bedbug* Mayakovsky

SCANDINAVIAN THEATRE / *Hedda Gabler* Ibsen / *Miss Julie* and *The Ghost Sonata* Strindberg / *The Difficult Hour* Lagerkvist / *The Defeat* Grieg / *Anna Sophie Hedvig* Abell

SPANISH THEATRE / *The Witches' Sabbath* Benavente / *The Cradle Song* Martínez-Sierra / *The Love of Don Perlimplín and Belisa in the Garden* Lorca / *The Dream Weaver* Buero Vallejo / *Death Thrust* Sastre

MASTERPIECES OF THE MODERN ITALIAN THEATRE

🔲🔲🔲

Edited by ROBERT W. CORRIGAN

SIX PLAYS

SIX CHARACTERS IN SEARCH OF AN AUTHOR

THE PLEASURE OF HONESTY

CRIME ON GOAT ISLAND

FILUMENA MARTURANO

THE ACADEMY

THE RETURN

COLLIER BOOKS, *NEW YORK*

CONTENTS

THE CONTRADICTIONS OF
THE MODERN ITALIAN THEATRE

By Robert W. Corrigan

MOST PEOPLE, if asked what they thought about the modern Italian drama, would probably reply that they didn' know there was any. To even the most sophisticated, the Italian theatre usually means the *commedia dell' arte*, grand opera, the neo-realistic films of Rossellini, Feltrenelli, and Fellini, and—well, of course—Pirandello. In some respect this response is fairly legitimate. It is also misleading. In fact this is but the first of a series of contradictions upon which the Italian theatre is built. It has not developed a repertoire of internationally famous modern plays, but it has one of the more vital theatres of Europe. Italian theatre has a popular nonliterary tradition which puts emphasis on the actor and stage spectacle, but it has also encouraged a verbose, intellectual drama passionately devoted to such weighty philosophic concerns as appearance versus reality, the nature of identity, the meaning of time, and the possibility of salvation. It demands great inventiveness of its actors, at the same time insisting that they work within well-established conventions and with traditional character types. Like the Italian people, it has a hot and mercurial temperament, but a melodic, slow, and non-rhythmic language which is not at all suited for the expression of dramatic conflict (although it is ideal for opera). Finally, because Italy is not so much a nation as it is a loose-knit federation (it never really had its French Revolution), it has no national drama but only a number of regional acting styles. All of these conditions explain why the Italian theatre seems to have maintained strong connections with older theatrical traditions while at the same time being remarkably inventive—thus explaining why we tend to speak of the Italian theatre and not of an Italian drama.

Nowhere are these contradictions more clearly observable than in the plays of Luigi Pirandello. One does not usually think of Pirandello as part of the *commedia* tradition, and yet in each of his plays he seems to be questioning, as did the *commedia*, the capacity of words to express life's most significant realities. And it is quite clear from his essay, "The Italian Theatre," that he believed he had inherited the mantel of Machiavelli, Gozzi, and Goldoni, as well as that his theatre —like theirs—is not in the classical, literary tradition but dominated by that romantic spirit and buoyancy which characterizes the popular Italian theatre of earlier times. There is no doubt that, with the inventiveness of an actor, Pirandello uses theatrical techniques and, as in the plays of his predecessors, we do find the comedic fusion of the serious and the comic in his approach to a dramatic situation.

But that is only part of the story. Basic to Pirandello's art is an Ecclesiastical sense of disillusionment, isolation, and abandonment. His is a drama of metaphysical anguish; neither he nor his characters can derive much hope from the thought that the rest of mankind is in the same fix. All of these contradictory elements are reconciled, or at least brought into balance, when we realize that the action of a Pirandello play is one of spiritual unmasking, wherein the intellectual and the comedian join hands. In the *commedia* tradition, pain exists but is the chief source of laughter because it is never taken seriously. Pirandello uses the same comic techniques as the *commedia*, but there is one crucial difference: the pain is real. As he said in an interview given in 1924:

My friend, when someone lives, he lives and does not watch himself. Well, arrange things so he does watch himself in the act of living, a prey to his passions, by placing a mirror before him; either he will be astonished and dismayed by his own appearance and turn his eyes away so as not to see himself, or he will spit at his image in disgust, or will angrily thrust out his fist to smash it. If he was weeping he will no longer be able to do so, if he was laughing he will no longer be able to laugh. In short, there will be some manifestation of pain. This manifestation of pain is my theatre.

After Pirandello, Ugo Betti is generally regarded as the most important dramatist to write for the modern Italian theatre. In the direct manner with which he comes to grips with great moral issues, Betti is a kind of Latin Ibsen. And, as with his Scandinavian counterpart, we discover the soul

of a poet resides beneath the reserved appearance of th
stern moralist. On the surface, his plays seem to fall outsid
the wide embracing limits of the Italian popular tradition. N
so. The theme of almost all his plays is justice, and the for
tends to be more rhetorical than dramatic. But all of h
work reveals his abiding belief in the divine quality of th
human imagination and its power to create in man a sens
of dignity. It is these qualities that relate him to his fore
bears. Failure to see that the driving force of Betti's theatr
is the transforming power of the imagination will lead one—
as it has some critics—to dismiss his plays as clichés, a
well as being verbose and solemn melodramas.

While it is true that his situations and plots seem fair
stereotyped, it also must be noticed that Betti has infuse
the techniques of traditional dramaturgy with new meaning
—religious meanings. In a radio interview two years befor
his death, Betti reaffirmed his lifelong aim:

> What I would like to do in my writings would be to p
> certain individuals and certain sentiments naked and alone o
> the bottom rung of a tall ladder and see if there is in them
> and in them alone, without any help or prop, the capacity, c
> rather the necessity, to climb. To climb: that is, to love, to b
> lieve in themselves and in others; to see in life and beyond it
> harmony, a justice; to feel within themselves an immort
> destiny. To be a valid proof, this ascent of man must start ver
> low: from the lowest rung, just that. It is in the despairin
> man, the skeptic, that it is important to detect a spark of ligh
> only then will such a spark be proof of something.

Such an allegorical approach to the theatre may seem fa
removed from the braggarts, doctors, and clowns of th
commedia, but they are not unrelated. In his belief in th
power of the imagination to assert itself with generative an
regenerative force, Betti carries on one of the essential ele
ments of the Italian popular tradition. However, he does n
fit many of the patterns that most aptly describe the develop
ment of the modern Italian theatre. Betti is just there an
cannot be ignored.

Eduardo de Filippo, on the other hand, fits all the pattern
—past and present—perfectly. He is unquestionably the fulle
contemporary embodiment of the commedia spirit. Eri
Bentley's perceptive essay on Eduardo's art can be foun
elsewhere in this volume. It is only necessary to add here tha
Eduardo is best described as a capocomico, or princip
comedian, whose function is to write, direct, act, and manag

his own company at the Teatro San Ferdinando in Naples. He is a consummate artist and one of the greatest actors in the world today. His scripts are in reality little more than scenarios, skeletons which the actor Eduardo (who insists upon being called by his first name) fleshes out, mesmerizing an audience with, as Harold Acton puts it, "half a word, a pregnant pause, a light gesture, and the immobility of those features which express anguish and defeat more often than joy and success. . . ." Eduardo is probably best known in this country for writing the script for the film "Marriage, Italian Style" (based on *Filumena Martuano*), which starred Marcello Mastroianni and Sophia Loren.

Since the Second World War the Italian theatre is almost impossible to describe. Betti, who died in 1953, wrote some of his finest plays just before his death. De Filippo has achieved a belated but much deserved international fame. The Piccolo Teatro of Milan has come into being and has emerged as one of the three or four most important theatres in the world. The Italian film-makers are the most exciting now working. But where are the playwrights? Practically every country in the world has come forth with at least one major dramatist during the past twenty years—except Italy. To be sure, one can cite contemporary Italian playwrights: Diego Fabbri, Vitaliano Brancati, Enrico Bassano, Valentino Bompiani, Carlo Terron, Federico Zardi, Luigi Squarzina, even the novelist Alberto Moravia. However, their plays are not known outside of their own country, and it is hard to find reasons why they should be.

Only the unmentioned Mario Fratti seems to have that kind of international sense of theatre that guarantees performance of his work elsewhere in Europe and in the United States. But it should be noted that he is a playwright in exile, now living in New York City. The failure of Italy to produce a single dramatist of international significance since the war leads us to a final contradiction: In the essay cited above, Pirandello sees the novella and the Italian romantic tradition—traceable to Boccaccio—as the dominating spirit of his country's theatre. He is probably correct in his assessment. But if he is, it explains why the films, not the drama, have thrived in postwar Italy. There is no performing art better suited to narrative expression than the film. So, the very force that gave rise to the peculiar Italian theatrical genius may also be the cause of its present decline.

MASTERS OF THE MODERN THEATRE

By Robert W. Corrigan

AFTER VISITING the United States in 1835, Alexis de Tocqueville described the kind of literature he believed an industrialized democratic society would produce. "I am persuaded," he wrote in *Democracy in America*, "that in the end democracy diverts the imagination from all that is external to man and fixes it on man alone.... It may be foreseen in like manner that poets living in democratic times will prefer the delineation of passions and ideas to that of persons and achievements. The language, the dress, and the daily actions of men in democracies are repugnant to conceptions of the ideal.... This forces the poet constantly to search below the external surface which is palpable to the senses, in order to read the inner soul.... The destinies of mankind, man himself taken aloof from his country, and his age, and standing in the presence of Nature and of God, with his passions, his doubts, his rare prosperities and inconceivable wretchedness, will become the chief, if not the sole theme of poetry." Any examination of the arts of the past century would seem to indicate that Tocqueville's prophecy has been fulfilled, and it is certainly clear that the theatre's general pattern of development during this time can be best described as a gradual but steady shift away from universal philosophical and social concerns toward the crises and conflicts of man's inner and private life. It is possible to discover foreshadowings of this change in direction and emphasis in the plays of the early nineteenth-century romantics—Buechner, Hebbel, Kleist, Gogol, Musset—but it was not until Ibsen that the theatre's revolutionary break with the past became clearly discernible. In fact, Ibsen's career as a playwright to a large extent parallels both in form and in theme the modern drama's increasing tendency to be concerned more with the conflicts of the individual's interior world than with the significance of his public deeds.

The causes of any revolution are always as difficult to untangle as its consequences are to assess, and any attempt on the part of the critic to describe them will inevitably result in oversimplification. But it is possible to discover certain basic changes in attitude which had been evolving in Europe since the time of Luther and which had begun to crystallize in Continental thought by the second half of the nineteenth century. And the works of the revolutionary playwrights—Ibsen, Strindberg, Chekhov, Shaw, and Hauptmann—were the first to express in the theatre certain of these radical shifts in the way man had come to think of nature, society, and himself. What follows is an attempt to set forth briefly some of the more important aspects of this revolution in the drama which Ibsen referred to as "a war to the knife with the past."

One of the dominant ideas of the modern *Weltanschauung* is the belief that it is impossible to know what the world is really like. Beginning with Luther's refusal to accept that there was any intelligible relationship between faith and works, the sacramental view of experience gradually disappeared. In rejecting the phenomenal world as an outward and visible manifestation of man's spiritual condition, Luther began a revolution in thought which, because of the achievements of science and technology in the past two hundred years, now makes it impossible for man to attach any objective value to the observations of his senses. This insistence on such a clear-cut division between the physical and the spiritual aspects of reality had a profound effect on the modern dramatist. Inevitably, it made him increasingly distrustful of his sensory responses to the "outside" world, and at the same time it tended to negate whatever belief he might have had in the objective validity of his subjective feelings and sensations. The modern artist no longer holds a mirror up to nature, at least not with any confidence; he can only stare at his own image. He becomes a voyeur to his own existence.

Probably no force in the nineteenth century did more to destroy man's belief in an established norm of human nature, and hence begin this process of internalization in the theatre, than the advent of psychology as a systematized field of study. In his book *"Modernism" in The Modern Drama*, Joseph Wood Krutch argued that the basic issue confronting all the dramatists of the past hundred years was the problem of "modernism." Briefly, modernism involves both the conviction and the practice that to be modern is to be, in many important ways, different from anyone who lived before. This does not mean that man has changed; human nature is the same, but man's way of looking at himself has changed significantly. It is this new view of man that creates the problem for the dramatist.

Good examples of this changed perception can be found in Ibsen's *Hedda Gabler* (1890) and Strindberg's *Miss Julie* (1888). Hedda and Julie have the distinction of being the first fully and consciously developed neurotic heroines in dramatic literature. By neurotic we mean that they are neither logical nor insane (in the sense of being random and unaccountable) but that the aims and motives of each has a secret personal logic of their own. The significant thing about both characters is that they are motivated by the premise that there is a secret, and sometimes unconscious, world of aims and methods, a secret system of values which is more important in human experience than rational ones. This approach to character is not, however, the same as the Romantic attitude which affirms the superior validity of the nonrational. We need only read Strindberg's famous Preface to *Miss Julie* or Ibsen's working notes for *Hedda Gabler* to discover that they did not believe, as did the nineteenth-century Romantic poets, that the irrational was a supernatural and unknowable force; rather, in giving detailed account of why their heroines behaved as they did, Ibsen and Strindberg insisted that neurotic behavior and mysterious events are always explainable in terms of natural causes. The significant difference is that neither of these characters can be explained or judged by a common standard; the actions of each character (and by extension, of each human being) are explicable only in terms of that peculiar combination of forces, frustrations, and desires which is unique to himself.

For us living in the middle of the twentieth century there is nothing very new in these psychological ideas; but, coming when they did, they were quite revolutionary, and they have created problems for the playwright which have not yet been solved. By convincingly demonstrating that normal people are not as rational as they seem, and that abnormal people do not act in a random and unintelligible way, psychology has made it difficult, if not impossible, for the dramatist to present his characters in a direct way. In earlier times when it was believed that there was a sharp distinction between the sane and the insane, the irrational "aberrations" of human behavior were dramatically significant because they could be defined in terms of a commonly accepted standard of sane conduct. It seems clear, for instance, that Shakespeare believed Lear on the heath to be insane, while it is equally clear that Macbeth at the witches' cauldron was not. But for the modern dramatist deeds do not necessarily mean what they appear to mean, and in themselves they are not directly revelatory of the characters who commit them. Miss Julie, Hedda Gabler, and Kostya Treplev of Chekhov's *The Sea Gull* are all suicides; but, unlike Othello's suicide, the meaning of each of their deaths cannot be clearly ascertained from the actions that preceded it. The plight of the modern dramatist in this regard becomes apparent when we realize that without Strindberg's Preface or Ibsen's Notebook we could never know for certain what the significance of each heroine's death really was. And the ambiguity of almost every interpretation of *The Sea Gull* is largely due to the fact that Chekhov never made the meaning of Treplev's suicide explicit.

All drama of the past is based upon the axiom "By their deeds shall ye know them." The significance of the dramatic hero was revealed by his deeds, and there was a direct relationship between the hero's overt acts and his inner spiritual condition. The significance of Oedipus, for instance, is revealed by his deeds, not by some explanation that he is suffering from an Oedipus complex; and there is a direct relationship between the act of tearing out his own eyes and his solving the riddle of the Sphinx. Even when a character commits a dissembling deed, it is to deceive the other characters in the play, not the spectators. Certainly one of the chief functions of the soliloquy in Elizabethan drama was to keep the audience informed as to what was going on. Hamlet may put on an antic disposition, but not before he tells the audience he is going to do so. However, beginning in the nineteenth century, the drama began to reflect man's growing distrust in the ability of his senses to comprehend the true nature of reality. Appearances are no longer believed to be direct reflections of ideal reality, like the shadows on the wall of Plato's cave; rather they are thought of as a mask which hides or distorts reality. And by the time of Pirandello, particularly in such plays as *Right You Are, If You Think You Are*

(1916), *Six Characters in Search of an Author* (1921), and *The Mock Emperor* (*Enrico IV*) (1922), appearances not only do not express reality, they contradict it, and the meaning of these plays is not to be found in appearance or reality but in the contradiction itself.

One of the great achievements of the Elizabethan dramatic form was its ability to express several levels of experience simultaneously. The world of Hamlet is both public and private, a world in which personal and familial relationships, fantasy and mystery, and political and psychological conflict coexist in a state of constant dramatic tension. One of the main reasons why the Elizabethan dramatic form works so successfully is that appearances can be taken at face value. But when the dramatist begins to distrust the validity of his sensory perceptions, it becomes difficult, if not impossible, for him to dramatize the complex totality of experience in a single form. Reality must be broken down into its component parts, and each part can be expressed only in a form peculiar to itself. Admitting individual differences in the works of each dramatist's writing of any given period, it is nonetheless possible to describe with some accuracy the dramatic form employed by the playwrights of the fifth-century Greek theatre, the Elizabethan and Restoration theatres of England, and the French neo-classic theatre of the seventeenth century. But in discussing the modern theatre we must always speak of forms, for there is no single, dominant form in the serious theatre of the past hundred years. It is for this reason that the evolution of the drama since the time of Shakespeare has been so aptly described as a process of fragmentation.

It is likely that every serious dramatist believes it his artistic duty to be true to his presuppositions about the real nature of the world in which he lives. However, once a playwright believes that the meaning of every human action is relative and intelligible only in terms of a unique and subsurface combination of forces, the dramatic events of the plot cease to have meaning in themselves, and they take on significance only as the secret motivations of the characters who participate in them are revealed. (The technique of earlier drama is just the reverse: the motivations of the characters are revealed by the events of the plot.) But how does the dramatist objectify the hidden and unconscious, and what happens to the theatre when he feels obligated to explain and probe into his characters' hidden lives? Explanation is always a dangerous business in the theatre (since the time of the ancient Greeks, exposition has always been the dramatist's most difficult problem), but the moment a playwright assumes that if he explains his characters he has written a play, that danger becomes mortal. All too often the writers of the modern theatre have forgotten that a dramatic situation requires not that we *understand* a character but simply that we *believe* in him. Dramatic action always leads to a judgment; it requires that something shall happen to and through the characters; something that is embodied in the events of which the characters are a part. Whenever the personality of the character, rather than the action of which the character should be a part, becomes the playwright's chief concern, dramatic process dissolves into explanation, and when that occurs, the range of the theatre is drastically reduced, if not unalterably damaged.

One has only to compare the plays of the mid-twentieth century to those of Ibsen, Shaw, or Strindberg to realize just how much the scope of the theatre has been narrowed. However, early evidence of the gradual loss of belief in dramatic heroes, who needed no explaining, can be found in the sentimental bourgeois drama of the eighteenth century. For the first time a character was no longer noble, responsible, or morally significant, and therefore dramatically interesting just because of his birth, position, power, or wealth. As a result, the dramatist was obliged to justify both his choice of characters and the situations in which they are engaged. The Romantic drama of the eighteenth and nineteenth centuries resisted a break with the past and attempted unsuccessfully to perpetuate the forms and figures of earlier times. Certainly the revolt of Ibsen and his contemporaries in the last quarter of the nineteenth century was in some measure due to their conviction that the dramatic conflicts of the Romantic drama were inflated and without significance, and that the nobility of its characters was artificial and contrived. In rejecting the artificialities of Romanticism, the modernists changed the theatre in many ways; but for all their dissatisfaction with their predecessors they were unable to forestall disbelief in the possibility of heroic characters who needed no explaining.

This was largely because as a literary movement nineteenth-century naturalism was so closely related to nineteenth-century biology. Darwin's theories of evolution (*Origin of Species*, 1859) and the discovery of new genetic laws had convinced many writers that man's existence, including his personality, was a phenomenon that could be explained in terms of scientific laws. As a result, increasingly, man's complex biological needs rather than his capacity to make moral choices were thought to be his most significant characteristic. Once such a view was accepted, however, the exceptional man, who because of his position and power had the greatest freedom of choice, ceased to be the fullest embodiment, and therefore the best representative, of those conflicts and choices that most clearly define the human condition. Instead, the lives of the poor—where the role of natural necessity is most readily observable—became the playwright's most suitable subjects. The drama of the common man, then, did not happen by accident, nor did it evolve because some dramatist or group of dramatists wanted it to. Given the problem of creating in a world in which all human actions tend to be explained in terms of psychological or sociological cause and effect, a world in which the possibility of deliberative and moral choice is doubted if not rejected outright, it is difficult, if not impossible, for the playwright to fashion a character of traditional heroic stature.

There is an old saw about no man being a hero to his valet. Neither is he one to his psychoanalyst. Nor can he be one to a playwright who views his actions as behavioral phenomena explicable in terms of some kind of laws—scientific or otherwise. Oedipus, for example, remains a hero of great stature so long as he is not suffering from an Oedipus complex. But once we learn to explain him in terms of repressed hopes and fears, traumatic childhood experience, or a vitamin deficiency in infancy, although he may remain interesting—in fact he may gain a new kind of interest, as Cocteau's *The Infernal Machine* attests—he loses stature. Even if we are able temporarily to accept the Elizabethan attitude toward heroes, which of us can understand a Hamlet or a Lear? And which of us can forgive an Othello or a Macbeth? But it is precisely because they seem mysteriously beyond our powers of understanding that they remain heroes for us. And it is a belief in a mysterious, unknowable quality in men that substantiates man's sense of his own importance in the universe. However, if a playwright comes to believe that all human actions are in reality predictable behavioral responses, and his moral judgments of these actions can be dissolved by psychological understanding, how can he pattern a tragedy or create characters with stature? If there an be no possibility for an appraisal of personality as such, why should Hamlet's death be any more significant than that of Rosencrantz and Guildenstern?

But the problem does not end here. For once the dramatist dismisses the possibility of passing moral judgments on his characters' actions, he comes face to face with an even more frightening spectre—guilt that has no form of expiation and thus turns into anxiety. It has long been known that art must ultimately fail in its attempt to come to grips with the facts of death. Perhaps this is also true of anxiety. How can there be drama in an Age of Anxiety? What kind of play will be produced when the central conflict is between something and nothing? Many of the arts may be able to express the condition of anxiety; but the theatre, because of the objective reality and irremovable presence of the living actor, and because the drama is essentially an embodiment of the conflict between at least two opposing recognizable and nameble forces, is incapable of dealing with anxiety, or it does so to its own great peril. Beginning with the Watchman in the opening scene of the *Orestia* right on through the ghosts of Elsinore and the tormented heroes of Schiller and Kleist, the theatre has always found a way to transform anxiety into fear; that is, give it a definite object. But when we come to such plays as Ibsen's *Ghosts* and *The Master Builder* and Strindberg's *There Are Crimes and Crimes*, and *The Ghost Sonata*, we discover that although this process of objectification is attempted, it is not totally successful. And when the transformation does not take place, the form and content of drama begin to change in uncontrollable ways, as some of the plays of Beckett and Ionesco, Pinter and Albee will attest. It is difficult enough to find a meaning for man in a world that views a return to nothingness as the ultimate reality, but it is next to impossible to create a dramatic "action" which can encompass the terror of being on the edge of the abyss. Kierkegaard, and more recently Paul Tillich, have declared that this threat of nothingness is the central anxiety of modern man. Many modern playwrights have sought to overcome the despair of this situation by maintaining that the only meaning of life is to be found in that death which is inevitable. But this is not an assertion that gives meaning to any of the particularities of life; in fact, it drains them of meaning. At best, it is a method of redeeming existence from meaningless anarchy by showing that the pattern of life is simple and imperturbable. But such a pattern, though it may appear to conquer chaos, is too abstract to live successfully in the theatre.

In life as we experience it, we are conscious of our physical natures, our social situation, and our unique psychic existence; and we live on all three of these levels simultaneously. For this reason it is impossible for us to act or make a choice without some element of human behavior—what we do out of physical necessity or because of social habit—playing a significant role in our decision. At the same time, because of the simultaneity of our being, it is impossible for us to understand completely the individuality of our actions. But in the theatre we see life as pure deed, that is, life in which the arbitrariness of human behavior has been eliminated and in which the mysterious transformations of individuality have been fixed. Thus, in contrast to a person in life, who is recognized by the continuity of his being and finally can be known only through intuition, a character in a play is an identity who is defined by the coherence of his acts. For this reason the deeds of a dramatic action are always public, and the characters best suited to drama are men and women who, either by fate or choice, lead a public life and whose deeds are of public concern. This explains why kings, princes, and nobility have traditionally been the most suitable subjects for drama. But as the increasing dominance of the machine in modern life has gradually destroyed the direct relation between a man's intention and his deeds, public figures have ceased to be our most appropriate heroes because, as W. H. Auden points out, "the good and evil they do depends less upon their characters and intentions than upon the quantity of impersonal force at their disposal."

Our world, it would seem, has become almost too big for the playwright. Power is too impersonal, great deeds are collective achievements, and the great man is one who is capable of withstanding some of the pressures of a mass society and manages, somehow, to maintain a face and stance more or less his own. Compare, for example, the achievement of a Lindbergh (our last "lone" hero) to that of a Colonel Glenn, who was interchangeable with five other astronauts. Or, how can the power of a Napoleon be envisioned today? In our times power is so enormous that it is barely visible and those who govern are little more than incidental and easily replaceable expressions of that power. Power is like an iceberg; the largest part is submerged—it bstraction, anonymity, and bureaucracy. Government, like modern physics, has lost its physical reality and can be expressed only in statistics and formulae. Indeed, the true men of action in our time, those who transform the world, are not the statesmen and politicians but the scientists. Unfortunately, their most significant actions are not suitable subjects for the theatre, because their deeds are concerned with things, not people, and are, therefore, speechless.

But what are the implications of this for the theatre? Who are the true representatives of a world whose heroes are nameless? As the Swiss playwright Duerrenmatt put it: "Any small-time crook, petty government official, or policeman better represents our world than a senator or president. Today art can only embrace victims if it can reach men at all; it can no longer come close to the mighty. Creon's secretaries close Antigone's case."

That there has been a shift in attitude toward the heroic is easily seen when we examine any one of the many modern adaptations of the Greek tragedies. For example, today most people find Anouilh's *Antigone* much more a reflection of their attitudes and thus more immediately interesting than Sophocles' tragic working of the theme. The characters and the dilemma of their situation seem more human. Antigone is not a hard and almost inhuman girl, with such a monomaniacal fixity of purpose that she rejects all other feelings and desires. In the modern version she is, humanly, both weak and strong. She has a lover in Haemon, whom she rejects; but she is also a helpless little girl who runs to "Nanny" for comfort and strength; as she approaches death, she is afraid and seeks the consolations of even the most callous of guards. Creon is not a blind and power-mad tyrant; he is a businessman king who is caught in the complex web of compromise and expediency which will not allow abstract moral principles to upset the business of government.

However, what the play gains in humanity it loses in tragic force. The sense of Antigone's aloneness and Creon's moral blindness, and of the inevitable destruction implicit in their conflict, has been softened. Anouilh's Antigone is not alone and unloved, and his Creon is not blind. We pity their situation because they are two quite attractive people caught up in a situation which neither of them likes but which they cannot control. They are victims in a disordered world which they have not created and which they have no moral obligation to correct. As the play ends, we are left with an ambiguity that allows for no reconciliation.

One of the most important functions of the hero, both in art and life, is to supply those images, values, and ethical standards which people aspire to and which they would like, if possible, to incorporate into their own lives. It would seem, however, that increasingly our modern industrialized society not only does not need heroes, but it actually suppresses or perverts our need of them. In their important book *Industrialism and Industrial Man*, Kerr, Dunlop, Harbison, and Myers convincingly demonstrate that "like ideologies, the great personality—the one great figure around whom historians so frequently weave their story—began to seem less important. Instead of ideologies and dominant personalities, we became increasingly attentive to the inherent nature of the particular industrializing system and the basic strategy and forces at work within it." Only the system, then, is important, and it fills men's remaining need for heroes by promoting celebrities, those heroes of the surface who play well their constantly shifting roles.

Furthermore, specialization—the key operative principle of an industrial society—produces not only pluralism in our economic system but also a pluralistic deviation of heroic types. However, when there are and can be so many heroic types—one cannot even begin to count all the heroes of the popular imagination—you begin to get a leveling; and with that leveling not only is the stature of heroism diminished but the individual's sense of his own identity is actually invalidated.

Traditionally, the hero is always best described in terms of those forces that urge him to spiritual redemption. Maxwell Anderson once wrote that "from the point of view of the playwright, the essence of a tragedy, or even a serious play, is the spiritual awakening, or regeneration, of his hero." But the one thing that characterizes the hero of surfaces—and this is certainly in large measure due to industrialization and bureaucracy—is precisely the fact that he lacks the dimensions of spiritual awareness, personal morality, and social responsibility. Paul Tillich wrote in his *The Religious Situation* that "the fundamental value in ethics of a capitalistic society is economic efficiency—developed to the utmost degree of ruthless activity." Such an ethical standard is hardly conducive to the creation of great heroes in the drama

That we live in an antiheroic age is a commonplace. Carlyle proclaimed its coming in the nineteenth century when he said: "We shall either learn to know a hero . . . when we see him, or else go on to be forever governed by the unheroic." This transformation has occurred; we have accepted it; we are even used to it. Whatever nostalgia we may still occasionally feel is more than adequately taken care of by television. In the place of the hero we have the celebrity, that triumph of the ordinary. In our time, hero worship has become horizontal; indeed, we even look down to a "man like myself."

While the advent of psychology as a systematized field of study may have been the most powerful single force to shape the modern theatre, actually the process of internalization had begun much earlier. For instance, it is clear from Hebbel's essays on the drama that the despair of old Anton's "I don't understand the world any more" in the final scene of *Maria Magdalena* is much more than an expression of the age-old frustration of the parent who does not understand the behavior of his children. It also reflects his dimly understood but tremendously painful realization that it is no longer possible for him to comprehend what the world has become or to imagine what the future will be like. Until the Industrial Revolution, patterns of life were passed on from father to son with the confidence that these patterns would satisfy the needs and desires of each new generation. Such confidence was justified, for life changed so gradually and imperceptibly that when changes did occur they were easily assimilated into the shared life of the community. But by the middle of the nineteenth century the effects of the Industrial Revolution had begun to be felt on all levels of society. Technology, with its ever increasing capacity to transform man's way of living, not only made the future so unpredictable that it soon became impossible for him to imagine what his life would be like twenty years hence, but in its singular concern with the individual's functional qualities technology tended to isolate him from his fellows and invalidate his spiritual values and metaphysical concerns. At the same time, the discoveries of the nineteenth-century archeologists, and the ensuing interest in anthropology, tended to break down provincial and absolutist attitudes concerning human nature. Early anthropologists like Mannhardt, Robertson-Smith, Tylor, and the great James Frazer made it clear that human nature was not something fixed and unchanging but only that kind of behavior exhibited in each culture. In fact, as early as 1860 scholars were demonstrating that human nature is so plastic that it can, as Frazer was later to point out in the Preface to the first edition of *The Golden Bough* (1890), "exhibit varieties of behavior which, in the animal Kingdom could only be exhibited by different species." Furthermore, by the middle of the century, democracy was finally beginning to be established both as a way of life and as a form of government. Today we tend to forget what a revolutionary idea democracy is and the shattering effects that it had upon the values of eighteenth- and nineteenth-century Europe. Alexis de Tocqueville told us long ago: "Not only does democracy make every man forget his ancestors, but it hides his descendants and separates his contemporaries from him, it throws him back forever upon himself alone and threatens in the end to confine him entirely within the solitude of his own heart." In short, by the middle of the nineteenth century every established view of God, human nature, social organization, and the physical universe was beginning to be seriously challenged if not invalidated. And this revolutionary climate had a profound effect on the theatre.

Of all the arts, theatre is the only art that has always concerned itself with human destinies. Dramatic action is historical in the sense that the perpetual present of each moment on the stage is created out of past events and is directed toward a definite, if yet unknown, future. In previous ages the destiny of any dramatic action was significant because the ever-changing events in the lives of dramatic heroes could be meaningfully related to eternity, that is, to some permanent value or idea such as Fate, the Gods, or Heaven and Hell, which transcends the human condition and which is believed in by the dramatist and/or his audience.

In the plays of Buechner and Hebbel we discover the first indications in the theatre of that sense of alienation from both God and Society which underscores the fact that man's belief in eternity had been shaken. And one of the most significant aspects of Ibsen's work (at least after *Peer Gynt* 1867) is the fact that the realm of ultimate value has either disappeared or has become so mysterious that it has ceased to have dramatic relevance. In its place we find instead a belief in some form of social ideal or societal structure:

irst, as the agent of some unknown Destiny, and then as Destiny itself. But when society begins to assume the role of Destiny, that is, is thought of as the determining force for good or evil in the lives of men, man cannot help but feel eventually that the meaning of his Destiny has been drastically reduced. For Society, as Robert Bolt writes in the Preface to his *A Man for All Seasons,* "can only have as much idea as we have what we are about, for it has only our brains to think with. And the individual who tries to plot his position by reference to our society finds no fixed points, but only the vaunted absence of them, 'freedom' and 'opportunity'; freedom for what, opportunity to do what, is nowhere indicated. The only positive he is given is 'get and spend' . . . and he did not need society to tell him that. In other words we are thrown back by our society upon ourselves, which of course sends us flying back to society with all the force of rebound."

Any mind capable of spiritual aspiration seeks in the actions of the dramatic hero that which affirms the vitality of the free will in any given situation. Man's free will may be defeated by the forces of Destiny—in fact, the great plays have always testified that the destroying forces of Destiny are as much a part of the hero's character as his free will; it may be paralyzed and thus incapable of action; it may be submerged by the battle in such a way as to become part of that Destiny; it may even turn out to be an illusion; but it must always be an active force if we are to believe that we are partaking in human greatness. Such a Destiny must be greater than an aggregate of human beings or an expression of social patterns.

Ironically, the revolt of Ibsen and Shaw against the conventional nineteenth-century drama was motivated by a desire to enlarge the range of Destiny in the theatre. In their attempts to present man in his total historical and social setting, they were rebelling against the narrow and private worlds that had been dominating the stage since the Restoration. But in spite of their efforts, nothing could change the fact that in the two hundred years since Shakespeare the world of the spirit had greatly diminished. The Ekdals' attic and Mrs. Warren's drawing room were not—and never could be—the same as Elsinore or Cleopatra's barge.

Nonetheless, the pioneers of the modern drama had revitalized the theatre precisely because they believed that

significant social issues should be dealt with in the theatre
Thus for nearly three decades the theatre had a vitality o
spirit and a forcefulness of manner which it had lacked fo
more than a century for the very reason that its contex
had been reduced. To the playwright writing at that time th
human and social problems, which were the source ma
terials of the naturalistic play, appeared capable of solutio
if only man and society would learn to use their commo
sense; which usually meant one of two things—the acceptanc
of a less rigid standard of social morality or the espousal o
some form of socialism. But with the collapse of the es
tablished social order in the first World War, the validit
of these too-easy solutions was impugned, and beginning wit
the plays of the early German Expressionists (written 1912-
1916) the positive optimism of the Edwardian era gav
way to a sense of bewilderment, exasperation, and defeat
ism, only occasionally tempered by the slim hope that th
war had brought man to the threshold of a "New Age." Th
theatre reflects these changes from confidence to doubtin
and despair, from complacent faith in cherished values to a
anxious questioning, from a rigorous but rigid morality t
the mystic evangelism, the fanatical polemics, and the frivo
lous apathy of a disintegrating world. These changes ar
most apparent in the Jekyll and Hyde theatre of the Ger
man Expressionists whose nerve-shattered playwrights alter
nated between a militant idealism and grotesque nightmares
But one need only compare Shaw's *Heartbreak House* t
Major Barbara, Pirandello's *Right You Are, If You Thin*
You Are to *Liolá*, or Hauptmann's *Winter Ballad* to *Th*
Weavers to realize that the effects of the collapse of the ol
order were widespread and were reflected in the works o
established writers as well as those of the new generation
Immediately after the war the theatre on the continent wa
dominated by attitudes of emotionalism and cynicism, bu
these gradually gave way to feelings of frustration, futilit
and despair, and by the middle of the 1920's the seriou
drama of Europe had become almost totally introspectiv
and psychological in its orientation.[1]

[1] Because they were essentially isolated from the main currents of Euro
pean history in the first two decades of the century, the Irish and America
theatres were not immediately effected by the spreading paralysis which wa
transforming the rest of modern drama. But it is clear from O'Casey's *Th*
Plow and the Stars (1926) and *The Silver Tassie* (1927) that the Abbe
Theatre could not withstand for long the theatre's introspective tendencie

Obviously, this tendency toward paralyzing introspection has by no means been accepted by everyone writing for the theatre. In fact, a large segment of the modern theatre might be best described as a reaction against the despair and dehumanizing implications of the modernist position. These "resistance movements" have sought to discover the means, both formal and substantive, whereby the possibility and validity of selfhood and human integrity, personal responsibility, and morally significant judgments could be reasserted in the theatre. Some playwrights—especially Eliot, Fry, Betti, and Claudel—have turned to orthodox Christian belief to provide a metaphysical structure for their drama. Others, like Lorca and Synge, have written out of the traditions and value systems of premodern hieratic societies. Probably the largest group of all is composed of those dramatists who have sought to escape the deadly strictures of modernism by turning to classical mythology.

All of these writers shared one common and fundamental attitude: each of them was in some way rebelling against the conditions of the modern world. They were not only conscious of that lack of a sense of community which inevitably occurs in an increasingly democratic society; more important, they were aware of man's growing sense of his own isolation. The modern world, with its growing collectivism, paradoxically tends to throw man back upon himself, while at the same time it increasingly tends to destroy the individual's sense of his own selfhood. This creates an impasse which the modern dramatist, for the most part, has been unable to overcome.

Joseph Warren Beach, in analyzing the problems of modern fiction, describes the reaction of many writers to this condition in this way: "One of the hardest things for man to bear is spiritual isolation. The sense that he stands alone in the universe goes terribly against his gregarious instincts. He has an over-powering impulse to construct a system which will enable him to feel that he does not stand alone but is intimately associated with some force or group infinitely

---

and there was no serious American drama until O'Neill's plays were first produced right after the war. In the twenty years between O'Neill's *Beyond the Horizon* (1920) and *The Iceman Cometh* (1941) the American theatre repeated the Continental cycle in its own terms, and by the beginning of the Second World War all of the Western theatre had reached that No Man's Land between comedy and tragedy, between pathetic aspirations and ridiculous bewilderment, between never-beginning action and never-ending talk.

more powerful and significant than himself." It is clearly evident in the work of all those playwrights who have rebelled against modernism that they too are seeking to construct a system that will restore meaning to life and validity to art. In the end, however, they have not been completely successful, because they have all too often had to deny the realities of the modern world in the process. Furthermore, they have not accepted the wisdom of Brecht's statement that "when one sees that our world of today no longer fits into the drama, then it is merely that the drama no longer fits into the world." By insisting upon values that we may once have cherished but which no longer in actuality exist, the playwrights of the resistance have not been able to revitalize the theatre or it's audiences. And most important, they have not succeeded in stretching the imaginations of men in order that they might conquer that sense of isolation and despair that pervades the modern world. And this brings us to the playwrights of the mid-twentieth century.

In an age dominated by space orbits and telestars, the fear of nuclear war, the tension of cold war diplomacy, and the insecurity of a defense economy, our greatest uncertainty is whether or not in the midst of epochal disorder man has any good chance, to borrow Faulkner's phrase, of prevailing; and if he does, what kind of man will prevail?

This uncertainty has had a profound effect on our theatre, and if there is one thing that characterizes the work of almost all of our serious playwrights of the last two decades it is that their plays express the contemporary theatre's tremendous concern to find a metaphor for universal modern man as he lives on the brink of disaster—a metaphor that expresses the inalienable part of every man, that irreducible part of each of us that exists after all the differences have been stripped away and which is beyond and beneath all that is social, political, economic, religious, and ideological. In short, they are searching for a metaphor of man left face to face with himself.

Such an idea of the theatre has tremendous implications for the drama, and we are just now becoming aware of them. First of all, it abolishes the traditional linear plot because our contemporary playwrights are not interested in presenting an action in any Aristotelian sense but are, rather, dramatizing a condition. Whenever one asks what the central action of a Beckett, Ionesco, or Pinter play is, he comes a cropper; "action" for the contemporary playwright is an artificial concept. He is concerned with showing life as it is, and in life there is no central action, there are only people, and the only thing that is basic to each individual is the ontological solitude of his being. The dramatist's only concern is to create in his plays a situation which will reveal the private drama that each man has inside himself and which is enacted every day in the random, apparently meaningless, and undramatic events of our common routine. "History," said James Joyce's Stephen Daedalus, "is a nightmare from which I must awake." The rapidity of historical change and the apparent powerlessness of the individual to affect Collective History has led in the theatre to a retreat from history. Instead of tracing the history of an individual who is born, grows old, and dies, many modern playwrights have devoted their attention to the timeless passionate moments of life, to states of being. They want to express the paradox, the contradiction, and the incompleteness of experience. They are attempting to suggest the raggedness, the confusion, the complexity of motivation, the "discontinuous continuity," and the basic ambiguity of all human behavior. They are, in short, pursuing the premises of modernism to their fullest and most logical conclusions. The writers of the contemporary theatre are facing the "facts of life." If the dramatic meaning of their plays is that drama is no longer possible, they would contend that any other meaning would be artificial, illusory, false; if the dialogue in their plays consists of meaningless clichés and stereotyped phrases, they would insist that this is the way we talk; if their characters are constantly changing their personalities, these playwrights would point out that no one today is really consistent or truly integrated. If the people in their plays seem to be helpless puppets without any will of their own, they would argue that we are all passively at the mercy of blind fate and meaningless circumstance. They call their theatre "Anti-Theatre," and this they insist is the true theatre of our times. If they are correct, so be it! Then history has again followed its own inexorable laws. The very forces that gave life and strength to the modern theatre have caused its decline and death.

But the theatre is always dying, and with equal regularity, like the phoenix, it is resurrected. No one can say with certainty what its new form will be, but that there will be a future seems certain. First, largely because of the development of college and university theatre programs in this country and the large increase in the number of professional repertory theatres here and abroad, there are more people who have experienced good theatre than ever before. And this enlarged audience wants and needs theatre, and it will not be satisfied for long with the maimed rites of psychological and moral cliché, or impassioned jeremiads from prophets of doom, or the meandering contemplations of writers who are morbidly consumed in introspection and self-analysis. Fortunately, there are audiences who want and need the theatre, and they go to the theatre in the hopeful anticipation that the stage will be capable of accommodating all of the terrible-wonderful emotions and insoluble dilemmas of our shared life together. This demand insistence by audiences on a drama that deals with the significant issues and concerns of our public life will, I believe, force our playwrights to open up new frontiers in the drama and thus extend the boundaries of the theatre. The second great hope of the theatre is that, in spite of the overriding temper of despair and the dominance of antitheatricality in current drama, our playwrights still find human action significant, still find it necessary to write plays, and, in the very act of writing, attest to the miracle of life. We live in one of the most dramatic ages in the history of mankind, and if the past is any kind of reliable guide to what the future of the theatre will be, we have good reason to believe that the theatre of tomorrow can be as dramatic as the world in which we live today.

MASTERPIECES OF THE

MODERN ITALIAN THEATRE

LUIGI PIRANDELLO

1867–1936

LUIGI PIRANDELLO was the master of the modern Italian theatre, and no dramatist brought the intellectual and emotional unrest of post-World War I European society to the stage with more originality or excitement than this great experimenter, who was, appropriately, born in the Sicilian town of Chaos. In all his plays written after he left Sicily, Pirandello inverts the central convention of modern dramaturgy: instead of pretending that the stage is not a stage but a living room, he insists that the living room is not a living room but is really a stage. In short, Pirandello saw all human life as theatrical; people are characters who act out a series of continually shifting roles in the myriad dramas of life. In addition to his theatricality, Pirandello's significant contribution to modern drama was the development of a dramatic form capable of expressing the drama of ideas in a theatrically exciting way. All his characters in some way struggled between their own private individuality and the public pressures exerted by the society in which they lived. No one has given form to this typically Italian struggle between private anarchy and the strict rules of the community more effectively than Pirandello. He saw the inconsistency of everything, and man's life as a futile grasping at the unattainable. But for all his concern for ideas, Pirandello did not have any answers. His theatre has been called *il teatro dello specchio,* the mirror theatre, but it is a mirror that gives a grotesque reflection of life. Like the mirrors of a fun house in an amusement park or Alice's looking glass, it shows a queerly logical yet irrational world behind the mirror—a world in which reality has been reduced to an illusion. But in this illusion lies the only true reality. At first this philosophical mirror world tends to confuse us, but before long we are chiefly conscious not of ideas but of great human suffering. In his preface to *Six Characters,* Pirandello tells us that he is not representing people just for the sake of representing them, but because of their universal significance.

THE NEW THEATRE AND THE OLD[1]

By Luigi Pirandello

YOU MAY BE familiar with the anecdote of the poor peasant who, when he heard his parish priest say that he could not read because he had left his glasses at home, spurred his wit and conceived the fancy idea that knowing how to read depended upon having a pair of eyeglasses. Consequently, he journeyed to the city and went to an optometrist's shop and demanded "Glasses for reading."

But since no pair of glasses succeeded in making the poor man read, the optometrist, at the end of his patience, after having turned his shop upside down, snarled, "But, tell me, can you read?" Amazed at this, the peasant answered, "That's a good one, and if I knew how to read, why would I have come to you?"

Well, now, all those who have neither a thought or feeling of their own to express, and think that to compose a comedy, a drama, or even a tragedy it is enough to write an imitation of someone else, should have the courage and the frankness of naive wonder of this poor peasant.

To the question, "But really, have you something of your own to tell us?" they should have the courage and the frankness to answer "That's a good one! And if we had something of our own to say, would we write like someone else?"

But I realize that this might really be asking too much.

Maybe it would be enough that all these persons should not become so angry when somebody calmly points out that while it is true that no one forbids them the exercise of writ-

[1] "Teatro Nuovo e Teatro Vecchio" ("The New Theatre and the Old") by Luigi Pirandello is from *Saggi, Poesie e Scritti Varii*, edited by Manlio Lo Vecchio-Musti. © Arnoldo Mondadori Editore 1960. The translation by Herbert Goldstone is from *The Creative Vision: Modern European Writers on Their Art*, Edited by Haskell M. Block and Herbert Salinger, Published by Grove Press, Inc., Copyright © by Grove Press, Inc., 1960.

ing and rewriting a theatre already written, doing this means that they do not have eyes of their own but a pair of borrowed glasses.

It has been said and repeated that, in general, the imitative or decorative faculty in the nature of the Latin character is superior to the creative or inventive, and that the whole history of our theatre, and in general of our literature, is fundamentally nothing but a perpetual repetition of imitated manners; and that, looking at our literary history, we certainly find very many glasses, and very few eyes, and that our writers did not disdain glasses but were proud to use ancient lenses to see in the manner of Plautus or Terence or Seneca, who in their turn had seen in the manner of the Greek tragedies, Menander, and of middle Athenian comedy. But these—shall we say—visual aids were at least made at home from rhetoric which always came from our own optometrist shop; and these glasses passed from one nose to another, through generations and generations of noses, until suddenly, with the rise of Romanticism, the cry was raised, "Gentlemen, let us try to look with our own eyes." They tried; but alas, they were able to see very little. And the importation of foreign glasses began.

An old story. And I should not have mentioned it if, truly, things had not everywhere reached such a state that to obtain public favor it is not necessary to have a pair of one's own eyes, as to have a pair of someone else's eyeglasses, which make you see men and life in a certain manner and with a given color, that is, as fashion urges or current public taste commands. And woe to whoever disdains or refuses to put them on his nose, or who is obstinate enough to want to look at men and life in his own way; his vision, if simple, will be called bare; if sincere, vulgar; if intimate and acute, obscure and paradoxical; and the natural expression of this new world will always appear filled with the greatest defects.

I will speak again of these defects. The greatest and best known has been in every age that of "writing badly." It is distressing to acknowledge it, but all the original visions of life are always badly expressed. At least they were always so judged at their first appearance, especially by that plague of society, the so-called cultivated and nice people.

Recently I have much enjoyed reading a piece of Clive Bell[2] attacking these same people. Here and there, he says, a man

[2] Twentieth-century British art critic and aesthetician.

of powerful intellect is able to succeed in forcing the gates; but cultivated people do not like originality, not as long as it looks original. The company of the man of original talent is not pleasant, at least not until he is dead. Cultivated people adore whoever gives them, in some unsuspected way, just what they have learned to expect, and, fundamentally, they do not like art any more than do the Philistines; except that they want to have the sensation of seeing the old cloaked in the new; and, for that reason, they prefer those pastry cooks who sprinkle a little art on their common thoughts and feelings. Because of this, culture (so understood) is even more dangerous than Philistinism: it pretends to be on the side of the artist; it has the "charm" of its exquisite taste, yet it can corrupt because it can speak with an authority denied the Philistines; and because it feigns an interest in art, often the artists are not indifferent to its judgments. It is necessary, therefore, to free the artist and also the public from the influence of the opinion of the cultivated. And the liberation will not be complete until those who have already learned to scorn the opinion of the petty bourgeoisie will also learn to ignore the disapproval of people constrained by their limited power of feeling to consider art an elegant entertainment.

Gentlemen, for the cultivated fifteenth century Dante wrote badly; *The Divine Comedy* was badly written, and not only because it was not composed in Latin, but in the language of the people and really badly written in that same popular idiom. And Machiavelli? He writes *The Prince* and shamefully has to excuse himself and confess that he was not cultivated enough to write it better. And to the fanatic admirers of the flowery Tasso did not also Ariosto's *Orlando Furioso* seem badly written? And Vico's *New Science* appeared not only badly but terribly written; he had the curious fate of starting to write in a completely different manner, so as to seem somebody else when he decided to please all those who were accustomed to read with the glasses of that rhetoric which he later habitually professed.

To conclude this discussion of eyes and eyeglasses, the joke, nevertheless, is that all who wear the glasses (and all cultivated people wear them, or at least one supposes that they must have them, and the more so as they may pretend not to be aware of it), preach that in art it is absolutely necessary to have one's own eyes; yet at the same time they criticize anyone who uses them, whether well or badly, because, let us make it clear, while these people say writers should use their own eyes, they must be and see exactly as the cultivated people's eyes, which, however, are only glasses, for if they fall and break, then it is good night.

Ever since foreign importation began in the theatre world, these eyeglasses have been bought—it is too obvious to point out—in Paris, a market which has become international only for such wares. In fact, the most renowned French factories are now on the decline, and not a few have lost all credit. The illusory eyeglasses of the Sardou[3] firm were once greatly used almost everywhere. Someone, and not without profit and consideration, still continues using them among us, incredible as it may seem. But nothing is often more incredible than the truth. A pair of lenses for the near-sighted, very powerful, and strongly recommended for acute and precise clarity, were those of the firm of Becque[4] with the trademark of "Parisian." And another pair, justly valued for a certain idealizing virtue, were those of the house of de Curel.[5] But there came from far-off Norway, first on the German market and then on the French, the powerful glasses of Henrik Ibsen, to impose themselves through a very different investigating power of ideal and social values. The vogue lasted a long time, though few succeeded in adjusting these eyeglasses to their noses; then, after they recognized this difficulty as almost insurmountable, there came into fashion the monocles of the firm of Bataille[6] and Bernstein,[7] which sold widely in all the countries of the world. And, finally, and alas, without the least fault nor the slightest pleasure of the inventor, there is a certain Pirandello lens, called a diabolical brand by the malicious, which makes you see double and triple and slanted, and in short, makes you see the world upside down. Many still use these lenses, despite the fact that I do not miss any occasion to make them know that such lenses ruin their eyesight. On the one hand for support, and on the other for the good digestion of the honest citizen, a pair of lenses can be found today, lenses at a good price and easily used, for colored diversion and natural comfort, and in two colors: a comic eye and a sentimental eye. Every barber with the slightest dramatic aspiration is able to supply them,

[3] Victorien Sardou (1831–1908), French playwright, known for his advocacy of the well-made play form.

[4] Henry Becque (1837–1899), French realist dramatist, author of *The Vultures* and *The Parisian Woman*.

[5] François de Curel (1854–1928), French playwright, popular in the early twentieth century for his psychological dramas.

[6] Félix-Henry Bataille (1872–1922), French boulevard playwright.

[7] Henri Bernstein (1876–1956), popular French naturalistic playwright.

confident of quickly acquiring a fine reputation and of making a hatful of money.

But I must speak to you of the new theatre and the old, and I have spoken to you until now of eyes and eyeglasses: that is, of original creation and the exercise of imitation. This carries its own explanation. I do not want to criticize even this copying exercise which was and always will be typical of all the old theatre. I do not criticize it—do you know why? —even to irritate the devotees of that other vice of civil society, that is, "pure" literary criticism. To them, every debate on the theatre appears almost unworthy of their attention and consideration, unless as a pardonable exception it is used as an expressive form by some poet who is otherwise important and respected. And even then, if this "pure" literary criticism talks about theatre, naturally it avoids wasting a word or casting a glance, even in passing, at all that stage armament which sustains the habitual conception of a theatre, "played," as they say, according to its well-defined "rules," and spoken in its well-defined gibberish and regulated scene by scene with means and effects of its own stage. Everyone agrees that a work of the theatre should be understood as neither more nor less than a work of art; and that only on this condition is it worth discussing. Very well. But let us reflect a little. To refuse all literary expression to the products of such a trade by being hermetically silent about it—as one does when the monopoly is controlled by those writers of comedies who are proud to declare themselves of a "trade" acquired through assiduous training on the stage, and who feel they must defend the stage as their small, exclusive, inviolable domain protected all around by so many posters stating "entrance prohibited to outsiders"—may be right, without doubt, in so many ways; but, excuse me if I should point out to you that nevertheless out of that profession, when a sudden inspiration invests and ennobles it, although leaving it for the most part a trade, so many beautiful and great comedies have come. What then?

Even in England in Shakespeare's time, even in Spain at the time of Lope de Vega and Calderón de la Barca, or even in France at the time of Molière, the theatre was a trade reserved to the "specialist," to those who knew the stage, and they remade fifty times the same plots, filled with the same spirit common to a whole generation, and the priority of the ideas did not matter at all and the personality of the writer very little, and the greater part of the comedies, written in twenty-four hours, served as a spectacle for an evening and then was discarded among the rummage. There was no artistic seriousness, in the sense of high literary criticism and of cultivated and nice people. But *La vida es sueño*,[8] to cite only one example, was still forged at that smithy. And what then?

It then appears clear to me that in the field of art every polemic, every critical attitude, every theory, if postulated and developed systematically and abstractly, *a priori* or *a posteriori*, whether discussed according to intellectual or moral criteria, or even from a purely aesthetic point of view, risks continually being disarranged and turned topsy-turvy or remaining bewildered at the disconcerting appearance of the created work, which is without original sin and finds citizenship and status in the kingdom of art from wherever it comes; the crux is that it got there.

Until now, we have anticipated a brief preface on original creation and imitative exercise (eyes and eyeglasses) apropos of the new theatre and the old; and a negative judgment on the polemics of art stated and developed systematically and abstractly. If you let me pause a little on this point, I will give you reasons for both prefaces.

Let us ask: is it possible or not to recognize in the work of the theatre a value of art, of achieved expression, from the assumption of its "newness," understanding by newness a harmony between the content and the particular spirit of revision and reconstruction of intellectual values which animates our times in every field: politics, science, philosophy, art itself? Are not the comedies or dramas in harmony with this spirit of new theatre, that is, in this sieve, grain from which we can extract the best of the living work of art—while those comedies and those dramas which do not absorb this new spirit remain chaff, without any hope of salvation? Let us examine this a little. Is is possible, then, that criticism may direct with a certain sureness the activity of writers, instead of following it and explaining it, and that it may direct it with maximum profit for all, and especially of the young still in search of an expression of their own, toward particular problems, without which there is no hope of constructing new and vital works? If this were so, we should without ado immediately ask literary criticism to set forth such problems. But probably criticism would answer that to enunciate them, or to define them, is as good as to resolve them, and, therefore,

[8] Calderón's *Life Is a Dream.*

o destroy them as problems; and that this is the task of authors and not of critics.

Everyone sees that in this way the question is badly put; and that, so put, it cannot be resolved. To resolve it, as a work of art, we must look fully into the fundamental problems of form and the aesthetic fact; and we will then see clearly that the "new" in art is nothing more than one of the many necessary values of every created work. We need not discuss in abstraction, stating and denying as exterior and existent for themselves, certain indeterminate problems from which we determine the "new." The open minds, the creative spirits find them indeed, but without searching for them—here is the essential point—and attack them, but without perhaps even knowing them in their abstract terms, and, without study, resolve them. Because it is not true that these problems are of a particular time, or that creative spirits can assume them from time.

If these minds are truly creative, the problems belong to the minds themselves and are not an indistinctive and indeterminate fact in time; but indistinct and undetermined points of the active spirit itself, which just because he has them himself as a part of his nature, as a living effort, can find the strength to free himself from them by expressing them. And they are active problems just because they are not enunciated by criticism but are expressed through the means of art. That is to say, they are not defined by the pure intellect which chills and solidifies them, and naturally kills them, as problems, merely by enunciating them; but they have to be represented through the means of art in a form which is the construction and the *raison d'être* of their eternal life.

What is our time outside of the meaning and value that we give it? I say, we, with our spirit.

Now, think! Who can give meaning and value to his time, not a particular meaning and value functioning in the moments of the life of a single individual, but universal, in which each person can always find himself, if not the man who can speak with the most absolute disinterestedness, so that his voice can sound as his own in the breast of whoever listens? Not the person who satisfies material ambitions for himself in life, but the one who affirms "my kingdom is not of this world" and nevertheless affirms that he has a kingdom; who, therefore, creates life for himself and for all; who, therefore, succeeds in making consistent his own organic and total

vision of life; who, therefore, is like the whole and pur
spirit which is able to reveal itself fully; he is the poet, th
maker, the creator: he will be able to give to his time ¿
universal meaning and value because with his own absolut
disinterestedness he makes all the concerns of his frank an
lively senses (his own new eyes), thoughts and relationship
of concepts, feelings, images assume in him an autonomou
and complete organic unity, and he wants to realize that unit
in himself which life freely wants for itself, so that he, in thi
sense, is a spirit servant of the spirit, the creator servant o
his creation. In the organic wholeness of life he has a plac
like all the others; he has created not to dominate and rule
but to systemize. And for that reason, Christ, poet, maker
creator of reality, called himself son of man and gave mean
ing and value to life for all men.

The problems of time, therefore, do not exist for hin
who creates.
They exist for those men, undoubtedly worthy of th
greatest respect because they are enlightened and enlighter
others, but who do not have truly creative qualities in thei
spirit; these people take them truly from time, where th
creative spirits have placed them.
In fact, every creation, every vision of life, every revela
tion of the spirit, necessarily carries within itself problems
questions, logical contradictions, the more decisive and eviden
as these creations, visions, and revelations are organic an
comprehensive: and this simply because mystery is congenita
to the spirit, and to look with new eyes, to express frankly, t
reorganize life is to project life once more in mystery. T
make: to create, anew, from nothing: that nothing is fel
again necessarily by all with greater strength. Little by little
however, the anxiety of every first intuition will be appeased
as well as the dismay or also the annoyance which humanit
always experiences in looking again at these objects: for
tunately, our nature is such that it is allowed to sleep. Bu
at first an almost general elevation of the spirit makes rebor
those problems, those questions, the warning of those contra
dictions which have always been the same, but which nov
reappear as new because they have a new value. It is almos
impossible that the new sense of life may be hit upon directl
from the beginning. The problems appear obscure, and th
spirit which agitates them, paradoxical. The so-called "logic,
unmasked, has been driven out of life.

The sense of revelation is obscure if we blame its expression, especially when we deal with a work of art. The case is different if it is a question of religious revelation or a new philosophical revelation.

Because if we treat of a relevation in which faith enters as a necessary and essential element, the problems that revelation brings with it are naturally set aright if we accept faith; or, otherwise, they immediately lose any consistency and, for that reason, any stimulus and power to create doubt, to make intellectual systems waver, and finally, to be discussed passionately.

And if we treat of problems set forth in new intellectual constructions of philosophy, through the same technical and conventional language in which they are stated, they already appear connected to certain currents of thought already expressed, and the troublesome sense of the "new," which they are able to awaken is, for that reason, always somewhat limited and relative; but they are immediately evaluated perfectly, in their precise terms, and this annuls every spiritual restlessness over whatever may appear indistinct, imprecise, and ambiguous in its expressions. Every mind which becomes conscious of them has in so doing immediately tested them in all their parts. Furthermore, by their conceptual nature, that is, abstracted from life, in the light of criticism they can be displaced, completed, annulled, or resolved.

But not the problems represented in a new work of art. They remain and always will remain as they have been fixed: problems of life. Their irreducibility consists in their expression as representation. Think of Hamlet: to be or not to be. Take this problem from Hamlet's mouth, empty it of Hamlet's passion, conceptualize it in philosophical terms, and in the light of criticism you may play with it as long as you like. But leave it there on Hamlet's lips a living expression, an active representation of the torment of that life, and the problem of being or not being will never be resolved in eternity. And not only for Hamlet, a single spirit in a definite moment of his life, but for every spirit who contemplates that form of life, and—for this is Art—lives it. And these problems are in that form, and will always be, for everyone, problems of life. Thus, they live through the form, through the expression.

They are able to live in this way because their expression is finished, completed.

The perfect form has detached them entirely, both alive

and concrete; that is, fluid and indistinct from time and from space, and has fixed them forever, has gathered them into itself, that which is incorruptible, as if embalming them alive.

At so great distance of time, humanity without still having resolved them, has adjusted itself to them. It has succeeded in putting itself in that state of aesthetic contemplation in which it calls them beautiful, still feeling them as problems of life.

With the meaning and value they have assumed, organized in that way, humanity can now contemplate them without any anguish. It knows, and by now is accustomed to know that, in that vision of life, mystery appears in this way. For it is not the sense of mystery which terrifies men, since they know that mystery is in life; the unusual way of representing something new is what terrifies. Now that way is no longer new. But has it for that reason become old? No. How can it become old, if it is represented in action, in perfect, incorruptible form? Only the time has come in which we have discovered it "created," in which all the reasons of its being are seen to consist in the necessity of its being what it is; and no longer new, never old, not arbitrary, or obscure, or imprecise, or unfinished, but finally necessary in every way: *that*, and that alone which it had to be.

But it might be instructive to read once more about the anger stirred up in the heart of Voltaire, for example, even at a distance of two centuries. And an almost contemporary critic of Michelangelo, in a solemn attack, harshly criticizes him for having made an arbitrary and absolutely illogical work, depicting in the "Pietà" the Virgin as a girl scarcely eighteen who holds on her knee the thirty-three year old Son. Now we understand what depth of poetry Michelangelo reached in the representation of that Madonna, the Virgin, who conceived through grace and is always the girl of the "Annunciation," compared to the Son, the Redeemer, who has had to bear all the pain of the world. But how that same critic boasted of having opened Michelangelo's eyes and of inviting him to correct properly his inconceivable aberration! As if one might wish to enlighten Hamlet's mind in order to help him resolve in some way the confusion of his problems.

Now we would laugh and no longer think of this; but because it is a matter of Hamlet and of Michelangelo's "Pietà"—artistic expressions for which we have finally found the *ubi consistam* of aesthetic evaluation which explains the being of their life: which the form represents.

Still, because contemporary criticism does not give enough weight to the absolute difference between the philosophical problem set forth through concepts in an intellectual construction and the problem of life expressed in the immediate representation of art—creator of form, in this sense inviolable —very often today this criticism of contemporary works of art avoids probing as deeply as it could, not merely into the representation of a spiritual debate accidentally expressed in the work, but into the very objects of that debate, and tries instead to discover its logical contradictions and looks only at the conceptual design of the work of art. This has happened to me and to my work. But the conceptual framework, on the one hand, is absolutely nothing more than a pretext, a stimulus to create, and, therefore, in the evaluation of the created work (which is considered in itself and by itself) could not and must not find a place. On the other hand, the conceptual framework is at best no more than a scheme, a skeleton, which becomes immediately incorporated, wholly reabsorbed, in the whole of the expressive elaboration of the work, and not even from this side, therefore, can it lead to a just aesthetic evaluation. And just as bad, it seems to me, is criticism generally done by those who still would like to do it according to its correct principles, based, I mean, upon expression. Especially when these people come upon new material expressed for the first time.

We have declared what seemed to us the reasons for which this first expression must at the beginning appear muddled, obscure, arbitrary, paradoxical: a "badly written" work. These difficult judges, among other things, do not consider that the very fury with which they penetrate into the limits of the problems represented in the work of art in order to combat them and destroy them, and define them in themselves, this very fury from which they then resolve the judgment that the work of art is not completely expressed, is, instead, the surest and clearest testimony that the incriminated expression is still that which it had to be: so that they have been able to draw out and fight these problems face to face as alive and present, and which are therefore represented, and perfectly so, in an achieved form.

But it is natural that conflict and misunderstanding exist for those who have eyes and create, and not for those who have glasses and copy in a final draft the obscure, abstruse expressions of creators who "write badly" and diligently clean up all those "errors," so that one fine day when a taste will have developed for the new expression, these qualities will reveal themselves as their necessary "traits."

Think that even Goldoni,[9] who today seems as simple and accessible as it is possible to imagine, whose style seems so pure and faithful to the reality of his characters lifted bodily from the pressure of the life of his time; even Goldoni was not recognized in his own time. And how they criticized him! They said that he wrote badly, and they all said it to him, right away, even those who with due reservations accepted his theatre and followed him. They seemed to say to him, "Yes you are right; those who criticize you understand nothing, but if only you knew how to write a little better!"

And this is natural, if we think that the spirit always brings to life its creations with great and slow labor and that every time it succeeds in establishing one of them it experiences the need of resting for a while. In this way, therefore, certain periods come after the recognition of every original expression, certain periods in which spirits no longer truly create but devote themselves to small discoveries of illuminating the details of the vision of life which is present at that moment, so that all remains impregnated in it; and we have established, besides, a heavy burden of clichés which have meaning for all in that moment and perhaps have none after the advent of a new original expression; we have established, I was saying, a world absolutely determined, perhaps more by expression than by conception, which is not really the same for all, naturally, but which is stamped with the same characteristics. Take the writings of men of a certain time, anonymous in the sense that they are called neither Shakespeare nor Dante, and you can recognize, without looking at the date, those written by our fathers, grandfathers, and ancestors. There are some who write with great clarity of expression, with grace, with a beautiful periodic style. There! These men write well. And why does Carlo Goldoni write badly? Because his expressions, in order to define a new vision of life, necessarily had to be different from those that were in the ears of all, already composed, already studied and for that reason very clear, and which anyone, by Jove, with a bit of talent and good will, could embellish gracefully. And that clumsy Goldoni. . . .

I believe that every creator, besides his great sins, ought

---

[9] Carlo Goldoni (1707–1793), Italian popular dramatist who used *commedia dell' arte* materials and conventions in the writing of his plays.

to feel on his conscience the secret afflictions of his contemporary admirers, almost as a sense of shame because of his inevitable bad writing. And Goldoni should have more remorse than anyone. The dialogue of Carlo Goldoni must have appeared, even to his admirers, insipid and specious, compared to the language of the *commedia dell' arte;* and badly written, legalistic, and formless enough to make you sick compared to the style of the serious compositions of the time.

The *commedia dell' arte* which was, indeed, played spontaneously, but which was incapable of imposing itself as a true improvisation, was at bottom only the quintessence of the commonplace, based on generic themes and ready-made patterns contrived to frame the same repertory of stereotyped phrases, typical, and traditional jokes and epigrams, and ritualized blows and retorts, phrased as though in a manual of etiquette. It was natural for everyone that on the stage it should be so spoken: since a taste had been developed for conventions which ruled that language, one went to the theatre to admire the undisguised witticisms, the false naturalness, and false spontaneity; and the style of Goldoni had to appear fallacious because it was psychological, insipid because it was natural, and it undid with its dialogue the fixity of those lines and loosened the rigidity of the masks, cutting apart little by little their consistency and expressing it—a new and unknown spectacle—through the free play of all the liberated muscles.

But why couldn't Goldoni, who still experienced in life the struggling fate of the innovator, fix himself as an absolute value, so that he could face those who have made almost a fetish of him and who, with the intention of praising him, exclaim, "Oh, the good 'old' Goldoni!" (and that "old" expresses, more than a real intrinsic recognition, a spirit of polemic with "new") and altogether deny him any value in himself and regard his production as an outdated moment in the history of the Italian theatre, and deny that it can be the expression of a created and insurmountable world in the eternal kingdom of art?

This too—I think—comes about through the ambiguities to which the abstract and systematic evaluations are subject.

It is natural that each finished work—a created world unique in itself, and beyond comparison, which no longer can be new or old but simply "that which it is" in itself and for itself eternally, finds in its very "uniqueness" the reasons, first, of its incomprehension, and then, always, of its frightening solitude: the solitude of things which have been expressed in this way, immediately, as they wanted to be, and, therefore, "for themselves alone." And because of this single fact alone they would be impossible to know, if each person wanting to know them did not make them escape from that being "for themselves alone," making them exist for him, as he interprets and understands them.

Who knows Dante as he was for himself in his poem! Dante in his existence for himself becomes like nature: we should have to go out of ourselves to understand him as he is for himself, and we can not, and each one understands him as he can in his own way. Dante remains truly alone in his divine solitude. Nevertheless, each age makes him its own; each age echoes in its own way his unique voice.

But actually, the voice of Dante speaks eternal things; he speaks from the very insides of the earth. His is a voice of nature which will never go out in life, and our necessity to echo it does not mean we misunderstand or do not understand him.

Instead, it is possible at the same time to misunderstand and no longer understand the voice of one who, though creating, and in the most accomplished forms, his own organic vision of life, did not endow real and free "movements" of the spirit with his expression, but rather created according to a "pose" or "attitude" of the spirit.

And this "attitude" in itself, usually abstracted from expression, can be overcome, indeed is necessarily overcome, and at a certain point becomes, so to speak, historical, as soon as unexpected agitations of the spirit have displaced the elements of that panorama thus contemplated from a fixed point. Yet, in the movements of the spirit we can never lose interest: the Middle Ages of Dante, not represented according to an attitude of his spirit, as is the eighteenth century of Goldoni, but in the movements of a spirit which need not contemplate its own age because it has all the passions alive in itself, or when it does contemplate, does not stand still a moment because its glance is not attached to time, but from time is attached to eternity and then follows it swiftly and presses it closely, moving it with its doubts and unfolding it with its revelations—this Middle Ages of Dante, just because it is all gathered in the movement of a spirit, can no longer become outmoded; it will always be, in one way or another, echoed in every age. It is possible always, in substance, for every age to receive into itself, one way or another, the spirit of Dante and to feel its perpetual presence; and on the other hand, it is necessary to refer in a certain sense from one's own age to those past times to enjoy the value of the expression of an attitude of the spirit, which can be enjoyed only in its particular flavor and which can not re-echo; it is necessary, in other words, to bring ourselves back to the age of Goldoni.

Goldoni's attitude was good-naturedly satirical: an expression of a wide-awake moral consciousness which remained intact and kept itself whole in reflecting those contingencies it could then satirize, with the satisfaction of feeling them overcome, yet unable to detach them from the spiritual limits of his own time; and hence the good nature of this satire, which might appear superficial in a period of trial and fundamental upheaval of every established value.

Because of the frankness and transparency of his form, it is and always will be easy to go back to Goldoni, to feel alive, in the life of the representation offered by his spiritual attitude, the rapidity of his wit and the organic wholeness of life so observed and represented. All this is united in a form which, in truth, embalms it forever, together with the freshness and the gaiety of its own expressions, with the happiness of a spirit which created for the joy of creating. The way Goldoni expresses everything will always be a model of correct representation, so fluid and scintillating, so clear and quick, so careful and spontaneous and truly diverting. His propriety of style, not only in dialect, is absolute; nothing is ever said through approximation or in a way that may not be the most frank and savory, just as there is never in conception any emptiness or unbalance in feelings or intellect: conception, elaboration, and expression are exquisitely blended to create a graceful world. Grace, which is one of the most attractive and rarest qualities of human nature, finds in Goldoni its perfect expression, never attained before him; certainly it can not be reached again with such immediacy and in such fullness.

When this fresh expression of life burst on the mummified stage of the Italian theatre and restored to it breath, warmth, and movement, they spoke of a reform. It was the new theatre. Today, can we say that it is old theatre because the spiritual attitude from which it grew is in itself superseded by the change of values with the passing of time?

In art what was created new remains new forever. Goldoni had witty, lively eyes with which he saw anew and created the new.

Any new writer today who copies and does not create,

that is, who wears glasses, although in the latest style, and
claims that with them he sees the liveliest problems and newest
values in his time, if he wears glasses, will copy and will
create old theatre.

The new theatre and the old. It is always the same question:
of eyes and eyeglasses; of the work of creation and the exercise of copying.

An ape was boasting to a fox, "Can you name an animal
so clever and shrewd that I, if I wished, could not imitate?"

And the fox rejoined, "And can you name an animal foolish
and stupid enough to want to imitate you?"

This is a little fable of Lessing's, composed at the time of
the famous Silesian school led by Martin Opitz, when the
German poets endeavored to imitate the graces of the Italian
arcadians, bitterly complaining to the good God that they
could not become the lap dogs of their ladies.

And as an epilogue to this fable (Lessing's, I repeat, and
not mine) in the way of a moral, not for my contemporary
playwrights of every land but for the German writers of the
eighteenth century, there was the sarcasm of this request, "O
authors of my nation, do I have to express myself more
clearly?"

PREFACE TO

SIX CHARACTERS
IN SEARCH OF AN AUTHOR[10]

By Luigi Pirandello

IT SEEMS LIKE yesterday but is actually many years ago that
a nimble little maidservant entered the service of my art.
However, she always comes fresh to the job.

She is called Fantasy.

A little puckish and malicious, if she likes to dress in black
no one will wish to deny that she is often positively bizarre
and no one will wish to believe that she always does everything in the same way and in earnest. She sticks her hand in
her pocket, pulls out a cap and bells, sets it on her head,
red as a cock's comb, and dashes away. Here today, there
tomorrow. And she amuses herself by bringing to my house—
since I derive stories and novels and plays from them—the
most disgruntled tribe in the world, men, women, children,
involved in strange adventures which they can find no way
out of; thwarted in their plans; cheated in their hopes; with
whom, in short, it is often torture to deal.

Well, this little maidservant of mine, Fantasy, several years
ago, had the bad inspiration or ill-omened caprice to bring
a family into my house. I wouldn't know where she fished
them up or how, but, according to her, I could find in them
the subject for a magnificent novel.

I found before me a man about fifty years old, in a dark
jacket and light trousers, with a frowning air and ill-natured,
mortified eyes; a poor woman in widow's weeds leading by

[10] Translation Copyright, © 1962, by Paul Avila Mayer. Preface translated
by Eric Bentley. Reprinted by permission of E.P. Dutton & Co., Inc., publishers of *Naked Masks: Five Plays* by Luigi Pirandello, edited by Eric
Bentley. Copyright, 1922, 1952, by E.P. Dutton & Co., Inc., renewal, 1950,
by Stefano, Fausto and Lietta Pirandello.

one hand a little girl of four and by the other a boy of rather more than ten; a cheeky and "sexy" girl, also clad in black but with an equivocal and brazen pomp, all atremble with a lively, biting contempt for the mortified old man and for a young fellow of twenty who stood on one side closed in on himself as if he despised them all. In short, the six characters who are seen coming on stage at the beginning of the play. Now one of them and now another—often beating down one another—embarked on the sad story of their adventures, each shouting his own reasons, and projecting in my face his disordered passions, more or less as they do in the play to the unhappy Manager.

What author will be able to say how and why a character was born in his fantasy? The mystery of artistic creation is the same as that of birth. A woman who loves may desire to become a mother; but the desire by itself, however intense, cannot suffice. One fine day she will find herself a mother without having any precise intimation when it began. In the same way an artist imbibes very many germs of life and can never say how and why, at a certain moment, one of these vital germs inserts itself into his fantasy, there to become a living creature on a plane of life superior to the changeable existence of every day.

I can only say that, without having made any effort to seek them out, I found before me, alive—you could touch them and even hear them breathe—the six characters now seen on the stage. And they stayed there in my presence, each with his secret torment and all bound together by the one common origin and mutual entanglement of their affairs, while I had them enter the world of art, constructing from their persons, their passions, and their adventures a novel, a drama, or at least a story.

Born alive, they wished to live.

To me it was never enough to present a man or a woman and what is special and characteristic about them simply for the pleasure of presenting them; to narrate a particular affair, lively or sad, simply for the pleasure of narrating it; to describe a landscape simply for the pleasure of describing it.

There are some writers (and not a few) who do feel this pleasure and, satisfied, ask no more. They are, to speak more precisely, historical writers.

But there are others who, beyond such pleasure, feel a more profound spiritual need on whose account they admit only figures, affairs, landscapes which have been soaked, so to speak, in a particular sense of life and acquire from it a universal value. These are, more precisely, philosophical writers.

I have the misfortune to belong to these last.

I hate symbolic art in which the presentation loses all spontaneous movement in order to become a machine, an allegory—a vain and misconceived effort because the very fact of giving an allegorical sense to a presentation clearly shows that we have to do with a fable which by itself has no truth either fantastic or direct; it was made for the demonstration of some moral truth. The spiritual need I speak of cannot be satisfied—or seldom, and that to the end of a superior irony, as for example in Ariosto[11]—by such allegorical symbolism. This latter starts from a concept, and from a concept which creates or tries to create for itself an image. The former on the other hand seeks in the image—which must remain alive and free throughout—a meaning to give it value.

Now, however much I sought, I did not succeed in uncovering this meaning in the six characters. And I concluded therefore that it was no use making them live.

I thought to myself: "I have already afflicted my readers with hundreds and hundreds of stories. Why should I afflict them now by narrating the sad entanglements of these six unfortunates?"

And, thinking thus, I put them away from me. Or rather I did all I could to put them away.

But one doesn't give life to a character for nothing.

Creatures of my spirit, these six were already living a life which was their own and not mine any more, a life which it was not in my power any more to deny them.

Thus it is that while I persisted in desiring to drive them out of my spirit, they, as if completely detached from every narrative support, characters from a novel miraculously emerging from the pages of the book that contained them, went on living on their own, choosing certain moments of the day to reappear before me in the solitude of my study and coming—now one, now the other, now two together—to tempt me, to propose that I present or describe this scene or that, to explain the effects that could be secured with them, the new interest which a certain unusual situation could provide, and so forth.

For a moment I let myself be won over. And this con-

---

[11] Ludovico Ariosto (1474–1532), Italian Renaissance poet, best known for his *Orlando Furioso*.

descension of mine, thus letting myself go for a while, was enough, because they drew from it a new increment of life, a greater degree of clarity and addition, consequently a greater degree of persuasive power over me. And thus as it became gradually harder and harder for me to go back and free myself from them, it became easier and easier for them to come back and tempt me. At a certain point I actually became obsessed with them. Until, all of a sudden, a way out of the difficulty flashed upon me.

"Why not," I said to myself, "present this highly strange fact of an author who refuses to let some of his characters live though they have been born in his fantasy, and the fact that these characters, having by now life in their veins, do not resign themselves to remaining excluded from the world of art? They are detached from me; live on their own; have acquired voice and movement; have by themselves—in this struggle for existence that they have had to wage with me—become dramatic characters, characters that can move and talk on their own initiative; already see themselves as such; have learned to defend themselves against me; will even know how to defend themselves against others. And so let them go where dramatic characters do go to have life: on a stage. And let us see what will happen."

That's what I did. And, naturally, the result was what it had to be: a mixture of tragic and comic, fantastic and realistic, in a humorous situation that was quite new and infinitely complex, a drama which is conveyed by means of the characters, who carry it within them and suffer it, a drama, breathing, speaking, self-propelled, which seeks at all costs to find the means of its own presentation; and the comedy of the vain attempt at an improvised realization of the drama on stage. First, the surprise of the poor actors in a theatrical company rehearsing a play by day on a bare stage (no scenery, no flats). Surprise and incredulity at the sight of the six characters announcing themselves as such in search of an author. Then, immediately afterward, through that sudden fainting fit of the Mother veiled in black, their instinctive interest in the drama of which they catch a glimpse in her and in the other members of the strange family, an obscure, ambiguous drama, coming about so unexpectedly on a stage that is empty and unprepared to receive it. And gradually the growth of this interest to the bursting forth of the contrasting passions of Father, of Stepdaughter, of Son, of that poor Mother, passions seeking, as I said, to overwhelm each other with a tragic, lacerating fury.

And here is the universal meaning at first vainly sought in the six characters, now that, going on stage of their own accord, they succeed in finding it within themselves in the excitement of the desperate struggle which each wages against the other and all wage against the Manager and the actors, who do not understand them.

Without wanting to, without knowing it, in the strife of their bedeviled souls, each of them, defending himself against the accusations of the others, expresses as his own living passion and torment the passion and torment which for so many years have been the pangs of my spirit: the deceit of mutual understanding irremediably founded on the empty abstraction of the words, the multiple personality of everyone corresponding to the possibilities of being to be found in each of us, and finally the inherent tragic conflict between life (which is always moving and changing) and form (which fixes it, immutable).

Two above all among the six characters, the Father and the Stepdaughter, speak of that outrageous unalterable fixity of their form in which he and she see their essential nature expressed permanently and immutably, a nature that for one means punishment and for the other revenge; and they defend it against the factitious affectations and unaware volatility of the actors, and they try to impose it on the vulgar Manager who would like to change it and adapt it to the so-called exigencies of the theatre.

If the six characters don't all seem to exist on the same plane, it is not because some are figures of first rank and others of the second, that is, some are main characters and others minor ones—the elementary perspective necessary to all scenic or narrative art—nor is it that any are not completely created—for their purpose. They are all six at the same point of artistic realization and on the same level of reality, which is the fantastic level of the whole play. Except that the Father, the Stepdaughter, and also the Son are realized as mind; the Mother as nature; the Boy as a presence watching and performing a gesture and the Baby unaware of it all. This fact creates among them a perspective of a new sort. Unconsciously I had had the impression that some of them needed to be fully realized (artistically speaking), others less so, and others merely sketched in as elements in a narrative or presentational sequence: the most alive, the most completely created, are the Father and the Stepdaughter who naturally stand out more and lead the way, dragging themselves along beside the almost dead weight of the others—first, the Son, holding back; second, the Mother, like a victim resigned to her fate, between the two children who have hardly any substance beyond their appearance and who need to be led by the hand.

And actually! actually they had each other to appear in that stage of creation which they had attained in the author's fantasy at the moment when he wished to drive them away.

If I now think about these things, about having intuited that necessity, having unconsciously found the way to resolve it by means of a new perspective, and about the way in which I actually obtained it, they seem like miracles. The fact is that the play was really conceived in one of those spontaneous illuminations of the fantasy when by a miracle all the elements of the mind answer to each other's call and work in divine accord. No human brain, working "in the cold," however stirred up it might be, could ever have succeeded in penetrating far enough, could ever have been in a position to satsify all the exigencies of the play's form. Therefore the reasons which I will give to clarify the values of the play must not be thought of as intentions that I conceived beforehand when I prepared myself for the job and which I now undertake to defend, but only as discoveries which I have been able to make afterward in tranquillity.

I wanted to present six characters seeking an author. Their play does not manage to get presented—precisely because the author whom they seek is missing. Instead is presented the comedy of their vain attempt with all that it contains of tragedy by virtue of the fact that the six characters have been rejected.

But can one present a character while rejecting him? Obviously, to present him one needs, on the contrary, to receive him into one's fantasy before one can express him. And I have actually accepted and realized the six characters: I have, however, accepted and realized them as rejected: in search of *another* author.

What have I rejected of them? Not themselves, obviously, but their drama, which doubtless is what interests them above all but which did not interest me—for the reasons already indicated.

And what is it, for a character—his drama?

Every creature of fantasy and art, in order to exist, must have his drama, that is, a drama in which he may be a character and for which he *is* a character. This drama is the character's *raison d'être*, his vital function, necessary for his existence.

In these six, then, I have accepted the "being" without the reason for being. I have taken the organism and entrusted to it, not its own proper function, but another more complex function into which its own function entered, if at all, only as a datum. A terrible and desperate situation especially for the two—Father and Stepdaughter—who more than the others crave life and more than the others feel themselves to be characters, that is, absolutely need a drama and therefore their own drama—the only one which they can envisage for themselves yet which meantime they see rejected: an "impossible" situation from which they feel they must escape at whatever cost; it is a matter of life and death. True, I have given them another *raison d'être*, another function: precisely that "impossible" situation, the drama of being in search of an author and rejected. But that this should be a *raison d'être*, that it should have become their real function, that it should be necessary, that it should suffice, they can hardly suppose; for they have a life of their own. If someone were to tell them, they wouldn't believe him. It is not possible to believe that the sole reason for our living should lie in a torment that seems to us unjust and inexplicable.

I cannot imagine, therefore, why the charge was brought against me that the character of the Father was not what it should have been because it stepped out of its quality and position as a character and invaded at times the author's province and took it over. I who understand those who don't quite understand me see that the charge derives from the fact that the character expresses and makes his own a torment of spirit which is recognized as mine. This is entirely natural but of absolutely no significance. Aside from the fact that this torment of spirit in the character of the Father derives from causes, and is suffered and lived for reasons that have nothing to do with the drama of my personal experience, a fact which alone removes all substance from the criticism, I want to make it clear that the inherent torment of my spirit is one thing, a torment which I can legitimately—provided that it be organic—reflect in a character, and that the activity of my spirit as revealed in the realized work, the activity that succeeds in forming a drama out of the six characters in search of an author is another thing. If the Father participated in this latter activity, if he competed in forming the drama of the six characters without an author, then and only then would it by all means be justified to say that he was at times the author himself and therefore not the man he should be. But the Father suffers and does not create his existence as a character in search of an author. He suffers it as an inexplicable fatality and as a situation which he tries with all his powers to rebel against, which he tries to remedy; hence it is that he is a character in search of an author and nothing more, even if he expresses as his own the torment of my spirit. If he, so to speak, assumed some of the author's responsibilities, the fatality would be completely explained. He would, that is to say, see himself accepted, if only as a rejected character, accepted in the poet's heart of hearts, and he would no longer have any reason to suffer the despair of not finding someone to construct and affirm his life as a character. I mean that he would quite willingly accept the *raison d'être* which the author gives him and without regrets would forgo his own, throwing over the Manager and the actors to whom in fact he runs as his only recourse.

There is one character, that of the Mother, who on the other hand does not care about being alive (considering being alive as an end in itself). She hasn't the least suspicion that she is *not* alive. It has never occurred to her to ask how and why and in what manner she lives. In short, she is not aware of being a character inasmuch as she is never, even for a moment, detached from her role. She doesn't know she has a role.

This makes her perfectly organic. Indeed, her role of Mother does not of itself, in its natural essence, embrace mental activity. And she does not exist as a mind. She lives in an endless continuum of feeling, and therefore she cannot acquire awareness of her life—that is, of her existence as a character. But with all this, even she, in her own way and for her own ends, seeks an author, and at a certain stage seems happy to have been brought before the Manager. Because she hopes to take life from him, perhaps? No: because she hopes the manager will have her present a scene with the Son in which she would put so much of her own life. But it is a scene which does not exist, which never has and never could take place. So unaware is she of being a character, that is, of the life that is possible to her, all fixed and determined, moment by moment, in every action, every phrase.

She appears on stage with the other characters but without understanding what the others make her do. Obviously, she imagines that the itch for life with which the husband and the daughter are afflicted and for which she herself is to be found on stage is no more than one of the usual incomprehensible extravagances of this man who is both tortured and torturer and—horrible, most horrible—a new equivocal rebellion on the part of that poor erring girl. The Mother is completely passive. The events of her own life and the values they assume in her eyes, her very character, are all things which are "said" by the others and which she only once contradicts, and that because the maternal instinct rises up and rebels within her to make it clear that she didn't at all wish to abandon either the son or the husband: the son was taken from her and the husband forced her to abandon him. She is only correcting data; she explains and knows nothing.

In short, she is nature. Nature fixed in the figure of a mother.

This character gave me a satisfaction of a new sort, not to be ignored. Nearly all my critics, instead of defining her, after their habit, as "unhuman"—which seems to be the peculiar and incorrigible characteristic of all my creatures without exception—had the goodness to note "with real pleasure" that at last a *very human* figure had emerged from my fantasy. I explain this praise to myself in the following way: since my poor Mother is entirely limited to the natural attitude of a Mother with no possibility of free mental activity, being, that is, little more than a lump of flesh completely alive in all its functions—procreation, lactation, caring for and loving its young—without any need therefore for exercising her brain, she realizes in her person the true and complete "human type." That must be how it is, since in a human organism nothing seems more superfluous than the mind.

But the critics have tried to get rid of the Mother with this praise without bothering to penetrate the nucleus of poetic values which the character in the play represents. A very human figure, certainly, because mindless, that is, unaware of being what she is or not caring to explain it to herself. But not knowing that she is a character doesn't prevent her from being one. That is her drama in my play. And the most living expression of it comes spurting out in her cry to the Manager, who wants her to think all these things have happened already and therefore cannot now be a reason for renewed lamentations: "No, it's happening now, it's happening always! My torture is not a pretense, signore! I am alive and present, always, in every moment of my torture: it is renewed, alive, and present always!" This she *feels*, without being conscious of it, and feels it therefore as something inexplicable: but she feels it so terribly that she doesn't think it *can* be something to explain either to herself or to others. She feels it and that is that. She feels it as pain and this pain is immediate; she cries it out. Thus she reflects the growing fixity of life in a form—the same thing, which in another way, tortures the Father and the Stepdaughter. In them, mind. In her, nature. The mind rebels and, as best it may, seeks an advantage; nature, if not aroused by sensory stimuli, weeps.

Conflict between life-in-movement and form is the inexorable condition not only of the mental but also of the physical order. The life which in order to exist has become fixed in our corporeal form little by little kills that form. The tears of a nature thus fixed lament the irreparable, continuous aging of our bodies. Hence the tears of the Mother are passive and perpetual. Revealed in three faces, made significant in three distinct and simultaneous dramas, this inherent conflict finds in the play its most complete expression. More: the Mother declares also the particular value of artistic form—a form which does not delimit or destroy its own life and which life does not consume—in her cry to the Manager. If the Father and Stepdaughter began their scene a hundred thousand times in succession, always, at the appointed moment, at the instant when the life of the work of art must be expressed with that cry, it would always be heard, unaltered and unalterable in its form, not as a mechanical repetition, not as a return determined by external necessities, but, on the contrary, alive every time and as new, suddenly born *thus forever!* embalmed alive in its incorruptible form. Hence, always, as we open the book, we shall find Francesca alive and confessing to Dante her sweet sin, and if we turn to the passage a hundred thousand times in succession, a hundred thousand times in succession Francesca[12] will speak her words, never repeating them mechanically, but saying them as though each time were the first time with such living and sudden passion that Dante every time will turn faint. All that lives, by the fact of living, has a form, and by the same token must die—except the work of art which lives forever in so far as it *is* form.

[12] Francesca da Rimini, heroine of the tragic tale of illicit love recorded in Dante's *Inferno*.

The birth of a creature of human fantasy, a birth which is a step across the threshold between nothing and eternity, can also happen suddenly, occasioned by some necessity. An imagined drama needs a character who does or says a certain necessary thing; accordingly this character is born and is precisely what he had to be. In this way Madame Pace is born among the six characters and seems a miracle, even a trick, realistically portrayed on the stage. It is no trick. The birth is real. The new character is alive not because she was alive already but because she is now happily born as is required by the fact of her being a character—she is obliged to be as she is. There is a break here, a sudden change in the level of reality of the scene, because a character can be born in this way only in the poet's fancy and not on the boards of a stage. Without anyone's noticing it, I have all of a sudden changed the scene: I have gathered it up again into my own fantasy without removing it from the spectator's eyes. That is, I have shown them, instead of the stage, my own fantasy in the act of creating—my own fantasy in the form of this same stage. The sudden and uncontrollable changing of a visual phenomenon from one level of reality to another is a miracle comparable to those of the saint who sets his own statue in motion: it is neither wood nor stone at such a moment. But the miracle is not arbitrary. The stage—a stage which accepts the fantastic reality of the six characters—is no fixed, immutable datum. Nothing in this play exists as given and preconceived. Everything is in the making, is in motion, is a sudden experiment: even the place in which this unformed life, reaching after its own form, changes and changes again, contrives to shift position organically. The level of reality changes. When I had the idea of bringing Madam Pace to birth right there on the stage, I felt I could do it and I did it. Had I noticed that this birth was unhinging and silently, unnoticed, in a second, giving another shape, another reality to my scene, I certainly wouldn't have brought it about. I would have been afraid of the apparent lack of logic. And I would have committed an ill-omened assault on the beauty of my work. The fervor of my mind saved me from doing so. For, despite appearances, with their specious logic, this fantastic birth is sustained by a real necessity in mysterious, organic relation with the whole life of the work.

That someone now tells me it hasn't all the value it could have because its expression is not constructed but chaotic, because it smacks of romanticism, makes me smile.

I understand why this observation was made to me: because in this work of mine the presentation of the drama in which the six characters are involved appears tumultuous and never proceeds in an orderly manner. There is no logical development, no concatenation of the events. Very true. Had I hunted it with a lamp I couldn't have found a more disordered, crazy, arbitrary, complicated, in short, romantic way of presenting "the drama in which the six characters are involved." Very true. But I have not presented that drama. I have presented another—and I won't undertake to say again what!—in which, among the many fine things that everyone, according to his tastes, can find, there is a discreet satire on romantic procedures: in the six characters thus excited to the point where they stifle themselves in the roles which each of them plays in a certain drama while I present them as characters in another play which they don't know and don't suspect the existence of, so that this inflammation of their passions—which belongs to the realm of romantic procedures—is humorously "placed," located in the void. And the drama of the six characters presented not as it would have been organized by my fantasy had it been accepted but in this way, as a rejected drama, could not exist in the work except as a "situation," with some little development, and could not come out except in indications, stormily, disorderly, in violent foreshortenings, in a chaotic manner: continually interrupted, sidetracked, contradicted (by one of its characters), denied, and (by two others) not even seen.

There is a character indeed—he who denies the drama which makes him a character, the Son—who draws all his importance and value from being a character not of the comedy in the making—which as such hardly appears—but from the presentation that I made of it. In short, he is the only one who lives solely as "a character in search of an author"—inasmuch as the author he seeks is not a dramatic author. Even this could not be otherwise. The character's attitude is an organic product of my conception, and it is logical that in the situation it should produce greater confusion and disorder and another element of romantic contrast.

But I had precisely to *present* this organic and natural chaos. And to present a chaos is not at all to present chaotically, that is, romantically. That my presentation is the reverse of confused, that it is quite simple, clear, and orderly, is proved by the clarity which the intrigue, the characters, the fantastic and realistic, dramatic and comic levels of the

work have had for every public in the world and by the way
in which, for those with more searching vision, the unusual
values enclosed within it come out.

Great is the confusion of tongues among men if criticisms
thus made find words for their expression. No less great than
this confusion is the intimate law of order which, obeyed in all
points, makes this work of mine classical and typical and at
its catastrophic close forbids the use of words. Though the
audience eventually understands that one does not create life
by artifice and that the drama of the six characters cannot
be presented without an author to give them value with his
spirit, the Manager remains vulgarly anxious to know how the
thing turned out, and the "ending" is remembered by the Son
in its sequence of actual moments, but without any sense and
therefore not needing a human voice for its expression. It
happens stupidly, uselessly, with the going off of a mechanical
weapon on stage. It breaks up and disperses the sterile experiment of the characters and the actors, which has apparently
been made without the assistance of the poet.

The poet, unknown to them, as if looking on at a distance
during the whole period of the experiment, was at the same
time busy creating—with it and of it—his own play.

SIX CHARACTERS
IN SEARCH OF AN AUTHOR

by LUIGI PIRANDELLO

1921

SIX CHARACTERS
IN SEARCH OF AN AUTHOR[13]

Adapted by Paul Avila Mayer

CHARACTERS

FATHER

MOTHER

STEPDAUGHTER

SON

BOY (*nonspeaking*)

LITTLE GIRL (*nonspeaking*)

MEMBERS OF THE COMPANY

DIRECTOR

LEADING MAN

LEADING LADY

SECOND FEMALE LEAD

INGENUE

JUVENILE

OTHER ACTORS AND
  ACTRESSES

STAGE DOOR MAN

FIRST STAGE MANAGER

SECOND STAGE MANAGER
  (*prompter*)

STAGEHANDS

[13] Translation Copyright, © 1962, by Paul Avila Mayer. Reprinted by permission of the translator, and by permission of E.P. Dutton & Co., Inc., publishers of *Naked Masks: Five Plays* by Luigi Pirandello, edited by Eric Bentley. Copyright, 1922, 1952, by E.P. Dutton & Co., Inc., renewal, 1950, by Stefano, Fausto and Lietta Pirandello.

ACT ONE

DAYTIME. THE PRESENT. THE STAGE OF A THEATRE

[N.B. *There are no acts or scenes in the play. The performance will be interrupted twice, once when the* DIRECTOR
and the CHARACTERS *withdraw for a conference and the*
ACTORS *take a "break," and a second time when a stage
hand lowers the curtain by mistake.*

*When the audience enters the theatre, the curtain is up.
The stage is empty and in semi-darkness. Only one or two
work lights provide illumination. The atmosphere is that
of an empty theatre in which no play is being performed.
And this is precisely right. For, throughout the evening,
the audience should feel that it has stumbled onto a play
that occurs rather than that it is witnessing a carefully
rehearsed performance.*

*To the left and right of the stage, temporary rehearsal
steps are in place leading down from the stage into the
orchestra section of the theatre. On the stage are as many
chairs and tables as are required for the rehearsal which
is about to take place. Toward the rear of the theatre,
partially out of sight, is an old, upright piano.*

As the house lights dim, a STAGEHAND *enters from the
wings. He carries several pieces of wood and some car-
penter's tools. Crossing to a position under one of the work
lights, the* STAGEHAND *begins to nail two of the pieces of
wood together. At the first sound of his hammering the*
FIRST STAGE MANAGER *rushes in from the wings. The* FIRST
STAGE MANAGER *carries a clip board holding various appropriate papers.*]

FIRST STAGE MANAGER. Hey! What do you think you're doing?
STAGEHAND. What's it look like? I'm nailing.
FIRST STAGE MANAGER [*looking at his watch*]. At this hour?
Rehearsal's starting. The Director'll be here any minute.
STAGEHAND. Well, let me tell you something. I've got to have
time to do my work, too.
FIRST STAGE MANAGER. You'll get it, but you can't do this now.
STAGEHAND. Then when?
FIRST STAGE MANAGER. After the rehearsal. Now, come on.

Get all this stuff out of here and let me set up. [*During the next few moments, mumbling and grumbling to himself, the* STAGEHAND *gathers up the pieces of wood and his tools, and exits; as he does so, the* FIRST STAGE MANAGER *moves to the center of the stage, calls off-stage.*] O.K., Charlie, light 'em up. [*He looks up toward the lights; nothing happens.*] Hey, Charlie! [*Still nothing happens.*] Charlie, are you deaf? Turn on the lights.

CHARLIE'S VOICE [*off-stage*]. Sorry!

[*Immediately, one by one, the lights come on. After satisfying himself that all the lights are working, the* FIRST STAGE MANAGER *moves around the stage adjusting tables and chairs, preparing for the rehearsal which is about to take place.*

As he does so, the ACTORS *and* ACTRESSES *of the company enter. One at a time, then in groups of two and three, they straggle casually onto the stage. There are nine or ten of them in all, as many as would be required to perform Pirandello's "Rules of the Game." Their clothing is suitable for the weather outside of the theatre so that the audience feels that the* ACTORS, *too, have just entered the house. However, without exaggerating their costumes in any way, all of the* ACTORS *wear light colored, gay clothing which will be in sharp contrast to that worn by the* CHARACTERS *when they enter.*

During the short scene which precedes the entrance of the DIRECTOR, *the action is improvised. Various members of the company greet one another; some find seats; others remain standing; some smoke; three of the younger members of the company find their way to the piano where one plays while the other two move through a few simple steps; one member of the company reads aloud a short paragraph from a topical trade publication. The atmosphere is that of a natural and animated prelude to the rehearsal of a play.*

After a few moments, the action is interrupted by the entrance down the side aisle of the theatre of the SECOND STAGE MANAGER *and the* DIRECTOR. *As they near the stage, the* SECOND STAGE MANAGER *begins to clap his hands and call for attention.*]

SECOND STAGE MANAGER. All right, let's go, let's go!

[*The music and the dancing stop; the* ACTORS *all move forward and gather at the center of the stage as the* SECOND STAGE

MANAGER *and the* DIRECTOR *come up a set of temporary stairs onto the stage. The* DIRECTOR, *from his dress and manner, gives the impression of being a man of parts.*]

DIRECTOR. Hello everybody.

[*The* ACTORS *ad lib greeting without referring to the time of day; as they do so, the* DIRECTOR *turns to the* FIRST STAGE MANAGER.]

DIRECTOR [*continues*]. John, have you got the props?

FIRST STAGE MANAGER. They're backstage. Do you want any now?

DIRECTOR. Later. [*To the* ACTORS; *briskly.*] Well suppose we get started. [*Noticing a gesture from the* FIRST STAGE MANAGER.] Hello! Someone missing?

FIRST STAGE MANAGER. Our leading lady.

DIRECTOR. Again! [*Looking at his watch; after a momentary hesitation.*] We're ten minutes late already. We'll begin without her. But let me know the minute she gets here. I'll have a few things to . . .

LEADING LADY [*rushing down the center aisle; carrying a small dog*]. No, no, for heaven's sake, I'm here! I'm here! [*Breathlessly.*] I'm so sorry! I couldn't get a taxi! [*Coming up a set of temporary steps onto the stage.*] Anyway you haven't started yet, and besides, I'm not even in the first scene. [*Handing the small dog to the* FIRST STAGE MANAGER.] Tie him near a radiator, won't you, sweetie?

[*The* FIRST STAGE MANAGER *exits with the dog.*]

DIRECTOR. Must you bring that . . . oh, never mind! [*To the* ACTORS; *more businesslike.*] Come on, let's go. Act One of "Rules of the Game." Places, please.

[*Some of the* ACTORS *retire to the side of the stage; others take up "places" in the playing area; the* LEADING LADY, *however, ignoring the others, moves to the front of the stage and practices striking several different dramatic poses; the* DIRECTOR *turns to her.*]

DIRECTOR [*continues*]. Am I to understand you now think you're in this scene?

LEADING LADY. What? Good heavens, you know very well I'm not! [*Crossing to a chair, she sits, sulking.*]

SECOND STAGE MANAGER [*reading from the "book" as the* LEADING LADY *seats herself*]. "The house of Leo Gallant.

An unusual room being used both as a dining room and a study. In the center of the room a large table is laid. Nearby, a writing desk is covered with books and papers. The decor throughout is luxurious. There are three exits: stage rear, a door leading into Leo's bedroom; stage left, a door leading into the kitchen; stage right, the main exit."

DIRECTOR. Pay attention, please. [*Pointing to the areas where the various exits will be.*] There's the main exit, there's the bedroom, and there's the kitchen. [*To the* LEADING MAN.] You'll exit, of course, into the kitchen.

SECOND STAGE MANAGER. "Scene One": [*He hesitates, looks up from the "book."*] Do you want me to go on reading the stage directions?

DIRECTOR [*impatiently*]. Yes, yes, go on.

SECOND STAGE MANAGER [*reading*]. "When the curtain rises, Leo Gallant, dressed in a cook's hat and apron, is busy beating an egg in a bowl. Phillip . . ."

LEADING MAN [*interrupting; to the* DIRECTOR]. Excuse me but is it really necessary for me to wear a cook's hat?

DIRECTOR [*annoyed; pointing to the "book"*]. That's what it says.

LEADING MAN. But I'll look ridiculous!

DIRECTOR. Ridiculous? Of course you'll look ridiculous. What do you expect me to do about it? Is it my fault that . . . [*He names a popular play of the day.*] . . . was cancelled? Can I help it if things are in such a muddle that we're reduced to reviving a play of Pirandello's which no one understood when it was written and which makes even less sense today?

[*Some of the* ACTORS *laugh; the* DIRECTOR *crosses slowly toward the* LEADING MAN; *during the next few moments, offstage voices are heard, raised in argument.*]

DIRECTOR [*continues*]. You *will* wear a cook's hat! And you will beat an egg! But do you think for one minute that you're just a man on stage beating an egg? You are not! You represent the shell of the egg you are beating!

[*Several of the* ACTORS *laugh or comment at this; the* DIRECTOR *glares about him.*]

DIRECTOR [*continues*]. Be quiet and listen to me! This is important! [*To the* LEADING MAN.] The shell of the egg stands for reason; its contents for instinct. You are an empty eggshell, without instinct, and therefore blind. In "The Rules of the Game" you represent reason and your wife

represents instinct. Each of you is incomplete. Each of you
becomes a puppet presentation of yourself rather than a
whole person. Do you understand?

LEADING MAN. I most certainly do not.

DIRECTOR. Neither do I. But let's get on; it's going to be a great
flop anyway! All right . . .

[*As the* DIRECTOR *turns toward the* SECOND STAGE MANAGER,
he sees the STAGE DOOR MAN *backing onto the stage; he
throws his hands in the air.*]

DIRECTOR [*continues*]. Now what?

[*Embarrassed, the* STAGE DOOR MAN *hurries forward in a most
apologetic manner. The* SIX CHARACTERS *enter immediately
after him.*]

[*The* FATHER *is in his late forties, a pale man with reddish
hair thinning at the temples. He wears a moustache. His
mouth is large and sensuous. The* FATHER *is dressed conservatively in a jacket and trousers. His manner varies
between two extremes. He is either relaxed and quite charming, or rough and almost violent.*

The MOTHER *is in her early forties, a small, weary woman. She seems thoroughly defeated by life, as if she has
been overwhelmed by some dreadful disgrace. She is dressed
in mourning and when her veil is lifted we will see a chalk
white, wax-like face. Her eyes are almost always downcast.*

The STEPDAUGHTER *is dashing and impudent. She is very
beautiful. She, too, wears mourning but with great elegance.
Her attitude toward the* BOY—*who is 14, a frightened, de-
jected figure, also dressed in mourning—is one of contempt;
on the other hand, she displays the greatest tenderness and
affection for the* LITTLE GIRL. *About 4 years old, the* LITTLE
GIRL *wears a white dress with a black sash at the waist.*

The SON *is 22, tall, severe in manner. He treats his* FA-
THER *with resentment and his* MOTHER *with superciliousness
and indifference. He is dressed properly, conservatively, but
is clearly not in mourning.*]

STAGE DOOR MAN [*to the* DIRECTOR]. Mister, I'm sorry, but . . .
[*He hesitates.*]

DIRECTOR [*roughly*]. Yes, yes, what is it?

STAGE DOOR MAN. These people, they say they gotta see you.

[*He shrugs hopelessly as the* DIRECTOR *and the* ACTORS *turn
in surprise toward the* SIX CHARACTERS.]

DIRECTOR. But I'm in rehearsal! [*To the* SIX CHARACTERS; *impatiently.*] Who are you? What do you want?

[*The* FATHER *comes forward, half followed by the others; the* STAGE DOOR MAN *lingers for a moment, then turns and exits quietly.*]

FATHER [*coming forward*]. We are here in search of an author.

DIRECTOR. An author? What author?

FATHER. Any author.

DIRECTOR [*waving them away toward the wings*]. I'm very sorry, there's no author here. We're not doing a new play.

STEPDAUGHTER [*coming forward a step; vivaciously*]. So much the better. Then we can be your new play.

JUVENILE [*as the other* ACTORS *murmur among themselves*]. Well, listen to her!

FATHER [*momentarily stymied; to the* STEPDAUGHTER]. If there is no author here . . . [*Turning back to the* DIRECTOR; *hopefully.*] . . . perhaps you would be our author . . .

DIRECTOR. Are you trying to be funny? I told you before . . . [*Again he gestures towards the wings, indicating that they should leave.*]

FATHER [*instantly; tensely*]. Oh, please, don't say that. No, not funny. Never funny. We have come to bring you a play, a terrible play of suffering and anguish.

STEPDAUGHTER. If we're a hit, we might make your fortune for you.

DIRECTOR. I'm sorry but you've got to get out of here. We've no time to waste on lunatics.

FATHER. Why do you jump to conclusions? You know very well that life is full of infinite absurdities, absurdities which do not need to *seem* true simply because they *are* true.

DIRECTOR. What the devil are you talking about?

FATHER. I am saying that when the ordinary order of things is reversed, people often cry out of madness. For example, when we labor to create things which have all the appearance of reality that they may pass for reality itself. But if this is madness, it is also the very essence of your profession, is it not?

[*Some of the* ACTORS *grumble a little among themselves at this suggestion.*]

DIRECTOR. Then the theatre is full of madmen, is that what you're saying?

FATHER. Making what isn't true seem true . . . for fun . . .

Isn't that your purpose, bringing imaginary characters to life?

DIRECTOR [*speaking for the entire company*]. I think that you should understand that those of us in the theatre feel it is a creative art, and a very worthwhile occupation. If our playwrights, in recent years, have only given us commercial plays to perform, I'll have you know that we are proud also to have given life, on this very stage, to immortal works.

[*Some of the* ACTORS *nod in approval and applaud these words.*]

FATHER [*immediately*]. Yes! Exactly! To living beings more alive than those who breathe and wear clothes. Less real, perhaps, but more true. We are in complete agreement.

DIRECTOR [*as some of the* ACTORS *look astonished*]. Wait a minute! You've lost me. You said before. . . .

FATHER. I spoke only because you said you had no time to waste with lunatics. Surely no one knows better than you that nature uses the instrument of human fantasy to unfold her creative work at the highest level.

DIRECTOR [*completely lost*]. What is all this? Where does all this get us?

FATHER. It's quite simple if you'll only try to understand. You were born as man. But one can be born in other ways . . . as a tree . . . or a stone . . . as water . . . or a butter- fly . . . [*Gesturing to include himself and the other* CHARAC- TERS.] . . . or even as a character in a play.

DIRECTOR [*suddenly understanding; amused and ironical*]. And you and your friends were born as characters?

FATHER. Exactly! Alive, just as you see us here! [*Several of the* ACTORS *laugh at this; the* FATHER *looks pained.*] I wish you wouldn't laugh at us. Because, as I said before, we carry such suffering and horror within us . . . [*He half turns toward the* MOTHER.] . . . as you should have guessed from this woman who is, as you can see, dressed in mourn- ing.

[*Saying this, the* FATHER *extends his hand and leads the* MOTHER *toward the center of the stage. She crosses toward him in a solemn and tragic manner. As she does so, the* BOY *and the* LITTLE GIRL *move solemnly with her. The* SON, *however, turns and moves upstage, away from the other* CHARACTERS. *The* STEPDAUGHTER *moves downstage where she leans in a provocative pose against a proscenium arch. All of these movements are performed simultaneously with a unified rhythm and solemnity which first astonishes the* ACTORS, *then causes them to break into applause, as if for a performance being presented for their benefit.*]

DIRECTOR [*open-mouthed for a moment; then angry*]. Wait a minute! [*To the* ACTORS.] Be quiet, all of you! [*To the* CHARACTERS.] This has gone far enough. I've told you, I'm busy! [*To the* FIRST STAGE MANAGER.] For God's sake, get them out of here!

FIRST STAGE MANAGER [*to the* CHARACTERS]. All right, now you've got to leave. Please. Come on, let's go, let's go.

FATHER. But no, look, we . . .

DIRECTOR [*shouting*]. Don't you understand? I'm in rehearsal! Write me a letter!

LEADING MAN. We don't have time for practical jokes!

FATHER [*quietly; as if astonished*]. You don't believe us. I know it's difficult, but . . . [*Coming forward; with determination.*] . . . surely, in your profession, you're accustomed to seeing the characters created by an author spring to life in yourselves here on the stage, every night? Or is it, perhaps, that there is no script . . . [*He points toward the "book."*] . . . there that contains us?

STEPDAUGHTER [*moving forward; to the* DIRECTOR; *coquettishly*]. We are really six most interesting characters . . . but lost, somehow . . .

FATHER [*brushing her aside*]. Yes, that's it exactly. [*To the* DIRECTOR.] You see, the author who created us was never able to finish his play. And this was really a crime. Because anyone fortunate enough to be born a character . . . why, he can laugh at death. A man must always die; even an author must always die; but a character lives forever. And without having to have extraordinary gifts or accomplishments. Who was Sancho Panza? Who were the Three Musketeers? Yet they will live forever because like seeds fallen into rich soil they were fortunate enough to find a fertile fantasy which raised them, nourished them, and gave them eternal life.

DIRECTOR [*more weary than impatient*]. Yes, yes, but what is it you want here?

FATHER [*passionately*]. We want to live!

DIRECTOR [*sardonic*]. Through all eternity?

FATHER. Oh, no. Just for a moment . . . in you.

CHARACTER LADY. How extraordinary!

LEADING LADY. They want to live in us?

JUVENILE [*indicating the* STEPDAUGHTER]. That's all right with me . . . as far as she's concerned.

FATHER. You must give us a chance! Our play is here for the making! [*To the* DIRECTOR *and the* ACTORS.] If you and your actors are willing, we can work it up among ourselves, very quickly.

DIRECTOR. Work what up? We're not here to do improvisations. We're here to do legitimate plays.

FATHER. Exactly! And that's why we came to you, to do our play!

DIRECTOR. But there's no script!

FATHER. The script is inside us! [*Some of the* ACTORS *laugh.*] Don't you see? We *are* the script! We *are* the drama! And our passions are so strong that they are forcing us to cry out to you to let us play it!

STEPDAUGHTER [*sneering, impudent, shameless*]. Yes, my passion! Ah, if you only knew! My passion . . . for him! [*The* STEPDAUGHTER *points to the* FATHER *and moves forward as if to embrace him; when he flinches and moves away from her, she breaks into loud scornful laughter.*]

FATHER [*shouting*]. Stop it! Stop that laughing! We've had enough of you! I forbid you to speak!

STEPDAUGHTER. Oh, you do! [*Turning to the* ACTORS.] Then perhaps you'll permit me, ladies and gentlemen. Let me show you how I, who have been an orphan for only two months, can dance and sing.

[*With a malicious mischievousness, she sings and dances for a moment; her song is an animated and slightly suggestive French love song. While she is singing and dancing, several of the younger* ACTORS *raise their arms toward her, as if to join her in her dance. She moves away from them, however, in each instance. When she finishes her song, the* ACTORS *break into applause. When the* DIRECTOR *rebukes her, the* STEPDAUGHTER *stands quietly where she is, without moving, as if her thoughts were far away.*]

ACTORS [*laughing and clapping*]. Bravo! Very good!

DIRECTOR [*angry*]. Be quiet, all of you! [*To the* STEPDAUGHTER.] What do you think this is, a nightclub? [*To the* FATHER, *lowering his voice slightly*.] What's the matter with her? Is she crazy?

FATHER. No. It's worse than that.

STEPDAUGHTER [*running lightly to the* DIRECTOR]. Yes, worse! Far worse! Oh, won't you let us play it for you? Then you'll see that . . . [*Turning to the* LITTLE GIRL; *leading her to the* DIRECTOR.] . . . when this little angel here . . isn't she beautiful? . . . [*Picking up the child and kissing her.*] . . . you darling, you darling . . . [*Putting the child down, adding, almost involuntarily but with great feeling.*] . . . well, when God suddenly takes this dear little child away from her poor mother, and this imbecile . . . [*She seizes the* BOY *and drags him forward.*] . . . does the stupidest of all stupid things, like the idiot he is . . . [*She pushes the* BOY *roughly back toward the* MOTHER.] . . . then you'll see me run away. Yes, I'll run away and you'll be rid of me. Not now, but believe me, soon enough. After all that has happened between him and me . . . [*She indicates the* FATHER *with a leering wink.*] . . . I can't stay here any longer, watching the misery of my mother because *of that* [*Spitting out the last word, she whirls and points to the* SON.] Look at him! Just look at him! So cold . . . aloof . . superior . . . because he's the legitimate son. He despises me, he despises him . . . [*She points to the* BOY, *then to the* LITTLE GIRL.] . . . he even despises the baby there because we're bastards! Do you understand? We're bastards! [*Crossing to the* MOTHER, *embracing her.*] And he won't even recognize his own mother, this poor woman who is the mother of us all. He treats her with contempt, as if she were only the mother . . . of us three. [*All of this has been spoken in great excitement; now she turns and softly spits out two words at the* SON.] You swine!

MOTHER [*to the* DIRECTOR; *in anguish*]. Please . . . for the children's sake . . . I beg you . . . [*She sways on her feet begins to faint.*] Ah! My God!

FATHER [*running to support her; as the* ACTORS *look on in consternation*]. A chair! Bring the poor widow a chair!

OLD CHARACTER MAN. What's happened? Has she really fainted?

DIRECTOR [*to the* FIRST STAGE MANAGER *who is bringing a chair to the* MOTHER]. Quickly! Quickly!

FATHER [*when the* MOTHER *is seated, the* FATHER *begins to lift her veil*]. I want you to see her face.

MOTHER [*trying to prevent him from lifting her veil*]. No, no! For God's sake, don't!

FATHER [*pushing her protesting hands aside*]. Let them see you. [*He lifts the veil, revealing her chalk white, wax-like face.*]

MOTHER [*rising; covering her face with her hands; to the*

DIRECTOR; *in desperation*]. Please, please . . . don't let him go on with this . . . it's too horrible!

DIRECTOR [*as the* MOTHER *sits down again; stunned*]. I don't understand. [*To the* FATHER.] This lady is your wife?

FATHER [*quickly*]. Yes, my wife.

DIRECTOR. But, if you are still alive, how can she be a widow?

[*Some of the* ACTORS *smile and laugh at this.*]

FATHER [*hurt; sharply*]. Don't laugh! For the love of Christ, don't laugh! This is her tragedy. She has had a lover, the man who rightfully should be here.

MOTHER [*with a cry*]. No! No!

STEPDAUGHTER. He has the good luck to be dead. He died two months ago which is why we are still in mourning.

FATHER. But the reason he isn't here is not because he is dead. Just look at her. Surely you can see that her story isn't in the love of two men . . . two men for whom she was incapable of feeling anything, except possibly a little gratitude—for him, not for me. No, her story, her tragedy is in the children, the four children she had by these two men.

MOTHER. Did you say I had these two men? Had you the nerve to suggest I wanted them? [*To the* DIRECTOR; *pointing to the* FATHER.] It was his doing! He forced me to go away with the other man!

STEPDAUGHTER [*immediately; indignantly*]. That isn't so!

MOTHER [*amazed*]. It isn't?

STEPDAUGHTER. It isn't so! It isn't!

MOTHER. What do you know about it?

STEPDAUGHTER. I know! [*To the* DIRECTOR.] You mustn't believe her! Don't you realize why she's saying it? Because of him! [*She points to the* SON.] She's torturing herself, destroying herself, because of that son of hers, because of his indifference. She wants to make him believe that if she left him when he was two years old, it was because he . . . [*She points to the* FATHER.] . . . made her do it!

MOTHER [*vigorously*]. But he did make me! As God is my witness, he did! [*To the* DIRECTOR; *pointing to the* FATHER.] Ask him! Ask him if he didn't! [*To the* STEPDAUGHTER.] You don't know anything about it.

STEPDAUGHTER [*quietly*]. I know that you were happy with my father, that you lived together in peace and contentment. I know that you used to sing. Can you deny it?

MOTHER [*shaking her head*]. I don't deny it.

STEPDAUGHTER. He loved you. He loved you every day of his

life. [*To the* BOY.] Isn't it true? Go on—tell them! Why don't you say something, you little fool?

MOTHER. Leave the poor child alone. Why do you want to make me seem ungrateful? I don't want to say anything against your father. But can't you understand it wasn't my fault? I didn't want to leave my baby; I didn't want to leave my home.

FATHER. What she says is true. It was my doing.

LEADING MAN. My God! What a show!

LEADING LADY. And we're the audience this time.

JUVENILE. For a change.

DIRECTOR [*more interested*]. Let's hear what they have to say. [*He moves downstage, then faces up toward the* CHARACTERS.]

SON [*without moving; slow, cool, ironical in tone*]. Oh, yes! Now you'll hear a fine piece of philosophy. He's going to tell you about the "demon of experiment."

FATHER [*to the* SON]. What a cynical idiot you are. [*To the* DIRECTOR.] He mocks me because of this expression which I use in my own defense.

SON [*contemptuously*]. Words! Words!

FATHER. Yes!! Words!! Words that bring consolation . . . to all of us . . . when we are faced with something so horrible, when we must live with such guilt . . . words that say nothing but bring peace.

STEPDAUGHTER [*contemptuously*]. And dull your sense of remorse! That above all!

FATHER [*quickly*]. I have eased my remorse with far more than words!!

STEPDAUGHTER. Oh, yes! There was a little bit of money, too! [*To the* ACTORS; *swinging her body sensuously.*] The money he offered me in payment, ladies and gentlemen.

[*There is a sensation of horror among the* ACTORS.]

SON [*to the* STEPDAUGHTER]. My God, you're revolting!

STEPDAUGHTER [*innocently*]. Revolting? But there it was, in a pale blue envelope, on the little mahogany table in the room provided by Madam Pace. [*To the* ACTORS.] You understand about Madam Pace? One of those ladies who runs a very elegant dress shop, a very *special* dress shop, where decent girls from poor families are led along, step by-step, until . . . [*The* STEPDAUGHTER *throws a contemptuous glance at the* FATHER.]

SON [*bitterly*]. She thinks she's bought the right to lord it

over all of us with that money he was going to pay her . . .
but which, thank God . . . and I want to emphasize this
. . . he had no reason to pay!

STEPDAUGHTER. But it was a near thing, a very near thing
indeed! [*She laughs.*]

MOTHER [*rising; in protest*]. Have you no shame?

STEPDAUGHTER [*in an outburst of anger*]. Shame? This is my
revenge! I am trembling with desire . . . to live that scene!
I can see the room . . . here is the window . . . there the
fireplace . . . the bed . . . and over here, in front of the
window, the little mahogany table . . . and the pale blue
envelope with the money inside. I can see it all so clearly.
I have only to reach out and pick the money up. But you
gentlemen should turn your backs, because I am almost
naked. No, I don't blush any more! he's the one who does
the blushing now. [*Pointing to the* FATHER.] How pale he
was . . . and stammering . . . as he . . . [*She pauses; smiles.*]

DIRECTOR [*in horror*]. Just a minute . . .

FATHER. Thank God! Put your foot down! All these accusations! You've got to let me explain!

STEPDAUGHTER. This is no place for your lies!

FATHER [*to the* STEPDAUGHTER]. I'm not going to . . . [*Turning desperately to the* DIRECTOR.] I only want to tell how it
really was!

STEPDAUGHTER. Oh, yes, of course you do! You want to tell
it your way!

FATHER. But don't you see this is the cause of the whole
trouble? In the words, the very words we use. Each of
us has inside him his own special world. And how can we
ever really understand each other if I put into the words
I speak the sense and value of things as I see them while
whoever is listening inevitably translates them into the sense
and value they have for him. We think we understand each
other but we never really do. [*Gesturing to include all of
them.*] Look at us here. [*Pointing to the* MOTHER.] All my
pity, all the pity I feel for this poor woman she takes as a
special form of terrible cruelty.

MOTHER [*a cry*]. But you sent me away!

FATHER [*dispassionately*]. There. Listen to her. I sent her
away. She believes that.

MOTHER [*in a lowered voice*]. You know how to talk. I . . .
[*She hesitates, turns desperately to the* DIRECTOR.] You
must believe me. After he married me . . . who knows why
. . . I was a poor, shy sort of girl . . .

FATHER [*interrupting; quickly*]. But it was for just those qualities, the shyness, the humility, that I loved you. I married
you for that very humility, believing . . . [*During this
speech, the* MOTHER *has turned her head away from the*
FATHER *and made a gesture of contradiction; seeing this,
he stops, opens his arms wide in a gesture of hopelessness.*]
Ah! You see? She won't listen. It's frightening, this deafness . . . [*He taps his forehead.*] . . . this mental deafness
of hers. A good heart, yes, for the children, but the brain,
deaf, a deafness which was my constant despair.

STEPDAUGHTER. Oh, yes! Now ask him what good all his
intellectuality, his celebrated mental abilities have done us?

FATHER [*quietly; with a touch of regret*]. If we could only
foresee the evil that may result from the good we think
we are doing.

[*During the last few minutes, with ever-increasing anger the*
LEADING LADY *has been watching the* LEADING MAN *flirting
with the* STEPDAUGHTER. *Now, very annoyed, she steps
forward toward the* DIRECTOR.]

LEADING LADY. I beg your pardon but are we going to rehearse today?

DIRECTOR. In a little while. Let's hear them out.

JUVENILE. Yes.

INGENUE. I think it's fascinating.

LEADING LADY [*with a meaningful glance at the* LEADING MAN].
If you like that sort of thing.

DIRECTOR. But you must explain everything clearly.

FATHER. Very well. Now, look here. I had a poor, ineffectual
man working for me—my assistant. Well, over a period of
time, he becomes attached to her. [*He points to the*
MOTHER.] There was nothing wrong about it. Far from it.
He was a good man, very modest and self-effacing, very
much like her. The two of them were incapable of doing
anything wrong, or even thinking it.

STEPDAUGHTER. So he thought it—for them—and then urged
them on!

FATHER. That isn't true. I thought that what I was doing
would be good for them, and I must confess for myself,
as well. Things had come to the point that I couldn't say
a word to either of them without their automatically ex-
changing a sympathetic glance. I could see them silently
asking each other how to handle me, how to prevent me
from getting angry. And this was enough, as I'm sure you

understand, to keep me in a constant rage of intolerable exasperation.

DIRECTOR. Why didn't you fire your assistant?

FATHER. I did! But then I had to watch this poor woman wandering around the house like some forlorn lost animal, like one of those strays you take in out of pity.

MOTHER [*protesting*]. But . . .

FATHER [*turning on her; forestalling what she is about to say*]. The son. You want to tell him about the son, don't you?

MOTHER. He took my baby away from me!

FATHER. Not out of cruelty! I sent him away to the country so that he could grow up strong and healthy.

STEPDAUGHTER. And just look at him!

FATHER. Is it my fault he grew up that way? I sent him to live with good people who had a farm because she . . . [*He points to the* MOTHER.] . . . didn't seem to be strong enough . . . although it was because of that very weakness, that humility that I married her in the first place. A mistake, perhaps, but what was I to do? I was a healthy young man with a young's man's normal appetites. All my life I've sought to lead a life of solid morality.

[*The* STEPDAUGHTER *breaks into loud cynical laughter at this.*]

FATHER. Stop it! Make her stop! She's driving me mad!

DIRECTOR [*to the* STEPDAUGHTER]. Yes, for God's sake be quiet! Let him finish what he has to say!

[*At the* DIRECTOR'S *rebuke, the* STEPDAUGHTER *is silent, a half smile on her lips; the* DIRECTOR *again moves downstage, facing up toward the* CHARACTERS.]

FATHER. I couldn't go on living with her . . . [*He indicates the* MOTHER.] . . . not so much because of the irritation she caused me, or the boredom, the awful boredom, but because of the guilt and pity I felt for her. She was so unhappy.

MOTHER. So he sent me away!

FATHER [*instantly*]. But well provided for . . . to the other man . . . that she might be free of me.

MOTHER. And to free himself.

FATHER [*nodding*]. I admit it. And a great deal of harm resulted. But I meant well, and I did it more for her sake than my own, I swear it! [*Folding his arms; turning to the* MOTHER.] Didn't I keep track of you? Didn't I keep track of you until that fellow suddenly carried you off to another town, no forwarding address, nothing. Did I ever bother you? Wasn't I content to watch from a distance? I wanted to watch; certainly I did; but without any ulterior motives; simply out of pure interest. I just wanted to watch the incredibly tender family that was growing up around you. [*Indicating the* STEPDAUGHTER.] She can testify to that.

STEPDAUGHTER [*conveying a sordid innuendo in her tone*]. Oh, I most certainly can. When I was just a little girl . . . with braids down to my shoulders and panties you could see underneath my short skirt, I used to see him standing by the door of the school, waiting for me. He came to watch me, to see how I was growing up.

FATHER. This is monstrous!

STEPDAUGHTER. Oh? Why?

FATHER. Monstrous! Monstrous!!! [*Turning to the* DIRECTOR *in excitement; then controlling himself and continuing in a conversational tone.*] After she went away . . . [*He indicates the* MOTHER.] . . . my house seemed to be empty. She had been such a disappointment to me, but she had filled my house. Suddenly I was like a fly caught between a window and a screen. I—buzzed around in the emptiness . . . [*Indicating the* SON.] The boy was educated away from home. When he came back to me I didn't know him. He didn't seem to be my son at all. With no mother to link him to me he grew up entirely on his own, quite apart from me. He had neither intellectual appreciation for me nor affection for me. So then, in a strange way, I found myself attracted to her . . . and her family. At first I simply wanted to see what had resulted from my efforts. Then the thought of her, and them, began to fill the emptiness I felt around me. I had to know that she was happy, and at peace. I wanted to think that she was fortunate because she was so far removed from the complicated torments of my spirit. And so, to have proof of this, I would go to see the little girl coming out of school.

STEPDAUGHTER. Oh, indeed he would! He used to follow me along the streets after school until I got home. He would smile at me and wave. I looked at him, not without interest, wondering who he was. I told my mother and she guessed immediately that it was him.

[*The* MOTHER *nods.*]

STEPDAUGHTER. She didn't want me to see him and kept me home from school for several days. But when I did go back, there he was paper bag in his hand. He came up to me, put his arms around me and caressed me, and then he opened the paper bag and took out a beautiful big straw hat with flowers on it, a present for me.

DIRECTOR. We've wandered a bit from our story, haven't we?

SON. Yes! This is literature, literature!

FATHER. Literature indeed! This is life! Passion!

DIRECTOR. That may be, but it won't play.

FATHER [*quickly*]. I agree with you. This is only the background. I'm not suggesting that this part should be staged. As you can very well see . . . [*He indicates the* STEP-DAUGHTER.] . . . she is obviously no longer the little girl with braids down to her shoulders . . .

STEPDAUGHTER [*interrupting; again with a sordid innuendo in her tone*]. . . . and pretty little flowered panties which you could see underneath my skirt . . .

FATHER [*instantly; desperately changing the subject*]. Now we come to the plot! New, complex . . .

STEPDAUGHTER [*coming forward; proud and gloomy*]. As soon as my father died . . .

FATHER [*interrupting; taking up the story*]. . . . they fell into the most wretched poverty. They came back here and because of her stupidity . . . [*He indicates the* MOTHER.] . . . I knew nothing about it. If she could not bring herself to get in touch with me, she might at least have asked her son or her daughter to let me know they were in need.

MOTHER [*to the* DIRECTOR]. How was I to know he felt this way?

FATHER. That was always your mistake, never to have understood any of my feelings.

MOTHER. After all those years, and all that had happened . . .

FATHER. Was it my fault you disappeared? [*To the* DIRECTOR.] I tell you, one day they were here, the next they were gone. He'd found a job somewhere else and they vanished overnight. I could find no trace of them anywhere. So, naturally enough, as the years went on my interest in them dwindled. But after they returned, then the whole thing exploded violently and unexpectedly into . . . what else can I call it but melodrama? . . . when I was driven by the demands of my miserable flesh, which is still alive with desire . . . [*He pauses, turns passionately to the* DIRECTOR.] Can you understand the guilt, the misery of a moral man, living alone, trying to divert himself with reading and music, and able to think of nothing but women? Do you know what it means to detest casual affairs and still be driven to them? Not to be old enough to do without a woman, or young enough to go and look for one without shame and loathing? Did I say misery? It's a horror! Knowing, all the time, that no woman will give herself to me for love . . . realizing that . . . I should do without, shouldn't I? Of course. Or at least, as far as the world is concerned, seem to do without. Because we all try to appear to our fellow men at our best, dressed in a costume of dignity and propriety. But we all know the unconfessable things that lie within the secrecy of our own hearts. [*Painfully.*] One yields, one gives way to temptation, only to rise again immediately afterwards, God knows, determined to re-establish our dignity and propriety, as if dignity were like a gravestone, concealing, burying out of sight the memories of our awful shame. And we're all like this, I think, except that some of us lack the courage to admit to . . . certain things.

STEPDAUGHTER. But have the courage to *do* them! All of them!

FATHER. Yes, all of them! But only in secret! The courage is not in the doing, but in the admission of guilt. The moment that a man admits his real feelings, society at once says he's different, calls him a cynic. That's not true. He's not a cynic, but he is different. He is better, much better, because he is not afraid to reveal with his intelligence the blush of shame, the shame to which most men close their eyes. And woman . . . is she really different? She looks at you, tantalizing, invitingly. You take her in your arms. And no sooner does she feel herself in your grasp than she closes her eyes. It is the sign of her mission, the sign by which she says to man: "Blind yourself; I am blind."

STEPDAUGHTER. And when she no longer closes her eyes? When she no longer feels the need of hiding her shame from herself? When instead she sees, dry-eyed and dispassionately, the shame of the man who blinds himself without love? [*To the* ACTORS; *pointing to the* FATHER.] What disgust, what unutterable disgust I feel for all this "philosophy" of his! What is it but an elaborate excuse for his own lechery! I can't listen to any more! When he simplifies life to one ingredient . . . lust . . . throwing aside every human concept of virtue . . . decency . . . idealism! After all he's done, what could be more revolting than these . . . crocodile tears!

DIRECTOR [*moved by the* FATHER's *speech*]. Yes, but what

he says is true. I know that in my own case I . . . [*He stops; becomes more businesslike.*] But let's come to the point. This is still only a discussion.

FATHER. Very well. But a fact is like a sack. It won't stand up when it's empty. To make it stand up you must first pour into it all of the reasons and emotions which have caused it to exist. I couldn't possibly have been expected to know that after the death of that man, when they returned here in such utter poverty, she . . . [*indicating the* MOTHER.] . . . in her ignorance would go to work in a place like Madam Pace's.

MOTHER [*to the* DIRECTOR]. How was I to know? I needed work. It never entered my head for a minute that the old hag had her eye on my daughter.

STEPDAUGHTER. Poor Mama. Do you know what that woman did? She told me that Mama was so inefficient, so unsatisfactory, that she would have to let both of us go unless I took on . . . some *special* work. So I did. I paid for us, while . . . [*Indicating the* MOTHER.] . . . this poor creature thought she was sacrificing herself for me and the two children.

DIRECTOR [*immediately; suddenly understanding*]. And it was there, one day, that you met . . .

STEPDAUGHTER [*pointing to the* FATHER]. Him! Him! Yes, an old client. There's a scene for you to play!

FATHER. With the interruption . . . just before . . .

STEPDAUGHTER [*treacherously*]. Almost in time!

FATHER [*crying out in a loud voice*]. No, in time! In time! Because, fortunately, I recognized her in time. And I took them home. You can imagine what the situation is like now, for both of us. Living together in the same house . . . I cannot look her in the face.

STEPDAUGHTER. It's absolutely ridiculous. How can I possibly pretend, after all this, to be a proper young lady, well brought up and in complete accord with his damned aspirations for a life of "solid morality"?

FATHER. For me the whole drama lies in this one thing: that each of us believes himself to be a single person. It isn't true. With some people we are one person, with others we are quite a different person altogether. But to ourselves we retain the illusion of being always the same person to everyone. And we realize it isn't true when suddenly, to our horror, we are caught up into the air by some giant hook, frozen in time, suspended for all to see. Then we recognize that all of us was not in that particular action, that it would be an atrocious injustice to judge us by that action and that action alone . . . keeping us suspended, in pillory, as if our life were made up of only that one moment. Now do you understand the treachery of this girl? She surprised me in a place where she should never have known me, and in an action that should never have existed for her. And now she is trying to make the entire reality of my life from that one, fleeting, shameful moment. How unjust it is. Ah! [*Regaining control of himself.*] And, as you will see, the drama takes on a tremendous conflict because of this situation. [*Turning toward the* SON.] Then there are the others . . . him . . .

SON [*scornfully*]. Leave me alone! I have nothing to do with all this!

FATHER. What are you talking about?

SON. I have nothing and I want nothing to do with it. Because, as you very well know, I wasn't meant to be mixed up in all this with the rest of you.

STEPDAUGHTER. We're not good enough for him! He's so superior! But, as you may have noticed, ladies and gentlemen, when I look at him . . . he lowers his eyes. He knows the harm he's done me.

SON [*not looking at her*]. Me?

STEPDAUGHTER. Yes, you! I owe my life on the streets to you! Because you denied us, by the attitude you adopted, I won't say the intimacy of your home but even the mere hospitality which makes guests feel at ease. We were intruders who had come to disturb the kingdom of your legitimacy. I'd just like . . . [*To the* DIRECTOR.] . . . you to see some of the scene which took place between him and me. He says I've "lorded" it over everybody. But it was his behavior, his coldness, that forced me to take advantage of the thing he calls "revolting." The result was that when I went into that house with my mother, who is his mother as well, I went into the house as if it were mine.

SON [*coming forward*]. It's all great sport for them, isn't it, ganging up this way, always putting me in the wrong. But just imagine how I felt that fine day when an arrogant young woman arrived at the door, demanding to see my father with only a secretive smile hinting as to the nature of her business with him. And then when she came back again, more brazen than ever, bringing the little girl with her . . . I saw her treating my father . . . in such a mysteri-

ous way, asking him for money in such a tone of voice that
I knew he *had* to give it to her, had some obligation to do
so.

FATHER. As indeed I have. It is an obligation I owe your
mother.

SON. How was I to know that? When did I ever see her or
hear of her? Until one day she arrived with her . . . [*Indicating the* STEPDAUGHTER.] . . . and the boy and the little
girl, this time with all their luggage. Then I was suddenly
told, "This is *your* mother, too, you know." And as time
went on I began to understand . . . [*Indicating the* STEPDAUGHTER.] . . . from her attitude, why and how they had
come to live with us. I won't even begin to express what I
feel about it. I don't even allow myself to think about it.
So you see no action can be expected from me in this
affair. I am an unrealized character dramatically and I
find myself very much ill at ease in their company. So
please leave me out of it.

FATHER. Ridiculous! It's just because you're like that . . .

SON [*exploding in anger*]. What do you know about it? What
do you know about me, or what I am like? When did you
ever concern yourself about me?

FATHER. I admit it! I admit it! But isn't that a dramatic situation in itself? This aloofness of yours which is so cruel to
me and to your mother? Think of her returning home and
seeing you for the first time a grown man, not even recognizing you, yet knowing you were her son . . . [*Pointing to
the* MOTHER *who is crying*.] Look there, she's crying.

STEPDAUGHTER. Like the fool she is.

FATHER [*indicating the* STEPDAUGHTER'S *distaste for the* SON].
She can't stand him, as you can see. [*Indicating the* SON.]
He says he has nothing to do with all this, but, as a matter
of fact, the whole action hinges on him. Look at the little
boy, clinging to his mother, always frightened and crying.
It's his fault . . . [*Indicating the* SON.] . . . that the boy
is like that. [*Indicating the* BOY.] Perhaps his position is
the most painful of all; more than anyone else he seems
to feel himself an outsider in my home. He's humiliated to
be taken in by me, by my charity . . . [*Lowering his voice;
confidentially*.] He's very much like his father . . . humble
. . . quiet . . .

DIRECTOR [*in a professional tone*]. Oh, we'll cut him out.
You've no idea what a nuisance children are on the stage.

FATHER. He won't be a problem. He disappears very soon, and the baby, too. She's the first to go.

DIRECTOR. Fine. Good. [*Walking around; with more interest.*] Yes, I think this is all very interesting. There might be the makings of a very exciting play here.

STEPDAUGHTER [*trying to intrude*]. When you've got a character like me!

FATHER [*angry; pushing the* STEPDAUGHTER *aside*]. You be quiet!

DIRECTOR. Yes . . . it's quite new . . .

FATHER. Nothing like it has ever been done.

DIRECTOR. You've got nerve, I'll say that, coming in here and throwing the idea at me . . .

FATHER. Well, you understand, born as we were for the stage . . .

DIRECTOR [*suddenly alarmed*]. You're not actors?

FATHER. No, no. I said we were born for the stage because . . .

DIRECTOR. Are you trying to put something over on me?

FATHER. Oh, no. I only act the part for which I was cast, the part which I was given in life. But because I have read a great deal and am very emotional, I became a little theatrical without even meaning to.

DIRECTOR. Well, that might be, of course. But still, without an author . . . I could give you the name of an author who, perhaps, might . . .

FATHER. No! No! Look here! You be the author!

DIRECTOR. Me? What are you talking about?

FATHER. Yes, you! You! Why not?

DIRECTOR. Because I've never written anything in my life, that's why not.

FATHER. But you could do it, couldn't you? It can't be very difficult. So many people do it. And it couldn't be very hard with all of us here, alive, right in front of you.

DIRECTOR. Well . . . I am almost tempted . . . it would be rather an interesting experiment . . . it might almost be worth trying . . .

FATHER. It is! And you'll soon see what marvellous scenes will come out of it. I can tell you now . . .

DIRECTOR. You tempt me . . . you do tempt me! All right, let's take a crack at it! Come with me. There's an office upstairs. [*Turning to the* ACTORS.] We'll take a short break. But don't go too far away because I'll want you all back here in ten or fifteen minutes. [*To the* FATHER.] Let's see what we can do. With luck, we might be able to turn it into something sensational.

FATHER. There's no *might* about it. They'd better come too, don't you think? [*He indicates the other* CHARACTERS.]

DIRECTOR. Yes, yes, bring them along. [*He starts to exit, then turns back to the* ACTORS.] Remember, no more than fifteen minutes.

[THE DIRECTOR *and the* CHARACTERS *exit into the wings; the* ACTORS *look at one another with astonishment.*]

LEADING MAN. Is he serious?

JUVENILE. The whole thing is crazy.

OLD CHARACTER MAN. Does he really expect to rough out an entire play in a quarter of an hour?

JUVENILE. We can do improvisations!

LEADING LADY. I have a contract! If he thinks I'm going to have anything to do with some classroom exercises . . .

INGENUE. I don't understand. There doesn't seem to be any part for me at all.

OLD CHARACTER LADY. Still, I would rather like to know who those strange people are . . .

OLD CHARACTER MAN. They're probably either escaped lunatics, or it's some sort of a practical joke.

JUVENILE. But he's really taking them seriously.

LEADING LADY. It's vanity. Now he sees himself as a writer.

LEADING MAN. If the stage has come to this . . .

OLD CHARACTER LADY. I do believe, though, that I'm rather enjoying it.

FIRST STAGE MANAGER. Well, there's no point in just standing here. Let's get some coffee while we've still got the time.

[*Still talking among themselves, the* ACTORS *leave the stage. The curtain remains up. The lights go on. The action is suspended for a brief intermission.*]

ACT TWO

[*As the lights dim on the audience, a call bell sounds back-stage signalling for the* ACTORS *to return. Before they do so, however, the* SON *enters followed by the* MOTHER.]

SON. What a joke! What a monstrous joke! With me for its punch line!

[*The* MOTHER *moves toward the* SON, *trying to make his eyes meet hers, but before she can do so, the* SON *turns away from her. The* MOTHER *moves forward again, persisting in her efforts to make his eyes meet hers.*]

MOTHER. And isn't my punishment the worst of all? [*As the* SON *turns away again, the* MOTHER *looks up toward the heavens, cries out in anguish.*] Ah! God! God! Why are You so cruel? Isn't it enough that I must endure this fantastic life, this never-ending torment? Must You insist on my exhibiting it to others as well?

SON [*speaking to himself but with the intention that the* MOTHER *should overhear his words*]. Why must it be put on the stage at all? What for? He complains that he was discovered in a moment of his life that should have remained hidden. Then why must he put it on display? And what about me? Must my shame be exposed as well? Must everyone know about my parents, my mother running off with another man, my father . . . a lecher? Can't I at least be allowed to conceal this shameful business?

[*The* MOTHER *covers her face with her hands. At this moment, the* ACTORS, *other* CHARACTERS, *and other members of the company enter.*]

DIRECTOR. All right, let's go. Let's go, please. Is everybody here? [*Looking around him.*] Let me have your attention. [*To the* FIRST STAGE MANAGER, *calling him by name.*] John, we'll have to set the scene.

[*The* FIRST STAGE MANAGER *nods "yes," begins to write down the needed items on a piece of paper held by his clip board.*]

DIRECTOR. See what there is backstage—for a bedroom. A three fold with a door will do.

[FIRST STAGE MANAGER *nods and writes.*]

DIRECTOR. We'll need a bed, that's the main thing.

FIRST STAGE MANAGER. There's the old iron one, with the green bedspread.

STEPDAUGHTER. No, no, not a green one. It was yellow with big flowers on it, velvet, very soft and comfortable.

FIRST STAGE MANAGER. I'm sorry, Miss, but we haven't anything like that.

DIRECTOR. It doesn't matter. Use whatever we have.

STEPDAUGHTER. Doesn't matter? Madam Pace's celebrated bed?

DIRECTOR. This is only for a run-through. Now please don't make things harder. [*To the* FIRST STAGE MANAGER.] Just do the best you can.

STEPDAUGHTER. Don't forget the little table, the little mahogany table for the pale blue envelope.

FIRST STAGE MANAGER. There's one small table, painted gold.

DIRECTOR. Fine, fine, we'll use that.

FATHER. A mirror, too.

STEPDAUGHTER. And a screen! I must have a screen! Otherwise I can't play the scene.

FIRST STAGE MANAGER. Don't worry, Miss, we've plenty of screens.

DIRECTOR [*to the* STEPDAUGHTER]. What about clothes hangers? You'll need some, won't you?

STEPDAUGHTER. Yes, several.

DIRECTOR [*to the* FIRST STAGE MANAGER]. Bring as many as you can find. [*He gestures for the* FIRST STAGE MANAGER *to go and prepare the scene.*]

FIRST STAGE MANAGER. Right.

[*The* FIRST STAGE MANAGER *hurries off. During the next few minutes, while the* DIRECTOR *is talking to the* SECOND STAGE MANAGER *and later to the* ACTORS *and the* CHARACTERS, *the* FIRST STAGE MANAGER *re-enters and supervises several* STAGE HANDS *as they bring in scenery, furniture and props for the bedroom scene. The items used should be real, somewhat battered and soiled from backstage use, and unobtrusive.*]

DIRECTOR [*turning to the* SECOND STAGE MANAGER; *handing him some papers; pointing to the table where he was sitting before when acting as prompter.*] Sit where you were before.

[*As he hands him the papers.*] Look, here's an outline of the action, scene by scene. Now what I want you to do . . . [*He hesitates.*]

SECOND STAGE MANAGER [*quickly*]. Take it down in shorthand?

DIRECTOR [*surprised*]. Can you? Do you know shorthand?

SECOND STAGE MANAGER [*separating a pad of blank paper from the other papers on his table*]. Enough to get some of it, anyway.

DIRECTOR. Wonderful! Then follow each scene as they play it and get as much of the dialogue as you can. At least the important speeches. [*He turns back to the* ACTORS, *waves them toward one side of the stage.*] O. K., let's clear the stage, please. Be sure you can see everything that's going on, and pay attention.

LEADING LADY. Excuse me, but . . .

DIRECTOR [*anticipating her question*]. Don't worry, you won't have to do any improvising.

LEADING MAN. Then what will we be doing?

DIRECTOR. If you'll be patient, and just listen and watch, everyone will get written parts later. Right now we're going to have a run-through and they're going to do it. [*He points to the* CHARACTERS.]

FATHER [*as if suddenly awakened from a distant daydream*]. We . . . I'm sorry, but what do you mean by a "run-through"?

DIRECTOR. A rehearsal . . . for the company. [*He indicates the* ACTORS.]

FATHER. But if we're the Six Characters . . . ?

DIRECTOR. That's right; you're the characters. But on the stage the characters do not perform. The actors perform. The characters remain there . . . [*He points to the* SECOND STAGE MANAGER.] . . . in the script . . . [*As an afterthought.*] . . . when there is a script.

FATHER. There, you've just said it! Since there is no script and you're lucky enough to have right in front of you, alive, the six characters themselves . . .

DIRECTOR. You really want to be the whole show, don't you? You want to conceive it, supervise the writing, direct it, and then act it out in front of the public yourselves?

FATHER. Of course. That's the reason we're here.

DIRECTOR [*sardonically*]. What a great show that would be!

LEADING MAN. What do you think we're here for?

DIRECTOR. You're not going to tell me, after all, that you're actors? [*Some of the* ACTORS *laugh; the* DIRECTOR *gestures toward them.*] You see? The whole idea is laughable. [*Remembering.*] That reminds me. I must give out the parts. Well, that won't be difficult. It's pretty much a matter of type. [*To the* SECOND FEMALE LEAD.] You'll be the Mother. [*To the* FATHER.] We'll have to find a name for her.

FATHER. Amelia.

DIRECTOR. But that's you wife's real name. We certainly don't want to use that.

FATHER [*confused*]. Why not, since it is her name? [*Turning toward the* SECOND FEMALE LEAD; *still confused.*] Still, if this lady is to . . . [*Pointing to the* MOTHER.] . . . I see this woman as Amelia. [*To the* DIRECTOR.] Do it any way you like. I don't know what to say any more, I'm already beginning to . . . I don't know . . . to sound . . . false . . . as if my words weren't my own any longer but were somehow distorted, unreal . . .

DIRECTOR. Don't worry about it. We'll find a way to make the words sound right to you. That's our business. And as for the name, if you want Amelia, Amelia it'll be. Right now we'd better finish up the casting. [*To the* JUVENILE.] You'll be the son . . . [*To the* LEADING LADY.] . . . and, of course, you'll be the stepdaughter.

STEPDAUGHTER [*very excited*]. What !!!??? That woman—me!? [*She bursts out laughing.*]

DIRECTOR. Stop that laughing!

LEADING LADY [*genuinely hurt and angry; for despite the somewhat flamboyant characteristics of her profession, the* LEADING LADY *is a very real person, never a caricature*]. No one has ever laughed at me like that! [*Almost in tears.*] If I'm not going to be treated with respect, I'll leave!

STEPDAUGHTER. No, no, you mustn't. Please forgive me. I wasn't laughing at you . . .

DIRECTOR. You should be flattered to be played by . . .

LEADING LADY [*interrupting; angrily*]. "That woman" . . .

STEPDAUGHTER. But I really didn't mean that you . . . [*She hesitates, groping for words.*] . . . I was . . . thinking about myself . . . that I can't see anything at all of me . . . in you . . . because you're simply so unlike me.

FATHER. That's it exactly! [*To the* DIRECTOR.] You see, what we're trying to express . . .

DIRECTOR. Stop it! Stop! For God's sake forget whatever it is you're "trying to express." Don't you realize that the way you feel, inside yourself, is completely unimportant and irrelevant?

FATHER. But, to us, our feelings, our emotions . . . [*He stops, confused.*]

DIRECTOR [*impatiently*]. Are only the raw materials with which my actors will work. They will take them and make them real to any audience by voice and gesture. And if this little story holds the stage at all, it will be thanks to the talents of my actors!

FATHER. I don't mean to contradict you, but we are the ones who are suffering; we ourselves, as we are before you, with these bodies, these faces . . .

DIRECTOR. Make-up and costumes will take care of all that.

FATHER. But our voices, our gestures . . .

DIRECTOR. Now look here; Let's get this straight once and for all! You, as you are, cannot exist on the stage. This actor . . . [*He points to the* LEADING MAN.] . . . will play you. And that's the way it's going to be!

FATHER [*slowly*]. Very well. I understand. And now, I think, I also understand why the author who conceived us didn't want to finish his play, to put us on the stage. I don't want to offend your actors, God knows, but when I think that I shall see myself represented by . . . [*He shakes his head in bewilderment.*]

LEADING MAN [*rising; very serious; crossing toward the* FATHER; *as several of the younger* ACTRESSES *giggle and laugh*]. By me, if you have no objection.

FATHER [*humbly, melifluously*]. I'm very flattered, of course, but . . . [*Nodding toward the* LEADING MAN.] . . . it still seems to me that no matter how hard this gentleman tries with all his serious intentions and professional abilities, nevertheless . . . [*He hesitates.*]

LEADING MAN [*impatiently*]. Yes? Go on!

FATHER [*continuing*]. . . . it will still be impossible for him to portray me as I really am. It will be . . . apart from the make-up . . . rather his interpretation of how he thinks I feel, and not at all what I really feel within me. And it seems to me that whoever comes to criticize us should take that into account.

DIRECTOR. My God, he's thinking about the critics already! Well, we've no time to worry about them! Right now we'd better get to work and try to get the show into shape [*Looking around at the bedroom scene which is now all set up.*] Let's go now. [*To the* ACTORS.] Move aside, please. Let us see what it looks like. [*To the* STEPDAUGHTER.] What do you think? Is the set all right?

STEPDAUGHTER. To tell the truth, I don't recognize it at all.

DIRECTOR. Well, you didn't expect us to build a duplicate of Madam Pace's bedroom with scrap pieces of scenery, did you? [*To the* FATHER.] You said a room with flowered wallpaper, didn't you?

FATHER. Yes, white.

DIRECTOR. This isn't white; it's striped but that doesn't matter. And the furniture we have seems to be about right. [*To a* STAGEHAND.] Move that table a couple of feet downstage, will you?

[STAGEHAND *does so;* DIRECTOR *takes charge, adopts a more positive tone; to the* ACTORS *and the* CHARACTERS.]

DIRECTOR. All right, we'll begin. Act One, Scene One—the stepdaughter.

[LEADING LADY *comes forward.*]

DIRECTOR. No, no, wait. I meant her. [*He points to the* STEPDAUGHTER, *speaking to the* LEADING LADY.] You stand and watch . . .

STEPDAUGHTER [*interrupting*]. How I shall live it!

LEADING LADY. I'll make it live, too, don't you worry about that! Just wait until it's my turn to play it!

DIRECTOR. Ladies! Ladies! No more arguing, please. The first scene is between the stepdaughter and Madam Pace. [*Suddenly realizing that* MADAM PACE *is not present.*] But . . . where is Madam Pace?

FATHER. She's not with us.

DIRECTOR. Then what are we supposed to do now?

FATHER. But she's alive! She's alive, too!

DIRECTOR. If you say so, but where is she?

FATHER. Let me show you. [*Turning to the* ACTRESSES.] I wonder . . . if you ladies would be so kind as to lend me your hats . . .

TOGETHER [*several of the* ACTRESSES]. What? Our hats? I told you so, he is crazy!

DIRECTOR [*as some of the* ACTORS *laugh*]. What do you want with women's hats?

FATHER. Nothing important. I only want to use them for a moment to decorate your set. And if one of the ladies would be so kind as to lend me her coat as well.

TOGETHER [*several of the* ACTRESSES; *as before*]. Now he wants a coat! What for? I think it's fascinating!

FATHER. I only want to hang them up here for a moment. Please. It's only a small favor. Won't one of you help me?

TOGETHER [*as several of the* ACTRESSES *pick up hats and a coat, carry them over to the set, hang them up in appropriate positions*]. Why not? All right? Here's mine. This is hilarious! Now we're providing the props!

FATHER [*as they complete hanging up the hats and the coat*]. Fine! That's right. Fine! Now we're ready for our show.

DIRECTOR. Would you mind if I asked you exactly what you think you're doing?

FATHER [*moving toward the* DIRECTOR, *away from the set*]. Not at all. I only thought that if we prepared the scene for her . . . perhaps she might be attracted by the articles of her trade . . . and appear among us. [*He turns back toward the set.*] Look! Look!

[*The door of the set has already opened and* MADAM PACE *is standing in the doorway.* MADAM PACE *is an ugly woman, terribly fat and wearing an incredible, carrot-colored wig. She is rouged and powdered and dressed with pretentious elegance in a long silk gown. She carries a lace handkerchief in one hand, a cigarette in a long holder in the other hand.*

As the FATHER *turns and sees* MADAM PACE, *she comes forward into the set and begins to play her scene with the* STEPDAUGHTER *who moves quickly forward to greet her. The* STEPDAUGHTER *is humble and polite to* MADAM PACE; *her attitude is that of an employee to her employer.*

As this happens, the ACTORS *are startled—in some cases, frightened; instinctively the* ACTORS *move back several paces, away from the set.*]

STEPDAUGHTER. Here she is! Here she is!

FATHER [*radiant*]. There! What did I tell you?

DIRECTOR. What kind of a trick is this?

JUVENILE. Where did she come from?

INGENUE. They must have been hiding her backstage.

LEADING LADY. It's a cheap trick to impress us!

FATHER [*coming forward; dominating the protests*]. Stop it! Stop it, all of you! What you are seeing is truth itself! Why must you try to destroy it? Why must you call it a trick? This miracle of birth, this reality, called to life by the scene which we have just created, has more right to be here than any of you because it is more true! Which actress among you will play Madam Pace? Well, this is Madam Pace herself! At least admit that the actress who will play

her will be less true than what you see before your very
eyes, Madam Pace in person. As you see, my stepdaughter
recognized her immediately and went to greet her. Now
stay where you are, quietly, and watch the scene!

[*The* DIRECTOR, *the* ACTORS, *and other* CHARACTERS, *and the
other members of the company all turn to watch the scene
which is taking place between the* STEPDAUGHTER *and*
MADAM PACE. *The scene has already begun but it is being
played softly, in normal lowered tones of voice. When the
group turns to listen to the scene, not a word that is being
spoken can be clearly heard. It is all so soft, so muted,
that it blends into a vague, unintelligible murmur of conversation.* MADAM PACE *has put one hand under the* STEP-
DAUGHTER'S *chin, lifting the girl's head to hers as they
speak. After a few moments, the* ACTORS *grow disappointed
and restive.*]

DIRECTOR. Well? Well?

LEADING MAN. What are they saying?

LEADING LADY. I can't hear a word!

JUVENILE. Louder! Louder!

STEPDAUGHTER [*leaving* MADAM PACE *who is smiling at her
with a magnificent smile; turning to the* ACTORS]. Louder?
Well, how loud? These are not things I can shout about
at the top of my lungs. I should shout about them, it's
true, to his shame . . . [*She indicates the* FATHER.] . . . and
for my revenge. But for Madam Pace it's quite a different
story. It could mean prison for her.

DIRECTOR. Oh, fine! [*Shaking his head in dismay.*] I'm sorry,
my dear, but you simply must realize that in the theatre
you have to be heard. And we can't even hear you from
ten feet away. Pretend that there's an audience in the theatre
and that a performance is taking place. Pretend that you are
alone in that room with Madam Pace, where no one can
hear you, and then speak up so you'll be heard! [*The* STEP-
DAUGHTER, *a malicious smile on her lips, slowly but firmly
shakes her head "no."*] No? What do you mean?

STEPDAUGHTER. There is someone who will hear us if we don't
keep our voices down.

DIRECTOR [*in dismay; confused*]. What's this? Have you someone else to spring on us?

FATHER. No, no. She is referring to me. I have to be there,
behind that door, waiting. Madam Pace knows that. In
fact, with your permission, I will take my place now.

DIRECTOR [*stopping him*]. Wait a minute. Now we must respect certain conventions of the theatre. Before you go on . . .

STEPDAUGHTER. Oh, let him go! I tell you I'm dying of my passion to play that scene, to live that scene again! If he's ready, believe me, I'm even more ready!

DIRECTOR [*shouting*]. But don't you understand? First we must finish the scene between you and Madam Pace!

STEPDAUGHTER. Oh, for God's sake! She's only been telling me what you already know; that my mother's work is unsatisfactory, that I must *cooperate* if she is to continue helping us . . .

MADAM PACE [*coming forward; dignified; full of self-importance; speaking in a mixture of Spanish and heavily accented English*]. My good sir, you realize I do not take advantage of her . . . [*She breaks into a stream of Spanish.*]

DIRECTOR [*almost frightened*]. What? What? What's she saying?

STEPDAUGHTER [*laughing*]. It's the way she speaks, half in English, half in Spanish. I know it sounds ridiculous.

MADAM PACE. Ah, how unkind of you people to laugh at how I speak. I speak as best I can.

DIRECTOR. No, no, please don't be offended. Speak exactly as you do. Don't pay any attention to them . . . [*He gestures toward some of the* ACTORS *who are laughing.*] The effect will be wonderful! We couldn't ask for anything better. It will provide some comic relief and ease the crudeness of the basic situation. Please go on, just as you were. It'll be fine that way.

STEPDAUGHTER. Of course it will! Whenever "certain suggestions" are made in that kind of language, the effect is always marvelous. It makes everything sound like a joke. How ridiculous it is to hear that an "old señor" wishes to "amuse himself" with me—isn't that true, Madam Pace?

MADAM PACE. Not so old, *cara mia*. And if you do not like him, if he is not to your taste, he won't give you any trouble.

MOTHER [*rising; taking advantage of the consternation of the* ACTORS, *she rushes across the stage to* MADAM PACE, *tears off her red wig and throws it to the floor*]. You witch! You devil. You've murdered my daughter!

STEPDAUGHTER [*rushing to restrain her* MOTHER]. No, Mother, no! In the name of God!

FATHER [*also hurrying to restrain the* MOTHER]. Please, please! Calm yourself, Amelia! Come; sit down!

MOTHER. I can't stand looking at that woman!

STEPDAUGHTER [*to the* DIRECTOR]. My mother can't stay here. It's asking too much.

FATHER [*to the* DIRECTOR]. They mustn't be here together. That's why Madam Pace wasn't with us when we arrived. [*Gesturing to* MADAM PACE *and the* MOTHER.] If the two of them are here together, it gives the whole thing away in advance.

DIRECTOR. It doesn't matter. It's not important now. This is only a run-through . . . just to give us a rough idea of how it will play. Everything will be useful . . . because I can collect all the various scenes and motivations . . . it's bound to be confusing at first . . . but I can sort it all out later. [*Turning to the* MOTHER; *leading her to a chair*.] Come, my dear Madam; please sit down again.

STEPDAUGHTER [*during the past few moments, she has moved upstage; now she turns downstage toward* MADAM PACE]. Madam Pace, shall we continue?

MADAM PACE [*offended; pointing to the* MOTHER]. Ah, no thank you. I am not going to do nothing more *con tue madre presente*.

STEPDAUGHTER. But . . . you must introduce me to the "old señor" who wishes to "amuse him" with me . . . [MADAM PACE *shakes her head "no"; the* STEPDAUGHTER *takes charge; imperiously*.] We must play the scene; that's all there is to it! [MADAM PACE *shakes her head adamantly; the* STEPDAUGHTER's *tone is curt*.] You can go.

MADAM PACE. Ah, I go! I go! I most certainly go! [*Furiously she picks up her wig and exits through the door of the set; as she does so, the* ACTORS *laugh and applaud;* MADAM PACE *glares at them as she exits*.]

STEPDAUGHTER [*to the* FATHER]. Now you must make your entrance. [*As he starts toward the door of the set*.] There's no need to actually do it. [*As he stops, turns back toward her*.] Pretend that you've already entered. [*Moving into the mood of the scene; in a lowered voice*.] I am standing over here with my eyes lowered, a picture of modesty. You approach me and say, in that very special tone, "Good evening, Miss . . ."

DIRECTOR [*moving toward the* STEPDAUGHTER]. Wait a minute. Are you directing or am I? [*To the* FATHER *who has turned toward the* DIRECTOR *with an expression of suspicion and perplexity on his face.*] Try it the way she said. Go to the back of the set . . . you don't have to go out . . . and then come forward as if you've just entered.

[*The* FATHER *carries out these instructions; as he moves upstage he seems pale and troubled; but when he turns and comes downstage he has adopted the reality of his created life. The* ACTORS *watch the scene with quiet concentration.*]

DIRECTOR [*as the* FATHER *moves upstage; to the* SECOND STAGE MANAGER]. Now pay attention and get as much of it as you can!

The Scene

FATHER [*approaching the* STEPDAUGHTER; *in a "special" tone*]. Good evening, Miss.
STEPDAUGHTER [*her eyes lowered; with restrained disgust*]. Good evening.
FATHER [*lifting her chin with one hand; discovering first that she is young and pretty, to his surprise; then fearing that she may be a virgin*]. Ah . . . well . . . um . . . but . . . this is not the first time, is it?
STEPDAUGHTER. No, sir.
FATHER. You have been here before, then.

[*The* STEPDAUGHTER *nods "yes," lowers her eyes.*]

More than once? [*As she hesitates, he pauses for a moment, then lifts her head again, smiling at her.*] Well, then . . . there's no need for you to be so shy . . . may I remove that little hat?
STEPDAUGHTER [*immediately moving a step or two away from the* FATHER *to prevent his removing her hat; starting to remove it herself*]. No, sir, I'll take it off myself.

[*The* MOTHER *has been watching this scene together with the* SON *and the two younger children who cling to her skirts. As the scene has progressed, the* MOTHER *has watched with increasing horror, indignation, pain, and sorrow. Now she buries her face in her hands and groans aloud.*]

MOTHER. Oh! Oh! My God! My God!
FATHER [*stopping for a moment as if moved to pity for the* MOTHER; *then resuming*]. Well, give it to me. I will put it

down for you. [*He takes the hat from her hands, looks at it for a moment, then places it on a table.*] On such a lovely head as yours I would like to see a much more beautiful little hat. Would you help me choose one for you from Madam Pace's stock? [*He quickly takes a small, pale blue envelope from his pocket, puts the envelope unobtrusively down on the small table.*]

INGENUE [*speaking without meaning to*]. But . . . he's talking about our hats!

DIRECTOR [*angry; in a stage whisper*]. Shut up for God's sake. This is no time for jokes! Let them play their scene! [*To the* STEPDAUGHTER.] Go on, please.

STEPDAUGHTER [*continuing; to the* FATHER]. No, thank you, sir.

FATHER [*offering her a hat*]. What? Oh, now, you mustn't say "no." You have to accept one. I shall be most upset if you won't. Look how lovely some of these are . . . and it would certainly please Madam Pace . . . why do you think she left them here?

STEPDAUGHTER. Thank you, anyway, sir, but I couldn't wear it.

FATHER [*more expansively*]. Afraid of what they would say at home if you arrived wearing such an expensive present? Oh, come along! You'll be able to think of something to tell them.

STEPDAUGHTER [*tensely*]. It isn't that . . . I couldn't wear it, because . . . I am . . . as you can see . . . I'm surprised you haven't noticed . . . [*She indicates her black dress.*]

FATHER [*realizing*]. In mourning! Forgive me, I'm so sorry. Yes, I do see. I . . .

STEPDAUGHTER [*gathering all her courage; forcing herself to adopt a positive tone; repressing her anguish and nausea*]. Please, please, don't go on. It is very kind of you, and I thank you for it, but you must not feel embarrassed or sorry for me. Please try to put it out of your mind. Because, you see . . . [*She tries to smile, adding.*] . . . I am trying to forget that I am dressed this way.

DIRECTOR [*interrupting; to the* SECOND STAGE MANAGER]. Wait a minute. Don't write that last part down. We'll leave that out. [*Turning to the* FATHER *and the* STEPDAUGHTER; *gesturing for them to move downstage, clearing the set.*] This is excellent, excellent! [*Then, only to the* FATHER.] It's going even better than I hoped. But that's enough for now.

STEPDAUGHTER. But why can't we go on? The best is still to come!

DIRECTOR. Just be patient. You can go on later. [*Turning to the* ACTORS.] It must be played very naturally, with just a touch of lightness . . .

LEADING MAN. Um . . . there's a certain quicksilver quality in the man, isn't there?

LEADING LADY. It's not a difficult scene. [*To the* LEADING MAN.] Shall we try it now?

LEADING MAN. Yes. I'll go and get ready for my entrance. [*He goes off and takes up his position behind the door leading into the set.*]

DIRECTOR [*to the* LEADING LADY]. All right, here we go. The scene between you and Madam Pace is over. She exits . . . [*Gesturing for the* LEADING LADY *to take up her position in the set.*] . . . and you remain here. I'll have that scene written up properly later. You're here . . . [*Seeing that the* LEADING LADY *is moving away from him.*] Where're you going?

LEADING LADY. I've got to put on my hat.

DIRECTOR [*as the* LEADING LADY *picks up her hat, puts it on, starts to move back toward the set.*] Good. Very good. Now you'll stand here, your head lowered, your eyes toward the floor.

STEPDAUGHTER [*laughing*]. But she's not even dressed in black.

LEADING LADY. I shall be dressed in black . . . but *I'll* be chic!

DIRECTOR [*to the* STEPDAUGHTER]. Now you must be quiet! Just stand there and watch and perhaps you'll learn something about the theatre. [*Calling for attention.*] Is everyone ready? All right! Entrance!

[*As the* DIRECTOR *moves downstage so that he will be able to see the scene with more perspective, the door of the set opens and the* LEADING MAN *enters. He is playing the lively manner of an old roué. The scene that follows, as performed by the* ACTORS, *is totally different from the scene as it was performed by the* CHARACTERS. *However, it is never a parody, never a burlesque of their scene. It is played with absolute reality, absolute truthfulness. It is however, played very differently. The line readings are different, the gestures different, the expressions different.*]

LEADING MAN. Good evening, Miss.
FATHER [*immediately unable to control himself*]. Oh, no!

[*As he says this, the* STEPDAUGHTER *bursts out laughing at the way in which the* LEADING MAN *is walking.*]

DIRECTOR. Shut up there! And stop that laughing! We cannot have these constant interruptions!

STEPDAUGHTER [*moving forward a few paces*]. I'm very sorry, but it's only natural. This lady . . . [*She points to the* LEADING LADY.] . . . is standing exactly where I stood before. But if she is intended to be me, I can assure you that if anyone ever said "Good evening" to me in a voice like that I would burst out laughing exactly as I did just now.

FATHER [*coming forward*]. Well, yes. His manner, his tone . . .

DIRECTOR. Are exactly right, for him! [*Pointing to the area where the* FATHER *was standing before he came forward.*] Now you must be quiet and let us get on with the rehearsal!

LEADING MAN [*coming downstage; ready to argue with the* FATHER]. If I'm to play an old boy who's coming into a house of . . .

DIRECTOR [*waving the* LEADING MAN *back toward the set*]. For God's sake don't listen to them! Just do it again! It's going very well. [*Waiting for the* ACTORS *to resume.*] From the beginning.

LEADING MAN. Good evening, Miss.

LEADING LADY. Good evening.

LEADING MAN [*lifting the* STEPDAUGHTER'S *chin exactly as did the* FATHER; *expressing very distinctly surprise and pleasure, then fear.*] Ah . . . well . . . um . . . but . . . this is not the first time, I hope?

FATHER [*interrupting; correcting*]. Not "I hope"; "is it?"

DIRECTOR [*accepting this correction*]. Yes, "is it?" in a questioning tone.

LEADING MAN [*looking at the* SECOND STAGE MANAGER]. I remember it as "I hope."

DIRECTOR. Well, it's all the same. There's no difference between "I hope" and "is it?". Go on, go on with, perhaps, just a touch more lightness. [*Moving toward the set.*] Here, wait a minute. I'll do it. Watch me. [*Moving upstage, the* DIRECTOR *turns and comes forward toward the* LEADING LADY.] Good evening, Miss.

LEADING LADY. Good evening.

DIRECTOR [*lifting the chin of the* LEADING LADY]. Ah . . . well . . . um . . . but . . . [*He turns toward the* LEADING MAN, *showing him the proper way of looking into the face of the* LEADING LADY.] Surprise . . . pleasure . . . and then fear. [*To the* LEADING LADY.] This is not the first time, is it? [*To the* LEADING MAN.] Do you see what I mean? [*To the* LEADING LADY.] And then you say, "No, sir." [*To the*

LEADING MAN.] In other words, a little more lightness, a little more flexibility.

[*As the* DIRECTOR *moves downstage again, the* LEADING MAN *once again takes his place in the set.*]

LEADING LADY. No, sir.

LEADING MAN. You have been here before, then? More than once?

DIRECTOR. No, wait a minute. You've got to pause to let her get her nod in. [*To the* LEADING LADY.] You have been here before, then?

[*At his signal, the* LEADING LADY *raises her head a little, closes her eyes, then nods "yes" twice.*]

STEPDAUGHTER [*unable to contain herself*]. Good God! [*She covers her mouth with one hand to prevent herself from laughing aloud.*]

DIRECTOR. Now what's the matter?

STEPDAUGHTER [*quickly*]. Nothing. Nothing at all.

DIRECTOR [*after frowning at the* STEPDAUGHTER; *to the* LEADING MAN]. Continue.

LEADING MAN. More than once? Well, then . . . there's no need for you to be shy . . . may I remove that little hat?

[*The* LEADING MAN *says these last sentences in such a tone and with such gestures that the* STEPDAUGHTER *is unable to keep from laughing despite the hand pressed against her mouth. She explodes into a burst of loud, incredulous laughter.*]

LEADING LADY. I'm not going to stand here and be made a fool of by that woman!

LEADING MAN. Neither am I! Let's forget the whole thing!

DIRECTOR [*to the* STEPDAUGHTER; *shouting*]. Stop it! Stop it!

STEPDAUGHTER [*regaining control of herself*]. Forgive me . . . please forgive me!

DIRECTOR. Haven't you any manners at all? How dare you behave like this?

FATHER [*intervening*]. Oh, you're quite right, of course, but you must excuse her . . .

DIRECTOR. Excuse her? I've never seen such rudeness!

FATHER. Yes, but still, you must believe me, when they play it they make it seem so strange that . . .

DIRECTOR. Strange? What's strange about it?

FATHER. Well . . . you must understand . . . I do admire your
actors . . . this gentleman . . . [*He indicates the* LEADING
MAN.] . . . this lady . . . [*He indicates the* LEADING LADY.]
. . . but it is simply that they are not us.

DIRECTOR. Of course they're not! How can they be you if
they're actors as well?

FATHER. Exactly! Actors! And both of them seem to be very
good. But to us it all seems so different. They try to be us
. . . but they are not us at all!

DIRECTOR. In what way aren't they? What is it exactly?

FATHER. It is that somehow . . . the play is becoming theirs.
It isn't ours any longer.

DIRECTOR. But that's inevitable! I've told you so already.

FATHER. I know, I know, but . . .

DIRECTOR [*interrupting*]. Then stop all these interruptions!
[*To the* ACTORS.] It's always a mistake to rehearse with the
author present. He's never satisfied! [*To the* FATHER *and
the* STEPDAUGHTER.] Now we're going to try it again and
this time see if you can keep yourselves from laughing.

STEPDAUGHTER. Oh, I won't laugh. I promise I won't. My big
scene is coming up.

DIRECTOR. Very well. [*To the* LEADING LADY.] Now then,
when you say "You must not feel embarrassed or sorry for
me. Please try to put it out of your mind . . ." [*To the*
LEADING MAN.] . . . then you say, very quickly, "I understand, I understand," and then ask her . . .

STEPDAUGHTER [*interrupting*]. What's this? What?

DIRECTOR [*continuing*]. . . . why she is in mourning.

STEPDAUGHTER. But that's not right at all! When I told him
that I was trying to forget I was dressed in mourning, do
you know what he answered me? "Oh, very well. Then
suppose we take off this little dress."

DIRECTOR. Oh, very good! Just what we need! A riot in the
theatre!

STEPDAUGHTER. But it's the truth!

DIRECTOR. What has that to do with it? This is the theatre.
Truth is all very well and good, other places, but here only
up to a point.

STEPDAUGHTER. Then . . . what are you going to do . . .
instead . . . ?

DIRECTOR. If you'll just shut up, you'll see. Just leave it to me!

STEPDAUGHTER. No! I won't! You want to take all my agony,
and all the cruel reasons why I am what I am, and twist
them into a romantic, sentimental little "tear jerker."

When he asks me why I'm in mourning no doubt I'm to answer him, weeping bitterly, that my poor dear daddy died two months before. No! No! I won't have it! His answer to me must be, immediately, "Then suppose we take off this little dress"! And I . . . with my heart still grieving for my father, dead only two short months, I went there, behind that screen, and with these fingers, trembling with shame and disgust, unbuttoned my brassiere, took off my dress . . .

DIRECTOR. In the name of God, what is . . . !?

STEPDAUGHTER [*shouting*]. The truth! The truth!

DIRECTOR. Yes, yes, I don't deny that it's the truth . . . and I appreciate your horror, but you must understand that there are certain things which we cannot do on the stage.

STEPDAUGHTER. You can't? Then thank you very much for your time. There's no need for me to stay here any longer . . .

DIRECTOR. Wait a minute. Look . . .

STEPDAUGHTER. I won't stay here! I won't! You've worked it all out with him already, there in your office! I understand only too well! He wants to jump ahead to the place where he can act out the scenes of his spiritual torment, his celebrated remorse, but I want to play *this* scene, *my* scene, *mine!*

DIRECTOR [*tired; bored*]. Always your part! Well, I hope you don't mind my saying so, but there are other people in the play as well as you. Him . . . [*He points to the* FATHER.] . . . and her! [*He points to the* MOTHER.] On the stage you can't have one character doing it all, overshadowing all the others. The characters must be blended together into one harmonious portrait, a picture presenting what it is proper to present. And this is the whole difficulty here, to select and present only what is important and necessary, taking into consideration all the motivations of the characters and hinting at the unrevealed facets of each one. Ah, wouldn't it be nice if every character had a simple, straight-forward monologue, a chance to talk directly to the audience, to pour out all the exposition and every feeling in one great outburst. [*He sighs, turns to the* STEPDAUGHTER *and continues in a conciliatory tone.*] You must restrain yourself, Miss. Believe me, it's in your own interest. You only make a bad impression with all this fury, all this exaggerated disgust. After all, you yourself have confessed that there were others at Madam Pace's before him.

STEPDAUGHTER [*bowing her head; after a moment's thought*].
That's true. But remember, all those others *were him* to me.
DIRECTOR [*not understanding*]. The other men *were him?*
What do you mean?

STEPDAUGHTER. When someone goes wrong, the person who
is responsible for the first step is responsible for all the
other ones. And he was responsible for me, even before
I was born. Look at him now and see if it isn't true!

DIRECTOR. Suppose it is? Doesn't the guilt of such a responsibility seem anything to you? Give him a chance to play
his feelings!

STEPDAUGHTER. His own story in his own way, is that what
you mean? So that he can boast to you of all his noble
remorses, all his moral torments? You want to spare him
the horror of being found, one fine day, in my arms, after
he has asked me to take off my dress of mourning; the
child, the child whom he used to watch coming out of
school, already a whore!

[*She speaks these last words trembling with emotion; the
MOTHER is overwhelmed with anguish; she groans, then
breaks into hopeless sobbing; the emotion touches everyone;
there is a long pause. The* STEPDAUGHTER *waits until her
MOTHER's sobbing ceases, then continues in a gloomy but
resolute tone.*]

Today you see us here, as we are, still unknown to the
public. Tomorrow you will play us as you wish, in your
own way. But do you really want to see our drama, to see
it burst into life as it actually was?

DIRECTOR. Of course. I couldn't ask for anything better. I
want to use as much of it as possible.

STEPDAUGHTER. Then ask my mother to leave us.

MOTHER [*raising her head from her silent weeping; with a
sharp cry*]. No, no! You mustn't! I beg of you, please!

DIRECTOR. But I must see it as it happened, Madam.

MOTHER. I can't bear it! You're torturing me!

DIRECTOR. But since it has already happened . . . I don't
understand . . .

MOTHER. Can't you see? It is happening now! It happens
always! My torment is unending! I am always alive and
subjected at every instant to torment which repeats itself
over and over . . . I cannot even die. I must live it and
feel it . . . forever. [*Indicating the two small children.*]
My two little ones, have you ever heard them speak?

[*Shaking her head "no."*] They can't speak any longer. But they still cling to me in order to keep my torment vivid and alive. And this one . . . [*She points to the* STEP-DAUGHTER.] . . . has run away. She has run away from me and is lost, is lost. If I see her now it is only for one reason, to renew my suffering, to renew the suffering which I must have because of her.

FATHER [*solemnly*]. What you are seeing is our eternal moment. She . . . [*He indicates the* STEPDAUGHTER.] . . . is here to trap me, to hold me suspended through all time, in pillory for that one fleeting and shameful moment of my life. She cannot give up that scene and you really cannot spare me of it either.

DIRECTOR. Well . . . if you say so. I never said that I didn't want to play it. Actually, it will form the nucleus of the whole first act, right up to the surprise entrance of the mother just before the curtain.

FATHER. That's right. Because this is my punishment. All of our agony and passion culminates in that final, terrible cry!

STEPDAUGHTER. I can still hear it ringing in my ears. That cry has driven me crazy! Present me any way you like; it's not important. Even completely dressed provided that I have my arms, only my arms bare. Because you see I was standing like this . . . [*She approaches the* FATHER, *puts her arms around him and leans her head up against his chest.*] . . . with my head leaning on his chest and my arms around his neck, when I saw a vein pulsing in my arm, here. And, somehow, the pulsing of that vein in my naked arm awakened such disgust in me that I closed my eyes, so, like this, and let my head sink down on his chest. [*Turning to the* MOTHER.] Cry out! Cry out, Mama! [*Once again she buries her head on the* FATHER'S *chest, lifting her shoulders as if to protect herself from the cry which she knows must come; then in a voice filled with torment, she almost shouts.*] Cry out as you cried then!

MOTHER [*crying out; coming forward to separate them*]. No!!! No!!! My daughter! My daughter! [*Pulling the* FATHER *away from the* STEPDAUGHTER.] You monster! You monster! This is my daughter! Don't you realize she's my daughter!

DIRECTOR [*stepping back toward the footlights; caught up in the action; enthusiastic*]. Wonderful! My God, it's wonderful! [*Clapping his hands together.*] And then a quick curtain. That cry, and then curtain! Curtain!

[*At the repeated "Curtain! Curtain!" by the* DIRECTOR, *a* STAGE-
HAND *lowers the main curtain leaving the* FATHER *and the*
DIRECTOR *outside of the curtain on the apron of the stage.*]

DIRECTOR. That damn fool! I said "curtain" meaning the act
would finish here, and he's actually let the curtain down.
[*Leading the way through the curtain; exiting behind it with
the* FATHER *following him.*] But the play is good; it's very
good. With a great first act curtain! It has to end that way.
I'll guarantee the first act, anyway.

[*They disappear behind the curtain.*]

ACT THREE

[*When the curtain rises, we see that the scenery used to create the room in* MADAM PACE'S *establishment has been removed. It has been replaced with a small cut-out of a fountain.*

The ACTORS *are seated to one side of the stage; the* CHARACTERS *to the other. The* DIRECTOR, *lost deep in thought, is standing in the center of the stage.*]

DIRECTOR [*finally resolving his thoughts*]. Well . . . suppose we go on to the second act. [*Quickly; to the* CHARACTERS.] Now if you'll just leave it to me, as we've agreed, we can work this out very quickly.

STEPDAUGHTER [*coming forward*]. We'll begin with our entrance into his house . . . [*She points to the* FATHER.] . . . in spite *of him!* [*She points to the* SON.]

DIRECTOR. Don't jump ahead so. You promised to let me do this my way!

STEPDAUGHTER. Yes . . . just so long as it's clear it was against his wishes.

MOTHER [*from her chair; shaking her head sadly*]. For all the good that came of it . . .

STEPDAUGHTER [*turning suddenly toward her* MOTHER]. That's not important! The more harm done to us, the more guilt for him.

DIRECTOR [*impatiently*]. Yes, I know! I've taken it all into account! If you'll only stop these constant interruptions!

MOTHER [*pleading; to the* DIRECTOR]. Please, make them understand that I followed my conscience, that I tried every way . . .

STEPDAUGHTER [*interrupts; disdainfully*]. To appease me, to persuade me to forget my revenge! [*To the* DIRECTOR.] Go ahead, do as she asks. Because it's true; I enjoy it enormously. Just look . . . the more she begs him, the more she tries to crawl into his heart, the colder he is, the more aloof!

DIRECTOR. Are we going to do the second act or not?

STEPDAUGHTER. I won't say another word. But remember, the whole act can't take place in the garden, no matter how much you want it to. It simply can't be done.

[108]

DIRECTOR. Why not?

STEPDAUGHTER [*indicating the* SON]. Because he spends all his time shut up in his room, alone, away from the rest of us. [*Turning toward the* LITTLE BOY.] And then there's the boy—poor, pathetic, bewildered little devil. All of his part takes place indoors, as I've told you.

DIRECTOR [*impatiently*]. Yes, yes, but you must understand that we simply can't change the scenery three or four times in one act.

LEADING MAN. We used to be able to . . .

LEADING LADY. It made the illusion easier . . .

FATHER [*in an outburst*]. The illusion! Damn it, don't say illusion! You mustn't use that word! It's too cruel!

DIRECTOR [*astonished*]. What! Why?

FATHER. Yes, cruel! Surely you understand that by now!

DIRECTOR [*indicating the* LEADING LADY]. What do you want her to say? She was speaking of the illusion created for the audience . . .

LEADING MAN. By our performances . . .

DIRECTOR. The illusion of reality.

FATHER. I understand you well enough but you do not understand us. Forgive me, but . . . you see . . . for you and your actors all of this is only . . . and quite rightly, I suppose . . . a sort of game.

LEADING LADY [*interrupting indignantly*]. A game indeed! We're not children! We're professional actors! This is a serious business to us!

FATHER. I don't deny it. What I meant, when I used the word "game," was that . . . [*To the* LEADING LADY; *indicating the entire company with a gesture.*] . . . all of you are dedicated, as you yourself just said, to the creation of the illusion of reality.

DIRECTOR. Exactly!

FATHER. But when you consider that we, as you see us now . . . [*He gestures to include the other* CHARACTERS *and himself.*] . . . have no other reality outside of this illusion . . .

DIRECTOR [*confused; looking toward the* ACTORS *who are also confused*]. Now what's that supposed to mean?

FATHER [*with a slight smile*]. What else can it mean . . . except that what is for you an illusion, which you are able on occasion to create, is our only reality. [*He pauses, moves closer to the* DIRECTOR.] Think about it for a moment. [*Looking into the eyes of the* DIRECTOR.] Can you tell me who you really are? [*He points a long index finger at the* DIRECTOR.]

DIRECTOR. Who I am? I'm myself!

FATHER. And if I were to say to you that that isn't true, that you are me?

DIRECTOR. I would say you were crazy!

[*Some of the* ACTORS *laugh.*]

FATHER [*indicating the* ACTORS *who are laughing*]. They're quite right to laugh because, to them, this is really nothing but a game. [*To the* DIRECTOR.] It's only in fun that . . . [*Indicating the* LEADING MAN.] . . . this gentleman here, who is "himself" must also pretend to be "me" while I, on the contrary, am "myself" and am right here before you. You see, I've trapped you!

DIRECTOR [*not understanding; irritated*]. But you said all this before! Must we go through it again?

FATHER. No, no, that's not my intention at all. In fact, I want to ask you to abandon this game of illusion . . . [*Looking at the* LEADING LADY, *as if warning her not to say anything.*] . . . which you and your actors are accustomed to play here. Let me ask you again, very seriously, who are you?

DIRECTOR [*turning to the* ACTORS; *astonished and irritated*]. What a lot of nerve he has! He who calls himself a character comes and asks me who I am?

FATHER [*with dignity but without haughtiness*]. A character may always ask a man who he is. Because a character has his own complete identity, marked by his own special characteristics, limited to his own precise existence. As a result, a character is always "somebody," generally a "nobody."

DIRECTOR. That may all be true, I don't know. But you're asking your question *of me,* the Director, the Boss, do you understand that?

FATHER [*lowering his voice; with mellifluous humility*]. But only to know if you really see yourself. Here you are, at this very moment filled with the solid reality of your own existence. But let me ask you to think back to some moment of your life in the past—ten years ago, let's say. Can you remember the exact circumstances in which you were living, the feelings which you felt and which others felt for you? [*The* DIRECTOR *gestures that he can remember, vaguely; the* FATHER *continues quickly.*] But remember, once *they were* your reality! Don't you feel . . . I won't say

this stage . . . don't you feel the very earth itself sinking
from beneath your feet when you realize that all your solid
reality as of this moment is destined to become the half-
remembered dream of tomorrow?

DIRECTOR [*not understanding a word the* FATHER *has just
said*]. What? What are you talking about?

FATHER. I only want to show you that while we . . . [*He
indicates himself and the other* CHARACTERS.] . . . have no
other reality beyond this one single illusion, you have no
reality at all. For what you feel at this moment, all of
your thoughts and actions of today are destined to become
an illusion of the past to you tomorrow.

DIRECTOR [*trying to make fun of the* FATHER]. Oh, fine! What
you're saying, then, is that you and your drama, which
you want to perform here, are more real than I am?

FATHER [*completely serious*]. Beyond any doubt.

DIRECTOR. You don't say?

FATHER. I thought you realized that from the beginning.

DIRECTOR. You're more real than I am?

FATHER. If your reality can change from day to day . . .

DIRECTOR. Of course it changes! My reality, as you call it, is
always changing, just like everyone else's!

FATHER [*with a cry*]. Not ours! Don't you see? That is the
great difference! Our reality doesn't change; it cannot
change; it cannot ever be other than it is because it is
fixed, forever! That is what is so dreadful, so terrible, this
immutable reality! It should make you shudder just to come
near us!

DIRECTOR [*suddenly struck by an idea; in an outburst*]. Just
one thing: I should like to know when you have ever seen
a character who comes out of his part and pleads, as you
do, and proposes things and offers explanations? What is
all this? I've never heard of such a thing!

FATHER. You've never seen it happen before because authors
usually hide the details of their creative work. When the
characters have really come to life before their author, he
does nothing but follow their words, their gestures, the
action which they suggest to him. And he must want them
to behave as they themselves want to behave, for God help
him if he doesn't! When a character is born, he instantly
acquires his independence, even from his own author, to
the point that others may even imagine him in situations
for which his author never intended him, and he may
acquire a meaning of which his author never dreamt!

DIRECTOR. Yes, yes, I know all that.

FATHER. Well, then, what is so astonishing about us? Consider our tragedy, first brought to life by the imagination of our author and then, later, denied our lives. And then tell me if we, as characters, abandoned this way, alive yet without life, are not justified in doing as we have done and are doing even now before you? Ah, we did everything we could for a long time, a long long time, believe me, trying to persuade him to give us life. We all tried to move him, first me, then her . . . [*Indicates the* STEPDAUGHTER.] . . . and even this poor woman . . . [*Indicates the* MOTHER.]

STEPDAUGHTER [*coming forward; as if in a daydream*]. It's all true. I tried to tempt him, many times, when he was sitting at his desk at twilight, feeling a little melancholy, not even able to decide whether to turn on the lights or to let the shadows fill his room . . . and those shadows were filled with us, coming to tempt him . . . [*As if she can see herself there by the author's desk; annoyed by the presence of the* ACTORS.] Oh, if you would only all go away! If you would only leave us here alone, the mother with that son, I with the child, and the boy there alone, always alone . . . and then I with him . . . [*She points to the* FATHER.] . . . and then I alone, I, alone in the shadows . . . [*She makes a sudden motion as if trying to reach out and illuminate those shadows, as if trying to seize a life that avoids her grasp.*] Ah, my life! My life! What scenes we offered him! And I, I have tempted him more than all the others put together!

FATHER. Yes, and it may very well be your fault that he didn't give us the life we begged for! Your constant demands, your . . . "over-emotionalism" . . .

STEPDAUGHTER. Nonsense! He made me this way himself! [*To the* DIRECTOR.] I believe that he abandoned us out of dejection over the current condition of the theatre with its constant pandering to public taste as measured by the box office . . .

DIRECTOR. Oh, for God's sake! Now we really must go on! We must come to the action, ladies and gentlemen!

STEPDAUGHTER. It seems to me that we have too much action for you already, without staging our entrance into his house. [*She indicates the* FATHER; *then turns back to the* DIRECTOR.] You said yourself we couldn't change scenes every five minutes.

DIRECTOR. That's right. The idea is to group all of the actions together in one dramatic scene. We simply can't, for example, show your little brother returning home from school and wandering like some lost soul from room to room, hiding in corners and behind doors, and all the time thinking about a project which . . . what did you say it did to him?

STEPDAUGHTER. It consumes him . . . wastes him away.

DIRECTOR. I don't remember your saying that. And all the time you can see it growing in his eyes. is that right?

STEPDAUGHTER. Yes! Just look at him! [*She points to the* BOY *who is standing close to the* MOTHER.]

DIRECTOR. Yes, yes, and at the very same time the little girl is playing in the garden, blissfully unaware of what is happening. One in the house, one in the garden . . . now do you really think that's practical?

STEPDAUGHTER [*very emotional*]. But you must show her, playing in the sun, playing joyfully! That's my only reward; her gaiety, her holiday in that garden after all the misery and squalor of that loathsome room where the four of us were sleeping together . . . I with her . . . I, imagine it, with the horror of my contaminated body next to hers as she slept, holding me tightly with her little loving innocent arms. In the garden when she saw me, she would run to me and take me by the hand, to show me the flowers. She didn't care for the big flowers; instead, she would walk me around to show me the little ones she'd discovered, "wee, teeny ones" she called them, wanting to show them all to me, so happily, so happily!

[*Tortured by this memory, the* STEPDAUGHTER *breaks into long, desperate weeping, bringing her head down onto her arms and resting them on a table. All are deeply moved by her emotion; the* DIRECTOR *finally approaches her, speaking in a paternal tone, trying to comfort her.*]

DIRECTOR. We'll show the garden; we'll show the garden, don't worry about that. And you'll see, it'll be just the way you want it. We'll play it all in the garden. [*Turning to the* FIRST STAGE MANAGER.] Let's have those two Cypress trees we've still got hanging. They'll do as well as anything else.

[*The* FIRST STAGE MANAGER *calls off-stage asking for the Cypress trees to be lowered; after a moment, two Cypress trees are lowered from the flies down onto the stage. They come into place in front of the fountain. The* DIRECTOR *turns to the* STEPDAUGHTER.]

DIRECTOR. Ah, that's the ticket. At least this will give us a rough idea, anyway. [*To a* STAGEHAND, *off-stage.*] Now let me have a little sky!

STAGEHAND [*off-stage*]. Which one?

DIRECTOR. The light blue one. It should come down right behind the fountain. [*A plain white "cyc" comes down from the flies.*] Not the white one! I said the light blue sky! Never mind, leave it. It'll do. [*Calling off-stage, in the other direction.*] Hey, you on the lights: let me have some moonlight blues, plenty of blues! [*A flood of blue light comes in.*] Yes, that's it! Fine!

[*The scene is now a mysterious, moonlit garden, as the* DIRECTOR *requested; the atmosphere is such that it leads the* ACTORS *to move and speak as they would in a garden at night; everything is very soft and enigmatic.*]

DIRECTOR [*turning to the* STEPDAUGHTER]. And now, instead of the boy hiding himself in the rooms upstairs, let's have him hide in the garden, behind the trees. [*The* STEPDAUGHTER *nods weak assent. The* DIRECTOR'S *tone becomes more businesslike.*] You understand it's going to be rather difficult to find a child who can play that scene with you, the one in which she shows you the flowers. [*Turning to the* BOY.] Here, boy, come here a minute. Let's see how this is going to work. [*As the* BOY *does not move.*] Come on, come on. [*Crossing, he takes hold of the* BOY, *pulling him forward; he tries to hold the* BOY'S *head up but it keeps falling forward.*] Now be a good boy . . . come along . . . say, something's the matter with him . . . my God, doesn't he ever say anything . . . [*He turns the* BOY *around, leads him behind the trees.*] Come up here for a minute. Let me see you hide behind these trees. [*The* BOY *disappears behind a tree.*] Now poke your head out a little, as if you were spying on someone. [*The* DIRECTOR *moves downstage, studies the effect he has created; the* BOY *repeats the action of putting his head out from behind the tree; somehow this action makes the* ACTORS *uneasy, fills them with fright and dismay; the* DIRECTOR *speaks to the* CHARACTERS.] Now, if the little girl were to surprise him while he was spying and run over to him, wouldn't he have to say something then?

STEPDAUGHTER [*rising*]. But, surely . . . you're not hoping that he will speak . . . at least, not while *he* . . . is here? If you really want the boy to speak, you must send him away. [*Again she indicates the* SON.]

SON [*starting toward the* ACTORS]. I'll go! I'm delighted! There's nothing I'd like better!

DIRECTOR. No, no, wait! Where're you going! Stick around a minute!

[*The* MOTHER, *terrified that the* SON *might actually leave, rises; instinctively she holds out her arms toward the* SON *as if to pull him back; but she does not move toward him.*]

SON [*to the* DIRECTOR *who has taken hold of his arm; trying to exit into the wings*]. I have nothing to do with all this. Let me go! Please let me go!

DIRECTOR. What do you mean you have nothing to do with all this?

STEPDAUGHTER [*calm; sardonic*]. There's no need to hold him. He won't go away.

FATHER [*quietly*]. He has to play the terrible scene in the garden with his mother.

SON [*resolutely*]. I will not "play" anything. I've told you so from the beginning. [*To the* DIRECTOR.] Let go of me!

STEPDAUGHTER [*crossing quickly to the* DIRECTOR]. Please. [*She pulls down the arm with which the* DIRECTOR *was restraining the* SON.] Let him go. [*To the* SON.] Well . . . go!

[*The* SON *tries to exit from the stage but he is held as if by some occult power. He cannot leave; then, amidst the stupor and dismay of the* ACTORS, *he crosses and tries to exit from the other side of the stage; again he is unable to leave. The* STEPDAUGHTER, *who has been watching him scornfully, now bursts into laughter.*]

You see? He can't! He is forced to remain here. He is forever chained to us. But if I . . . and I really do run away when I can no longer stand even to be in the same room with him, and I must run away because I loathe the very sight of him . . . if I must stay here and put up with the disgust that wells up inside me every time I look at him, then you realize that he must also stay . . . with that precious father of his . . . and that mother who has no other son but him . . . [*Turning to the* MOTHER.] Come on, Mama, it's time . . . [*Turning to the* DIRECTOR; *indicating the* MOTHER'S *actions.*] You see, she has risen; she has to keep him here . . . [*To the* MOTHER; *as if drawing her across to the* SON *by an invisible string.*] . . . do what you must do; play your scene. [*Again to the* DIRECTOR.] A woman like that . . . you can imagine how reluctant she is to show her real feelings with all your actors here . . . but she's so desperate to be with him that . . . you see . . . she's ready to play the scene anyway!

[*The* MOTHER, *who has already neared the* SON, *turns as the* STEPDAUGHTER *finishes her speech and gestures that she consents to play the scene.*]

SON [*suddenly*]. Ah, but I'm not! And I won't do it! If I cannot leave, then I'll stay, but I repeat again, I will not be part of your sordid little drama!

FATHER [*very excited; to the* DIRECTOR]. You must force him to play it!

SON. No one can force me to do it!

FATHER. I will force you, then!

STEPDAUGHTER. Wait a minute, wait a minute! First the child must go to the fountain. [*She runs to the* LITTLE GIRL, *bends over her, takes the child's face between her hands.*] My poor little darling, you're frightened, aren't you? You don't even know where we are. It's a stage, baby. [*Pretending to answer a question from the* LITTLE GIRL.] What is a stage? It's a place where people pretend to be very serious, a place where they put on plays. We have a play to put on now. A very serious one, you know. And you're in it, baby. [*Embracing the* LITTLE GIRL; *holding her close for a moment; rocking her back and forth in her arms.*] Oh, my darling, what an ugly play, what an ugly play for you to be in! And what a horrible part there is for you! A garden, a fountain . . . [*Gesturing toward the fountain and the trees.*] . . . but these are only make-believe, you know. That's the whole trouble; it's all make-believe here. But perhaps a baby like you would rather have a make-believe fountain than a real one, so you can play in it, eh? Oh, what a mockery! To all the others it is only an illusion, a game, a joke! But not to you! For you, who are real, my little darling, it is a real fountain that you play by. A big, beautiful green fountain with lovely trees throwing their shadows over the waters and lots and lots of little ducks swimming around, breaking the shadows with trails of ripples. You want to catch one of the little ducks . . . [*Suddenly screaming in anguish.*] No, Rosetta, no!!! Ah!!! If only your mother would concern herself about you, but she can't stay away from that wretch of a son . . . [*very depressed.*] . . . what a hell of a mood it puts me in. And as for you . . . [*She turns from the* LITTLE GIRL; *takes hold of the* BOY.] What are you doing there, always with your hands in your pockets? It'll be your fault, too, if the baby drowns! [*Pulling one of the* BOY's *hands from a pocket.*] What have you got there? What are you hiding in your hand? [*As she pulls his hand toward her, she sees that he is holding a revolver.*] Where did you get this? [*The* BOY, *frightened, pales and pulls away; he does not answer.*] You idiot! If I'd been in your shoes instead of killing myself I'd have killed one of them, or both of them, the father and the son!

[*The* STEPDAUGHTER *now releases the* BOY, *pushes him behind one of the trees; she then takes the* LITTLE GIRL *by the hand and leads her to the fountain, putting her into the basin of the fountain so that she is completely hidden from sight. The* STEPDAUGHTER *then gets down on her knees and buries her head in her hands at the edge of the fountain.*]

DIRECTOR [*pleased*]. Wonderful! That was great! [*Turning to the* SON.] And, meanwhile . . .

SON [*with dignity*]. What is this "and meanwhile"? That isn't right. I tell you there was no scene between her and me! [*He indicates the* MOTHER.] If you'll just ask her, she'll tell you the same thing.

[*During the past few moments, the* JUVENILE *and the* SECOND FEMALE LEAD *have separated themselves from the group of* ACTORS *and taken up places near the* CHARACTERS; *the* JUVENILE *is studying the* SON, *whose part he is to play; the* SECOND FEMALE LEAD *is studying the* MOTHER.]

MOTHER [*slowly nodding "yes"*]. Yes, it's true. I went into his room . . .

SON. Into my room! Not into the garden!

DIRECTOR. That's not important. I've told you: we've got to consolidate the action.

SON [*turning to the* JUVENILE *irritated by his staring*]. What do you want?

JUVENILE. Nothing. I was just watching you.

SON [*turning toward the* SECOND FEMALE LEAD]. And you're watching her . . . [*He indicates the* MOTHER.] . . . is that it? To play her part?

DIRECTOR. Exactly, and it seems to me that you should be grateful for their interest in you.

SON. Oh, sure; thanks a lot. [*Patiently.*] Hasn't it dawned on you yet that you'll never be able to stage this play? Because there's simply nothing of us in you at all. You study us from the outside—how preposterous! Don't you see that it's impossible for me to live in front of a mirror which not only doesn't reflect my likeness, but instead throws back my image twisted and distorted into . . . something grotesque . . . I don't know what to call it . . .

FATHER. He's right. He's absolutely right, you know!

DIRECTOR [*patiently waving the* JUVENILE *and the* SECOND FEMALE LEAD *aside*]. Very well; move away from them for a while.

SON. It doesn't really matter. I'm in no hurry.

DIRECTOR. Keep quiet now and let me hear your mother. [*To the* MOTHER.] Well? You said you went into his room . . . ?

MOTHER. Yes. I couldn't stand it any longer. I went into his room to empty my heart of all the anguish which was tormenting me. But as soon as he saw me come in . . .

SON [*interrupting*]. I ran away. There was no scene between us. I ran away in order to prevent a scene, because I never make scenes.

MOTHER. It's true. That's what happened.

DIRECTOR. But we must have a scene between him and you. It's the recognition scene!

MOTHER. Don't you think I want it, too? If you could persuade him to speak to me, just for a few minutes, so that I can tell him all that is in my heart . . .

FATHER [*approaching the* SON]. You must do it! For your mother's sake!

SON [*more determined than ever*]. I won't do anything.

FATHER [*seizing the* SON *by his jacket; shaking him*]. For God's sake do it! Don't you hear your mother begging you? Don't you ever have the guts to be a son?

SON [*taking hold of the* FATHER]. No, no, no! Once and for all, no!!

[*The* FATHER *and the* SON *continue to wrestle with one another; there is general excitement; the* MOTHER *tries to separate them.*]

MOTHER. For heaven's sake, stop it, stop it, please!

FATHER [*as they wrestle*]. You must obey! You must!

SON [*finally throwing his* FATHER *to the floor near the apron of the stage*]. What is all this? You're crazy! Get hold of yourself! Why must you insist on dragging out all our shame for everyone to see? I won't do it! I'll have no part in it! And I'm speaking for our author, as well! Even he didn't want us put on the stage!

DIRECTOR. But you came here, of your own free will . . .

SON [*indicating the* FATHER]. He insisted on coming, bringing us all with him. And then he told you not only the things that happened, as if God knows that wasn't enough, but he even added things that never happened at all!

DIRECTOR. Well then, won't you at least tell me what really did happen? You could do that. You rushed out of your room without saying a word, is that right?

SON [*after hesitating for a moment, then nodding in agreement*]. Exactly. I didn't want to get involved in a scene.

DIRECTOR. And then? What did you do next?

SON [*in anguish; painfully aware that everyone's attention is centered on him; moving a few steps across the stage toward the fountain*]. Nothing . . . I wanted some air . . . and crossing the garden . . . [*He breaks off, lost in gloomy memories.*]

DIRECTOR [*urging him to continue; deeply affected by the reluctance of the* SON, *and by his gloom*]. Yes? Crossing the garden . . . ?

SON [*exasperated; hiding his face in his hands*]. Why are you doing this? Why are you insisting I tell it? It's too horrible!

[*At this, the* MOTHER, *trembling all over, moans aloud and looks toward the fountain.*]

DIRECTOR [*noticing the* MOTHER'S *glance; turning toward the* SON *with increasing apprehension*]. The little girl . . . ?

SON [*not looking at the fountain; staring out at the audience*]. Yes. There in the fountain . . .

FATHER [*pitying; pointing to the* MOTHER]. She followed him . . . [*He indicates the* SON.]

DIRECTOR [*to the* SON]. So what did you do?

SON [*slowly; still looking out at the audience*]. I ran to the fountain, to fish her out, but I saw something so dreadful I stopped. I saw, behind a tree . . . horrible! . . . the boy, the boy, standing there, staring with the eyes of a madman, staring at the fountain where his little sister was drowned.

[*The* STEPDAUGHTER *has run to the fountain and is bending over the fountain, hiding the body of the child; her sobs echo in the background; there is a pause; then the* SON *continues slowly.*]

I began to walk toward him, and . . .

[*Behind the trees, where the* BOY *has remained hidden, a shot rings out.*]

MOTHER [*with a terrible, heart-rending cry; running with the* SON *and some of the* ACTORS *toward the* BOY; *the stage is in turmoil*]. Oh, my son! My son! [*Over the confusion, we hear her voice.*] Help me! Oh, God, help me!

DIRECTOR [*trying to force his way to the* BOY *who is carried off behind the white backdrop*]. Is he hurt? Is he really hurt?

[*By now everyone except the* FATHER *and the* DIRECTOR *has disappeared behind the backdrop; we hear excited whisperings from behind the backdrop; then, from both the right and left of the backdrop, the* ACTORS *return to the stage.*]

LEADING LADY [*re-entering from the left; full of sorrow and shock; there must be no doubt that the* BOY *is truly, in reality, dead*]. He's dead. That poor child . . . he's really dead. In the name of Christ, what is all this??? [*She begins to weep.*]

LEADING MAN [*re-entering from the right; laughing*]. What are you talking about, dead? It isn't real. It's all a trick. Don't let them kid you.

LEADING LADY. I saw!! That child is dead!!!

OTHER ACTORS [*together*]. It isn't a trick! It's true! It happened! Just as we saw it!

FATHER [*crying out*]. What do you mean a trick? It is reality, reality, ladies and gentlemen! Reality!

[*During this speech, the* STEPDAUGHTER, *the* SON *and the* MOTHER *unobtrusively exit behind the backdrop; now the* FATHER *turns and exits behind the backdrop.*]

DIRECTOR. A trick? Reality? What's going on around here? Let me have some lights! Lights!!!!

[*Suddenly both the stage and the auditorium are flooded in a blaze of light. The* DIRECTOR *shakes his head as if to clear it of some frightful nightmare; all of the* ACTORS *are looking around, their eyes filled with suspicion, fear, bewilderment, sorrow; the* DIRECTOR *finally realizes that all the* CHARACTERS *are gone.*]

DIRECTOR. They're gone! [*Very upset.*] My God, nothing like this has ever happened to me before in my entire life! [*Suddenly exasperated.*] They've cost me a whole day of rehearsal! [*Looking at his watch; to the* ACTORS.] Well, what are you hanging around for now? Go on, get out of here! There'll be no more rehearsal today! [*Ad libbing comments, the stricken* ACTORS *quickly leave the stage. The* DIRECTOR, *after a last look at them, turns toward the wings.*] You, electrician! Put out the lights! We're done for today! [*He has not quite finished saying this when the entire theatre is plunged into darkness.*] Hey, what're you doing? At least leave me enough light so I can get out of here!

[*Suddenly, as if by error, the background is illuminated by a green light. Through the white backcloth, we see the shadows of the* FATHER, MOTHER, STEPDAUGHTER, *and the* SON. *Seeing them, the* DIRECTOR *runs from the stage in terror.*]

THE PLEASURE OF HONESTY

by LUIGI PIRANDELLO

1917

THE PLEASURE OF HONESTY[1]

Translated by William Murray

CHARACTERS

FIRST MAID	MARCHETTO FONGI
MAURIZIO SETTI	SECOND MAID
MADDALENA RENNI	THE RECTOR
FABIO COLLI	THE DIRECTORS OF THE
AGATA RENNI	BOARD (*Four Men*)
ANGELO BALDOVINO	A NURSE

SCENES

ACT ONE—*The living room of the Renni household, in a provincial town of central Italy. Morning.*

ACT TWO—*The same room, in what has become the Baldovino household, about ten months later.*

ACT THREE—*The same, the following morning.*

TIME

The present.

[1] English Translation Copyright © 1962, by William Murray. From *To Clothe The Naked and Two Other Plays* by Luigi Pirandello. Copyright © 1962, by Stefano, Fausto and Lietta Pirandello. Reprinted by permission of E.P. Dutton & Co., Inc.

ACT ONE

An elegant living room in the Renni house. Exits lead to the front hall and Agata's bedroom. Another exit leads into a studio, not used in Act One. At curtain, the room is empty. Then a maid ushers in MAURIZIO SETTI. *He is thirty-eight years old, well dressed, casual, a good talker, worldly, with something of the adventurer about him.*

MAID. This way, please. I'll tell them you're here. [*She exits into the bedroom.*]

After a few seconds MADDALENA RENNI *enters. She is in her early fifties, chic, still beautiful, but resigned to her years. A devoted mother, she sees everything through her daughter's eyes. At the moment she is worried, anxious.*]

MADDALENA. Setti, at last! Well?

MAURIZIO. He's here. We arrived together this morning.

MADDALENA. And . . . it's all arranged?

MAURIZIO. Yes.

MADDALENA. You explained everything clearly?

MAURIZIO. Everything, everything. Don't worry.

MADDALENA [*hesitantly*]. You're sure? I mean, he understands—

MAURIZIO. Oh, God, I suppose so. I—I just told him what the situation was, that's all.

MADDALENA [*bowing her head, bitterly*]. The situation . . . oh, yes.

MAURIZIO. I couldn't very well not tell him, Mrs. Renni.

MADDALENA. I know, I know, but—

MAURIZIO. And then it all depends on how you look at it. I mean, who the person was, the circumstances, the time and the place. All these things matter.

MADDALENA. Yes, you're right. That's it exactly.

MAURIZIO. And you can be very sure I made all that perfectly clear to him.

MADDALENA. What kind of people we are? Who my daughter is? And he accepted? No difficulties?

MAURIZIO. No difficulties. Stop worrying.

MADDALENA. Stop worrying? How can I help but worry? Tell me about him.

MAURIZIO. Well, he's a good-looking man. No Adonis, but very presentable, you'll see. Unaffected, with a certain dignity about him. And from a very good family.

MADDALENA. But what kind of person is he? I mean, his character?

MAURIZIO. A good man, I'm sure.

MADDALENA. Can he talk? Does he know what to say?

MAURIZIO. Oh, Mrs. Renni, the Baldovinos have always been splendid talkers!

MADDALENA. No, I mean, can he be trusted? You see, even one indiscretion, one word without that certain—[*Just above a whisper, hardly able to express herself.*]—that certain . . . Oh, dear, I don't know how to put it! [*She begins to cry.*]

MAURIZIO. You mustn't take it so hard, Mrs. Renni.

MADDALENA. My poor Agata would just die!

MAURIZIO. No, you can rest easy on that score, Mrs. Renni. He's a most tactful man. I guarantee it. Very reserved, absolutely correct—a real gentleman. And extremely sensitive. There's no reason to worry. I guarantee it.

MADDALENA. My dear Setti, you have no idea how awful this is! I feel so lost . . . so helpless . . . To find yourself suddenly faced with such a decision! It's one of those disasters—well, you know, as if you opened a door into your private life and every passing stranger could walk in and snoop around.

MAURIZIO. Well, that's life . . .

MADDALENA. And that poor daughter of mine! That gentle heart! If you could see her, if you could hear her! It's so dreadful!

MAURIZIO. I can imagine. Mrs. Renni, I've done all I could to—

MADDALENA [*interrupting, clasping his hand*]. I know! I know! And can't you see I have no secrets from you? Because you're like one of the family. More than a cousin—a brother to our dear Fabio.

MAURIZIO. Is Fabio here?

MADDALENA. Yes, he's in there, with her. We can't leave her alone yet. The minute she heard you were back, she ran for the window.

MAURIZIO. Oh, my God! Because of me?

MADDALENA. No. Because she knows why you went away and with whom you'd be returning.

MAURIZIO. But—but I thought—I thought . . .

MADDALENA. She's almost in hysterics. So worked up it frightens me.

MAURIZIO. But—I'm sorry, but wasn't it all agreed? Didn't she give her consent?

MADDALENA. Yes. Of course.

MAURIZIO [*astounded*]. And she's changed her mind?

MADDALENA. No, no. How could she? What else can she do? She has to go through with it. She simply has to.

MAURIZIO. You're right. She must realize that.

MADDALENA. Oh, Setti, this will kill her!

MAURIZIO. Now, Mrs. Renni, you mustn't—

MADDALENA. It will kill her! Even if she doesn't do something foolish! It's partly my fault, I know. I thought . . . I thought Fabio would be more careful . . .

MAURIZIO *shrugs helplessly.*]

You shrug? Yes, you're right. What else can we do now but shrug, shut our eyes, and allow our shame to overwhelm us?

MAURIZIO. Now, Mrs. Renni, you mustn't feel that way. We're all of us doing our best—

MADDALENA [*hiding her face in her hands*]. No! Please don't talk like that! Please! It makes it worse! Believe me, Setti, I feel nothing but remorse for my weakness. That's all it was at first—just weakness.

MAURIZIO. I understand, Mrs. Renni.

MADDALENA. How can you understand? You're a man, Setti, and not even a father. How can you know what a mother feels when she sees her daughter growing older, beginning to lose the first flower of her youth? You no longer dare to be as strict as you think you ought to be, as your own honesty compels you to be. Ah, Setti, your own sense of honesty can become a mockery! When your daughter looks at you with eyes begging for understanding, for indulgence, what is a mother to say? I know the world . . . I've been in love . . . And so you pretend not to notice, and your pretense and your silence make you equally responsible until you come . . . you come to this! But I did think, I did think Fabio would be more careful.

MAURIZIO. Well, it's not always easy, Mrs. Renni.

MADDALENA. I know. I know.

MAURIZIO. If he could have done anything—

MADDALENA. I know. I can see he's as upset as I am, poor

man. And if he hadn't been really in love with her, d
you think any of this could have happened?

MAURIZIO. Fabio is a fine man.

MADDALENA. And we knew he was unhappy, separated from
that terrible wife of his. You see, the very thing that shoul
have prevented all this from happening is what has go
us into this mess! Tell me in all confidence, Setti: if Fabi
had been free, he would have married my daughter
wouldn't he?

MAURIZIO. Oh, undoubtedly.

MADDALENA. Don't lie to me. Please. You do believe tha
don't you?

MAURIZIO. Mrs. Renni, can't you see for yourself how much
he loves her? What a state he's in?

MADDALENA. It's true, then? It's really true? You don't know
how comforting it is to hear you say that, at such a time

MAURIZIO. My dear Mrs. Renni, you know I've never ha
anything but the highest respect, the most sincere an
devoted affection for you and Miss Agata.

MADDALENA. Thank you, thank you.

MAURIZIO. You must believe that. Or I would never hav
involved myself in the matter at all.

MADDALENA. Thank you, Setti. Believe me, when a woman
a serious young woman, has waited so many years, s
patiently, for a man worthy of her and has been unabl
to find one, when at last she does fall in love with a ma
and knows that this man has been wronged, embittered
unjustly hurt by another woman—believe me, it's impos
sible to resist the spontaneous impulse to show him that no
all women are like his wife, that there are women wh
will return your love and not trample you under their fee

MAURIZIO. Yes, that's it exactly! Trampled underfoot, poo
Fabio. You're quite right, Mrs. Renni. He didn't deserve i

MADDALENA. You say to yourself, "No, you can't. Yo
mustn't." And for a while you keep silent, you smothe
your feelings, your anguish—

MAURIZIO. And then it happens . . .

MADDALENA. Yes, it happens. And always when you leas
expect it. It was a wonderful spring night. I was leanin
out the window. Outside, the perfume of flowers, a sk
full of stars. Inside, my anguish, my love for her. An
everything in me cried out, "Why shouldn't she have a
this, too, just once—all those flowers, all those stars!". . .
And so I stayed there, in the shadows, knowing what woul

happen, all of us the helpless victims of an act of nature
for which the next day society and our own consciences
would condemn us. But at that moment, Setti, you're glad
it's happening, you know in every fiber of your being that
it *has* to happen, and you feel a strange sense of satisfaction and pride, even though you know you'll pay for it
tomorrow . . . That's the way it was, Setti . . . I know we
were wrong, but what could we do? It would be so easy if
afterward you could just disappear. But you can't. You have
to go on living, and by all the rules you threw away in a
single rash moment.

MAURIZIO. Yes, I know. And that's exactly why we have to
act calmly and sensibly now. You realize that you've all
given in far too much to your feelings.

MADDALENA. You're right, of course.

MAURIZIO. Well, now we have to put our feelings aside and
listen to the voice of reason, don't we?

MADDALENA. Yes, yes.

MAURIZIO. The fact is there's no time to lose. So—ah, here's
Fabio!

[FABIO *enters. He is forty-three, a likable and honorable man,
but with enough weakness in his make-up to suggest he
might be one of those men who are inevitably unlucky in
love. He is terribly upset and rushes to* MADDALENA.]

FABIO. Please! Go in there! Don't leave her alone!

MADDALENA. Yes, of course, But it seems—

FABIO. Please! Quickly!

MADDALENA. Yes, yes, yes! [*To* MAURIZIO.] Excuse me. [*She exits
into the bedroom.*]

MAURIZIO. Fabio! You, too?

FABIO. Please, Maurizio, don't say it! You think you found
a solution? I'll tell you what you did! You painted a corpse!

MAURIZIO. I what?

FABIO. All you've done is make it look possible!

MAURIZIO. But it was your idea! Now, listen—I'm not in this
because I enjoy it!

FABIO. I'm suffering, I'm suffering, Maurizio! That poor
creature in there! It's hell! And this solution of yours
doesn't make it any easier. In fact, it makes it worse,
because I know it's the only way out, understand? But
it's an external solution: all it can do is save appearances,
nothing else.

MAURIZIO. Doesn't that matter any more? Four days ago

that's all you could think about. And now that we have the chance—

FABIO. I can't go through with it! Does that seem so wrong?

MAURIZIO. Yes! Because that way you lose everything! Appearances don't matter? Of course they do, and you know it! You can't be objective about it, but I can. And I'm going to force you to go through with it, to paint the corpse, as you put it . . . He's here. We arrived together. Now, if we have to move quickly—

FABIO. Yes, all right. Tell me, tell me. Yes, I know it's the only way. You warned him I wouldn't turn over a penny of the estate?

MAURIZIO. Yes.

FABIO. And he accepted?

MAURIZIO. I told you, he's here with me. All he asks, and I don't think it's unreasonable, is the liquidation of his past. And only because he wants to be able to fulfill all the obligations he assumes toward you—and the conditions you imposed. He has a few debts.

FABIO. How many? A lot? I can just imagine!

MAURIZIO. No, only a few. My God, Fabio, what did you expect? He has a few debts. But he wanted me to tell you—he was very insistent on this point—that his debts are few only because he ran out of credit, not because of any reluctance on his part to make them.

FABIO. Oh, fine!

MAURIZIO. That's honest, anyway. You understand, if he still had any credit he wouldn't have to—

FABIO. All right, all right! That's enough! Now, tell me exactly what you said to him. What's he like? Shabby? A wreck?

MAURIZIO. He's a little run-down since the last time I saw him. But that's easily remedied. In fact, he looks better already. You know, with him it's largely a question of morale. The bad things he's been forced to do—

FABIO. Does he gamble? Swindle? Steal? What does he do?

MAURIZIO. He used to gamble. They won't let him any more. I found him so bitter it shocked me. We spent the whole night walking along the road near his home. Have you ever been in that part of the country?

FABIO. No.

MAURIZIO. I tell you, it was a fantastic night. We walked up and down that road, among the winking lights of great swarms of fireflies, and beside me all the time that man talking steadily, with the most terrifying frankness. And

like the fireflies, his words would flash in the air around
you, suddenly illuminating the very darkest corners of
your soul. I had the feeling after a while that we were no
longer on the earth but in some strange dreamland, a dark,
mysterious country where he ruled, where the most bizarre,
the most unbelievable things could happen and seem both
natural and usual. He guessed what I was thinking—he
notices everything—he smiled and talked to me about
Descartes.

FABIO. Who?

MAURIZIO. Descartes, the philosopher. Well, you'll see—he's
an extremely well-educated man, especially in philosophy.
He told me that Descartes—

FABIO. For God's sake, Maurizio, what the hell do I care
about Descartes?

MAURIZIO. Let me finish! You will care, you'll see. He told
me that Descartes, in examining our sense of reality, had
one of the most terrifying thoughts any human being has
ever had: that if our dreams had any regularity, we would
no longer be able to distinguish between sleeping and wak-
ing! Have you ever noticed how disturbing it is to have the
same dream more than once? You begin to think you're
dealing with something tangible, something real. Because
our whole knowledge of the world hangs on this very
slender thread: the re-gu-la-ri-ty of our experiences. We
who live regular lives, by certain set rules, cannot imagine
what can seem real or unreal to a man who lives outside
any such pattern, like Baldovino. That's why I eventually
found it so easy to make our proposition to him. He was
talking about some plans of his that seemed so impossible
to me, outrageous and impractical, that our scheme suddenly seemed ridiculously simple, so obvious and sensible
that anyone would have agreed to it. That surprises you?
Well, I wasn't even the one to bring up the money question.
He immediately said he didn't want a cent for himself and
wouldn't even discuss the matter. And you know why?

FABIO. Why?

MAURIZIO. Because he maintains it's much easier to be a
hero than a gentleman. Anyone can be heroic from time
to time, but a gentleman is something you have to be all the
time. Which isn't easy.

FABIO. Ah! [*Disturbed, irritated, gloomy, he begins to pace
up and down.*] So . . . so he's apparently a man of some
talent, eh?

MAURIZIO. Oh, a great deal of talent. Perhaps even a genius.

FABIO. Obviously he's never known how to use this talent.

MAURIZIO. Never. Even when he was a boy. We were class-mates in school, as I told you. With his ability he could have done anything. But he studied only what he liked, all the most useless things. And he says that a practical education is the enemy of wisdom because you have to learn so many things which, if you want to be really wise, you ought to do without. He had an expensive upbringing: all the tastes, habits, ambitions, even vices of his class. Then things went badly, his father went bankrupt and—well, it's no wonder . . .

FABIO [*resuming his pacing*]. And . . . and you say he's a handsome man?

MAURIZIO. Yes, very presentable. Why? [*He laughs.*] Admit it: now you're afraid I made too good a choice!

FABIO. Go on! I just—I just don't see where all this fits in, that's all. Talent, education—

MAURIZIO. Philosophy. Not entirely inappropriate in this case.

FABIO. Damn it, Maurizio, this is no time for jokes! I'm going out of my mind! I would have preferred someone else, that's all. A modest, unassuming, more respectable type—

MAURIZIO. —who wouldn't fool anyone! Come on, Fabio! You have to remember what kind of house this is! Do you think anyone would believe Agata would want to marry some homely, middle-aged nonentity? We had to find somebody more worthwhile, someone people could respect and believe in, so at least no one would wonder how Miss Renni could bring herself to marry an ugly, inferior man. And I have every reason to think—

FABIO. What?

MAURIZIO. —that she'll accept him. Not only that, but she'll thank me a little more warmly than you.

FABIO. Oh, yes! She'll pour out her gratitude! If you could hear what's going on in there! Did you tell him everything has to be done as soon as possible?

MAURIZIO. Of course. You'll see, he'll be a member of the family in no time.

FABIO. Now what do you mean by that?

MAURIZIO. Oh, God! I mean, well, you know . . .

[*The* MAID *runs in.*]

MAID. Mr. Colli, you're wanted in here!

FABIO. I can't now! I have to go with my cousin. [*To* MAU-

RIZIO.] I must see him—speak to him. [*To the* MAID.] Tell Mrs. Renni I can't come now.

MAID. Yes, sir. [*She exits.*]

MAURIZIO. The hotel is just down the block.

FABIO. I'm going mad! Mad! Between her in there, crying her eyes out, and you out here—

MAURIZIO. Listen, Fabio, we made no definite commitments. And if you don't want to go through with this—

FABIO. I want to see him first, talk to him.

MAURIZIO. Well, let's go then.

MADDALENA [*entering, very upset*]. Fabio! Fabio, come in here! Don't leave her alone now! Please!

FABIO. Oh, God!

MADDALENA. She's in hysterics! Please come!

FABIO. But I have to—

MAURIZIO. No. Go to her, Fabio.

MADDALENA. Yes! Please!

MAURIZIO. Shall I bring him here? We're under no obligation. You can talk to him here. Perhaps that's the best way. For Miss Agata, too.

FABIO. Yes, yes. Go get him. But no commitments, remember! We'll talk first! [*He exits into the bedroom.*]

MAURIZIO [*calling after him*]. In a few minutes! We'll be right back! [*He exits out the back.*]

MADDALENA [*following him to the door*]. You're bringing him here?

[AGATA *and* FABIO *rush in from the bedroom.* AGATA, *though beautiful, has a hard, suffering look, the result of her difficult situation. Desperate now, rebellious, dishevelled, she nevertheless gives the impression of a woman of character, a person who, once she knows what she must do, will avoid subterfuge and follow the dictates of her conscience.*]

AGATA [*freeing herself from* FABIO]. Let me alone! No! Let me alone! Let me go! I've got to go!

MADDALENA. Darling, where? Where do you want to go?

AGATA. I don't know! Away from here!

FABIO. Agata! Agata, please!

MADDALENA. You don't know what you're saying!

AGATA. Let me alone! I'll go mad, I'll die! There's no way out for me! I can't stand it! [*She collapses into a chair.*]

MADDALENA. Wait till Fabio sees him at least! Talks to him! And you see him, too.

AGATA. No! Me? No! Don't you understand how horrible

this is? Don't you see it's monstrous, what you want me
to do?

MADDALENA. But, darling—but you said yourself there was
no—

AGATA. No! I won't do it! I won't do it!

FABIO [*with desperate resolve*]. All right, then! If you don't
want to go through with it, we won't! You're right: it is
monstrous! I couldn't agree more! But are you brave
enough to face the situation with me?

MADDALENA. What are you talking about, Fabio? You're a
man and you can ignore the scandal! But what about us?
Two women alone in a town of this size! We'll be overwhelmed by the disgrace! It's entirely a question of choosing the lesser of two evils: a public scandal or—

AGATA. —or a private one! Mine alone! I'm the one who'll
have to live with this man! To see him every day! A man
who must be a scoundrel, a swine, to lend himself to such
a scheme! [*She leaps to her feet and again tries to escape.*]
No, no, I can't do it! I can't see him! Let me go! Let me go!

MADDALENA. But where? And what will you do? Face the
scandal? If that's what you want, I'll . . . I'll . . .

AGATA [*throwing herself into her mother's arms, sobbing helplessly*]. No . . . for your sake, Mother . . . no . . . no
. . . for you . . .

MADDALENA. For my sake? Darling, what have I got to do
with it? You mustn't worry about me. There's no way
we can spare each other the pain of all this. Nor can we
run away from it. We have to stay here and face it, all
three of us, because we're all to blame.

AGATA. No, Mother . . . not you . . . not you . . .

MADDALENA. I most of all, my child. And I'm suffering even
more than you.

AGATA. No, Mother! Because I feel for you as well as for
myself!

MADDALENA. And I only for you, and so it's worse for me.
I can't share my pain, because I live only in you, my
child. Now be calm—wait—we have to see—

AGATA. It's horrible! Horrible!

MADDALENA. I know. But let's talk to him first.

AGATA. I can't Mother, I can't!

MADDALENA. But we're right here with you. There's no
trickery involved. We aren't hiding anything. We'll be right
here all the time, both of us, Fabio and I—right beside you.

AGATA. But he'll come and live here, don't you see? Live here with us, Fabio! A man who knows what we're hiding from the world!

FABIO. And it will be in his own best interests to help us hide it, for his own sake, and he'll stick to the agreement. If he won't then so much the better for us. The minute he says he won't go along with it any more I'll find a way to get rid of him. In any case, we won't need him any longer.

MADDALENA. You see? Of course! It doesn't have to go on forever. Just for a little while.

FABIO. A few months, a year at most. Why should it be permanent?

AGATA. No, no! We'll never get rid of him!

MADDALENA. Let's meet him first. Setti assured me—

FABIO. We'll find a way, Agata! We'll find a way!

MADDALENA. He's an intelligent man, and—

[*The doorbell rings. A pause.*]

That must be him.

AGATA. Let's go, let's go. Mother! Oh, God! [*She drags her mother toward the bedroom.*]

MADDALENA. Of course. Fabio will talk to him. We'll go in there, the two of us.

FABIO. Don't worry, darling.

[MADDALENA *and* AGATA *exit.*]

MAID [*appearing in the entrance*]. Mr. Setti and another gentleman.

FABIO. Tell them to come in.

[*The* MAID *exits and* MAURIZIO *appears, followed by* ANGELO BALDOVINO. *He is about forty, with a serious, intelligent face. His hair is thinning and uncombed; he has a short reddish beard, a penetrating glance, and speaks slowly in a deep voice. He dresses conservatively, a bit shabbily, and wears a pince-nez, which he almost always carries in his hand and uses to emphasize his words. He seems abstracted: his appearance, his way of talking, of smiling, indicate a man nurturing in himself a host of bitter memories from which he has evolved a curious personal philosophy full of irony and pity.*]

MAURIZIO [*entering*]. Well, here we are. Fabio, my friend Angelo Baldovino.

[FABIO *bows*.]

[*To* ANGELO.] Fabio Colli, my cousin.

[ANGELO *bows*.]

FABIO. Please sit down.

MAURIZIO. You have things to discuss, so . . . so I'll leave you now. [*To* ANGELO, *shaking his hand*.] We'll see each other later, back at the hotel, all right? Good-by, Fabio.

FABIO. Good-by.

[MAURIZIO *exits*.]

ANGELO [*sitting down, his pince-nez on the end of his nose, his head tilted back*]. I must begin by asking you a favor.

FABIO. Go ahead, go ahead.

ANGELO. Mr. Colli, you must be frank with me.

FABIO. Of course. I ask for nothing better.

ANGELO. Thank you. However, I'm not sure you understand what I mean by this word "frank."

FABIO. Well . . . I don't know . . . open . . . sincere.

[*With one upraised finger* ANGELO *indicates the negative*.]

What then?

ANGELO. It's not enough. You see, Mr. Colli, inevitably we construct ourselves.

FABIO. We what?

ANGELO. Let me explain. I enter this house and immediately I become what I have to become, what I can become: I construct myself. That is, I present myself to you in a form suitable to the relationship I wish to achieve with you. And, of course, you do the same with me. But behind these fabrications we present to each other are hidden our most secret thoughts, our most intimate feelings, all that we really are quite apart from the relationship we want to establish with each other. Have I made myself clear?

FABIO. Yes, yes, very clear. Perfectly clear. My cousin told me you were very intelligent.

ANGELO. And now you probably think I'm only trying to prove how brilliant I am.

FABIO. No, no . . . I only meant . . . I agree, I agree with what you said, that's all.

ANGELO. So I'll begin by speaking frankly. For some time, Mr. Colli, I've been disgusted by the wretched subterfuge

I've had to resort to in my relationship with my equals,
if you don't mind my including you in this category.

FABIO. Not at all.

ANGELO. I look at myself—I'm always looking at myself,
Mr. Colli—and I say to myself, "Look at what you're
doing now! How disgusting, how revolting!"

FABIO [*disconcerted, embarrassed*]. No . . . really! Why?

ANGELO. I'm sorry, because it's true. So then you might
wonder why I do such things? And the answer is: because
I can't help myself. To want to be one thing or another is
easy, Mr. Colli. The whole problem lies in succeeding.
We're not alone, you see. We ride through life on the
beast within us. Beat the animal, but you can't make it
think. Try to persuade a jackass not to rush to the edge
of a precipice—beat it, whip it, kick it—it can't help going
there. And afterward it looks at you reproachfully. Can
you help feeling sorry for it? And I mean pity, not forgiveness. To forgive a jackass you'd have to be a bit of a
jackass yourself. But to feel sorry for it, that's something
else. Don't you think so?

FABIO. Oh, of course, of course. So now can we talk about us?

ANGELO. That's exactly what we're doing, Mr. Colli. I told
you all this to make you realize that, feeling as I do about
the situation, I must insist on maintaining my self-respect.
To pretend would be horrible, disgusting, unbearable. The
truth!

FABIO. Yes, exactly. Quite right. Now let's see if we understand each other . . .

ANGELO. I'll just ask you a few questions.

FABIO. What?

ANGELO. Just a few questions, if you don't mind.

FABIO. Oh, certainly. Go ahead.

ANGELO. Here we are. [*He takes a little black notebook from
his pocket and leafs through it.*] The basic facts. Since
we're going to be open with each other . . . You, sir, are
the young woman's lover—

FABIO [*interrupting quickly*]. Now just a minute! I don't
think that's nece—

ANGELO [*smiling calmly*]. You see? You won't even answer
the very first question.

FABIO. Of course not! Because—because—

ANGELO [*quickly, severely*]. Because it isn't true? You mean
you aren't her lover? Well, then—[*Rising.*]—you must

excuse me. I told you I had my self-respect. I could not lend myself to a sad and humiliating comedy.

FABIO. What do you mean? This way we'll only . . . I mean, there's no need to—

ANGELO. You're wrong. I can only maintain my self-respect, for whatever it's worth, if you speak to me as you would to your own conscience. Either that, Mr. Colli, or there's nothing to be done. I will not take part in clumsy fictionalizing. The truth! Will you answer the question?

FABIO. All right . . . Yes, I am. But for God's sake put away that notebook! You're alluding to Miss Agata Renni?

ANGELO [*still looking through his notes. A pause*]. Agata Renni. Yes. She's twenty-seven years old?

FABIO. Twenty-six.

ANGELO [*checking his figures*]. Her birthday is in September, we're in May. So that makes her nearer twenty-seven. And — [*The notebook again.*] —there's a mother?

FABIO. Now really!

ANGELO. I'm only being conscientious; nothing else, believe me. I intend to be conscientious in everything, Mr. Colli.

FABIO. Well, yes, Miss Renni has a mother.

ANGELO. How old, please?

FABIO. Oh, I don't know. Fifty-one, fifty-two.

ANGELO. That's all? You see, it would be better if there weren't a mother involved. The mother, Mr. Colli, is an enormous fabrication. But I knew there was a mother. So let's be generous and say fifty-three. You, Mr. Colli, must be about my age, more or less. I look older, I know. I'm forty-one.

FABIO. Oh, I'm older then. I'm forty-three.

ANGELO. My congratulations. You look much younger. Who knows? Maybe after a while I also . . . well . . . forty-three, yes. Now, if you'll excuse me, I must touch on another very delicate matter.

FABIO. My wife?

ANGELO. You're separated. No fault of yours, I know: you've been a perfect gentleman. But the world is not for the gentle, Mr. Colli. So the fault is mainly your wife's. And here you found a refuge. But life is little more than a loan shark: it exacts a very high rate of interest for the few pleasures it concedes.

FABIO. How true!

ANGELO. Who should know that better than I? And now, Mr. Colli, it's your turn to pay. You find yourself threat-

ened by the usurer and I am called in to settle your debt.
You can't imagine how happy it makes me to be able to
revenge myself like this on a society that has already cut
off my own credit. To impose myself on life! To be able to
say, "All right! This man took from life what he had no
right to take and now I'll pay what he owes, because if I
didn't a concept of honesty would disappear, the honor of
an entire family would be compromised!" Mr. Colli, it's a
great satisfaction to me! A revenge on life! That's the only
reason I'm doing it. Do you doubt that? You have every
right to because I'm like— May I strike a parallel?

FABIO. Of course, of course.

ANGELO. I'm like a man who wants to spend gold in a
country where the money is made of paper. Everyone
mistrusts such a man at first, it's only natural. You're
tempted now to turn me down, aren't you? But it's real
gold, Mr. Colli. I've never been able to spend it because
I have it in my soul and not in my pockets. Otherwise . . .

FABIO. Well, that's splendid of you! Truly splendid! I couldn't
ask for anything better, Mr. Baldovino. Honesty! Good
will!

ANGELO. I have my own family traditions, too . . . Do you
know what it means to be dishonest? The sacrifice of my
self-respect, endless bitterness, remorse, disgust . . . Why
shouldn't I want to be honest with you? You invite me to
a double wedding in this house: not only do I marry the
woman, but I espouse the concept of honesty.

FABIO. Yes, exactly. And it's enough. That's all I ask.

ANGELO. All? You think it's enough? What about the consequences?

FABIO. The consequences? I don't understand.

ANGELO. Oh, I see that you . . . Well, I realize how anxious
you are to extricate yourself from a painful situation.
Which is probably why you treat the matter so lightly.

FABIO. Treat it lightly? No, no. On the contrary.

ANGELO. Let me explain. Mr. Colli, am I or am I not to be
an honest man?

FABIO. But of course you are! It's the only condition I insist
upon!

ANGELO. Excellent. In my feelings, my desires, in all my acts
I am to be entirely honest. I feel this. I want it. And I intend to prove it to you. Well?

FABIO. Well what? I told you, that's all I ask of you.

ANGELO. But the consequences, my dear Colli, the consequences! Look: honesty, the honesty you want from me, what is it? Think about it. Nothing. An abstraction. A pure form. Let's call it an absolute. Now, if I'm to be honest, I must live the abstraction; I must lend substance to the form; I must embody the concept. And what will be the consequences? First of all, I shall have to be a tyrant.

FABIO. A tyrant?

ANGELO. Of course. Not because I want to be one, but because I am the form, I am the absolute. I shall insist that all appearances be respected, which, of course, will mean grave sacrifices from you, Miss Renni, and her mother. Your liberties will be restricted and you will have to observe all the abstract forms of social life. And—let's put all our cards on the table, Mr. Colli, so you'll grasp the full extent of my commitment—and you know what will happen? In all your dealings with me, face it, you will be judged, and not I. I have only one interest in the whole unpleasant business: the chance you give me of being an honest man.

FABIO. Yes. My dear sir . . . you understand . . . well, you said it yourself . . . I . . . I'm not really sure I follow you . . . I . . . oh, you're a marvelous talker, but . . . well, let's get back to earth again, for heavens' sake!

ANGELO. I? To earth? I can't.

FABIO. Why not? What do you mean?

ANGELO. I can't because of the very condition you impose on me. I have to deal in the abstract. The one thing I can't ever do is touch ground. Reality is not for me; it's for you. You can plant your feet in the earth. You talk and I'll listen. I'll be the intelligence that cannot forgive but pities.

FABIO [indicating himself]. The jackass?

ANGELO. If you like.

FABIO. I suppose you're right. Yes, you are right. Well, then— then I'll talk and you listen. That way maybe we'll reach an understanding.

ANGELO. We?

FABIO. Of course. Who else?

ANGELO. No, Mr. Colli, you have to reach an understanding with yourself. I know what I have to do. I told you all this—I don't usually talk so much—because I want you to realize what you're doing.

FABIO. Me?

ANGELO. Yes, you. For me it's easy. What do I actually do?
Nothing. I represent the form. The act—and an ugly one
—was committed by you and I appear to make amends.
I am to cover up the reality. But if I'm to succeed, in
the interests of all concerned, you must respect me, and
it won't be easy for you. You'll have to respect not me,
but the form, the form I represent: the honest husband
of a respectable woman. Don't you want to respect it?

FABIO. Of course I do!

ANGELO. And don't you understand that the more honest you
expect me to be, the more unyielding and tyrannous will
be the form? That's why I warned you to beware of the
consequences. Not for my sake, but for yours. You see,
I have a philosophy to lean on. And to justify my behavior, under such conditions, all I have to do is remind
myself that the woman I'm marrying is to become a mother.

FABIO. Yes. Exactly. Very true.

ANGELO. And in my relationship with her I shall always
bear in mind the baby that will be born. I shall have a
function to fulfill—a noble, worthy function, all bound up
in the innocence of the child. Is that all right?

FABIO. Oh, fine! Fine!

ANGELO. For me, but not for you. Mr. Colli, the more you
approve, the more trouble you pile up for yourself.

FABIO. How? Why? I don't see all these difficulties.

ANGELO. It's my duty to make you see them. You're a gentleman. The circumstances of life have forced you to behave
dishonestly. But you can't do without your honesty! So
you come to me and require me to take your place: I am
to become the honest husband of a woman who can never
be your wife, the honest father of a child you can never
acknowledge. Am I right?

FABIO. Yes. Yes, it's true.

ANGELO. But if the woman is yours, not mine; if the child
is yours, not mine—don't you understand that my honesty
isn't enough? You will have to be honest with me. There's
no other way. If I'm to be honest, we're all going to be
honest. There's no other way.

FABIO. What? I don't understand. Just a minute. You're
saying—

ANGELO. Ah! Now, at last, you feel the earth tremble under
your feet!

FABIO. No, but . . . I mean . . . if things are going to be
different—

ANGELO. Of course they are. You're going to make them different. These appearances you wish to save, Mr. Colli, are for all of us. You want to save them and I am here to help you. You also want to be an honest man. Think it over. It isn't going to be easy.

FABIO. But you know what our situation is . . .

ANGELO. Precisely because I do know. I'm speaking against my own interests, but I can't help it. I advise you to think it over very carefully.

[*A pause.* FABIO *rises and begins to pace up and down in consternation.* ANGELO *also rises and waits.*]

FABIO [*still pacing*]. Of course . . . of course you know . . . if I . . .

ANGELO. Yes. Yes, you'd better think some more about what I've said. And it might not be a bad idea to discuss it with Miss Renni. [*Glancing toward the bedroom door.*] Though that may not be necessary since—

FABIO [*turning on him*]. Since what?

ANGELO [*calmly, sadly*]. Oh . . . why shouldn't she listen, after all? . . . I'll go now. You can let me know what you decide. I'll be at the hotel. [*He starts out, then turns back.*] In the meantime, Mr. Colli, you can count on my complete discretion.

FABIO. I do count on it.

ANGELO [*seriously, slowly*]. I have many wrongs on my own conscience, and here I don't think anyone is to blame, really. One of life's misfortunes . . . Whatever your decision, I want you to know that I'll always be secretly grateful to my old schoolmate for having thought me worthy to assume such an honest obligation. [*He bows.*] Mr. Colli . . .

CURTAIN

ACT TWO

[*About ten months later, the living room of what has become the Baldovino household. A few new pieces of furniture are in evidence. At curtain,* FABIO *and* MARCHETTO FONGI *are on stage.* FONGI *is about fifty, an old fox, short, stooped, shrewd, and not devoid of humor. He is holding his hat and cane in one hand and has the other one on the knob of the open door into the studio.* FABIO *stands off to one side, as if anxious not to make his presence known.*]

FONGI [*speaking into the studio*]. Thank you, thank you, Baldovino. . . . Yes, of course. . . . I'll be delighted to come. Thank you. . . . I'll be back, I'll be back with the other members of the board in about half an hour. Until then . . .

[*He closes the door and turns toward* FABIO, *who now tiptoes up to him and winks conspiratorially.*]

FABIO [*softly, eagerly*]. Well? Do you really think it will work?
FONGI [*nodding first*]. He fell for it! He fell for it all right!
FABIO. I thought so. It's been nearly a week.
FONGI [*holding up and wiggling three fingers*]. Three million! Three million lire! What did I tell you? It couldn't miss! [*He takes* FABIO *by the arm and leads him toward the front door.*] What a comedy! Leave it to me! Leave it to me! We'll catch him red-handed! [*They exit.*]

[*The room remains empty for a moment, then the studio door opens and* ANGELO *and* MAURIZIO *enter.* ANGELO *has changed considerably: he is soberly well dressed, more at ease, well groomed, less obvious in his mannerisms.*]

MAURIZIO [*looking around*]. You know, you've really done all right for yourself.
ANGELO [*abstractedly*]. I suppose so. [*Smiling faintly.*] Everything handled with perfect decorum. [*A pause.*] Well, now, what about you? Where have you been?
MAURIZIO. Oh, here and there. Pretty far off the beaten track, actually.
ANGELO. You?

MAURIZIO. You don't believe me?

ANGELO. Off the beaten track? By which you mean you haven't been to Capri or Paris or the Riviera. Where have you been?

MAURIZIO. The land of rubber and bananas.

ANGELO. Africa?

MAURIZIO. The Congo. In the heart of the jungle. Oh, yes. Real jungle.

ANGELO. Ah! See any animals?

MAURIZIO. A few pygmies, some half-civilized natives.

ANGELO. No, I mean big game: tigers, leopards.

MAURIZIO. Oh, a handful of exhausted lions. Nothing much . . . What a strange look in your eyes.

ANGELO [smiling bitterly, he cups his hand and shows MAURIZIO his nails]. You see what we've come to? And we don't cut our nails to disarm ourselves, Maurizio. On the contrary: just to make us look more civilized, so we can hold our own in a far more desperate struggle than the one our ancestors fought with nothing but their claws. That's why I've always envied wild animals. And you, you rascal, all over Africa without even looking at the animals?

MAURIZIO. Oh, never mind about that. Let's talk about you. How's it going?

ANGELO. What?

MAURIZIO. I mean, with your wife? This—this arrangement?

ANGELO. How should it go? Everything's fine.

MAURIZIO. And—and your relationship?

ANGELO [a pause. He looks at his friend, then rises]. What did you expect?

MAURIZIO [cheerfully]. You look well, you know.

ANGELO. I keep busy.

MAURIZIO. Ah, yes. I heard Fabio organized a new syndicate of investors.

ANGELO. Yes. To get me into trouble. It's doing very nicely.

MAURIZIO. And you're in charge of it?

ANGELO. That's why it's so successful.

MAURIZIO. Yes, yes, so I was told. I'd like to get into it myself, but . . . Well, they say you're terribly strict.

ANGELO. That's right. I don't steal . . . [Going up to MAURIZIO and resting his hands on his friend's arms.] You know what it's like? To have hundreds of thousands passing through your hands? To think of all that money as just so much paper? Not to feel the slightest need for it or interest?

MAURIZIO. Oh, it must be great fun for you—

ANGELO. Divine! And not one mistake, not one failure! I work, I work hard. And they all have to go along with me.

MAURIZIO. Yes . . . that's it . . .

ANGELO. They complain, don't they? Tell me. They scream? They bite their nails?

MAURIZIO. They say—they say you could be a little less—well, a little less meticulous, that's all.

ANGELO. I know. I stifle them. I stifle everybody. Whoever comes close to me. But you see, there's nothing else I can do. For the past ten months I haven't been a human being.

MAURIZIO. No? What are you?

ANGELO. I've told you: almost a god! If you could only understand, Maurizio! I exist only in what seems to be. I bury myself in numbers, in financial speculations, but only for others. Not one cent of it—and I want it that way—not one cent of it is mine! I live here, in this beautiful house, and I can hardly see or hear or touch anything. Sometimes I'm amazed at the sound of my own voice, the echo of my own footsteps through these rooms; to discover that I need a drink of water or feel the need to rest. I live—do you see?—deliciously, in the absolute of a pure abstract form!

MAURIZIO. You ought to feel a little compassion for us poor mortals.

ANGELO. I do, but I can't help myself. However, I warned him, I warned your cousin well ahead of time. And I'm living up to the agreement we made.

MAURIZIO. But you seem to be taking malicious pleasure in it all.

ANGELO. Not malicious, no. Suspended in the air, it's like lying on a cloud: the joy of the saints as depicted in the great frescoes of our churches.

MAURIZIO. Still, you understand, it can't go on like this.

ANGELO [gloomily, after a pause]. Oh, I know. It will end. Soon, perhaps. But they'd better be careful! We'll see how it goes! [Looking into his eyes.] I'm saying this for their own sake. Open your cousin's eyes. He's too anxious to get rid of me as soon as possible. That disturbs you? You know something?

MAURIZIO. No, nothing.

ANGELO. Come on, be honest. I'm sorry for them. It's only natural.

MAURIZIO. I assure you I don't know anything. I spoke to Mrs. Renni, but I haven't even seen Fabio yet.

ANGELO. Oh, I know. They both thought, her mother and

your cousin, they both thought: "We'll get the girl married,
a mere formality. Then, after a while, on some pretext or
other, we'll get rid of him." That was the best they could
hope for, wasn't it? But they had no *right* to hope for it!
From the very beginning they've both been deplorably
frivolous.

MAURIZIO. Is that what you suspect? Who told you that?

ANGELO. They even made the question of my honesty the
basis for the whole agreement.

MAURIZIO. Well, then, how could they want you—

ANGELO. Don't be stupid. Logic is one thing, the human
animal another. You can quite easily propose a logical
solution to something and at the same time hope in your
heart of hearts that it won't work out. Believe me, I could
easily ingratiate myself with them both by giving them a
pretext for getting rid of me. I could, but I won't. I won't
for their own sake. Because they can't possibly really want
me to do that.

MAURIZIO. My God, you're incredible! You even deny them
the possibility that they might want you to do something
wrong?

ANGELO. Look. Let's suppose I went along. At first they'd
be relieved. They'd be rid of the crushing weight of my
presence. With me gone, they could tell themselves that
the concept of honesty I failed to maintain survives, at
least to some extent, in them. Agata would still be a married
woman, now separated from an unworthy husband, and
because her husband turned out to be a scoundrel, and
because she's still a young woman, she would quite naturally allow herself to be consoled in the arms of an old
friend. What would have been quite unthinkable for an
unattached young lady is easily condoned in a married
woman who has been absolved of her marriage vows. All
right? So I, as the husband, could compromise my honesty
and allow myself to be thrown out. But I didn't come into
this house merely as a husband. As a husband and nothing
else I would never have agreed to the proposition. There
would have been no real need for me. I was needed here
because the husband was soon to become a father. In a
reasonable amount of time, that's understood. Here a
father was desperately needed. And the father—oh, yes—
the father has to remain an honest man. Not even Fabio
could want anything else. Because if, as the husband, I
could leave here without hurting my wife, who would

probably resume her maiden name, as a father I would do a terrible injury to the child, who can bear no other name but mine. In the eyes of the law and of society the boy is my son. And the lower I fall, the more he'll suffer from it. Fabio can't possibly want me to do such a thing.

MAURIZIO. No. You're quite right.

ANGELO. So you see? And you know what would happen to me. You know me, Maurizio: I'd sink like a stone. To avenge myself for the wrong they'd do me by publicly disgracing me, I'd want the child, who legally belongs to me. I'd leave the boy here for two or three years, then I'd prove that my wife is an adulteress living openly with her lover and I'd take the child away. Down, down into the mud with me . . . You know I have this horrible beast in me, this creature I freed myself from by chaining it here, in the conditions imposed by our agreement. It's in their own best interest to see that I continue to respect those conditions, as I firmly wish to do, because, once unchained, today or tomorrow, who knows where the beast will lead me, what will become of me? [*Suddenly changing tone.*] Well, that's enough of this. Tell me: did they send you to me the minute you got back? Come on, out with it! What were you supposed to ask me? Quickly, now! [*Looking at his watch.*] I've spent too much time with you already. You know the baby is being baptized this morning? And first I have a lunch here with my board of directors. Did Fabio send you? Or Mrs. Renni?

MAURIZIO. Well, yes . . . both of them. It's about the baptism, in fact. This name you insist on—

ANGELO [*with a sigh*]. Oh, I know.

MAURIZIO. Well, now—really!

ANGELO. I know, the poor little creature. He's too tiny for such a big name. He'll be crushed by it.

MAURIZIO. Sigismund!

ANGELO. But it's a very old family name. It was my father's . . . and my grandfather's . . .

MAURIZIO. Not an argument that makes much sense to them, you understand.

ANGELO. Or to me. You know, I might never have thought of it myself. But is it my fault? A horrible name, yes— ludicrous, especially for a child—and I confess—[*very softly.*]—if he were my own son, really my son, I probably wouldn't have given it to him.

MAURIZIO. Ah, you see? You see?

ANGELO. See what? Under these circumstances what else can I call him? It's the same old story. It's not what I want; it's what appearances demand! The form, Maurizio, the form! You know that! Since I have to name him, I can't give him any name but this one! It's useless, you know! It's quite useless for them to insist! I'm sorry, but I will not give in. You can tell them that for me. And now I have to get back to work. This kind of thing is just a waste of time. I'm sorry to have to welcome you like this. Well, until later, eh? Good-by, Maurizio. [*He hurriedly shakes* MAURIZIO's *hand and exits into the studio.*]

[MAURIZIO *stands there, not knowing what to do. After a moment or two* MADDALENA *and* FABIO *enter softly, anxious to hear the news.* MAURIZIO *looks at them and helplessly scratches the back of his head. First* MADDALENA, *then* FABIO, *nods to him questioningly, she with suffering eyes, he sullen and frowning.* MAURIZIO *shakes his head, then shrugs and spreads his arms helplessly.* MADDALENA *collapses into a chair and remains there, crushed.* FABIO *also sits down, but resentfully, his clenched fists resting on his knees.* MAURIZIO *now sits down, nodding thoughtfully, and sighs deeply several times. No one dares to break the crushing silence.* FABIO *snorts despairingly.* MADDALENA *hardly breathes at all, but looks from one to the other, her expression more and more disconsolate. A long, long pause. Then* FABIO *bounds to his feet and begins to pace furiously up and down, clenching and unclenching his hands. After a moment or two* MAURIZIO *also rises, goes to* MADDALENA *and bows, offering her his hand.*]

MADDALENA [*softly, plaintively, taking his hand*]. You're going?

FABIO [*turning on them*]. Let him go! I don't know how he dares to show himself in this house! [*To* MAURIZIO.] Don't you ever set foot in here again!

MAURIZIO [*not daring to protest, turning just once to look at him, still holding* MADDALENA's *hand, softly*]. Agata?

MADDALENA. In there, with the baby.

MAURIZIO. Please say good-by to her for me. [*He kisses* MADDALENA's *hand, then turns away and spreads his arms wide.*] Tell her—tell her I'm sorry.

MADDALENA. Oh, she at least . . . she has the child now.

FABIO [*still pacing*]. Yes! And a fine time she'll have with it! Once the boy is old enough to fall under this maniac's spell!

MADDALENA. Yes! That's what I'm afraid of!

FABIO [*still pacing*]. It's already started with this business about the name!

MADDALENA [*to* MAURIZIO]. Believe me, Setti, it's been hell for ten months now!

FABIO [*still pacing*]. Imagine what kind of an education he'll want to give him!

MADDALENA. It's awful! We . . . we can't even read a newspaper any more.

MAURIZIO. No? Why not?

MADDALENA. Oh, he has some crazy idea about the press.

MAURIZIO. But . . . what's he like around the house? Harsh? Impolite?

MADDALENA. Nothing like that. Worse. He couldn't be more polite. He tells us to do the most dreadful things in the nicest possible way . . . giving such unexpected reasons and making them seem so unanswerable that we're always forced to give in to him. He's an appalling man, Setti, simply appalling! I can't even take a deep breath any more with him around!

MAURIZIO. My dear Mrs. Renni, what can I say? I'm absolutely annihilated! I never thought—

FABIO [*exploding again*]. You never thought! My God! I'd walk right out of here, if I didn't have to stay for the baptism! Don't you understand that I can't bear to listen to you? That I can't stand the sight of you?

MAURIZIO. You're right. Yes . . . I'll go, I'll go . . .

[*The* MAID, *a different girl from Act One, enters.*]

MAID. The rector is here.

MADDALENA [*getting up*]. Ah, show him in.

[*The* MAID *exits.*]

MAURIZIO. Good-by, Mrs. Renni.

MADDALENA. Must you really go? You won't stay for the baptism? Agata would be so happy. Well, come around, come around, Setti. I have great faith in you.

[MAURIZIO *again spreads his arms helplessly, then bows, glances at* FABIO *without daring to say anything, and exits, nodding, as he goes, to the* RECTOR, *who has just been admitted by the* MAID.]

MADDALENA. Come in, Father. Sit down.

RECTOR. My dear Mrs. Renni, how nice to see you!

FABIO. Good morning, Father.

RECTOR. Dear Mr. Colli! Mrs. Renni, I've come to make the final arrangements.

MADDALENA. Thank you, Father. Your assistant was here earlier.

RECTOR. Oh, excellent, excellent.

MADDALENA. Yes, and we've prepared everything in there. You were so kind to send us all those beautiful things from the church. It looks perfectly lovely! Adorable! Would you like to see—

RECTOR. And Mrs. Baldovino?

MADDALENA. Shall I call her?

RECTOR. Not if she's busy. I only wanted to know how she was.

MADDALENA. Fine now, thank you. All taken up with the baby, as you might imagine.

RECTOR. Of course.

MADDALENA. We can hardly tear her away.

RECTOR. And you, Mr. Colli, are the godfather?

FABIO. Uh . . . yes . . .

MADDALENA. And I'm the godmother!

RECTOR. Oh, I took that for granted! And—and the name? Is it to be that one—the one you—

MADDALENA. Unfortunately. [*She sighs.*]

FABIO [*angrily*]. Unfortunately!

RECTOR. Sigismund . . . Still, you know . . . after all . . . he was a saint . . . a king! I'm—I'm something of a dabbler in this field.

MADDALENA. Oh, we know! A scholar!

RECTOR. No, no! Nothing so exalted! Just a hobby of mine . . . Oh, yes . . . Saint Sigismund, King of Burgundy. Married Amalberga, daughter of Theodoric. She died and he was left a widower. He then married one of her ladies-in-waiting, I think. A terrible mistake. Horrible woman. She instigated him to commit—oh, yes—a dreadful crime —against his own son.

MADDALENA. My God! His own son? What did he do to him?

RECTOR. Well—[*a helpless gesture.*]—he . . . he strangled him!

MADDALENA [*to* FABIO]. You hear that?

RECTOR [*quickly*]. But he repented, you know. At once. And to atone for his crime he dedicated himself to the strictest penitence. He retired to a monastery. Dressed only in sackcloth. And his many virtues stood him in good stead during his ordeal.

MADDALENA. His ordeal?

RECTOR. Yes, he was martyred. After being tortured, he was . . . [*He closes his eyes, bows his head, and then, with one finger, makes a gesture of decapitation.*] In the year 524, if I remember correctly.

FABIO. Oh, grand! A splendid saint! He strangles his own son and dies on the scaffold!

RECTOR. Very often the worst sinners, Mr. Colli, make the greatest saints. And this man was also a sage, you can take my word for it. He was the author of the celebrated *Lex Gombetta*, the Burgundian Code. At least that's one opinion. There are others, of course. But Savigny says he was, and when Savigny says something he's usually pretty reliable. Yes, yes, I'm with Savigny on that . . . a very reliable authority.

MADDALENA. At least, Father, I'll be able to call him by his diminutive, that's some consolation: Dino.

RECTOR. That's it, that's it: Dino! Excellent! A lovely name for a child! Goes well with the little fellow, eh, Mr. Colli?

MADDALENA. Yes. But who knows if he'll let us use it?

FABIO. Just what I was thinking.

RECTOR. Well, after all, if Mr. Baldovino insists on naming him after his father, who are we to object, eh? Well, now, what time shall we perform the ceremony?

MADDALENA. I suppose that's also up to him, Father. Wait. [*She rings for the* MAID.] I'll tell him you're here. I think he's working. [*The* MAID *enters.*] Tell Mr. Baldovino the rector is here. Ask him to come in for a moment. He's in the studio. [*She indicates the studio door. The* MAID *goes to it, knocks, and enters. Immediately* ANGELO *appears.*]

ANGELO [*entering hurriedly*]. Oh, Father, how nice of you to come! I'm honored! Please, please sit down.

RECTOR. The honor is mine. Thank you, Mr. Baldovino. I'm sorry to disturb you.

ANGELO. Not at all, not at all. I'm delighted to see you. What can I do for you?

RECTOR. We . . . I . . . if you'd be so kind . . . well, we—we wanted to agree on a time for the baptism, you know.

ANGELO. That's entirely up to you, Father. We're at your disposal. The godparents are both here, the nurse is in there, I'm ready any time, and the church is just down the street . . .

MADDALENA [*surprised*]. The church?

FABIO [*trying to control his anger*]. What's that?

ANGELO [*turning to look at them in astonishment*]. Did I say something wrong?

RECTOR [*quickly*]. You see, Mr. Baldovino, it was all arranged— You mean you don't know?

MADDALENA. We arranged everything in the nursery.

ANGELO. Arranged? Arranged what?

RECTOR. For the baptism. It was decided to have it here. It's often done nowadays.

FABIO. Everything necessary has been sent over from the church.

ANGELO. It's often done? I'm sorry, Father, but I never expected to hear you say such a thing.

RECTOR. Well, all I meant was . . . it's . . . it's become the fashion. All the best families, well . . . you know what I mean.

ANGELO [*smiling, quietly*]. And don't you think, Father, that it would be more fitting if we were to give an example of Christian humility, that spirit which recognizes that in God's eyes there are no distinctions between rich and poor?

MADDALENA. I don't see how we offend God by holding a baptism in our own home.

FABIO. Of course we don't! I'm sorry, but you always deliberately ruin everything! You never do anything anyone else wants to do! And I find it more than a little strange that you, of all people, should presume to preach to us!

ANGELO. Now, Mr. Colli, don't force me to raise my voice, please. What do you want from me? A profession of faith?

FABIO. No! I don't want anything from you!

ANGELO. If you think I'm being a hypocrite—

FABIO. I didn't say that! It just seems unnecessary, that's all!

ANGELO. And who are you to judge? What do you know about it? I suppose you think I shouldn't care at all how we baptize the child. But even if I didn't, it wouldn't matter in the least. The act doesn't concern me, but the child, and we all know it has to be done. And we all approve. Well, let's see that it's done correctly. The child must be baptized in church, at the baptismal font, and without claiming any special privileges that would serve only to contradict the whole spirit of the ceremony. I can't understand why you force me to say all this in front of the rector, who can't help but recognize that a baptism celebrated in the proper

way, in its proper place, is a much more significant and
devout event. Isn't that so, Father?

RECTOR. Oh, yes! Yes indeed! No doubt about it!

ANGELO. Furthermore, it's not only up to me. Since the matter
concerns the child, let's hear what his mother has to say.
[*He rings for the* MAID.] You and I, Mr. Colli, will keep
quiet. We'll leave it to the rector.

[*The* MAID *enters.*]

Please ask Mrs. Baldovino to join us.

[*The* MAID *exits.*]

RECTOR. Well . . . really, I . . . I'd rather let you do the talking, Mr. Baldovino. You do it so well.

ANGELO. No, no. I intend to stay out of it. You can explain
how I feel and then—[*Turning to* MADDALENA *and* FABIO.]
—you can give your reasons. We'll let the mother make
her own decision. And we'll do as she says. Here she is.

[AGATA *enters. She is pale, erect.* FABIO *and the* RECTOR *rise.*
ANGELO *remains standing.*]

AGATA. Oh, the rector. Good morning, Father.

RECTOR. My warmest congratulations, Mrs. Baldovino.

FABIO [*bowing*]. Agata . . .

ANGELO [*to* AGATA]. It's about the baptism. [*To the* RECTOR.]
You'll excuse me, Father. [*He exits into the studio.*]

AGATA. Hasn't it all been settled? I don't see—

MADDALENA. Yes, everything's ready. It looks so nice.

FABIO. It's him again!

RECTOR. Yes, you see, Mr. Baldovino—

MADDALENA. He says we can't baptize the baby here.

AGATA. Why not?

MADDALENA. Because he says . . . he says . . .

RECTOR. May I, Mrs. Renni? [*To* AGATA.] Actually, he didn't
say we can't do it. He left it up to you. Because, as he put
it, it's really up to the mother to decide. So if you decide
to have the baptism here—

MADDALENA. But of course! We were all agreed!

RECTOR. I really don't see any harm in it.

FABIO. All the best people are doing it now.

RECTOR. That's what I told Mr. Baldovino. Didn't I tell him
that?

AGATA. Well? So what is there for me to decide?

RECTOR. Ah, you see ... because Mr. Baldovino pointed out—
and quite rightly, I must admit, with a sense of respect
that does him the highest honor—he pointed out that the
ceremony should more properly be celebrated in the church
without claiming—oh, he put it so beautifully—without
claiming any special privileges that would contradict the
spirit of—of Christian humility—oh, a beautiful phrase,
isn't it? A matter of principle, you see. Yes, a matter of
principle.

AGATA. Well, Father, if you approve of what he says—

RECTOR. Oh, as a matter of principle I can't help but approve,
Mrs. Baldovino.

AGATA. Then we'll have it in the church.

MADDALENA. Agata! You, too?

AGATA. I'm afraid he's right, Mother.

RECTOR. In principle, yes, of course. But if you—

FABIO. There's nothing wrong with doing it here.

RECTOR. Oh, of course not. Oh, there's nothing wrong with
that.

FABIO. He just wants to ruin everything, as usual!

RECTOR. If you decide on the church, Mrs. Baldovino—

AGATA. Yes, I have decided, Father. In the church.

RECTOR. Very well, then. It's only down the street. All you
have to do is let me know when. Any time, Mrs. Baldovino.
Good day. [To MADDALENA.] Mrs. Renni.

MADDALENA. I'll see you out, Father.

RECTOR. Don't bother, please. Mr. Colli.

FABIO. Father.

RECTOR. There's no need—

MADDALENA. No, no, Father. No trouble. This way. [They
exit.]

[AGATA, *very pale, is about to leave the room, but* FABIO,
*unable to control himself, goes up to her and addresses her
in a low, angry voice.*]

FABIO. Agata, for God's sake, don't push me too far!

AGATA. Not now, Fabio. Please. [*She indicates the closed door
into the studio.*]

FABIO. Always what he wants! Always!

AGATA. If what he wants is right—

FABIO. You've done everything, everything he wanted you to
do! From the moment he set foot in this house!

AGATA. Let's not go back over all that, Fabio. We all agreed to this arrangement.

FABIO. But it's what you want now, isn't it? It's what you want! All you had to do was force yourself to swallow the original idea! And you did swallow it, that very first day, when you heard us talking! And now look at you! You accept everything, everything I had to force myself to do for your sake! You want it this way! You want him to know, you want him to know!

AGATA [*quickly*]. Know what?

FABIO. You see? You see? I'm right! You want him to know that we haven't touched each other since then! Don't you?

AGATA. For my own sake, Fabio.

FABIO. No! For his! For his sake!

AGATA. I couldn't bear to have him think otherwise.

FABIO. Oh, yes! Because you want him to respect you! As if he didn't agree to everything with us!

AGATA. And what does that mean? Nothing, except that we're all in this together. He's living up to his part of the bargain; I intend to live up to mine.

FABIO. But I want what belongs to me! What I have every right to have, Agata! You! You! You! [*He seizes her and attempts to embrace her.*]

AGATA [*struggling to free herself*]. No! No! Stop it! Let go of me! I told you: I can't, I can't! Not until you get rid of him!

FABIO [*not letting her go*]. I will! I will! Today! I'll chase him out of here like the criminal he is!

AGATA [*stunned, unable to resist any longer*]. Criminal?

FABIO. Yes! Yes, a criminal! He's done it, Agata! He's been stealing from us!

AGATA. You're sure?

FABIO. Of course I'm sure! He's taken three million lire! I'll get rid of him today! And then we'll be together again! Darling—

[*The studio door opens and* ANGELO *appears. Finding them in each other's arms, he stops, surprised.*]

ANGELO. Oh, I beg your pardon. [*Severely, but with a shrewd smile.*] Good Lord, it's only me, you know, so it doesn't really matter. But it could have been the maid or somebody else. Next time lock the door.

AGATA [*angrily*]. There was absolutely no reason to!

ANGELO. Not for my sake, but for yours. [*To* FABIO.] Mr. Colli, you ought to know that.

AGATA. Exactly what I've been telling him. But now I think Fabio has something to say to you.

ANGELO. He does? Gladly. What is it?

AGATA [*scornfully*]. Don't you know?

ANGELO. Should I? [*Turning to* FABIO.] What is it?

AGATA [*to* FABIO]. Tell him!

FABIO. No, not now.

AGATA. I want you to tell him now, in front of me!

FABIO. I think we ought to wait.

ANGELO [*scornfully*]. Perhaps you need witnesses?

FABIO. No, I don't need anyone! I know that you've stolen three million lire from us!

ANGELO [*very calmly, smiling*]. No, more. Much more. Something over five million. Wait. [*He takes out his wallet and extracts from it five notarized receipts which he glances over, adding them up.*] Yes, five million six hundred and seventy-two thousand, nine hundred and twenty-eight lire! Well over five million, Mr. Colli. You underestimated me.

FABIO. It doesn't matter, I don't care. You can keep the money and get out!

ANGELO. Not so fast, not so fast, Mr. Colli. I don't blame you for being in such a hurry, but the situation is much more serious than you think.

FABIO. Oh, come now! No more of your preaching!

ANGELO. I'm not preaching, no. [*Turning to* AGATA.] I'd like you to hear this, if you don't mind. [*She looks at him, coldly silent. He turns back to* FABIO.] If you're anxious to make a thief out of me, perhaps we can reach some sort of agreement about that, too. But I want you to realize first that you aren't being fair to me. Look. [*He shows them the receipts, spreading them out like a fan.*] From these receipts, as you can see, Mr. Colli, the sum figures as savings and unexpected earnings of the syndicate I head. But that doesn't matter. We can fix all that. [*To* AGATA.] All I had to do, you see, was stick these in my pocket and keep quiet. That's what they wanted me to do. [*Indicating* FABIO *and alluding to his partners.*] If I had fallen into the trap set for me by that crooked little man, that Marchetto Fongi who was here this morning. [*To* FABIO.] Oh, I don't deny the trap was set with a certain amount of skill. [*To* AGATA *again.*] You don't understand these things, Agata, but they arranged it so that my personal accounts would

show a large surplus, which I could have simply accepted
without anyone finding out about it. Of course they expected me to fall for it and keep the money, at which
point they would have produced other documents and
caught me with my hand in the till. [*To* FABIO.] Isn't that
how you planned it?

AGATA [*with barely disguised contempt, looking at the silent*
FABIO]. Did you do this?

ANGELO [*quickly*]. No, Agata, you mustn't take it so hard!

AGATA. Not take it so hard?

ANGELO. If it upsets you so much, then—then I'm the one
in trouble, not him.

AGATA. Why?

ANGELO. Because it means his situation has become intolerable.
And if his is intolerable, mine is even worse.

AGATA. Worse? How can it be worse?

ANGELO [*gazing intently at her, then looking away, disturbed*].
Because . . . because if I were to become human . . . to
become a man in your eyes, I . . . I couldn't go on. Oh,
Agata the worst possible thing would happen to me: I
. . . I'd no longer be able to look anyone in the face again
. . . [*He passes a hand over his eyes and tries to control
himself.*] No . . . enough of this. We have to find some
solution and quickly. [*Bitterly.*] I thought I'd give myself
the satisfaction today of making fools out of my directors,
out of this Fongi. And out of you, too, Colli, for thinking
you could trap me, a man like me, with such a childish
scheme. But now I realize that if you had to stoop so low,
to try to make a criminal out of me, just to get her back,
without even understanding that my disgrace would reflect
on your own son, well—the pleasure of honesty isn't worth
it, not at that price. [*Holding the receipts out to* FABIO.]
Here.

FABIO. What am I supposed to do with them?

ANGELO. Tear them up. They're the only proof I have. The
money is in the safe, every cent of it. [*Looking him sternly
in the eye, then speaking harshly, contemptuously.*] But
you'll have to steal it yourself.

FABIO [*stung*]. Me?

ANGELO. Yes, you. You.

FABIO. Are you mad?

ANGELO. Why go halfway, Colli? I told you from the very
beginning that if you wanted me to be an honest man,
I'd be one. So now, if you want to make a criminal out

of me, you'll have to commit the crime. You steal the money, I'll play the thief. And then I'll go away, because I know now I can't stay here any longer.

FABIO. You *are* mad!

ANGELO. You think so? From the beginning I've had to do the thinking here for all of us. I'm not suggesting you send me to jail. You couldn't do that. You'll take the money for me, that's all.

FABIO [*trembling, advancing on him*]. For you? What do you mean?

ANGELO. Don't be offended. Just my way of putting it. You'll cut a splendid figure, Colli. All you have to do is take the money out of the safe, just long enough to prove I stole it. Then you can put it back, so your investors won't suffer. After all, they put their trust in me out of their regard for you. It's clear, isn't it? I'll look like a criminal. That's all you want from me, isn't it?

AGATA [*violently*]. No! I won't let you do it! [*The two men stand facing each other. Then, to enhance the effect of her protest.*] And what about the baby?

ANGELO. We have to go through with this, Agata.

AGATA. No! I can't, I won't let you!

[*The* MAID *appears in the main entrance.*]

MAID. The directors and Mr. Fongi.

FABIO [*quickly, dismayed*]. We'll talk about this tomorrow!

ANGELO [*readily, strongly, defiantly*]. I've made up my mind. You can go ahead right now!

AGATA. And I tell you I won't let you! Do you understand? I won't let you! I don't want you to!

ANGELO. All the more reason why I should.

FONGI [*entering with four directors*]. Excuse us. May we?

[MADDALENA *now enters, followed by the nurse carrying the baby. Everyone flocks around the infant with exclamations, congratulations, greetings, etc., while* MADDALENA *proudly shows off the child.*]

CURTAIN

ACT THREE

[*The Renni–Baldovino living room the following morning.*
ANGELO, *dressed in the same shabby suit he first appeared in, is sitting with his elbows on his knees and his head in his hands, staring gloomily at the floor.* MADDALENA *is talking to him urgently.*]

MADDALENA. But you don't have any right to do this, you ought to know that! It has nothing to do with either you or Fabio any more. Not even with her. It concerns the child, the child!

ANGELO [*looking up and staring at her ferociously*]. And what do I care about the child?

MADDALENA [*stunned, but quickly recovering*]. Oh, God, that's right. But I'm only reminding you of what you said yourself about the baby, that in the long run he would be the one to suffer the most. Blessed words. What an impression they made on my daughter and—and what anguish they cause her, now that she's a mother and nothing but a mother! You ought to understand that.

ANGELO. I don't understand anything anymore, Mrs. Renni.

MADDALENA. That's not true. You pointed it out to Fabio only yesterday.

ANGELO. What?

MADDALENA. That he couldn't go through with this because of the child.

ANGELO. I pointed it out? No, Mrs. Renni. I don't care what he did or what he'll do. I knew very well he'd try something like this. [*Looking at her, more irritated than contemptuous.*] And so did you, Mrs. Renni.

MADDALENA. I? No! No, I swear it!

ANGELO. What do you mean, no? Why else would he have organized this syndicate?

MADDALENA. I don't know. Perhaps—perhaps to give you something to do.

ANGELO. Yes, to get me out of the house. That was certainly the original purpose. He was hoping to keep me busy elsewhere, so that behind my back he and Agata could—

MADDALENA [*quickly interrupting*]. No, not Agata! Not her!

[159]

Fabio, yes—that was probably what he wanted. But I can
assure you that Agata—

ANGELO [*shrugging, impatiently*]. My God, are you so blind?
You can really tell me this about her, to my face?

MADDALENA. It's the truth.

ANGELO. And doesn't it frighten you? [*A pause.*] Don't you
understand what it means?

MADDALENA. What?

ANGELO. That I have to leave here and that, instead of coming to me, you should be trying to convince your daughter
to let me go.

MADDALENA. But why? Why? I don't see—

ANGELO. Never mind why. The important thing is that I leave.

MADDALENA. No, no! She won't let you!

ANGELO. Please, Mrs. Renni, don't make me lose my head
like the rest of you! Don't deprive me of my last remaining strength! I can still see the consequences of what others
do blindly. Blindly, you know, not because they're all fools
but because they live, and when you're alive, Mrs. Renni,
you live and you don't see. I can see, because I came into
this house in order *not* to live. Do you insist on bringing
me back to life? Is that what you want? Be careful, because if life were to seize me in its grip and make me as
blind as everybody else . . . [*He stops and makes a visible
effort to overcome the onrush of his human feelings, the
suppression of which always makes him look ferocious.
Then he resumes, calmly, almost coldly.*] Look . . . look
. . . all I wanted to do, quite simply, was point out to Colli
the consequences of what he was about to do. That is, by
wanting to make a thief out of an honest man—

MADDALENA. You?

ANGELO. Not me, not the real me, Mrs. Renni, but the man
you all wanted in this house, the man I became, the man
none of you understood. To make a thief out of such a
man Colli himself would have to take the money.

MADDALENA. How can you expect him to do that?

ANGELO. He wants to make me look like a criminal.

MADDALENA. But he can't! He mustn't!

ANGELO. He'll take the money, I tell you! He'll pretend to
steal it. If he doesn't, I will! Would you really force me to
steal it?

[MAURIZIO, *very worried, enters hurriedly.* ANGELO *sees the
expression on his face and laughs loudly.*]

I suppose you're also here to beg me "not to commit this act of madness"?

MADDALENA [*quickly, to* MAURIZIO]. Yes, yes! Please, Setti, you persuade him!

MAURIZIO. Don't worry, Mrs. Renni. Of course he won't do it. Because he knows it's an act of madness. Not on his part, but on Fabio's.

ANGELO. Did he ask you to come here and fix everything?

MAURIZIO. Of course not! I'm here because you asked me to come. In your note last night. Don't you remember?

ANGELO. Oh, yes. And did you really bring me the money I asked you to loan me?

MAURIZIO. I didn't bring you a penny!

ANGELO. Because, like the bright fellow you are, you understood I was only bluffing? Good for you! [*He indicates the jacket he has on.*] However, you can see I'm dressed for departure—as I wrote you in my note—in the same suit I came in. But an honest man dressed like this, eh? What else can he want from an old school friend but a small loan in order to make a decent exit? [*He goes up to* MAURIZIO *and takes him by the arms.*] Remember, Maurizio, I've always been very particular about keeping up appearances.

MAURIZIO [*confused*]. What the devil are you talking about?

ANGELO [*turning to look at* MADDALENA *and laughing again*]. Look at the way that poor woman stares at me . . . [*Friendly, casual.*] Now, I'll explain, Mrs. Renni. You see, the only real mistake Fabio made—and it's really quite understandable, I sympathize with him completely—was simply in thinking I would fall into his trap. The mistake is not irreparable. Colli will be made to understand that since I came into this house to play a game it amused me to play, I must play it out to the end. Yes, right up to the crime itself. But not a real crime, you understand. You can't actually expect me to pocket all that money, to really steal it. But the game is so enjoyable I'm willing to pretend to steal it. And don't worry, I mean about the threat I made: that in three or four years I'd come back and claim the child. I only said that to impress Colli. It's pure nonsense. What do I want with the child? Or were you afraid I'd blackmail you?

MAURIZIO. Go on, Angelo, stop it. No one thinks that.

ANGELO. And suppose it had occurred to me?

MAURIZIO. I said stop it!

ANGELO. No, not blackmail . . . But I did want to play the game out to this point, so I could enjoy the exquisite pleasure of seeing you all on your knees, begging me now not to take the money you all worked so hard to make me steal.

MAURIZIO. But you didn't steal it.

ANGELO. No. Because I want him to steal it, with his own hands.

[FABIO *appears in the doorway, very upset and pale.*]

And he will steal it, I promise you.

FABIO [*approaching* ANGELO *in near terror*]. I *will* steal it? But then—oh, my God!—did you give—did you give anyone else the key to the safe?

ANGELO. No. Why?

FABIO. My God! My God! But then? Could anyone have found out? . . . Could Fongi have told anyone? . . .

MAURIZIO. Is the money missing?

MADDALENA. Good heavens!

ANGELO. Don't worry, Colli. It's not missing. [*He pats the inside pocket of his jacket.*] I have it.

FABIO. Ah, so you *did* take it?

ANGELO. I told you, I always go all the way in everything!

FABIO. What *are* you trying to do?

ANGELO. Don't worry. You see, I knew a gentleman like you would find it very difficult, perhaps impossible, to remove that money from the safe, even for a few minutes, even as a joke. So I went and took the money out of the safe last night.

FABIO. You did? And why, may I ask?

ANGELO. Why, to give you a chance, Colli, to make a magnificent gesture of restitution. Think of the effect on your board of directors!

FABIO. You still insist on this foolishness?

ANGELO. You see, I really did take the money. So now, if you won't do what I tell you, I'll stop pretending and we'll play the game for keeps. I'll be the criminal you wanted me to be.

FABIO. I only wanted to— But don't you understand? I've changed my mind. I don't want to go through with this.

ANGELO. But now I do want to go through with it.

FABIO. With what?

ANGELO. Exactly what you wanted. Didn't you tell Agata,

right here, yesterday, that I had the money in my pocket? Well, I do have it in my pocket.

FABIO. But you haven't got me in your pocket, by God!

ANGELO. Yes, I do. You, too, Colli. And this morning I shall preside over our regular board meeting. I'm going to make my usual report. You can't stop me. Naturally, I'll say nothing about these surplus earnings Fongi so cleverly arranged and I'll give him the satisfaction of catching me red-handed. Oh, don't worry, I'll give a wonderful imitation of a criminal caught in the act. Then, later on, you and I will settle everything back here.

FABIO. You won't do it!

ANGELO. I will, I will, my dear Colli.

MAURIZIO. But you can't just voluntarily pretend you're a thief when you aren't one!

ANGELO [*firmly, threateningly*]. I told you I've made up my mind. I'll actually steal the money if you persist in opposing me!

FABIO. But why? In God's name, why? If I myself beg you not to do this?

ANGELO [*turning to look at him and speaking in a low, serious tone*]. And how can you expect me to remain in this house any longer, Colli?

FABIO. I told you I was sorry—really sorry . . .

ANGELO. For what?

FABIO. For what I've done.

ANGELO. But there's no need to be sorry for what you've done, my dear Colli, because it's only natural—but for what you haven't done!

FABIO. And what should I have done?

ANGELO. What should you have done? Why, after a few months you should have immediately come to me and told me that even if I wanted to abide by our agreement, which was costing me nothing, and you wanted to abide by it, which was only natural, there was someone else in this house who counted more than either of us, someone whose dignity and nobility of spirit made it impossible for us to go on with this farce. And then I would at once have shown you how absurd the whole idea was, that any honest man could lend himself to such an arrangement.

FABIO. Yes, yes, you're right! [*Indicating* MAURIZIO.] In fact, I was angry with him for having brought someone like you here!

ANGELO. No, he was absolutely right to bring me, believe

me! What did you want in this house? An honest medi-
ocrity? As if any ordinary man would accept such an
arrangement, unless he were a scoundrel. I was the only
one able to accept it. Just as I'm able, you see, to accept
the idea of passing for a thief.

MAURIZIO. But how can you? Why?

FABIO. Why? Just for the fun of it?

MAURIZIO. Who's forcing you to? No one wants you to do it!

MADDALENA. No one! We're all begging you not to!

ANGELO [to MAURIZIO]. You, out of friendship . . . [To
MADDALENA.] You, because of the child . . . [To FABIO.]
And you? What's your reason?

FABIO. The same as hers.

ANGELO [looking into his eyes]. The child? That's all? Nothing
else?

[FABIO does not answer.]

I'll tell you the real reason: because you realize now the
effect of what you've done. [To MADDALENA.] Mrs. Renni,
you think he's concerned with the good name of the child?
An illusion! [Indicating MAURIZIO.] He knows that my
past . . . unfortunately . . . yes, that my present way of
life . . . the birth of a child . . . might help to bury the
memory of so many other sad events . . . my old life . . .
[Indicating FABIO.] But now he has a lot more to think
about than just the child, Mrs. Renni. Oh, a lot more.
[Turning to the others.] And what about me? Don't I
count for anything? Do you think I can stay here forever,
a light by which you can all see and nothing else? I, too,
am made of flesh and bone. I, too, have blood in my veins
—a thick, black blood, bitter with the poison of my
memories. And I'm afraid! Yes, I'm afraid! Yesterday, in
here, when this man, in front of your daughter, hurled his
accusations in my face, I fell blindly—more blindly than
any of you—into another and far more subtle trap, a trap
that has been lying in wait for me during the ten months
I've been in this house, living with a woman I hardly dared
even to look at. And this childish little trick of yours, Colli,
was all I needed to make me aware of the abyss at my
feet. . . . I planned to keep quiet, you understand? To
swallow your insult in front of her, to let her think I was
a criminal. Then I would get you alone and prove to you
it wasn't true, and force you in secret to play our game
out to the end. But I was unable to keep quiet. My flesh

cried out in protest! And you . . . she . . . all three of you
. . . can you still dare to prevent me from doing what
I must do? . . . I tell you that to resist this force within
me I am compelled to steal that money!

[*They all look at him in silence. A pause.* AGATA, *pale and
determined, now enters. She takes a few steps into the room
and stops.* ANGELO *looks at her. He tries to remain composed and grave, but his eyes betray a hint of terror.*]

AGATA [*to her mother,* FABIO, *and* MAURIZIO]. I want to talk
to him. Alone.
ANGELO [*almost stuttering, his eyes lowered*]. No. No, please.
You see, I—
AGATA. I must talk to you.
ANGELO. It's . . . it's useless, Agata . . . I told them . . . I
told them all I had to say.
AGATA. And now you'll hear what I have to say.
ANGELO. No, no . . . please . . . It's useless, I tell you. Enough
. . . enough . . .
AGATA. I insist. [*To the others.*] Please leave us alone.

[*They exit.*]

I didn't come here to tell you not to go . . . I came to tell
you that if you do go, I'll go with you.
ANGELO [*he appears about to faint, then barely recovers. He
speaks very softly*]. I understand. You don't want to beg
me for the child's sake. A woman like you doesn't ask for
sacrifices; she makes them.
AGATA. I'm not making any sacrifice. I'm only doing what
I must.
ANGELO. No, no, Agata, you can't. Not for the baby's sake
nor for yours. And at any cost I must prevent you.
AGATA. You can't, I'm your wife. You wish to leave? Fine.
I approve and I'll follow you.
ANGELO. Where? What are you saying? Have pity on yourself,
and on me . . . and don't make me tell you . . . try to
understand by yourself, because I . . . because I . . . face
to face with you I . . . I don't know what to say . . .
AGATA. There's nothing else to say. Everything you said that
first day you came here was enough for me. I should have
come in at once and offered you my hand.
ANGELO. Oh, if you only had, Agata! I swear to you I hoped
for a moment that you would. I mean, come in . . . I

would never have dared even to touch your hand . . . but it would have ended right there.

AGATA. You wouldn't have accepted?

ANGELO. No. Out of shame, Agata, out of shame. Face to face with you, as I'm ashamed now.

AGATA. Of what? Of having spoken honestly?

ANGELO. That's easy, Agata. It's very easy to be honest, you see, as long as it's only a question of saving appearances. If you had come into the room that day to tell me you couldn't go through with the deception, I couldn't have stayed here a minute longer. As I can't stay here now.

AGATA. So you thought I agreed with Fabio?

ANGELO. No, Agata. But I waited, and when you didn't come in . . . But I spoke that way only to show him that to expect me to be honest was impossible. . . . Not for me . . . but for all of you! . . . So you ought to realize that now— since you've changed the conditions—it becomes impossible for me . . . Not because I don't want to be honest, but because of what I am . . . because of all I've done. . . . You see, only the part I agreed to play here in your house—

AGATA. We asked you to play it!

ANGELO. And I accepted.

AGATA. But you warned us in advance what the consequences would be. You tried to dissuade him. Well, I accepted, too.

ANGELO. And you shouldn't have, you shouldn't have, Agata. That was your mistake. My voice was never heard in this house. Never. It was only the voice of a grotesque mask I chose to wear. And why? Here you were, all three of you, a portion of this poor suffering humanity of ours, exulting in the joys and undergoing the torments of living. In this house a poor, weak mother had made the sacrifice of allowing her daughter to have an illicit love affair! And you, in love with a good man, allowed yourself to ignore the fact that this man was already married to someone else. You all realized you had done wrong, that you were to blame. And so you tried to escape the consequences of your action by bringing me into your house. And I came, speaking a language in these rooms that stifled and paralyzed you—the language of an abstract concept, a fictitious and unnatural honesty which you finally had the courage to rebel against. I knew very well that in the long run neither Fabio nor your mother would accept the conditions of such an arrangement. Their humanity was bound to rebel against it. I heard their groans and protests. And believe me, I

enjoyed watching them intrigue against the most serious of
the consequences I had told them to expect right from the
very beginning. But it was dangerous for you, Agata. The
only danger I could see was that you'd accept all the consequences, to the bitter end. And you did accept them. In
fact, you were able to accept them because, unfortunately
for you, the moment you became a mother the young girl
in love died, she simply ceased to exist. Now, more than
anything else, you are a mother. But I—I'm not the father
of your child, Agata. Do you understand what that means?

AGATA. Then it's for the child's sake you want to go away?
Because you aren't the real father?

ANGELO. No, no! What are you saying? Try to understand!
By the very fact that you'd want to come with me you
make the child mine, more sacred to me than if he were
my own son—the pledge of your sacrifice and your esteem.

AGATA. Well, then?

ANGELO. But I tell you this only to remind you of my own
reality, Agata. Because you can see nothing but your child!
You're still talking to a mask, the mask of a father.

AGATA. No, no. I'm talking to you, to the man behind that
mask!

ANGELO. And what do you know about me? Who I am?

AGATA. This is what you are. The man I see before me.

[*Overwhelmed*, ANGELO *bows his head.*]

You can raise your head and look at me, Angelo, as I
can look at you. Otherwise, in your presence we'd all
have to lower our eyes. If only because, of all of us, you
had the courage to be ashamed of what you had done with
your life.

ANGELO. I never thought I'd hear anyone speak to me like
this. [*Violently, as if recovering from a spell.*] No . . . no
. . . Agata . . . please go! Believe me, I'm not worth it!
Do you know what I have here? In my pocket? I—I have
more than five million lire!

AGATA. You'll return the money and we'll go away.

ANGELO. Return it? Do you think I'm crazy? I won't return
it! Not—one—cent—of—it!

AGATA. All right, then the child and I will follow you down
that road as well.

ANGELO. You—you'd come with me—even . . . even as a
criminal? [*He collapses into a chair. He hides his face in
his hands and weeps.*]

AGATA [*she looks at him for a moment, then goes to the door and calls*]. Mother!

[MADDALENA *enters, sees* ANGELO *weeping, and stops, dumfounded.*]

You can tell those gentlemen we have no further use for them here.

ANGELO [*immediately rising*]. No, wait! . . . The money! [*He tries to control himself, to dry his tears, but he can't find his handkerchief. At once* AGATA *offers him hers. He understands the significance of this act which, by its very simplicity, unites them for the first time. He kisses the handkerchief and dabs at his eyes as he stretches out his hand to her. Then he gains control of himself with a deep sigh that expresses immense joy.*] Yes, I know now. I know what to tell them!

CURTAIN

UGO BETTI

1892–1953

UGO BETTI, after Pirandello, is generally regarded as the most important dramatist to write for the modern Italian theatre. In fixing Betti's position within the broader perspective of modern drama, it is possible to note the influence of Pirandello, Ibsen, Chekhov, German expressionism, and the post-war French dramatists, but finally he created a symbolic style of drama that was uniquely his own. Certainly few writers in the twentieth century have come to grips with great moral issues more directly, forcefully, and imaginatively than did Betti in the twenty-five plays he wrote from 1926 until his death in 1953. With a flinty moral integrity, he spent a lifetime creating dramatic situations which forced his characters to face unflinchingly the problem of evil. Unlike so many modern plays in which the moral issues are dissolved by psychological explanation or by those mists of fantasy which are at one with the spectator's moral evasions, Betti's plays affirm both man's need to struggle with real alternatives and his capacity to do so. The dominant themes of all his work are justice and the individual's need for judgment (Betti's lifelong interest in this theme was certainly to a large degree occasioned by his own adult career as a chief justice in the Italian courts), the redemptive and transforming power of love, and a belief in the power of the human imagination to transform the quality of life. But in dealing with each of these themes there is no attempt to whitewash man's sense of his own guilt, nor the attendant need to avoid moral responsibility. Betti's attitude in this regard is best expressed in a newspaper article he wrote shortly before his death: "It is not very popular these days to attribute responsibility to oneself; the general practice is to blame others, history, laws, parents, etc. The fact is, that vast picture of our life has an author, carries a signature: Our own! We are responsible for it."

RELIGION AND THE THEATRE[1]

By Ugo Betti

TO APPROACH a subject like this in a truly meaningful way, it seems to me that it is necessary first to force oneself to a humble objectivity and even to a certain detachment. This subject is too important and we are bound to it by too jealous a commitment to allow ourselves to dismiss it with pat solutions or lyrical effusions. It is necessary to examine it with a dispassionate eye instead of imagining what we would like it to be. The point is to understand to what extent the movement which is drawing the theatre towards religious, Christian themes is authentic.

I am speaking, of course, of the theatre today, which is history in the making, a phenomenon still in the process of taking shape. In my opinion, only the theatre of today is in every respect truly theatre, that is, actual collaboration between speakers and listeners in the common effort to formulate the dialogue of our epoch and to give expression to its aspirations.

In the meantime, there is indeed one point worthy of consideration: that such a subject—Christ and the theatre, and even more generally, religion and the theatre—has assumed, in the conscience of many, a new importance precisely at a time when large areas of disbelief, or at least indifference, seem to spread both in the individual soul and in the world.

At least, such is the appearance. Nonetheless, it is precisely now that a confused instinct leads many playwrights and many audiences to converge on themes, problems, figures, and events which, consciously or not, revolve like the wheels of a mill,

[1] "Religion and the Theatre" by Ugo Betti, translated by Gino Rizzo and William Meriwether. Reprinted by permission of *The Tulane Drama Review* and Ninon Tallon Karlweis, exclusive agent for Ugo Betti. Copyright © 1960 by *The Tulane Drama Review*, Vol. V, No. 2, December 1960, pp. 3-14.

spun by the visible or hidden current of the same stream: Religion.

This may be religion viewed as a good already attained, which must now be exalted and asserted; or as a good yet to be attained, towards which one is moved by an indistinct desire if not by a precise aim; or as the inner re-elaboration of certain principles in order to make them alive and integral; or even religion viewed as an enemy to be attacked, but not without a wealth of distress and remorse.

Many contemporary plays are indeed religious in an obvious way, and since they represent edifying episodes and settings which are peculiarly sacred, they could, in fact, be performed just as well in a church square as on the stage of a theatre. In general, these works are so well known that I find it unnecessary to name them. Their titles are frequently displayed on the billboards, and audiences, even in the most sophisticated cities, and perhaps especially here, flock to see them.

But if we wish to interpret this religious character in broader terms, the field is considerably widened. One may go so far as to say that it is above all the theatre which corroborates an observation that is only surprising at first sight: if our epoch has affinities with any other, it is more with the passionate Middle Ages than with the brilliant and tolerant Renaissance. In some respects, our epoch, too, is eager for universal systems, and it is not so much preoccupied with living and prospering in them, as in fighting for them, in asserting that they *are* universal and absolute: in a word, religious. This need for universal systems often demands to be heard in the theatre, although through very different and frequently incongruous voices. But, if considered as an indication, perhaps the more these voices appear incongruous—incongruous because they are unconscious: a spontaneous movement and not a pre-established plan—the more their importance as a symptom must be recognized. We are concerned with the theatre, that is, with an art. This is not an area where a rigorous, logical consistency—critical, political, or philosophical—is essential; here, what is often alive and positive is precisely that which, on the plane of logic and orthodoxy, may seem unclear.

That part of the contemporary theatre which is insensitive to this need may be said to consist of plays which are little above the level of entertainment and, if listened to attentively, sound to us a little out of tune with the times, and basically antiquated. What truly sets these plays in motion, perhaps under the pretense of real problems, is a basic indifference to any problem whatever, an air of routine which is at times good-natured, at times impertinent, and fundamentally nihilistic even though gay on the surface. It is, in short, the survivor of the facile, post-romantic hedonism of the nineteenth century under a different guise, scarcely modernized by a certain irony. They are anachronistic plays; although numerous, they are not part of the picture. The true picture, surveyed in its entirety, induces us to conclude that all, or almost all of the contemporary theatre that counts draws its life from needs which, although variously expressed, are essentially religious.

The basic authenticity of these needs seems to me unquestionable. They are born, ultimately, of the ineradicable need of modern man to feel reassured by certain hopes. But it is equally unquestionable that such a deep authenticity is combined with countless other heterogeneous motives which contaminate it and at times end by overwhelming it.

The first of these contaminations is that of "religiosity," I mean a religion which is no longer a precise issue and necessity—and maybe even a painful error—but a benign substitute, a flexible fall-back, a comfortable *flou* which evades precisely the dilemmas that are well defined (the "either-or," the clearcut boundaries between good and evil, the responsibility towards others and towards ourselves), a poetic way of making us always right and never wrong. Closely related to this is the vague humanitarianism with which the modern age pads every edge a little, and, pushing them towards a meaningless philanthropy, has diluted all principles and relationships of politics, family, justice, and, naturally, religion. It is used to make us all feel good and at peace with our conscience, without any great effort. How much shrewdness, even if unconscious, under this sugar-coating! In the theatre we can taste its flavor towards the third act, in the reconciliations and effusions which resolve everything, and perhaps a grand finale accompanied by organ music. Not that I am disturbed by the sound of organs or by the effusions at the end, quite the contrary. But I think that one has to pay for those results and suffer for them; and when I see them given away free, I become suspicious. This extreme need for love, this great flame—Christ—is, I think, something else.

Another contamination comes from the decadent self-gratification by which an emotion, originally religious, is little by little cherished and nurtured in and for itself, a perturbation savored like a quivering sensation, a rare experience: confessions in which suddenly glow the oozings of I don't know what sexuality; martyrdom, guilelessness, ecstasy, whose cruelty or self-annihilation is pierced (even though very remotely) by some kind of inversion. (I cannot avoid thinking of certain moments in *The Cocktail Party*.)

Next to this there is the trap of the décor. The religious issue often implies, especially for us Latins, an ostentatious background. Gold, music, purples, rays falling from high stained-glass windows, angels' tresses on frescos; one feels, at times, that the poet writing, let's say, *The Martyrdom of St. Sebastian*, or the director staging an *auto sacramental*, has ended by being more attracted to all this than to the rest— more to gestures, colors and drapery than to the sentiment.

Another contamination, it seems to me, is the one caused by the intellect: too intently bent on its inner polemics, on its own way of "being Christian," on more and more subtle doubts and hypotheses expressed through self-questioning and increasingly more labyrinthine crises so that these gradually fascinate the intellect, but perhaps more for their complication and subtlety *per se* than for their substance. Then, once the contact with facts has been weakened, the self-revelations and the polemics come close to resembling an agonizing chess game of words, a dry equation of algebraic signs. In all this, apart from a certain gratification, there is no want of a real ferment which I would also call useful if I didn't see that certain scrupulous self-examinations end, almost without exception, by acknowledging their own inanity and by characteristically returning to the initial propositions, which would indicate a certain lack either of courage at the conclusive moment or of concreteness in the premises.

Not even the theatre seems to me immune from such indulgences, whose real place is in diaries and essays, although the physical weight and near coarseness, peculiar to the theatre, reject by their very nature all that is of little weight, and easily reveal, in the harsh brightness of the footlights, the quasi-arbitrariness of certain arabesques: arabesques that are almost a luxury (whether or not literature, as action, fulfills a commitment of a religious nature); antitheses that are mainly verbal ("he will bear, then, the martyrdom of not having suffered martyrdom"); complications that are refined and, I would say, marginal (martyrs who spend their last vigil in self-contemplation, examining with subtle syllogisms their own spiritual experience—whether it is one of fear, of pride, of forgiveness, or what have you). Inquiries of this kind are certainly not superfluous, but since they deal with exceptional cases, they evade the real, important issues, the central ones, those shared by everybody—the issues of the people we meet on the street, whose conscience, in regard to religion, is not preoccupied with such fine points, but with other problems which are humbler and probably more important and, in the end, more meaningful and universal; with other and far more dangerous doubts which, finally, are also our own doubts and dangers; with other and truer anguishes.

Such an excess of subtlety, such an eagerness to attach importance to the least coils of one's conscience—in short, such a lack of coarseness—probably betrays a certain lack of seriousness, in the moral sense of that word—a nursing of one's own perturbation, which, from the beginning, carries within it the punishment of sterility. Nevertheless, in spite of all its errors and lack of concreteness, there is something positive in all this. Undoubtedly, there is the need to discuss certain situations anew, to react to passive resignation, to live one's faith and not to accept it as a free gift, to enrich it with a suffering and an effort of one's own. Indeed, there is in all this a rich possibility, and an important one, which can be understood especially by comparing it with another of the dangers which threaten the authenticity—let us say it: even the usefulness—of the religious issue in art, and specifically in the theatre: the opposite danger, which I will call habitual complacency.

But at this point I must honestly admit that these pages (I realize it as I go on) cannot avoid being, above all, a confession. In the long run, all the issues inevitably confront me already conditioned by my preoccupations as a writer. The confusions and misrepresentations to which the originally religious impulse of a play is subject, the contaminations of which I have spoken so far, are contaminations which beguile me too; they are the traps that I should like to avoid and to which, when I have finished writing, I suspect, once again, I have succumbed. Religiosity without rigor; the extreme need to love and be loved which, however, remains so indolent; an accommodating and soft humanitarianism; the sensation more alluring than feeling; the frame which enamors more than the picture; the condescension in showing or believing one's own intelligence and in putting oneself on display; certainly, all these faults are mine too, for it would be strange if I were immune to the malaise affecting practically all the literature of our age. On the other hand, precisely the fact that I am tainted with these faults (and the fact that I am involved, as an old craftsman, in such difficulties), precisely this gives me the right, my only right, to have my say, although a crude and unqualified theoretician, in the tremendous subject of this essay.

It is in this spirit of making a confession that, coming now to speak of the danger represented by habitual complacency, I will begin with a humble disclosure: rarely, after seeing a religious play, especially if explicitly and programmatically religious, rarely, I say, have I returned home and gone over it in my mind without experiencing a certain dissatisfaction —but not because I had been irked by the "contaminations" of which I have already spoken. In general they were works without faults, works entirely dedicated to the humble—and lofty and ancient—task of being religious and nothing else; interpretations of glorious miracles; representations of edifying sacrifices; vicissitudes of Carmelite nuns led to the scaffold or of Jesuits put to the test; by and large excellent works, and unobjectionable in every respect. And yet I experienced a sense of disappointment.

This disappointment was due first of all, if I may say so, to reasons of pure dramatics. From the first scene it was altogether too obvious how the whole thing was going to end. No matter how cleverly or ingenuously the author had shuffled his cards, everything happened exactly as it had been arranged and also, unfortunately, as it had been foreseen. Battles were won and lost at the very outset—won, naturally, by the good cause and lost by the evil, won by the spiritual and lost by the material, won by faith and lost by disbelief. But, in a religious work, what other solution can conflicts of such a nature have? The posing of such conflicts is enough to give us their solution. Perhaps the fault (I am still speaking from a dramatic point of view) of the plays which disappointed me consisted precisely in this: from the very beginning every passion and every character appeared already labeled and defined, or (if the author had ably managed to deceive us) they had been labeled and defined in the author's own mind. They entered into the plays, then, already judged and without hope, judged *a priori* and not brought in to struggle with real alternatives of victory and defeat, but to run through a fixed (and, therefore, habitual) trajectory, measured by a yardstick which allows no error. (I repeat once more that I am speaking from a dramatic point of view.) That's why plays which had Freedom as their goal seemed to the man of the theatre somewhat lacking in freedom, why plays having Life as their subject matter seemed in want of life. Don't misunderstand me: those plays did not lack emotive power. The great crosses shedding their light on the darkness, the sacred chants rising above Error, those immolations, those miracles, those heroic deeds—sublime flowers of a sincere, and severely tried, faith—had the power of making the lady next to me wipe away her tears and even of filling my heart with palpitations. I do not wish to sound irreverent, but such an emotive power seemed to me somewhat automatic and physical. If you will forgive me the analogy, it recalled to my mind the emotion by which, undoubtedly, both young and old are assailed when they watch the flag go by from a crowded sidewalk, and behind the flag the marching step of an heroic troop amidst the sounding of trumpets and the roll of drums. A slight shiver runs antomatically through the crowd, but it is a slight shiver that remains such: not one of those who experience it would dream, a moment later, of leaving his own business to join the army, heaven forbid, or of immolating himself. Thus the tears that flowed down the cheeks of the lady at my side left me with the suspicion that they would have very little influence on what she would do once she was back home. Those tears did not change that woman. The sacrifice of the Carmelite nuns had certainly moved her, but, nonetheless, it would not occur to her the next day, or six months hence, to refrain from certain actions and habits. In sum, that emotive power and those plays fell short. The conventional targets they reached no longer amount to much. The true targets, the dangerous targets of today—that is, certain objections widespread in the world, certain disbeliefs, certain discouragements—are probably beyond the range of fire, and the sacrifices of the Carmelites or of Thomas à Beckett cannot even scratch them.

That contrast between good and evil, then, had a very mediocre effect on a world whose characteristic is precisely this: to believe very little in the real existence of good and evil. For some time the world has suspected that vice and virtue are only products like vitriol and sugar, that certain moral conflicts are mere conventions sanctioned by smart people to keep the fools in check. Above all, I fear that several of the ladies in the audience, or several of their friends, are rather sceptical about what Someone said to each and every one of them: "Verily I say unto thee, Today shalt thou be with me in paradise." I am of the opinion that today many people are scarcely convinced that they will be resurrected after death in order that they may be judged. At any rate, they don't believe in it strongly enough to conform their actions to such a conviction. That is all. It is very simple: one must try to convince them again.

In regard to such a situation, what is the thinking of many Catholics, particularly writers and critics? Their thinking strikes me as curiously rosy. I say "curiously" because the reality of today, on the crust of the world, from the big atheisms to the small indifferences, from the apocalyptic thundering in the far away horizon to the most trivial episodes of everyday exchange and intercourse, the reality of today does not seem to me to encourage a great optimism, but rather, it appears such that persons in a position of high responsibility solemnly avow their concern over it, and even speak of crusades. The optimism of a complacent conscience, however, does not allow concern. What strikes one and causes one to envy them is a kind of soft, quiescent contentment, always repeating that "all is well"—the words of those who live off the fat of the land, and know it. The frame of mind that is at the bottom of this acquiescence seems to me the same as that of the critic who concluded that "tragedy" ended the very moment in which Christ spoke, because wars stop when victory begins. That critic was speaking only of the theatre, but his words leave us nonetheless perplexed. Then wars would be over for mankind; which would mean, to remain in the field of art and the theatre, that Art and Theatre are over too, if it is true that art is always tragedy. With Art and Theatre finished, we are left with only an elegant delight with which to garland our leisure. Leisure, nothing but leisure, if everything were said and done; and our efforts and conflicts would be, to a great extent, superfluous since we have been given the Truth which resolves them once and forever.

I am speaking with the timidity of one who is groping through a maze of problems that are too big for him, and who, at this point, sees himself reduced to the modest resource of a hesitant common sense. We were indeed given a final victory and truth. This is sure. But why these landslides around us, then? And still others announce their coming with far-off thundering. Why these defeats here and there? And why, today and perhaps again tomorrow, this flood of cruelty and hatred, greater than ever before in history? What is the dam that gave way? And, on the other hand, this giving way—was it useless? Is this vast perturbation which is in us and in many others, useless too?

Is error useless—totally useless—and is this effort in our time to fight against it, but at the same time to know it and therefore to love it and extract from it a beneficial suffering, useless too? Should the fact that we have already arrived make our journey useless? We have arrived, but are we surrounded by the everlasting calmness of a haven, by the still waters of a harbor? Why then, should Bernanos' abbess say to her novice, "Our rules are not a refuge. It isn't the rules that guard us, but we who guard the rules"? Has the danger ceased to exist; is vigilance useless; is doubt itself forbidden, even though it was allowed Christ when He said, "Remove this cup from me," or when He cried with a loud voice at the ninth hour, "Eli, Eli, lama, sabachthani"? Is it a lie, then, this hope we have that Man's life is useful, that it is an ascending, even though difficult, path towards the ever fuller, more intimate, and enlightened discovery of that Truth? Granted the stability and perfection of that Truth, how is it possible not to think that our humble ways, the ways in which we, frail men, gradually become convinced of it and prove to ourselves its eternal validity, may change with time, just as, with time, they lose their efficacy? And don't we see around us so much weakness and bewilderment, and, indeed, a pressing need to be convinced on a new basis in the face of certain new objections, thus more firmly reassuring ourselves of those certainties without which we cannot live? Happy are they who are calm, sure, strong, and no longer need anything, or at least think they don't. But how can we avoid thinking, also, of those who are weak, without faith, and without hope? Is it not true that we must think of them before all?

When I think of men without hope an image often comes to my mind. I imagine them as inhabitants of an arid planet, without water or earth. Since these two elements—the source of life and the place where it exists—are totally unknown to the senses of these men, they are also totally unknown to their minds. But one day, having split, by chance, the rock on which they live, they discover some strange objects that are embedded in it. These objects are also rocks, but different from the others. These men cannot even fathom what a grain of wheat or a fish is, but what they now have before their eyes is a petrified grain and a petrified fish, and they do not know it. Their wise men carefully examine and re-examine those curious scales, those peculiar shapes, those inexplicable formations. And finally these very same shapes and formations, irreconcilable with all other hypotheses, will necessarily and of themselves create an hypothesis which is almost unbelievable, and yet the only one possible. Each one of these two fossils cannot but presuppose a certain unknown element. One will call forth the sea, the other, the earth. Bent over those scales, these men will finally behold what they never have and never will see in their mortal lives, but which, somewhere, if those scales exist, must certainly exist as well—the blue, infinite ocean, the green, marvelous pastures: Life.

No other way could have convinced them: not even an oath. It would have been an inane declaration, words of an unknown language. Only now are they convinced, since they themselves have discovered those scales.

I fear that it is not always possible or useful to speak of faith to those who despair, or to describe that fresh water, that earth in flower, to them. They do not know, and perhaps they do not want to know, what freshness and gardens are. They do not live in such a world, or they do not believe they do.

However, it can be demonstrated that they do belong to it. But demonstrated, perhaps, in one way only. One must enter their refuge and dig into it and know it. In order to do this, we must go to that rocky land and accept it as it is. The proofs must be found there, for it would be of no use to bring them from outside. I believe that by studying man carefully one will undoubtedly discover that, just as the grain of wheat presupposes the earth and the fish, the water, man presupposes God.

I realize that, even at this point, these are nothing but justifications. The means whose validity I am supporting are none but the means which, in writing for the theatre, I, myself, have tried to follow, although in part, unconsciously. But what else should I uphold if not these confused efforts—more than ideas—which have impelled me for so many years? All I can do is try clumsily to prove again certain things to someone, starting from zero. I believe, truly believe, that if we search untiringly at the bottom of all human abdications we will always end by finding, under so many "no's," a small "yes" which will outweigh every objection and will be sufficient to rebuild everything. One must not be afraid of that desert. On the contrary, everything must actually be razed to the ground first, one must find himself on that arid planet, and must have gone there without panaceas in his pocket. When we have truly suffered and understood human baseness, we will find at the bottom (since in error not all is error) several illogical and, I would say, strange needs: "illogical" because they cannot be measured by the yardstick of human reason, "strange" because unknown or, rather, opposed to the mechanism of the advantage of the world in which we live and in which we have discovered them. They deny this world and paint a different one, revealing a "bewildering incongruity between our existence and what it ought to be according to the aspirations of our soul." (I wrote these words twenty-five years ago as an introduction to my first play.)

They are inexplicable needs. But in the soul of the unjust man, and even in the soul of the judge who betrays justice, we will discover that, in the end, he, himself, cannot breathe or survive without justice. Underneath the most hardened bitterness we will, at a certain point, discover in the cruel, selfish, lost souls, a need for mercy, harmony, solidarity, immortality, trust, forgiveness, and, above all, for love: a mercy and a love which are far greater than the pale imitations offered by this world. This is a thirst which all the fountains of the earth cannot quench. Each of these mysterious needs is one side of a perimeter whose complete figure, when we finally perceive it, has one name: GOD.

CRIME ON GOAT ISLAND

by UGO BETTI

1950

CRIME ON GOAT ISLAND[1]

Translated by Henry Reed

CHARACTERS

AGATA   ANGELO

SILVA   EDOARDO

PIA

The time is the present.

[1] *Crime On Goat Island*, by Ugo Betti, translated by Henry Reed, published by Chandler Publishing Company, San Francisco. Copyright © 1961 by Chandler Publishing Company. Reprinted by permission of the publisher, and of Ninon Tallon Karlweis, exclusive agent for Ugo Betti.

ACT ONE

[*The action of the play takes place in a lonely house, surrounded by a barren, sun-baked tract of heathland. The scene throughout is a room on the ground floor—almost a basement—used as a kitchen. A shaft of sunlight strikes in through the bars of a window. Beyond the open door at the back of the stage, the parched, arid countryside can be seen. Other doors lead to the inner apartments of the house. Against one of the walls, in a recess, is a well.*

As the curtain rises, EDOARDO, *a dull, stupid-looking old man, is drinking a glass of water.* PIA *is seated at some distance from him. He is seeking an opportunity to linger; but she gives him none.*]

EDOARDO. Good water, this is, very good . . . It's nice and cool in here: wish I didn't have to get up. I'm getting a bit too old, you know, now, to drive that broken-down lorry all over the place. And in this heat as well. [*After a pause.*] You won't forget to tell your sister-in-law I'll be back this way on Monday, will you? And every Monday from now on. If any of you want anything, just come out and wave, will you? [*He waits for a reply; there is none.*] Has your sister-in-law gone to the post-office?

PIA. Yes.

EDOARDO. I wanted to ask her about the things I brought her last week. Were they all right? Was she satisfied?

PIA. Yes.

EDOARDO. Ah. Has your niece gone to the post-office with her?

PIA. No.

EDOARDO. Your niece is quite well again by now, I suppose?

PIA. Very well, thank you.

EDOARDO. Ah, good. That's good. [*He taps his glass.*] Do you think I might have another glass, please?

[PIA *gets up, takes his glass, and fills it from a jug. He drinks; then he rises, still reluctant to go.*]

EDOARDO. You say you won't need any flour next time?

PIA. I've given you the list, haven't I?

EDOARDO. Yes, yes, yes, all right, never mind. [*He takes it out, and looks at it.*] Yes . . . Very well, then: till next Monday, then, eh? [*He moves towards the door.*] It's not only the sun, it's the air as well. [*At the door he turns back to her.*] It's the wind: it burns: it burns right into you . . . Well, I'm off now . . . Give my respects to your niece and sister-in-law, won't you?

PIA. Good-bye.

[EDOARDO *goes.* PIA *wanders idly over to the window and watches the lorry depart. Silence falls over the place once more, and she goes over to the well. She takes a rope with a little hook on the end, and lets it dangle into the well, patiently maneuvering it about. A shadow falls across the shaft of sunlight. A man outside stands looking in through the window, unobserved, watching her. After a few moments, he addresses her, politely.*]

THE MAN. Have you dropped something down the well?

PIA [*starts; sharply*]. What do you want?

THE MAN. I wanted to ask if this is the way to Goat Island?

PIA. This is Goat Island. This is it, here. Where do you have to get to? [*Then, as he fails to reply.*] Which way did you come?

THE MAN [*vaguely*]. Oh . . . from over there, along the road.

PIA. There's nothing else along this way: this is the only house. If you want the post-office, you'll have to go back the way you came.

THE MAN. Oh. Is that very far?

PIA. Are you walking?

THE MAN. Yes.

PIA. A couple of hours then.

THE MAN [*appears to ponder this for a moment*]. Thank you. Good day.

PIA. Good day.

[*He disappears.* PIA *goes over to the window to watch him go. Then she returns to the well, and resumes her task.* THE MAN *reappears, this time at the door.*

He comes in soundlessly, He is a robust, healthy-looking young man with fair hair and complexion. He stands a moment, looking at PIA, *and then raps with his knuckles at the door-post.* PIA *turns round with a start, and says with a mixture of fear and harshness:*]

PIA. Who told you you could come in here?

THE MAN [*politely*]. Forgive me: but I've just realised this is the house I was looking for.

PIA. What do you want? [*She calls.*] Silvia! Silvia!

THE MAN. There's no need to be frightened. I'm sorry to come here looking so dirty and untidy. It's the road: it's thick with dust. [*His voice is very courteous and pleasant.*] This is the house that used to belong to Professor Enrico Ishi, isn't it?

PIA. The Professor died several months ago.

THE MAN. I know. Are you his widow?

PIA. No.

THE MAN. You must be his sister, then: Pia.

PIA. Yes.

THE MAN. You're young. Is his widow not in?

PIA. She'll be back shortly.

THE MAN. Ah, then I'll wait for her. And the daughter: Miss Silvia, how is she? Is she getting on well at the University? Is *she* at home?

PIA. I don't know. I think she is.

THE MAN. Do you mind if I sit down? [*At a vague shrug from PIA he does so.*] Thank you. It's very beautiful round here. Lonely: but very attractive, somehow. Don't you think so?

PIA. No. Nor would you if you had to stay here long. We don't come from these parts.

THE MAN. Why doesn't anything seem to grow round here?

PIA. It's because of the goats. They eat everything up.

THE MAN. Goats? Have you a lot of them?

PIA. We make our living from them.

THE MAN. Who do you have to look after them?

PIA. We look after them ourselves. Myself, and my sister-in-law, and the girl.

THE MAN. Haven't you a herdsman?

PIA. No.

THE MAN. You'd find a herdsman very useful. It's much better for the animals. They get used to obeying him. Haven't you any servants, either?

PIA. We used to have a peasant-woman who came in. We manage by ourselves now.

THE MAN. Will you excuse me a moment, please? I've left some of my things outside.

[*He goes out, returning immediately with a suitcase and a sack. He sits down again.*]

THE MAN. I think this is a very pleasant house, whatever you say. You can see it sticking up from the distance, like a tower.

PIA. It's not a house, it's a hovel. Did you notice the balcony, upstairs?

THE MAN. What about it?

PIA. You can't go out onto it; it's crumbling to pieces. At night, whenever there's a wind, the shutters start to rattle: whang-whang, all night long. You can't sleep for it. It drives my niece almost crazy.

THE MAN. Whang-whang. But surely all you have to do is to go up and tie the shutters back . . . or else pull them down? I . . . could do that for you.

PIA. Yes: and you and the balcony and everything else would all come down together. It it weren't dangerous, we'd have fixed it ourselves, long ago.

THE MAN. Have you and the widow and the girl been here a long time without a man in the place?

PIA. Five years: ever since my brother went away.

THE MAN. I suppose your sister-in-law doesn't ever think of getting married again?

PIA. I don't suppose the idea's ever entered her head. [*A pause*.] What is it you've come for?

THE MAN. Me? Oh, I was a friend of your brother's. I was with him when he died, as it happened. I heard what must have been his very last words. It all happened out there . . . in that hell-hole in Africa they shut us all up in.

PIA. Were you taken prisoner with my brother? [*He nods*.] Did you get on well with him?

THE MAN. Your brother had other companions who'd been taken prisoner with him: men from his own country, who spoke the same language. Yet, gradually, somehow he singled me out for his own special friend. I was the only one he ever talked to. We were together the whole time.

PIA. Are you a foreigner?

THE MAN. Yes. I'm not really supposed to be staying in this country. I haven't a permit to settle here.

PIA. You speak the language perfectly.

THE MAN. Yes. [*With a smile*.] I'm so fond of talking: perhaps that's why.

PIA. Where do you come from?

THE MAN [*with a laugh, and a vague wave of the hand*]. Miles away . . . it's very hot in my country: as hot as it is here. But it can be cold as well. In winter we have to wall up the windows with bricks and plaster, and keep great big stoves burning the whole time, It's not so bad then. [*He laughs again*.]

PIA. What do you work at there?

THE MAN. I used to study. I studied a great deal. And I thought a great deal too. My name's Angelo. Angelo Useim.

PIA. Why ever haven't you gone back home?

THE MAN. I didn't want to. [*He speaks with frankness and dignity.*] I wanted to come to this country; to come to this house.

[*There is a pause.*]

PIA. [*her curiosity aroused*]. Did my brother ask you to do anything for him . . . ? Is that the reason you've come here? Did he ask you to bring us some message or other?

ANGELO. Yes: that was the reason.

PIA. A message for me?

[ANGELO *vaguely indicates no.*]

For the girl?

[ANGELO *again, vaguely indicates no.*]

Ah, then it must be for his wife . . . his widow. I don't think she'll be long. You don't know her, of course?

ANGELO. No.

PIA [*a note of hostility in her voice*]. My sister-in-law is a woman we . . . all admire very much. I have always felt very small beside her. [*She laughs.*] When the shutter bangs at midnight it says: Agata! Agata!

ANGELO. Is that your sister-in-law's name?

PIA. Yes. The whole place is called Agata. We owe her the privilege of being allowed to rot ourselves away here. Do you know what the trouble with this place is? [*He looks inquiringly at her.*] Loneliness: day after day after day of loneliness. It could drive anyone mad . . . I'm hoping to get away before very long . . . fortunately. Were you an officer?

ANGELO. Yes.

PIA. I'm a school-teacher. I teach languages. I've been abroad a great deal . . . Sprechen Sie Deutsch? . . . Vous le trouvez joli, cet endroit?

ANGELO [*haltingly tries to repeat the last words, but gives up with a laugh*]. No, it's no use: I don't understand.

PIA. I once spent a whole year in Vienna. Have you ever been there?

ANGELO. No.

PIA. Lovely . . . lovely city! I used to stay with very important people there. Every night we went to theatres or parties . . . in evening-clothes. Every day was crowded with excitement. Can you dance?

ANGELO. Yes.

PIA. I can't believe I'm the same woman here as I was there. I seem to have become almost a savage. I've neglected myself: I'm only a bundle of rags now. Horrible.

ANGELO [smiles]. Do you think a man has eyes, and can't see with them? You're not horrible. Did you have love-affairs in Vienna?

PIA [laughs]. Ah, love-affairs . . . ! You men are the same everywhere, aren't you? I was going to ask you if you'd like a drink of water? It's very cool. And you must be thirsty.

ANGELO. Yes, I would; thank you very much.

[He comes to the table; she brings the water to him. He drinks.]

ANGELO. It's very pleasant in here.

PIA. It's the only cool spot there is.

ANGELO. Do you know? I've been in exactly the same state as you are. You've been a long while here without a man. I was a long while out there without a woman.

PIA. Ah, yes. In the prison camp. You must all have been very bored.

ANGELO. Well, it was not so pleasant as Vienna . . . A man wants a woman. He needs a woman.

PIA [maliciously]. Still . . . they did let you out in the end.

ANGELO. Certainly, they did . . . It's an unfortunate thing, but men, are full of . . . sin. It is the way they are made. [Calmly, almost sadly.] And the way I am made perhaps makes me even more addicted to that sort of thing than most men. I am driven to it: driven to sin. Aren't you?

PIA [with an embarrassed laugh]. Oh, dear . . . Surely . . . you must know that those things aren't half so important to a woman as they are to a man. We . . . don't think about such things so much as you do.

ANGELO. A man is always a man, and a woman is always a woman. What are men and women bound to think about when they're alone together?

PIA [laughs]. I'm sure they can find many other things to think about . . .

ANGELO [*still serious and amiable*]. Have you a husband? Or some man or other . . . ?

PIA [*expostulating*]. Please . . . I must ask you . . .

ANGELO [*courteously; he does not move towards her*]. Are we alone in the house?

PIA. Whatever do you mean? My niece is in there: and I shall most certainly call her if you go on . . . talking like that. My sister-in-law will be back at any moment.

ANGELO [*as before*]. If your sister-in-law lets me stay here tonight, will you be nice to me?

PIA. Are you crazy? Really, I don't know whether to be angry with you or to laugh at you. It's easy to see you're a foreigner. You'll have to learn to think very differently about things like that if you're going to stay in this country.

ANGELO [*as before*]. You won't?

PIA. I've told you not to talk like that! We've hardly known each other for ten minutes, and you think you can . . . Good heavens, don't you see how silly it is?

ANGELO. I see. [*Then, as if he had completely forgotten the matter.*] Look: when I came in, weren't you trying to get something out of the well? Have you dropped something down it?

PIA. Down the well? Yes. [*She returns to the former subject.*] Please, you mustn't think I meant to offend you. But you must realise that you can't make the same kind of . . . approaches to women everywhere you go. Women aren't all like the kind of women you've probably been used to since you came back from the prison-camp. Perhaps that's what's given you such silly ideas.

ANGELO. Yes. What was it that fell in?

PIA. Where?

ANGELO. Into the well.

PIA. A goatskin. We've a lot of them. [*She points to a pile of goatskins. They form a sort of couch.*]

ANGELO. You didn't manage to fish it out?

PIA. It must have got caught. There are hooks on the inside down there.

ANGELO. What will you do, then?

PIA. Go down and fetch it up. Why do you ask?

ANGELO. I'd like to make myself useful, that's all. I'm very obliging: I'm always anxious to be of use to people. Besides I must make people . . . *like* me, mustn't I? . . . especially as I haven't a penny to my name. You say someone will have to go down the well?

PIA. Yes.

ANGELO. How?

PIA. We have a ladder.

ANGELO. What about the water?

PIA. It's only a few feet deep.

ANGELO. Isn't it dangerous?

PIA. No.

ANGELO. I can do it for you. I'll get the skin back for you right away.

PIA [*laughing*]. Do you really want to?

ANGELO. Certainly.

[PIA *takes a rope-ladder from a corner and lowers it down the well, fixing it to a hook.* ANGELO *leans over the parapet, and calls down.*]

Hi, there! Look out! I'm coming down! [*He turns to* PIA, *laughs and begins to take off his shoes, and turn up his trousers.*]

PIA. You men are extraordinary creatures aren't you? [*He looks at her inquiringly.*] I . . . was thinking about what you said a few moments ago; I just don't know how a man can want such a thing of a woman, before he can even so much as tell whether they—well,—like or understand each other even. It's like . . . it's the way animals behave. [*Her embarrassment causes her to laugh again.*]

[*A few moments before this, another woman—*AGATA—*has appeared in the outer doorway. She stands watching them, unnoticed, though in no way furtively.* ANGELO *is still preparing to descend the well.*]

ANGELO. You are sure it isn't dangerous?

PIA. No, no, don't worry . . . I was saying that you men think all women are exactly the same. You can't really have meant you liked me. Why should you? I think it must be the hot weather: it's given you a touch of the sun.

[ANGELO *has taken off his jacket, and is preparing to clamber over the parapet of the well.*]

PIA. I think you probably behave in just the same way to every woman you meet. It doesn't mean a thing; it's just a form of greeting with you; it doesn't mean anything at all.

[ANGELO *disappears over the side of the well as she speaks. She leans over and calls down.*]

PIA. Is it cold down there?

ANGELO [*a hollow echo*]. Cold . . .

PIA. Are you right at the bottom?

ANGELO. Yes.

PIA. Have you found it?

ANGELO. Not yet.

PIA. I expect you'll find a lot of other things down there as
well: clothes, probably . . . Wait, I'll go and get the lamp.

She runs away from the well, almost bumps into AGATA. *The
two women whisper together for a moment or two, and then
go off together. The stage remains empty. The voice of*
ANGELO *comes up from the well. He is singing: a kind of
dirge.*]

ANGELO.

> Esevi—uttu—sehe
> Bi—be—ba
> Esevi—uttu—sehe
> Bi—be—ba.
> Agliela cicha
> Falhu manà.
>
> Bibete bibete
> Bibete bà.
> Agliela cicha
> Falhu manà
> Bibete bibete
> Bibete bà.

During this, AGATA *has returned, and sits waiting at the table.*]

ANGELO. I'm bringing up a whole pile of stuff from down here.

*He is coming up the well again; he throws up from the inside
a goat skin, and a bundle of rags, dripping with water;
eventually he himself appears, and climbs over the parapet,
carrying a bottle. He sees* AGATA *instead of* PIA, *but looks at
her without surprise.*]

ANGELO. Look at all these things I've fished up. [*He indicates
the bottle.*] There are a lot of these, a whole string of them,
hanging from one of the hooks. I suppose they were left
behind from Professor Ishi's time?

AGATA. Yes.

ANGELO. Is it sweet?

AGATA. It's juniper.

ANGELO. Was it made here? Do the peasants make it?

AGATA. Yes.

ANGELO. Do you mind if I have a drop? I'm exhausted. Ar you the Professor's widow?

AGATA. Yes.

ANGELO [*pointing to* SILVIA, *who at this moment, comes i with* PIA]. And this young lady must be your daughter . . Miss Silvia.

AGATA. Yes.

ANGELO. Pretty. Young. Forgive me: I must dry myself, othe wise I may catch cold.

[PIA *hands him a towel. He begins to dry himself.*]

I'm a strong man: very strong. But I'm delicate as we I get ill very easily, if I overstrain myself . . . [*He holds ou an elbow to* PIA.] You: come and take hold of my elbow [*To* SILVIA.] And you come and take hold of the other on

[*They obey shyly.*]

Now, I'll put my hands together, as though I were prayin Like that. Now: pull as hard as you can, both of you, an see if you can pull my hands apart. Go on! Pull. [*They d so, without effect, and then laugh and stop.*] You can' can you? No: and four men couldn't either. I'm ver strong. All the same, I have to take care; I have to hav my meals regularly. I'm clean, too. [*He laughs.*] Why, it a pleasure to have me in the house, I'm so clean!

PIA [*teasingly*]. Your skin's as white and soft as a woman'

ANGELO [*pleased*]. Yes: you wouldn't think I'd been throug so many hardships, would you? But the good thing is: always sleep very well. That's because I never do anybod any harm.

PIA [*teasing*]. And those pretty curls: they make you look lik a pet lamb.

ANGELO. Well, if it comes to that, you three have very fin skins too . . . from what I can see of them. Not like th women of my country: their faces are all covered wit freckles. And they get great breasts much too early for m liking. Though I'm bound to say they're pretty good giving a man what he wants. They know how to satisf you when you make love to them; they know what you lik

AGATA. You were a prisoner, I gather?

ANGELO. Yes. But whatever happens to me I always say

never mind! I expect that'll make you think I'm frivolous.
I'm not: I'm a very thoughtful type of man, as it happens.
You'll be saying I talk too much about myself: the reason
is that I have to make people understand me. And deep
down, what I most need in life is affection. That was what
I felt the lack of so badly in the prison-camp. [*He shakes
his head, and laughs, then he holds up his hand with the
thumb sticking up; he pretends to seize it with the other
hand and tear it off; but he is only closing it in his hand;
he shows the hand which now appears thumbless, and
laughs again.*]

AGATA. Have you been free for long?

ANGELO. Yes. [*He still speaks with simple dignity.*] I've been
rather a long time getting here, simply because of the
money; I had none. I've sometimes had to make good the
deficiency by rather unpleasant methods. Still, what's it
matter? Why's a man given the gift of cunning, if he's never
to use it? And certainly, I'm cunning enough. But I've
worked as well, sometimes.

PIA [*goodnaturedly teasing him*]. Ah, that *is* bad news.

ANGELO. Yes; I worked in a large mill: I used to keep the
account-books. But I soon grew tired of that. The people
were such illiterate fools; and always covered with flour.
And besides, I couldn't get this house off my mind.

AGATA [*coldly*]. Why?

ANGELO. Because I'd heard so much about it. The house with
the three women. All women. [*He laughs.*] Why it smells of
women! [*Seriously again.*] What was the use of my earning
money at the mill and buying myself a smart gray tweed
suit, if my soul was sunk in gloom the whole time? What
I love most of all is to sit and think: to reduce complicated
things to their simplest terms. And I love to read: to close
the book with my finger still between the pages. Perhaps
even to fall asleep over the book and then wake up and
realise how my thoughts have gone wandering on by themselves. A charming habit, reading: I know the young lady
is fond of it too. Aren't you?

SILVIA [*rather embarrassed*]. Yes.

ANGELO. And what about the shutter? I know the shutter robs
the young lady of her slumbers. Eh? I know a lot, don't I?

SILVIA [*as before*]. Yes.

ANGELO. And what about your studies? How are they going?
The University must cost a lot of money?

SILVIA. Yes, it does rather.

ANGELO. Still, it's good to learn why things are as they are, isn't it? I suppose you're on holiday at the moment?

SILVIA. I've not been very well this year; mother wanted me to stay at home and get better.

ANGELO. Which you seem to have done, to judge from the color in your cheeks. [*To the others.*] But more than anything else in the world do you know what I like? Talking.

PIA. So we've noticed. You haven't stopped for a single second since you came in.

ANGELO [*gently*]. Yes, I'd willingly go without food in order to talk. Arguments, beautiful conversations! Talking; discovering how well you agree with other people. And even if you disagree at first, if you just go on talking and questioning and answering, never raising your voice, never protesting, keeping your wits about you, slipping in a little joke every now and then, do you know what you eventually discover? That you have really been in complete agreement from the very start. Do you know why?

PIA [*mockingly*]. Tell us.

ANGELO. Because men agree with each other by nature—and women of course, even more so. We agree, without realising it. We are all brothers and sisters. [*He takes on the voice of a severe inquisitor.*] "Ah, brothers and sisters, eh? Brothers and sisters. And what about sin? How do you manage to explain sin, if we're all brothers and sisters?" [*As though replying.*] Sin? . . . well, yes, sin does get born, certainly it does. The earth's black yeast ferments. I'm a very great sinner myself. The black yeast of the earth lures me more and more, even in a single day, towards woman: yet I despise it all. My soul craves simply for the innocent intimacy of a brother and sister. And if the innocent intimacy turns into sin? Well, it isn't the end of the world, even if it does. The One who created us created the material world that it might delight the eternal soul in us which craved for desire and love, and needed an object for its passion. And sin: sin: what is it, after all? It's the means by which we satisfy and thereby conquer this infatuation of the soul. Women find these things difficult to grasp, I know; even educated women. But one thing is certain: our salvation lies in sin; and it's only our damnable pride that dares think otherwise.

SILVIA. But were you really out there with my father?

ANGELO. Certainly I was.

SILVIA. Forgive me for asking. So many families have been taken in.

ANGELO [*with a sudden, unexpected burst of anger that makes his voice sharp and falsetto*]. Do you doubt my word? Do you doubt my word?

SILVIA [*timidly*]. But did you really talk to him?

ANGELO [*gently once more*]. The whole time, for three long years.

SILVIA. What did you talk about?

ANGELO. Ah, many many things: all the things you need to talk about if you're to get through every day for three long years. He opened his heart to me. It was he who told me to come here. When he saw at last that he himself would never be able to come back again, he seemed to want me to come in his place. [*Silence.*] So I started out. I've seen the most wonderful places in the whole of Africa and Europe: but it was this house that always kept beckoning to me. I'd like to have come here better dressed than this. I also know that a stranger isn't a stranger if he comes bearing gifts. People make you much more welcome when you bring them presents. [*To* PIA.] And in fact, when I was in Algiers, I picked out a silk dress-length for you, in one of the finest shops I could find. And what silk! The shopkeeper sighed at the mere thought of parting with it. You couldn't really call it expensive even. [*To* SILVIA.] And I decided to bring *you* two huge gilt bottles of scent from Paris; everyone told me they were the best you could get. [*To* AGATA.] And for you, because you're the mistress of the house, I had to find an even more valuable present: so I chose a pair of earrings, with beautiful black stones set in them. And then . . . Well, I thought I ought to bring some cakes: the kind that stay fresh and soft for months. And I felt you'd like to have some sort of little animal in a cage, a quiet tame little creature: the kind you see nibbling nuts, holding them between their little hands. Oh, yes I took the greatest possible care I could to pick the sort of things you'd like. I chose them with great care . . . but of course I never actually bought them, because I was completely unprovided with cash! I hope you'll take the will for the deed. [*He laughs at great length, amused at his joke, which however fails to amuse the others.*] Please forgive me for joking, but I always think it's a man's duty to keep women cheerful. When a man makes a woman laugh, she feels somehow protected. You three must have been very melancholy here without a man to laugh and joke with you; especially with the shutter disturbing you at night! [*He laughs again.*]

AGATA. You'll forgive me, but would you mind talking seriously? Had you any particular reason for coming here?

ANGELO. Yes, an important one.

AGATA. You were actually present when my husband died?

ANGELO. Yes, I was there.

AGATA. Did he give you any message for us?

ANGELO. Yes.

AGATA. Then suppose you tell us what it was.

ANGELO. I'd have done so before now, only I'm afraid it doesn't concern all three of you.

AGATA. Whom does it concern?

ANGELO [*after a pause*]. You.

[*There is a silence:* PIA *and* SILVIA *rise and go out.*]

AGATA [*looking at the ground*]. What can my husband still want of me?

ANGELO. I'm sorry you should be so distressed.

AGATA. I am not distressed.

ANGELO. Are you frightened of something?

AGATA. I am not frightened. So you really don't know?

ANGELO. Know what?

AGATA. You are here on my husband's behalf. But I am quite sure he can't have told you the truth. He rarely did tell the truth; even when he thought he did.

ANGELO. What do you mean by the truth?

AGATA [*almost indifferently*]. It is simply that I have reasons for feeling resentful towards my husband; and I would prefer not to hear anything more about him.

ANGELO [*curiously*]. That I was unaware of.

AGATA [*after a moment*]. Do you know why my husband went away from here, and was taken prisoner and died, out there?

ANGELO. The war.

AGATA. No. My husband wanted to run away from me. [*Almost derisively.*] I am a woman who has been . . . "left." Though, in fact, I was alone even while he was here; I realised that afterwards.

ANGELO. You dislike your condition here: the continual loneliness of it?

AGATA. No. I still have relatives: I could go to them, no doubt,

if I wanted to. I just don't want to; that's all. Things have
turned out as they have; and life doesn't begin over again.

ANGELO. What was your husband's reason for leaving you?

AGATA [*indifferently*]. He was ashamed of himself. He was a
liar; rhetoric was the only language he knew.

ANGELO. Why did you marry him?

AGATA [*as before*]. I believed in him. I shared in his work. I
married him against everyone's advice. [*Ironically.*] Oh,
all his girl students adored him. He was almost a saint down
in the city.

ANGELO. However did you both come to live here?

AGATA. That was my doing. It's a long story. It was my doing.
Perhaps you ought to know. Enrico was beginning to come
up against a certain amount of opposition . . . I was proud
of the fact to begin with: the two of us, against the world.
Then I began to notice that all the trouble, the spite, the
petty worries, were beginning to waste and tarnish something between us also. It was my doing. [*Sadly.*] Ever since
I was a child I have wanted all or nothing. If I made a
blot on a page, I preferred to tear it right out; a victim
of rhetoric. I suggested to him—I had a little money of
my own—I suggested we should leave everything behind:
the city, the risks we ran. A revenge against the world. He
kissed me; it was all very moving. And what a farce it all
was! The two of us: alone, far away from everything. Our
aspirations, our fondness for each other, our sincerity. So
we came here. That was how it was.

ANGELO. And here?

AGATA. Wilderness; and silence.

ANGELO. How?

AGATA. Every day exactly the same, the absence of any kind
of distraction. Perhaps even one's feelings, if they're left to
themselves the whole time, begin to wear out. They burn
themselves up and become empty. I began to notice that my
husband hardly ever worked any more.

ANGELO. What did he do?

AGATA. He used to stay in bed. We fell into a habit of hardly
ever speaking to each other. Hours, days, without a word.
We no longer had anything to say to each other. Everything
became . . . terrifyingly simple: daytime, evening, supper,
silence: and the two of us. My husband began to avoid me.
The loneliness, the distance from everything, the wind . . .
[*She laughs.*] . . . and the goats.

ANGELO. The goats?

AGATA. Yes, all we could hear in the silence was the goats bleating. Goats are very important here; we earn our living from them.

ANGELO [*interested*]. The milk and cheese, I suppose? And the kids?

AGATA. Yes. Goats. Their eyes are . . . unfriendly and melan choly at the same time. They actually stare at you.

ANGELO. They recognize people. There are a lot of goatherds places where I come from.

AGATA. As I said, my husband and I hardly spoke to each other. After a time, it became . . . complete silence. Com plete silence fell on us. I believe even thought has need of words; it runs along on words, as though along a thread If you get out of the habit of words, something dark and shapeless forms in their place. The only words I was be ginning to hear . . . [*With the ghost of a laugh.*] were the bleating of the goats. I could hear them, hour after hour as I used to lie stretched on the turf. [*Pause.*] Until on day my husband ran away, and I never saw him again. He ran away. Everyone thought he'd merely gone away for a time. I've never told anyone the truth; I was too proud.

ANGELO [*curiously*]. What is it you blame him for?

AGATA [*indifferently*]. For having deceived me. For making me believe in things he didn't believe in himself.

ANGELO. Deceiving you. But you wanted to be deceived. You wanted to marry a man who was your intellectual superior

AGATA [*dropping her voice*]. You don't know what my husband did after he left here. Former . . . attachments, low women . . . degrading intrigues. That was what he wanted. [*With a sudden tremor in her voice.*] But the thing that still shock me most is my own immense credulity, the great faith I had in him. A whole life! The whole thing sacrificed! And now . . . this: just waiting for the years to pass.

[*A pause.*]

ANGELO. But the dead forgive us and we have to forgive them

AGATA [*with gloomy indifference*]. I don't believe in such things. In nature there is no forgiveness. [*With a shadow of a smile.*] It's a chemical matter. When a body becomes half-an-ounce too heavy it sinks; and that's the end of it And God: it's difficult to imagine Him as an impulsive old gentleman; first of all getting very angry and after a time calming down again. No: everything is final and ordained

ANGELO [*almost amused*]. Hell?

AGATA [*half smiling*]. I have imagined it ever since I was a child. I still do . . .

ANGELO. Even now?

AGATA. Rather than chaos, I still prefer to think of punishment. A punishment, inescapable, too. So that one doesn't have to think about it any more.

ANGELO. You suffered a great deal over all this, in fact?

AGATA. No, not really. That is what is so curious. I assure you I never suffered. It was something else. My faith had been shaken.

ANGELO. Faith . . . ?

AGATA. It's difficult to explain. On one occasion . . . [*She pauses.*]

ANGELO. Yes?

AGATA. It was after my husband had left. I was lying on the grass, as I often do. The goats were cropping round about, looking at me, going "beh" . . . It was a very peaceful day. I wasn't watching the goats; I could just hear them round about me: "beh" . . . I could smell them . . . I wasn't sad, I just felt indifferent . . . Do you understand? I realised how very little it mattered to me about my husband running away and dying; I no longer even cared about the house here, or the walls falling down; or even about my daughter. Nothing mattered any longer. I didn't care any more. And then, at last, I felt at ease, there, stretched out on the grass. I had ceased to think: yes, I had even ceased to think. I felt a sense of repose . . . And I was happy simply to feel my own weight on the ground; and there was nothing else in the whole world. And then . . . I felt a curious wish. You know the absurd ideas that suddenly occur to you when you're completely alone? I suddenly wanted to go "beh" myself, "beh . . . beh . . ."; and to munch the grass like the goats. One of them stared at me; and I went "beh." [*She laughs.*] Well . . . [*She pauses.*] I don't know why I'm telling you all this; it's all nonsense, of course.

ANGELO. Lady . . . you must prepare yourself for a surprise. Did you know that, in spite of all you say, your husband's thoughts centered continuously on this place, and on this house? Yes. He talked of it so much that after a while I even came to feel as if I had lived here myself. And he realised he could trust in me. It was he himself who said to me: "Go there, Angelo: those three women are alone, go and help them; go back in place of me."

AGATA [*coldly*]. Do you think that's enough to earn you your board and keep?

ANGELO. Lady: I was only repeating your husband's words. A man would be very useful here. Your husband also spoke of his books, and his work. He thought I might be able to go on with them.

AGATA. And is that the "surprise"?

ANGELO [*after a pause*]. No: the surprise was something else. I was trying to find some way of telling you that would not offend you.

AGATA. I can imagine what my husband must have told you about me. "A fool of a woman, unbearable."

ANGELO [*laughs*]. No, lady. Your husband actually told me a lot about you. He talked more about you than he did about the house, or his daughter, or anything else. I might almost say he never talked of anything except you. However: he never once spoke to me of the things you have spoken of. My dear good lady . . . those things are unimportant; they are trivialities. He talked of other things. [*With a change of tone.*] Listen, lady, memories are like flagstones, time and distance work upon them like drops of acid. Your husband had completely forgotten certain aspects of you. Others he remembered completely. Just think: two men alone: as though on an island; I know nothing of you, you know nothing of me. It becomes permissible to talk about anything. The most intimate things. In any case, there's always a way of embarking on subjects that are particularly delicate: you laugh, you pretend they're of no importance. And then somehow you find you can say the most amazing things. Perhaps when your husband talked, he didn't always say it was you he was talking about. He spoke simply of a woman. He was cunning; but I was cunninger still. I merely observed, and pieced everything together, till I understood it all. It was you. Always you. Your husband did nothing but talk of you; it was as if he were . . . ill.

AGATA [*in a low voice*]. Well, after all that: what did he say about me?

ANGELO. Well . . . [*He laughs shyly.*] Lady: out there, you were not . . . clothed. Forgive me saying it, but between us you were naked. The only thing your husband remembered of you was what you'd been to him on certain occasions, which he remembered with extraordinary clarity. The recollection made beads of sweat stand on his forehead. Your

slightest breath: there it was. I'm bound to say that I was
. . . interested. We were shut off from women, and talked
a good deal about them; everyone did. But in our case, it
was different. [*He laughs.*] Coming in here, I had never
seen your face before, but the rest of you . . . I had. I see
that you are thinking I have insulted you.

AGATA [*contemptuously*]. I know that among certain types of
men there is always a certain type of conversation.

ANGELO. But this was different. Lady: a man and a woman
embrace and make love to each other. And after a little . . .
there's no world any longer, no longer any memory, no
longer anything! For one moment, each of them becomes
something anonymous and isolated. As a stone might be.
And out of the stone there breaks a kind of cry. It is as
though a stone were painfully making a confession. It is
something extraordinarily lonely, lonely, a secret—the act
of love—meant to be unheard and unremembered. Your
husband, however disloyally, spied that out in you and told
me of it.

AGATA. It's disgusting to listen to you. What are you trying to
suggest?

ANGELO. Simply that I *know* you. You yourself don't know
who you are; but I do.

AGATA. And who am I?

ANGELO. Why do you suppose your husband, as he approached
his end, ignored the woman you were by day and remembered only the other? Because one was true and the other
not. Up to now you have behaved like a dead child in a
coffin.

AGATA. And how ought I to behave?

ANGELO [*he laughs as though he were ashamed of himself:
and says, as though quoting*]. "Love runs through the forest
with hair on end, calling on the monstrous black boar." [*He
laughs.*] There's no religion on earth that hasn't its legends
on that subject. I've studied these things. In your countries
you call her Pasiphaë; she turned into an animal, and gave
herself to the bull. It isn't a matter of the senses, understand, it's the soul! The raging unquiet soul which craves
to tear itself to pieces and cure itself of being human. That
is sacred, it's not a matter for shame. [*There is a long
pause: he lowers his voice.*] And that is you.

[AGATA *stands for a long moment motionless; then she takes
one of the soaking rags and slaps him across the face with*

it. ANGELO *puts his hand to his cheek, and speaks slowly, without anger.*]

ANGELO. I shall pay you back for that. I have thought of you unceasingly; I have desired you all this time. That is the reason I have come all this way to find you; I would have been unhappy in any other place. Night after night you approach my bed, undress, and we are together. We shall continue to be so, here. It is right; it is sensible. And you wish it too.

AGATA [*calls*]. Pia! Silvia!

[PIA *enters and looks at them; a moment later* SILVIA *follows her.*]

PIA [*taking a bowl and placing it on the table*]. You'll be hungry; there's some milk and cheese, if you'd like some. And bread.

ANGELO [*coming to the table and sitting down*]. Certainly I'd like some. I'd have asked you for them myself. But what about the rest of you? Aren't you having any supper? It's getting dark.

PIA. We eat very early here; we've become very countrified. In another half-an-hour we shall be in bed.

ANGELO [*tapping the bottle*]. Still, surely you'll have a drink; aren't you going to try this with me? [*Eating.*] Bring some glasses; it won't do you any harm for once in a while. It was put down by my friend, he'll like the thought of our drinking it together.

PIA. Shall I really bring some glasses?

ANGELO. Certainly.

[PIA *goes to fetch them.*]

ANGELO [*still eating*]. And light a lamp as well.

[SILVIA *lights a lamp and brings it to the table.*]

ANGELO. It doesn't matter if you haven't a room. [*He points to the heap of goatskins.*] I can sleep on those perfectly well; it'll be better than a bed, if you'll just spread them out a bit for me. I'm used to far worse than that.

[PIA *has uncorked the bottle.*]

[*Pouring out.*] Drink, my dears. You were a little flock without a shepherd, weren't you? You already find the voice of a man in here comforting. What good cheese this is;

excellent! [*Turning to* AGATA, *who remains apart.*] We've
innumerable, endless tales about goats and goatherds in my
country, you know, lady. I was thinking about what we
were saying a while ago. They say that when goatherds
have been away for months and months alone with their
animals, they actually grow tired of the language and habits
of human beings. So, when there's no one about, only the
goats, in the big grazing-grounds, the goatherds themselves
take to bleating. Yes. They keep it a secret, of course, but
you can soon tell, because when they do talk with human
beings afterwards, they are always rather bewildered. And
gradually—did you know this?—the goats themselves fall
in love with the goatherd? They keep their eyes fixed on
him, and never move away from him, they . . . butt him
gently. Yes. And eventually the shepherd begins to understand, and after a little while they . . . make love, there in
the meadows, pressing close together, closer than a man
and woman even . . . However, they say the best goatherd
is the devil. [*He tastes the wine for the first time.*] This is
good. Why aren't you others drinking?

[PIA *and* SILVIA *drink.* ANGELO *drinks again; then he goes over
to the parapet of the well, and speaks down into it.*]

Thanks, Enrico, the bottle was excellent. We'll have a go at
the others, all in good time. [*He turns to the women, winks,
and turns back to the well.*] It's true, Enrico, isn't it? You
do want me to stay here, don't you? At least till the hay is
all in? [*He pretends to wait for a reply.*] He says "yes."
Now we can put the top on. [*He does so.*] How on earth
have you managed without a man here? What about the
heavy work? And the winter? And what do you do for
company? [*He suddenly bursts into song.*]

> Esevi uttu sehe
> Bi be bo
> Esevi uttu sehe
> Bi be bo.

That's one of the songs we sing in my country. It's a very,
very long one. It means: if a man comes to your house,
you, woman, must take his boots off and wash him; and
after you've washed him you must dry him. And after
you've dried him, you must make him eat. And after you've
made him eat, you must make him drink. And after you've

made him drink, you must make him lie down. And so forth . . . Come on: you sing it too, all of you: join in the chorus. [*He begins again.*] Esevi uttu sehe . . .

[*He signs to them to join in the refrain.*]

PIA [*with him*]. Bi be bo.

ANGELO. What about you, Silvia? Come on, sing up . . . Esevi uttu sehe . . .

PIA *and* SILVIA [*with him*]. Bi be bo.

AGATA [*coming forward and interrupting*]. Look: I'm sorry to have to say that we can't possibly let you stay here. I've no doubt what you've told us is the truth; I know you must have been a friend of my husband's. But we haven't the resources here, and we have nowhere for you to sleep. You've had a rest, you've had some supper, and now I must ask you to leave.

ANGELO [*after a pause*]. I see . . . So I have to go?

AGATA. Yes. You told us your presence in this country is illegal. You might get into trouble.

[ANGELO *says no more, rises, dusts himself down, and goes towards the door; here he turns, and says politely:*]

ANGELO. Good night. [*He disappears.*]

[*After a pause,* AGATA *goes to the door, closes it and puts the chain across it.*]

SILVIA. We couldn't have let him stay. It's too cut off. There have been horrible cases: tramps and deserters coming into people's houses, and murdering them, or setting the place on fire. I didn't feel comfortable with that man in the house.

PIA [*lighting another lamp, and moving towards the door*]. Go to bed, Silvia. [*She pauses, and her voice becomes shrill.*] I'd like to know why we don't go back to the town! [*To* AGATA.] It's your fault, I'm tired of it. I don't want to be a servant here, working with my hands all day long. If that's what you want, you do it: you're the mistress here. But I'm leaving, do you understand? I shall find enough to live on . . . [*She pauses.*] What's that? [*She returns from the door.*]

AGATA [*stands looking at* ANGELO's *sack*]. He's left his sack behind. He's done that on purpose, so that he can come back. He will come back here.

[*Instinctively she turns to the door.* SILVIA *does the same.* PIA *runs to the window.*]

PIA. No, there's no one there now. [*She turns back.*] He's gone away. [*She approaches the sack and rummages in it.*] Just a couple of rags. They stink of sweat. How disgusting! [*In an outburst of hysterical revulsion, almost breaking down.*] How disgusting! How disgusting! It makes me feel sick! . . . [*She goes out.*]

SILVIA [*as she goes out with one of the lamps*]. Good night, mother.

AGATA. Good night.

[*She stands for a moment motionless. Then she takes the lamp and goes out. For some time, the stage remains empty. But the light of the lamp does not disappear; it still shines from the next room. Then someone re-enters cautiously, into the half-dark. It is AGATA. She advances into the room; and stands motionless for a long time, listening. Then she goes to the door, takes off the chain, and opens it. She comes slowly back. Then she goes over and sits on the pile of skins; and waits.*]

CURTAIN

ACT TWO

[AGATA *and* PIA *are busy sewing. In front of them, comfortably seated, is* ANGELO. *A considerable time has elapsed, the well is covered.*]

ANGELO. Have I ever told you that story about the bottle of Greek wine? The precious Greek wine? [*He smiles reminiscently.*] Well, I once happened to pass by a shop: a wineshop. There was a notice outside it, saying: "Exquisite Greek Wine: Why not try it?" etcetera . . . So of course, I thought: "Good, this means me." However, I didn't want to have to pay for it . . . being completely out of funds, as usual.

[PIA *laughs, immoderately.*]

So I went into the shop and said very grandly to the man: "Oh, ah, wine-merchant . . . I'd like to purchase a couple of dozen bottles of your Greek wine," I said. "I . . . ah . . . naturally, I should like to try a glass of it before I actually order it . . ." The old devil behind the counter (I can't tell you how blood-ugly he was) took one look at me: "You see what the notice says?" "But I . . ." "*Samples on payment only*, that's what it says." "But . . . but surely," I said, "surely a purchaser of a large quant— . . ." "If you want to sample that wine, you've got to pay for it," he said. And he sent me away, pff, just like that.

[PIA *again laughs rather more than the tale deserves.*]

ANGELO [*going over to the window*]. Between that old villain and me, from that day on, it was a fight to the death. Hasn't Silvia come in yet?
PIA. No.
ANGELO. Do you know where she's gone?
PIA. No.
ANGELO. Well, I let three weeks go by. Next time I went there, I went dressed as a kitchen-boy. [*Imitating.*] "Please sir, I've come from the Governor, and the Governor's butler has sent me to buy two or three crates of Greek wine for the Governor. So if you please, sir, will you kindly tele-

phone the palace of the Governor, so that I can ask whether it's three, or four, or five crates he wants."

[PIA *laughs*.]

ANGELO. And I saw the man was mine. He looked up the number himself, rang through to it for me, and passed the receiver over to me—oh, so affectionately! I'm bound to say the sounds I heard at the other end of the telephone were extremely strange and offensive. But I ignored them. Every time I answered I pretended I was speaking to the Governor's butler. And all the time, the wine-merchant was watching me with adoration in his eyes. "Have you spoken to the Governor's butler?" he said, when I'd finished. "Yes," I said. "It's five crates, they want, five . . . But first of all . . ." "First you'll want to taste it," he said, "won't you? Of course you will, I'll see to that for you, I'll give you a nice glass of it so you can really try it. Yes." And right there, on the counter, was the bottle with the label: saying: "Exquisite Greek wine. Why not try it, etc." But the wineman said: "No, no, not that, not that. I want to give you a drop of fresh I've specially uncorked for you." He ran into the room behind the shop, and came back with another bottle, and put it in front of me. And still he kept looking at me. He was just about to pour it out, when I stopped him: "Is it cold?" I said. "Cold," he said. "Greek wine," I said: "just opened?" "Greek wine," he said: "just opened." "Ah, then I'd like some ice in it," I said. "Ice?" he said. "Ice," I said. "You . . . you want some ice as well?" he said. Another minute and he'd have thrown his arms round me. "Bravo . . . Well done!" he said. "Ice in it. Straight away. I'll run and get it." He flew into the back room, I heard him breaking up the ice, back he came, and filled the glass right to the brim and placed it in front of me . . . and still he kept looking at me. I drank . . . Then I wiped the sweat off my face. "Like it?" he said. "Yes," I said. "Would you like another glass?" he said. I hesitated . . . It was then the brute exploded: he shouted at me in the most terrifying voice you ever heard, that either I had to drink another glass or he'd send for the police. So I drank another glass, and then I observed: "M'm, it's not bad . . ." "Hahahaha! Being clever, eh?" he said. "Coming in here to try and catch me out, eh? Well you've just fallen in your own trap, see, my lad! That wasn't the Governor's telephone number, it was my sister-in-law's, the midwife's!

That isn't Greek wine you've been drinking! That's seven-year-old vinegar!

[PIA *laughs*.]

"It's worse than sulphuric acid that is!" he shouted. "You'll be in hospital tonight! You'll be in the churchyard tomorrow!" [*He pauses: then, in flutelike tone.*] "Do you think I might have another glass?" I said. [*A dramatic pause.*] "Another glass?" "Yes." "Do you want to commit suicide?" "Yes." So I drank. And I drank again. Then I seized the bottle, emptied it, kissed the wineman tenderly on the forehead . . . and departed. [*Solemnly.*] After a few moments, I heard a tremendous row behind me. The brute had just discovered that while he was in the back room getting the ice, I'd changed the two bottles over. [*Pause.*] He had a stroke, and died on the spot.

PIA [*laughs and then says*]. You're a fraud, Angelo.

ANGELO. Why?

PIA. Not one of these things you tell us has ever happened to you. You're a rogue.

ANGELO [*pathetically*]. Yes: I'm a rogue. I'd be the first to admit it. You surround me with comforts, work for me, feed me, even look after my clothes and polish my shoes . . . while I—[*He breaks off.*] Haven't you even seen her?

PIA. Who?

ANGELO. Silvia.

PIA [*sharply*]. No.

ANGELO [*continuing*]. And do you know what you really ought to do? You ought to take a whip and thrash me.

PIA. Of course we ought.

ANGELO. Of course you ought. Because I'm lazy. I waste time doing all sorts of useless things; and I'm a bit of a liar as well. [*He rises and goes to look out of the window; then comes back and sits down again.*] I'm a parasite.

PIA [*shrilly and aggressively*]. Yes, you are! You're an idle good-for-nothing!

ANGELO [*gently*]. Never mind, my dear: everybody knows that some people are cut out for work, and others aren't. This morning I went out to chop the wood. Suddenly, I felt I had to have a rest for a minute, I sat down, and . . .

[SILVIA *has appeared in the doorway; the women turn and look at her; he goes on as if he had not seen her.*]

In a few moments I was deep in my own thoughts . . .
thoughts so lovely, so delicate it would have been a crime
to chase them away . . . merely to go back and chop wood.
I'd been travelling in great ocean liners in which even the
plates and dishes were made of gold. Well . . . What's the
point of it all? Here I am, thinking of America, thinking
of eternity. There isn't an eagle could fly as swiftly. That's
one's soul. Yes. Don't you agree with me, Silvia dear?
Of course you do. I've noticed lately that whenever you
come in, everything lights up: I always think that, every
time I see you. But today you're even more . . . vivid and
attractive than usual. What's the matter, my dear, don't
you feel well? Perhaps you didn't sleep well last night? [*To
the others.*] Yet she looks perfectly well, doesn't she?

PIA [*sharply*]. Say something, you silly little thing!

[SILVIA *has come forward without looking at anyone, and as
though she heard nothing.*]

ANGELO [*still affable and imperturbable*]. We were worried
about you, knowing you were out in this heat. It's dangerous, you know. Ah . . . now I can see you properly: you've
been out there too long. Of course you have. [*To the
others.*] This girl spends too much time out of doors! I'm
beginning to suspect there must be something in the house
she doesn't like. In which case . . .

PIA [*as before*]. Can't you open your mouth, you little fool!

ANGELO. . . . . In which case, we'll all be ready and glad to do
anything that may be necessary to put it right, won't we?
Tell her so, Agata. And you, Pia! Tell her.

[PIA *rises with deliberate hostility and goes toward the door.*]

ANGELO [*with sudden anger*]. Pia! I'm speaking to you.

[PIA *goes out.*]

ANGELO [*amiably once more*]. I allowed myself to speak like
that, though of course I'm only a mere underling here,
because I've been very sorry to hear that these are the last
few hours our little Silvia will be with us. She's going away,
leaving us. This very day, almost any minute, so I gather.
I'm very distressed to hear that. Studies . . . the University.

AGATA [*to her daughter*]. Have you let old Edoardo know?

SILVIA. Yes. He's going to blow his hooter from the road, I'll
go down with my bag.

AGATA. Is everything ready?

SILVIA. Yes.

ANGELO [*from the door, very quietly*]. But in any case old Edoardo will not be here until this evening. And we'd all be very glad if between now and then our little Silvia were persuaded to change her mind. [*He goes out.*]

[SILVIA *comes slowly forward and points to something among the garments that* PIA *and* AGATA *have been sewing.*]

SILVIA. I remember that jacket: Father used to wear it to go hunting in.

AGATA [*evasively*]. Yes, I think he did.

SILVIA [*with strange placidity*]. You'll have a lot of work to do on it. Angelo is fatter than father was.

AGATA. These things were getting moth-eaten. Now they'll be of some use to somebody at last.

SILVIA. There was something else in father's wardrobe. But it wasn't anything of any use to the rest of you. I've taken it.

AGATA. What was it? What do you mean? What was it you took?

SILVIA [*does not reply at once: then, suddenly, affectionately*]. Mother, I was bound to have to go away. I ought to have gone long ago, because of my classes. And . . . besides . . . it's so stifling hot here . . . and so lonely . . . I can't bear it any longer. The other night, there was that shutter again: I hardly closed my eyes. If I went on staying here I know I'd be ill again . . . [*She has begun to show signs of agitation.*]

AGATA [*who clearly wishes to avoid talking to her*]. Yes, darling, I can see it will do you good to go away for a time and be with your friends again. [*She is moving towards the door as she speaks.*]

SILVIA. Where are you going?

AGATA. There are some things I must get ready for you to take with you.

SILVIA. No, mother, wait. I came in specially to talk to you. There's something I must say to you before I go.

AGATA [*without looking at her*]. Very well: I'm here.

SILVIA. Mother, listen: these last few days we haven't spoken to each other very much. Perhaps we haven't had the opportunity. [*She speaks with difficulty.*] You know that there's . . . something we've never mentioned. Oh, mother, things have been happening here which I . . . can't . . .

Oh, I've been so miserable and uneasy! Sure you know what I mean.

AGATA [*not looking at her*]. You don't approve of that man being here, I suppose?

SILVIA. No.

AGATA [*evasively*]. We needed a man here. There are some things here a woman can't do.

SILVIA. But this man . . . doesn't do anything, anything at all.

AGATA. He probably needs a little time to get used to the place.

SILVIA. But he'll never do anything, mother.

AGATA. How do you know? If that's the case, we shall send him away. As soon as the hay's been got in.

SILVIA. But this man will never go away, he'll never go away.

AGATA. What makes you think that? In any case his staying in this country at all is an irregularity. We could have him arrested if we wanted to. We've no cause to worry.

SILVIA. Mother . . .

AGATA. What is it?

SILVIA. The other morning I went down to the post office; and then on to the village shop.

AGATA. Well?

SILVIA. Everyone looked at me.

AGATA [*pretending to be patient*]. Why?

SILVIA. And I had a talk with old Edoardo.

AGATA. You shouldn't have done that: he's an old fool.

SILVIA. He told me that everybody is gossiping about us and this man.

AGATA. What are they saying?

SILVIA. They say we're running ourselves into debt in order to keep him here.

AGATA. That's ridiculous. You know it is.

SILVIA. They say . . . it isn't nice, for three women to keep a man here in the house.

AGATA. Those people said exactly the same kind of thing when I sent you away to study in the city. A girl, they said, all by herself in the city, among all the men: that wasn't respectable either, they thought. In any case you're going away: *your* reputation at least will be safe. And I really don't know why the whole thing worries you so much. [*Going towards the door.*] As for those people down there, we all know how silly and nasty they are. They can think and say what they like; I don't care.

SILVIA [*sadly*]. Wait a minute, mother, wait! You don't care about those people. Don't you care about me either?

AGATA [*comes back slowly and sits down again: with a kind of weariness*]. Why do you ask?

SILVIA. Surely you care, you *must* care, if you see things making me suffer, mother? [*Cries out.*] Mother, I don't like that man to wear father's clothes like this! I don't like him to sleep in father's bedroom!

AGATA. You don't expect him to sleep on the floor, do you?

SILVIA. I don't like it! I don't like it! It's because of father: it used to be as though we were still expecting him to come back one day. It isn't like that any more.

AGATA [*her eyes on the ground*]. I see: it's because of your father. Yet I seem to have heard you laughing a good deal about the place these last months. Or haven't I? I thought you were the first to forget him.

SILVIA [*almost a cry*]. But I'm only his daughter!

AGATA. And I'm his wife, you mean? So I oughtn't to forget him? Is that it? [*With a change of voice.*] My dear child: the life a man and woman live together, my duties towards your father and his towards me, are a difficult problem: too difficult for an outsider to grasp. And sons and daughters *are* outsiders in these matters. They know nothing. Their judgments are only the conventional ones. Suppose we say no more about it, Silvia, shall we? In a very short time you'll be far away from here, and you'll find that many things here will seem very small and remote to you then. [*Trying to be friendly.*] You'll see all your friends again, you'll have plenty of amusements. You'll be well again there.

SILVIA [*with unwonted rebelliousness*]. My health! That's what you mean, my health! Mother! I've been wanting to speak to you for days. For days now, I've felt . . . frightened and worried . . .

AGATA [*almost with harshness*]. Go on then. You've been worried. What about?

SILVIA [*after a long silence*]. Pia.

AGATA. Pia?

SILVIA. Yes. She spends her whole time watching that man. I know she does.

AGATA. You think so?

SILVIA. Yes. I know I'm not mistaken.

AGATA [*after a pause*]. Well, Pia is rather like that. It's nothing to make a fuss about.

SILVIA [*agonized*]. Mother, it's the loneliness, the isolation here that frightens me . . . being here the whole time like this, bound and chained to the same thoughts the whole

time. The most incredible things begin to seem . . . ordinary, close at hand . . . inevitable . . . as if one were dreaming . . . I think that is the way all those horrible things
happen that one reads about in the . . .

AGATA [*not looking at her*]. But you're going away tonight,
darling.

SILVIA. It's a net, mother: it's a net . . . ! And we shall all of
us be caught in it.

AGATA [*her eyes lowered*]. All of whom?

SILVIA. Mother . . . I'm sure that that man . . . I'm sure he
and Pia . . .

AGATA. What do you mean?

SILVIA [*dully*]. You know what I mean.

AGATA. I don't think so. Angelo can't resist teasing people.
[*Suddenly.*] Silvia, I don't want to listen to any more of
this!

SILVIA [*calmly, dully*]. I've spied on them.

AGATA [*in an outburst of exasperation*]. Why? Why did you
do that? Why? Why? [*Controlling herself.*] In any case . . .
it's all nonsense. I don't believe you.

SILVIA. I've heard them. Don't you *know* what I mean?

AGATA [*roughly persuasive, and determined to break off this
conversation*]. No, no, my dear. I tell you no. You've made
a mistake. You've made it all up: it's all out of your own
head. You must stop, Silvia; I beg you. Please don't let's
waste any more time on it.

SILVIA [*stares at her in silence for a moment*]. Mother: from
the minute I came into this room you've been pretending
not to understand what I've been trying to tell you.

AGATA [*bitterly*]. Very well then, what is it?

SILVIA [*almost weeping*]. You know perfectly well what it is,
mother. That man . . . why, you yourself don't even take
the trouble to hide it . . . You and that man! . . . You and
that man! Why do you go on trying to pretend!

AGATA [*sadly*]. I haven't been pretending. I begged you. I
begged you to spare both of us words that never ought
to be uttered between a mother and daughter. But you
wouldn't have it. Why?

SILVIA. I've seen you! You and that man! A stranger. A
tramp. That's the reason I'm going away, surely you see
that?

AGATA. Exactly: You're going away. You could easily have
gone away and said nothing. [*A pause; sadly.*] Silvia, we
ought never to have started this conversation. You grew

up, and so did I, in a world in which a great many facts, and a great many ideas are taken for granted. Our books, our education, our friends, have made us used to accepting certain things. I have never asked you what you do with your time in the city. You are not a child any more. You're responsible for yourself. I haven't ever asked you anything, have I?

SILVIA [*after a pause*]. You are right. I've been silly. There's just this, mother: there are other things we haven't said yet. Do you think I'd have asked to talk to you if it hadn't been necessary?

AGATA. Silvia, Silvia: surely there's such a thing as good manners, even between a mother and daughter, isn't there? Surely there's *one* threshold where even those that are dearest to us have to pause and turn back . . . And whatever you have to say, I can't believe these things really matter so much. [*Bitterly.*] They're only trivialities.

SILVIA. Mother.

AGATA. Will you be quiet! Leave me alone, be quiet. Surely we all have the right to be left alone, haven't we?

[*There is a pause. When* AGATA *goes on, it is more in the hope of bringing the conversation to an end, than in the expectation of being believed.*]

You've got everything wrong. You've misinterpreted things.

SILVIA [*suddenly, with great gentleness*]. Oh mother, how you must have been suffering ever since I started to talk to you. To think of *you*: pretending, lying, humiliating yourself, anyone as proud and honest as you. Mother, what has happened, how can it have come about? You asked me what right I have to be talking to you like this. I'm your daughter. You are my mother.

AGATA [*pale, her eyes lowered*]. Your mother. A signed document: a receipt. Your mother. And because of that, no longer alive. Your mother. Quietly embalmed.

SILVIA [*gently, as before*]. No, mother, that's not true. I remember when I was little. I was in love with you, I'd like to have given up my whole life for you. I used to turn over the pages of your music for you and look up at you every now and then and watch the lamplight in your hair.

AGATA [*bitterly*]. It is a pity everything couldn't have stayed like that, like a picture, quietly yellowing with age; and no one would ever have thought of it again. [*Pause.*] Yes, it's a pity: everything has changed, I'm no longer the same woman. [*Pause.*] And neither are you, Silvia; I remember things too. I remember your sweet little voice. But no, no, you've grown up, Silvia, you're a woman, you're another person, I don't know what you are. You've no longer any need of me; and the sound of your voice even annoys me. Sometimes when a little bird grows up, its mother drives it from the nest, and pecks at it till it flies away. Nature is honest; we are not; we embalm our dead.

SILVIA. But to me you've always been the best thing in the world! Everything on earth was sweet and clean when you were there!

AGATA. And what did any of you know about me? I was alone. I've always been alone. Have any of you ever looked at me, or spoken to me, ever once wondered what I was thinking about when I was there, with the lamplight in my hair, or at night when I lay awake? Were you all so sure you knew me?

SILVIA. But your life here, mother, your beliefs . . .

AGATA [*bitterly*]. Beliefs. I've listened to lies, and I've told them. I've been cheated and I've cheated back. Were you all so sure you knew me? [*Almost desperately.*] Were you all so sure you knew me? [*Silence.*] Stop tormenting me, Silvia, stop!

SILVIA. And Pia? [*Almost shouting.*] What about Pia?

AGATA. What has Pia to do with it?

SILVIA [*stares at her in silence; then almost frantically*]. "What has Pia to do with it?" You know as well as I do. You've known it from the start! You even accepted that! You've let this horrible thing happen, you've let that man degrade you and Pia so that you're—like two mares in the same stable! You've been willing to cast aside whatever it is that makes you human! And if it were my turn tomorrow, you'd allow that too!

AGATA [*low-voiced and commanding*]. Lower your voice, Silvia! Pia's certain to be eavesdropping somewhere about; it only makes the whole thing even sillier.

SILVIA. I've seen it all, I've known about it, I've watched you both panting there, like . . .

AGATA [*with harsh vehemence*]. What claptrap, what a ridiculous fuss over something so small and petty! [*Suddenly in despair.*] What do you want of me? Leave me in peace, keep away from all this! Why are you behaving like this? Why are you here?

SILVIA [*imploring*]. Don't speak to me like that, mother.

AGATA. Whatever I am or do, what do I matter to any of you? Yes, what? Half my life, probably, I inflicted a kind of paralysis on myself. Well, it was all a mistake; I wore myself out, and all for nothing. The lies we told! The important thing is to know what you are and to be it: and then everything is simple. [*As though letting her thoughts wander.*] Like when you're tired and falling asleep: and you let all your thoughts slip away from you one by one; they drift far away and you feel relief from them; because you know they are foolish! Foolish and useless, all of them! And then at last: peace! The same peace that the grass knows, and animals, and stones. That is what I want: to be quiet. The rest can take care of itself.

SILVIA [*in a low, frightened voice*]. Don't talk to me like that, mother . . .

AGATA. I shan't take the slightest notice of anything you've said. Words, words: I heard them long ago from your father—and you are just like him. But even you don't matter to me, Silvia. You were wrong to make me speak: I never have in my life before now. All this wearies me, wearies me and bores me, I can't bear any more of it. Go away!

SILVIA. Mother, what has happened to you? It's *he* who's done all this! He came in here like a beastly animal . . .

AGATA. Darling: suppose I enjoyed . . . obeying him? His voice persuades me.

SILVIA [*shivering*]. I know. I've heard it: his voice; and yours. Do you think I don't realise? For three months now I've had to live through all this. You were unable to say no to him.

AGATA [*with bitter defiance*]. Exactly: I was unable to say no to him. Whatever he asked. And one thing is much the same as another, after all. Deep down, that was what I wanted: I was alone, the wind carried me away. Others called to me, but I didn't reply . . . It's all so simple, isn't it? It was what I wanted.

SILVIA. No, no, no, mother! This is unbearable! Oh, mother, I can't bear it!

AGATA. And who's asking you to bear it? What is it to do with you? Go away!

SILVIA [*suddenly*]. Mother, do you know what they are saying down in the village? They're saying it about me as well! About me as well, can't you understand? They say we're his little flock: the three of us. It's driving me out of my mind, I can't bear it! A little while ago I looked in papa's drawer. His revolver was there, I took it, I've got it here with me, here, in my bag.

AGATA [*shaking her*]. Go away, I tell you, Silvia! It's nothing to do with you! Your troubles are easily solved; all you have to do is go away!

SILVIA. I can't go away now! I've seen your face when you've gone into his room . . . And Pia's face . . . and your voices . . . You frightened me, I couldn't think of anything else . . . You've made me ill again! I'm ashamed for anyone to look at me! I can feel the stain of it on me, even when I'm asleep. [*She is on the ground, her arms round her mother's knees.*] Mother, let's go away, come away with me!

AGATA [*freeing herself*]. No.

SILVIA. Come away, I beg you, I beg you!

AGATA. No. Let me go.

SILVIA. I'll put an end to it all. [*Staring before her as though at a vision.*] I will kill him, mother. I've thought it all out, every detail. I shall call him in here, I shall tell him to look down, there, where father's clothes are: I shall make him bend over them. And then, from behind, close up to him, I shall shoot, right in the back of his head. I have the revolver.

AGATA [*looks at her, with intense calm*]. No, you won't shoot him; you won't do that; I know you won't. [*Suddenly.*] Silvia, what's *really* the matter with you? What is it? Why did you come in here, why have you been talking like this? Why have you been spying, why have you been shouting in this way? Why didn't you go away, why don't you want to go away now? Why? Why? [*She runs out of the room.*]

[SILVIA *still on her knees, continues to look at the door, her eyes wide and staring. Then she turns.* PIA *is standing before her. She has entered some moments earlier and has slowly advanced while the scene between* AGATA *and* SILVIA *has been in progress.*]

PIA. You look pale, Silvia. Is something the matter?

SILVIA [*absently, rigid*]. No, nothing. Do you know where Angelo is?

PIA. Do you want to speak to him?

SILVIA. I have something to say to him.

PIA. Now? This minute?

SILVIA. Yes, Now.

PIA [*lowering her voice*]. Do you know what you're going to
   say to him?

SILVIA. Yes, I know. [*Her gaze drops to her handbag.*]

PIA [*following her gaze*]. Sit down Silvia. You're shivering.
   I'll go and call him.

[PIA *makes* SILVIA *sit down.* SILVIA *obeys mechanically.* PIA
   goes out; her voice is heard calling.]

   Angelo! Angelo! [*Receding.*] Angelo! Angelo! [*Farther off
   still.*] Angelo! Angelo . . .

[SILVIA *shakes herself.* ANGELO *is at the other door. He advances cautiously.*]

ANGELO. Ah, Silvia dear, I didn't know I should find you here.
   Someone was calling me; I'm sure it wasn't you. Let them
   go on calling me. We do nothing but run after one another
   in this house. But I run about much more than your mother
   and your aunt: I'm just like a pussy-cat. [*He laughs.*]
   Silvia, my dear, I'd no idea I'd find you here; though to
   tell you the truth, I was very much hoping I would.

[SILVIA *slowly gets up from her chair.*]

   What are you getting up for? Are you going away already?
   No: stay in here; this is nice. Silvia: I've been wanting to
   talk to you for a long while. Silvia dear: I'll confess it
   frankly and with all my heart: I was looking for you. I
   was waiting till you were alone. I so very much wanted to
   talk to you before you went away. Oh, yes, I know you
   despise me; and you're right. And I know you are proud;
   and you're right to be that too. Still, I can see you are hurt
   and unhappy; and you're too young and sweet for me to
   allow that. That's why I came in. I felt I had to talk to you.

SILVIA. So did I.

ANGELO. You too? Ah, then: I'm glad. We both wanted to.
   Dear Silvia, tell me: I'm very anxious to know what you've
   finally . . . [*He breaks off.*]

[SILVIA *goes rather stiffly to the table where her bag is, and
   picks it up.*]

   Silvia dear: I think you have a few complaints you want to
   make about me. Very well: I'll accept them, and try and not
   deserve any more. I know I've been at fault . . . in some
   ways. Or is it your mother and aunt that have been at

fault? Even they can make mistakes. We'll try to correct them, shall we? Dearest Silvia, I'm sure you don't really mean to go away. What is it you don't like here?

[SILVIA *stretches out a hand, and points to her father's clothes.*]

What? Your father's clothes? Yes, you're right. You're quite right, my dear. It was unfeeling of me to think I might wear them. It's made you unhappy. My dear Silvia, they shall still be your father's. I won't touch them. Is that what you wanted? Is that all?

SILVIA [*breathing heavily; pointing to the clothes*]. Down. Bend down, and look at them. Look at them closely.

ANGELO [*surprised*]. Is there something there? Something I've not seen? [*He bends over them, picks up one of the garments, and turns to the girl.*] I can't see anything there.

[*He resumes his inspection of the clothes, and goes down on his knees.* SILVIA *approaches him, with her hand in her bag; she is standing over him.*]

PIA [*outside*]. Angelo! Angelo!

[SILVIA *moves away.* ANGELO *gets up from his knees and also moves away.* PIA *comes running in. She stops short, and looks at them: then she goes over to* ANGELO.]

ANGELO. What's the matter?
PIA [*whispering*]. She wants to kill you. She has the revolver.
ANGELO [*with a gesture, bids her be quiet; he stands reflecting for a few seconds without looking directly at* SILVIA; *then he says in a loud friendly voice*]. Thank you, Pia. What you've just told me is very important; it was a good thing you ran and told me. Now you can go.

[PIA *remains motionless, watching. He turns once more to the clothes, looks at them and bends over them, but in a very different way.*]

[*Slowly and amiably.*] Dear Silvia, I was just saying: I couldn't find anything among your father's clothes; I'll look closer, shall I? Like this. Is that better? Or must I bend lower down? Ought I to go down on my knees? Ah yes, I see now what it is I ought to find here. A sudden death. The death of a bull in the slaughterhouse. [*In the same amiable tone.*] Did you want to kill me?

[SILVIA *stares at him fascinated.*]

[*Suddenly at the top of his voice, furiously, in falsetto.*]

You wanted to kill me? [*In the same voice to* PIA, *who does not move.*] Go away Pia, you can leave us. [*To* SILVIA *in the same angry scream.*] You wanted to kill me?

SILVIA [*almost voicelessly*]. Yes.

ANGELO [*lower*]. You had a revolver.

SILVIA. Yes.

ANGELO. Give it to me.

[*She hands it to him. He takes it, still staring at her; then, to himself, as though unable to understand.*]

She wanted to kill me, to take my life. [*In tremendous surprise.*] She hates me! [*To* PIA.] She hates me, do you see? So long as she's alive my life's in danger. Do you understand? She hates me. She hates me.

[SILVIA *is suddenly shaken by sobs.*]

[*In the grip of a real terror.*] Oh, oh, oh, do you see, Pia? I might have been lying there smashed to pieces by now. She'd thought it all out, splendidly. [*Imitating it all, in a kind of pantomine.*] I was here . . . I was down on my knees like this . . . and she . . . Yes! You! Where did you intend to hit me? On the back of my neck, was that it? Here, here. And I'd have been there, like that! My face on the stones, my teeth broken in; like that, like that! and then, with my head, like a smashed egg, a mass of blood and brains . . . [*Suddenly, with tremendous fury, in falsetto, like some extraordinary trumpet.*] You beastly, filthy insect! You dirty little whore! Dirty little whore! [*He runs at the girl, strikes her, seizes her by her blouse and hair, and throws her to the ground, shrieking and babbling.*] You filthy little whore! You could do that . . . ! . . . you could do that! You wanted to kill me! Filthy little whore! Filthy little whore! [*He lets go of her.*]

[AGATA *has appeared; uncertainly, overcome, she goes to her daughter.* SILVIA *is lying on the ground.*]

SILVIA [*through her sobs*]. I wish I were dead.

[*There is a silence.*]

ANGELO [*suddenly, almost sadly*]. I've given way to violence! And been unjust as well! I'm ashamed, what a dreadful thing to have done . . . [*To* AGATA.] Our poor Silvia wanted

to . . . [*His teeth are almost chattering.*] She's sick. Really
and truly sick. We must do something; we must make her
get better. Oh, I'd give anything in the world, yes, my own
life even.

SILVIA [*as before*]. I wish I were dead.

ANGELO. I couldn't believe it: but this poor girl actually hates
me. It comes of being lonely; you have to be very strong
to be able to bear loneliness. If you're not strong, a poisoned
thought can worm its way in . . . and run through all your
veins. You turn into a machine, and finish up by committing
. . . Silvia might have done that . . . I escaped by a hair's-
breadth. Poor Silvia. She's too frail for this sort of life.

SILVIA [*sobbing, still prostrate*]. I wish I were dead.

ANGELO [*dropping his voice a little*]. She wishes she were dead,
she says. And out of pity for her you could almost wish . . .
Poor Silvia, poor delicate little thing, gnawed by such a
terrible disease. Poor Silvia, the best of us all: and in spite
of that, fated to go on through the years, rotting away and
befouling herself! Yes, rotting away and befouling herself! Cheated and mocked at; swollen, fat and sinful.
One could almost rather wish that she . . . that some
mysterious pity would bend down and pluck the flower,
gather it before it collapses into the mire and dirt. Gather it;
and save it, so that it shan't be lost. [*A pause.*] I don't
know whether I have dreamt it, or whether it was only a
thought; it seemed to me that it was evening, as it is now,
and that our Silvia was weeping. She was saying . . . that
she couldn't bear for a single night longer the awful noise
of the shutter rattling; whang, whang. That noise at night
has always been our dear girl's nightmare. And suddenly
she says: "I'll go and tear the shutter down." And I say
to her: "But dear Silvia, that would be very dangerous,
you might meet with an accident." And she smiles. Upon
my very word, she smiles; and she says: [*He lowers his
voice.*] "Dear Angelo, let Fate decide. Whatever happens, I
shan't have to hear the noise of the shutter any more. And
then I can sleep in peace."

[*A silence. Dusk is beginning to fall.* SILVIA *half-rises from
the floor, slowly.*]

SILVIA. Mother!

AGATA [*agitated*]. What do you want to say to me?

SILVIA. Mother, one day I was filled with despair and revulsion.
I went to his room, because I wanted to drive him away,

drive him away from the house . . . Mother, I am already
lost!

[AGATA *turns slowly and moves away from her.*]

Mother!

[*Silence.*]

AGATA [*without turning round to face her*]. I loved you so
much when you were little. You were so delicate, you filled
me with pity.

[SILVIA *rises to her feet; slowly; a little stiffly, she moves to
the door and goes out.*]

PIA [*in a low voice*]. Where is she going, now?

ANGELO. Why do you ask, you liar? You know as well as I do.
It's always been more than likely that sooner or later she'd
jump off that damned balcony. [*He looks up at the ceiling.*]
It might be happening at this very moment. [*He looks towards the clothes.*] And at this very moment too, I might
be lying there . . . with the flies already buzzing round my
corpse. [*He looks up at the ceiling.*] Have we the right to
interfere? It is destiny, itself, that must answer . . . yes or
no. [*He listens.*] You, Agata, you, what do you say? It's
you who should speak. Say something, for God's sake!
She's your daughter.

[AGATA *stands motionless, gloomily.*]

Or perhaps we are only playing with fancies? . . . Besides,
I . . . There. [*He looks up and listens.*] Oh, of course
nothing's going to happen. But I can still scarcely breathe;
I feel shaken. What ought we to do? How difficult it is to
keep ourselves innocent and human . . . and alive. Why,
why did our Silvia have to . . . How could she think of
anything so monstrous? Why? Why has she done this?

PIA [*exasperated, with a cry*]. Angelo, what a fool you are!

ANGELO. Why?

PIA. I should think your fright must have put you out of your
mind! Why do you think the girl did this? [*Contemptuously.*] Because she was in love with you.

ANGELO [*stands there, fascinated by this new thought*]. How
mysterious human actions are. Sometimes a single sail can
be blown upon by two different winds. I often think . . .
[*Suddenly, frantically, to* AGATA.] Call your daughter. Go

and fetch her. [*Shouting.*] Go and fetch her! Quick! Call her! [*He runs to the door.*] Silvia! Silvia! Silvia! Silvia!

He has gone out; his voice recedes in the house; then, from a change of tone, it is clear that he has found the girl, and is leading her back. He reappears holding her up, almost carrying her. She is half-fainting.]

Bring a chair. She's shivering with cold, she can't stand up. Take hold of her, bring her round; moisten her lips; make her drink something.

AGATA *and* PIA *bend over her;* ANGELO *stands for a long moment regarding them.*]

Ah, look! Yes, look! To see you all three there, close together like that, in love and harmony! How soothing and calming that is . . . Indeed, indeed, we've all been blind. And all the time it was so simple.

AGATA [*turning to him*]. What was simple?

ANGELO [*vaguely*]. Everything.

AGATA. What do you mean?

ANGELO. I mean our dear little girl isn't going away after all: tonight or any other night. Edoardo is coming: he'll go back by himself again, awful old man. [*A pause.*] The four of us. [*Silence.*]

PIA *suddenly begins to laugh, shrilly and hysterically, her teeth chattering.*]

Would you have liked it better if there'd been bloodshed here? Or there, outside, under the balcony? Pride, always our pride, our damnable pride. The four of us. Why should we spoil everything, what reason have we to hate each other?

PIA [*still howling with convulsive laughter*]. Angelo, you're insane . . .

ANGELO. I never even let myself tread on an insect. Whatever lives is delicate and lasts for only a short time, why do we have to behave cruelly to anything? Whatever our soul desires is always innocent. It is like a child stretching out its hand.

PIA. You're a fool, a fool! Agata, can you stand there and listen to him? [*Wildly.*] I'll go and throw myself off the balcony. I'll kill myself! I'll be the one! You filthy beast, you've ruined us! [*She is suddenly silent.*]

ANGELO. Pia, go and get my bag for me. It's I who am going
away. I'll be able to go with old Edorado: a good thing he'
coming, after all. It will solve everything.

PIA. *You!* . . . Go away? [*Screaming.*] Yes! Likely, likely
likely, isn't it?

ANGELO. Do you think I'm joking? I don't want to stay her
any longer, surrounded by mischief-making and spite . .
and my life in danger. [*He moves towards the door.*]
shan't be long. I've only a few old rags to fling together
that's all. [*He is at the door.*]

AGATA. Angelo, what are you doing?

ANGELO. I'm going away.

AGATA [*pleading*]. Wait.

ANGELO. No, I never turn back once I've made up my mind

AGATA [*imploring*]. But we hadn't decided anything yet
Angelo. Please wait.

ANGELO. No, I want to go away. I must look after my life afte
all: I must try to protect myself. You're all too much occu
pied with your own spite and jealousy to bother about me
I'm going.

AGATA [*still imploring him; her increasing distress is appallin,
to watch*]. No Angelo, wait. We shall be able to explai
everything.

ANGELO. We've already explained everything! It's a miracl
I'm still alive. And you're all still suspicious of me, you al
want to humiliate me.

AGATA. But no one is humiliating you . . .

ANGELO. Ingratitude; malice . . .

AGATA. I implore you, Angelo. I beg you. You can't go awa
like this. You've been here for months . . . Come . . . wai
a little . . .

[*A pause.* ANGELO *comes slowly back into the room.*]

PIA [*suddenly cries*]. But what on earth are you all doing
What is it? Are we all going mad? [*She throws herself o
ANGELO.*] You swine! You cheat! You miserable sponger

[*Almost calmly,* ANGELO *smacks her hard across the face. Sh
is suddenly silent. In the distance the noise of* EDOARDO'
motor-horn is heard.]

ANGELO. There it is, Silvia. Old Edoardo, with his lorry. Nov
it's stopping. It's up to you. You're free, Silvia. I won'
take advantage of what happened between us a few mc

ments ago. You are free to go or to stay. You can choose.
Hark . . . He's stopped; he's blowing his hooter.

[*It is heard again.* SILVIA *suddenly walks towards the door.*
ANGELO *stops her halfway; he says calmly to* PIA:]

You, Pia: shout to him: tell him she's not going, we'll talk
about it all later.

PIA [*goes to the window, and calls*]. She isn't coming! She isn't
coming!

[*The lorry is heard departing. A silence.*]

ANGELO. Well, that was all very simple. [*Amiably, to* SILVIA,
as he lets her go.] It's not that I forced you to stay, you
know, Silvia? We were all agreed from the start, really.
Only you all three wanted to . . . to feel yourselves a little
compelled in some way; that's to say, guided, protected. So
here we are: the four of us. There's nothing wicked or
sordid between us is there? We're brothers and sisters.
We've shouted and squabbled a good deal: and now . . .
how nice and peaceful it is. It's evening, the moon is coming up.

AGATA [*suddenly under her breath begins softly to sing, without words, the tune of the song*]. Esevi uttu sehe . . .

ANGELO. Close the doors, Pia. Shut them all up, and put the
bolts across. What's old Edoardo matter to us—What's the
whole world matter if it comes to that? It's from outside
that mosquitoes and doubts fly in. Close the place up.

[AGATA *and* PIA *do so,* AGATA *continuing to sing.*]

Out with them all. Ourselves alone. As if this house were
a walnut, black outside but sweet within. No, not a walnut;
an island, rather; in the sea; an island margined with silver,
and we four quite, quite alone on the wonderful grass, and
in every blade of grass the wind whistling lightly . . . and
over us the clouds . . . and . . . [*A pause.*] No one but
ourselves. Free. Free! And tonight we must celebrate! Let's
put all the best food in the house on the table! I'll go down
the well and fetch some bottles up, there are still some left.
You get everything ready, Agata; light the lamps. And you
help her, Pia. Quickly, quickly. [*He points to* SILVIA.] This
little sister of ours mustn't let us see she's been crying. Go
and comb her hair, wash her face, tidy her up. Why, she's
the reason we're having the party.

[*The two women begin to carry out his orders, at first a little
uncertainly, but after a few moments with some alacrity*
ANGELO *gets ready to go down the well.*]

ANGELO. Get out the very best tablecloth, and the best glasses.
My dear sisters! If one of you is in pain, the sun itself turns
dark for me. Quick, Pia, take Silvia, and make her tidy
herself up. [*Gaily.*] We all know Pia is a jealous girl; and
she's been known to speak a little sharply at times; but all
the same she's the most useful one of you about the house,
and very obedient. Silvia is the flower . . . [*As* PIA *and* SILVIA
go out.] Pia, make her put on that dress she was wearing
the day I came! And you, Agata . . .

[AGATA *is preparing the table; he is arranging the rope-ladder
over the side of the well.*]

AGATA. Me? I'm old.
ANGELO. You are the one that matters. I came for you from
far away; it's because of you I stay here. Whenever I look
at you, I always remember that where I come from, the
women are never let out alone at night in the countryside.
AGATA [*pausing in her preparations*]. Why not?
ANGELO. Because they might meet the devil. Everyone knows
that all women want to make love with the devil . . . It's
the devil who plays hard-to-get. [*He laughs.*]
AGATA [*interested*]. Well?
ANGELO. Well: sometimes, of course, you *have* to send them
out alone at night—to fetch the doctor, say, or on some
other errand.
AGATA. Well?
ANGELO. Well: as they're going along, suddenly, if there's a
moon, at the side of their own shadow they see there's
another one. It's a traveler, who's decided to go the same
way.
AGATA. What does he say?
ANGELO. Nothing. He just sniffs at them.
AGATA. Sniffs at them?
ANGELO. Yes. To see if they smell of smoke. Smoke is the
smell of human beings; no other creature lights fires and
boils pots on them. He sniffs.
AGATA. And what if they do smell of smoke?
ANGELO. Oh, he makes off at once. He knows they're just tarts
or housewives: tearful little creatures: the devil can't stand

them. Still, every now and then, just once in a while, he does meet one that doesn't smell of smoke.

AGATA. What does she smell of?

ANGELO. Nothing at all. In my country they say: she smells of the wind. The Almighty made a mistake over them. Something got mingled in their make-up that was intended for some other sort of creature, something stranger, more important, nearer to God. That's the reason why women of that kind are always melancholy. They are like you, Agata, hating it where there's smoke, hating it just as much where there isn't. Men love these women passionately, they say to them: "Soul of my soul!" But these women have often been known to poison their men. Nothing's right for them. Nothing at all, not even paradise. Those are the women the devil waits for at night. They have no fear; and off they go with him . . .

[*The last words come from the well; ANGELO is going down into it. AGATA stands thinking; suddenly she starts. A noise has been heard in the well.*]

AGATA. What's the matter?

ANGELO [*from inside the well*]. Nothing, the ladder has fallen in, that's all; it came off the hook.

AGATA. What shall I do?

ANGELO. Throw me a rope down, will you?

AGATA. Yes, straight away. I won't be a moment. [*She finds the rope, and goes towards the well with it; halfway there she pauses irresolutely, and lays the rope down.*]

ANGELO. Have you got it?

AGATA. I'm just getting it; wait just a moment, will you?

[*She turns.* SILVIA *comes in. She is gaily dressed, with flowers in her hair.* PIA *follows her, with a lamp.* AGATA *looks at her for a long moment.*]

They have dressed you up nicely, Silvia, haven't they?

PIA [*lifting the lamp in her hand, so that it shines on the girl.*] Angelo: where's Angelo gone?

AGATA. He's gone down the well. [*Motionless, averting her gaze.*] We have to throw this rope down to him.

CURTAIN

ACT THREE

[*It is still dark, just before dawn. The lamp is still burning on the table.* AGATA *is seated alone, in the half-dark. She sits there motionless for some time. Then* SILVIA *enters on tiptoe; she halts in the doorway.*]

AGATA [*in a whisper*]. Did you want something?

SILVIA [*also in a whisper*]. Mother, haven't you slept?

AGATA [*still with lowered voice*]. I never sleep very much.

SILVIA. Aren't you coming into the other room? We are going to have something to eat.

AGATA. Later on. Was there something you wanted?

SILVIA. No, nothing. Mother, why don't you come in there with us?

AGATA. Later on. What's the matter with you, aren't you very well? These mornings are chilly. Go on: go back to Pia. There's no point in your coming in here. [*A silence.*] Have you everything you want, in there?

SILVIA. Yes?

AGATA. Has anyone been for the milk? [*After a pause.*] One of these days we shall have to do some washing. [*There seems a great sense of peace in her voice.*]

SILVIA. Yes. [*A further silence.*] Mother, I'm rather frightened.

AGATA. You know it's only a joke, surely?

SILVIA. Yes, I know. [*A pause.*] But why don't you come into the other room? We can't even talk in here.

AGATA. Later on. [*A silence.*] Do you know what I've been thinking about? College: the professor of divinity: the words he used to use whenever he tried to describe to us the idea of eternity. He used to say: try to imagine a butterfly which every so often flutters its fragile little wings. It is placed upon a bronze globe. Now think how much time it would need for that butterfly, moving its wings every so often, to make a tiny mark on that bronze globe. And then think how long it would take for those weak wings to wear the whole of that bronze globe away. And then imagine that that bronze globe was as big as the earth and the sun together, bigger even than that, as big as the entire universe. And the little butterfly on that terrifying

globe has to wear away the whole globe till nothing remains of it. And when it has worn away the whole of that,
it has to wear away other globes: so many that you cannot
count them. And when it has destroyed every single one
of them . . . even then, eternity will still not have begun.
The idea of eternity eludes human thought. Or perhaps it
is the opposite idea that eludes human thought.

SILVIA. Mother: hasn't he spoken again? [*For the first time,
she casts a glance in the direction of the well.*]

AGATA. No. Only a few words. Nearly two hours ago.

SILVIA. Do you think . . . ?

AGATA. If you go very close and wait till your ear gets accustomed, you can hear him perfectly; you can hear him
breathing.

[SILVIA *takes two or three cautious steps toward the well.*]

He's only quiet because he's sulking at the moment. He
does sulk every now and then. [*She laughs quietly.*]

SILVIA. He was still talking up to two hours ago wasn't he?

AGATA. Yes.

SILVIA. What did he say?

AGATA. Nothing. He seemed a little impatient. He was making
rather a noise. [*She laughs quietly.*]

SILVIA. What is he doing now?

AGATA. Thinking.

SILVIA. And before: why was he making a noise?

AGATA. He hadn't understood; he didn't quite realise.

SILVIA. Realise what?

AGATA. Oh, that it's . . . just a joke, a little game.

SILVIA [*rather frightened*]. A game. I've been thinking: it's
two days and two nights now . . .

AGATA. Not quite, it's less than that. Besides, you others
agreed; you laughed, when I suggested it.

SILVIA. Yes, of course.

AGATA [*laughing quickly*]. What are two days and two nights?
and what about when he was in the war? That was much
worse. And besides, there are plenty of bottles down there
for him to pass the time with.

SILVIA. Bottles? What about them?

AGATA. Every now and then I hear him break the neck of one
of them.

SILVIA [*with a laugh*]. And does he drink it?

AGATA. Yes. I've heard him. He said so, too.

SILVIA [*laughs again*]. Is he getting drunk? Down there?

AGATA. I think so. That's how he's passing the time. You've no
need to worry, he isn't too badly off down there.

SILVIA. Are you sure?

AGATA. Quite sure.

SILVIA [*a little worried*]. There's nothing to be afraid of. After
all . . . two days and two nights . . . two days and two
nights . . .

AGATA. Less than that. He can stay there much longer than
that.

SILVIA. It will teach him a lesson; he deserved one, didn't he?

AGATA. Of course he did.

SILVIA. Of course: he deserved it.

AGATA [*vaguely*]. There was something wrong here. We weren't
quite at our ease. Oh, he's already changed, just a little.
When he calls up from down there sometimes, he almost
makes me want to laugh at him. [*A silence.*]

SILVIA [*suddenly*]. Mother, why don't you call to him? Just
to hear him? To hear what he says. Call to him, mother.

AGATA. No, better not. I've noticed he begins to get rather
lively when he knows there's someone here. He begins to
talk, and shout. He hopes someone will answer him. But
when he can't hear anybody . . . I've taken my shoes off.
If he can't hear anybody . . . it's then that he begins to
be a bit frightened . . . ? [*There is again the note of peace
in her voice.*] That's what we want. We must wait till he
begins to be a bit frightened.

SILVIA. Frightened of what, mother?

AGATA [*evasively*]. Oh, just frightened. Besides, you're speaking
quietly too, and going about on tiptoe; aren't you? Why is
that?

ANGELO [*suddenly from the well: hollow, echoing and much
magnified*]. Silvia!

[SILVIA *moves back from the well, frightened.*]

ANGELO [*calmly*]. Silvia. I know you are there. Answer me. I
heard you, you know. Answer me. Go on, answer me.

SILVIA [*to her mother, whispering*]. You answer him . . .

ANGELO [*calmly*]. Pia: is that you, Pia? I can hear you
splendidly. You've been going about on bare feet, all of
you. Pia! Silvia! [*A long silence. Then his voice begins to
sound slightly angry.*] Pia! Silvia! Pia! Silvia! Pia! Silvia!

PIA [*coming in, and whispering in an agonised voice*]. I can't
bear to hear him any more! We mustn't wait any longer.

It's dangerous. Throw the rope down to him, and have done
with it.

AGATA. You throw it to him.

PIA. I'm frightened. He sounds so fierce; he sounds like a
madman. I'm frightened.

ANGELO. Pia! Silvia!

PIA. I can't go on hearing him call out to me like that!

AGATA. Why did you come downstairs then? I told you to stay
up there, you can't hear anything upstairs.

PIA. You can hear upstairs; you can hear everywhere. And
from the road too. If anyone goes by, they'll be sure to
hear him.

AGATA. I don't think so. In any case, no one goes by.

PIA. All through the night, he's gone on . . .

AGATA. That's not true; it's just that you want to hear him.
Even when he's quiet.

ANGELO [*as though discouraged*]. Pia! Silvia! Pia! Silvia!

SILVIA. Why does he only call *us*? [*In sudden anger.*] Why
does he only call *us*, and not you?

AGATA. Because he knows you're easier to deal with; you're
younger than I am.

ANGELO [*in normal tones*]. Pia! Silvia!

AGATA. If you like, we can put the cover on the well. The lid
is there.

SILVIA. Yes, of course we could . . .

AGATA. You wouldn't hear so much of him then.

SILVIA [*suddenly penitent*]. No, no, don't let's cover it . . .

ANGELO [*quietly; too quietly*]. Ah, so Agata's there, as well,
is she? I know. [*Silence: then a long amiable echoing laugh;
and now his voice is cordial and amused.*] Clever girls. There
are times when I get angry down here. But then I see the
funny side of it too. Schoolteachers: a schoolteacher's joke.
I have to give it to you: clever girls. They once played a
joke like this back in my own country, on a man I knew;
it all ended up with a supper party, it was a wonderful
evening; ah, yes, I remember it. A magnificent dinner; I
was at that too.

AGATA [*gasping slightly*]. There. You hear him? What sort of
voice is that?

SILVIA [*surprised*]. A quiet one.

AGATA. Do you know what it means?

SILVA. What?

AGATA. Fright. It's beginning. The chill of fright. [*With an*

odd note of sadness.] He realises he's in danger, and refuses
to admit it. He is trying to master himself; and to master us.

ANGELO. My dears, you've been keeping me in after school a
bit, haven't you? . . . Never mind, I deserved it—I was
getting to be too cheeky. [*He laughs.*] I'm growing such
a thick beard; there's no razor down here. Luckily there
are a few bottles, however. I'll bring any that are left up
with me. [*He laughs.*] You'd better hurry up though, or I
shall empty the whole cellar and get really drunk. Do you
mind if I sing? [*He begins to sing "Esevi uttu sehe," but
after a few bars the song becomes fainter.*]

AGATA [*strangely compassionate*]. Oh, God! He really is
frightened.

[*The song has broken off.*]

PIA [*distressed and aggressive*]. Why are we doing this to him?
Why?

AGATA. He's told you himself. He was getting to be too cheeky.
We were all agreed about that, I think?

SILVIA [*almost as though in a dream*]. But we've done enough
to him, we can let him come up now, can't we?

AGATA [*laughing*]. Yes!

PIA. Now! At once!

AGATA [*laughing*]. Yes!

ANGELO [*suddenly, terrified, imploring, unrecognisable*]. Silvia
. . . for pity's sake . . . the rope . . . throw the rope down
to me for pity's sake . . . They want to kill me . . . Your
mother . . . she wants me to die down here . . . Quickly,
I've no strength left, I'm going to faint. If I faint, I shall
drown. Quick . . . Silvia . . . Pia. I'll leave you, I'll go
away. I'll do whatever you tell me. Don't make me die
down here . . . for pity's sake. [*He breaks off, pause.*]

[*Suddenly* SILVIA *runs and seizes the rope and carries it over
to the well, struggling to free it from various entanglements.* PIA *runs to help her; now they are at the side of
the well; and both suddenly stop.*]

[*His voice suddenly rising to a wild epileptic shriek, savage
and utterly inhuman.*] Murderers! [*Pause.*] Murderers! I'll
come up and rip your insides out, I'll tear you all three to
pieces! [*Pause.*] I'll get you condemned to death! I'll see
you hanged! Hanged! Hanged! Murderers!

[PIA *and* SILVIA, *terrified, run away from the well; the rope
has fallen from their hands.*]

ANGELO. You all plotted it! Murderers! You'll all three pay for
it! You unhooked the ladder yourselves! You, you, all of
you.

AGATA [*almost to herself*]. It isn't true. It just happened.

ANGELO [*now horrifyingly raucous*]. Murderers! I'll have you
hanged! Murderers! I'll rip your insides out! I'll tear you
to pieces!

[*It is no longer a voice, but an atrocious howl, alternating
with convulsive babbling.*]

PIA [*terrified, and forgetting to speak quietly.*] The cover!
Let's put the cover on, quickly!

SILVIA. He's climbing up . . . Oh God, I'm frightened.

PIA. Let's throw something . . . drop something on top of him
. . . a stone . . .

[*The noise from the well has died away into a kind of death
rattle, then into a heavy breathing. Then silence returns.*]

SILVIA. He's fallen.

AGATA [*after listening for a moment*]. He's breathing. [*To
the others, with a return of the same sadness of voice.*] He
can't climb up. He tried to climb up earlier, during the
night.

PIA. He tried?

AGATA. Yes, several times, I heard him. He can't get a grip
on the stones.

PIA. But sometimes people who are mad . . .

AGATA. No. As time goes on, he gets angrier. He also gets
weaker. If he hasn't managed it by now . . . I don't think
he ever will . . .

SILVIA [*her teeth chattering*]. But then, what are we to do?

[*A silence.*]

AGATA [*in a very low tone*]. Nothing. There is nothing to do.

[*The light of dawn has begun. In a little while it will be
daylight.*]

SILVIA. But what will happen then?

AGATA. Nothing.

SILVIA. What do you mean, nothing?

AGATA. I'm afraid it's already . . .

SILVIA. Already . . . what?

AGATA. Too late.

SILVIA. Too late . . . What do you mean?

AGATA. Oh, I don't ever expect to see him come up out of there again! Why, it would be like seeing . . . something monstrous coming up out of the earth . . . the devil. He'd tear us to pieces; I'm sure he would, he'd denounce us to the police, he'd get us hanged, all three of us. Nothing could save us. Surely you see that?

SILVIA. What then?

AGATA [*in a monotone*]. But I don't think he'll ever manage to get up again. [*Pause.*] You two go in the other room; try and eat a little. I'll come as well, now.

[*A silence.*]

PIA [*stammering*]. It isn't my fault. I had nothing to do with it. I've done nothing.

AGATA. None of us has done anything. It just happened. [*A silence.*] He happened to come here. Who asked him to come? The ladder happened to slip off the hooks. Nobody touched it; it happened by itself. And he gets the idea into his head that it's our fault. What can we do to help him? . . . What a strange chain of events . . . It was obvious things were not right here. It was all confusion; insecurity. It couldn't go on. [*A pause.*] It was as though he'd discovered for each one of us . . . a sort of root between us and the earth: a piece of gut, a bloody navel-cord; and he twisted it round his fist and dragged us along by it. He almost had us on all-fours, growing hair like goats. However, it was none of our choosing. It had to happen. And now it has happened.

SILVIA [*shivering*]. Mother, you knew it would happen. You could have prevented it.

AGATA [*half lost in thought*]. No. I couldn't.

SILVIA. But you'd realised . . .

AGATA. And you hadn't, I suppose? It's happened. And now one of us has to stay here quietly and think. It's an ungrateful task; I take it upon myself. [*Shaken for a moment.*] Do you think it doesn't horrify me too? [*Controlling herself; in a whisper.*] We shall leave here. It won't be long before the house and the well both collapse. There was a foreigner here; people will think he's gone; just as he one day arrived. In the meantime you can both go away.

SILVIA [*with a cry*]. But . . . I can't bear . . . This thing, down there . . . I can't bear it!

AGATA [*harshly*]. There are a lot of things you can't bear, aren't there? Fortunately, I'm here to bear them. Besides, in a little while, he'll have quietened down; there comes a point when things are seen to be inevitable and after that we do become quite calm once again. [*Lost in thought.*] Everything will happen very quickly. Dizziness; the water, though there's so little of it, will close over everything . . . and then be still again.

PIA [*hysterically*]. Oh, my God . . . Oh, my God . . . Oh, my God . . . I'm going away! I'm going away!

AGATA. Good. You go too, Silvia. Nobody will ask you anything.

PIA. I won't stay here a minute longer! My things are already packed. This house has always been a prison!

AGATA. Yes, my dear; go to Vienna. Go and dine out in your evening frock.

PIA. Yes, I *am* going! You frighten me!

ANGELO [*suddenly*]. Throw her on the ground, tie her up, she's mad! Pia! Silvia: don't let her do this. It's a crime! She's always laughed at you and despised you. Help me, help me; I can feel the cold of death on me. She was the one: she was responsible! It's her doing!

PIA. Yes, yes, it was Agata!

SILVIA. It was you, mother!

ANGELO. You! You!

AGATA [*suddenly, almost with a shout*]. Very well, then! Yes. It was I. I've been lying all this time.

PIA. It's been you all along! You unhooked the ladder!

AGATA. Yes, yes. It was what I wanted. Someone had to put a stop to all this. Like when a window keeps banging at night. Someone has to get up.

ANGELO. No! Silvia: she did it out of jealousy! Jealousy of you!

AGATA. Possibly . . . Before long this man would have tired of me, and humiliated me. For your sake, Silvia. [*Almost ironically.*] Rivals. And as you see, I've won.

ANGELO. Silvia! She killed your father! She killed him more surely than if she'd strangled him.

AGATA. Even that may be . . . He had cheated me and oppressed me. It was a long gloomy farce. Today I can breathe, at last. A pity that you lie out there now, under the earth, in Africa, dear Enrico; you cannot see the results.

PIA. I've always been frightened of you. You horrible, evil creature! You've killed the happiness in everybody.

AGATA. And in myself most of all. Perhaps I could have done better, if there'd ever been anyone in the whole world who needed me. But there never has been.

ANGELO [*suddenly*]. You gave yourself to a stranger, without a second thought, on a heap of goatskins.

AGATA. Yes.

ANGELO [*louder*]. And then sent your sister-in-law to sleep with me.

AGATA. Yes.

ANGELO [*louder still*]. And after that, your daughter! All three of you!

AGATA. I might protest a little there perhaps; but never mind; it's as true as makes no matter.

ANGELO. All three of you! All three of you!

AGATA. Yes. It was clear that it couldn't go on.

[*A silence.*]

This is something that must end today.

SILVIA [*hoarsely*]. Mother.

AGATA. What is it?

SILVIA [*a whisper, but gradually louder*]. I can't go away and leave him here. Nothing matters to me any more: myself, nor you, nor anyone else. I want him to come back up. I can't bear to live without him.

AGATA [*forcefully*]. That isn't true, Silvia. You two did nothing but follow after me, it was I who led you astray. Perhaps I wouldn't have let you stay immune. I feel sorry for you. [*Lowering her voice.*] And a little disgusted.

SILVIA [*passionately*]. I want him to come up! When he calls to me I want to leave everything else on earth! I want to obey him!

AGATA. Those were my words, not yours. It is I who've infected you.

SILVIA. I want him to come back! I'll throw myself down there to him! [*Weeping.*] Mother: perhaps at this very moment . . . I may be . . . I may . . .

AGATA [*seizing her and shaking her desperately*]. Be quiet, you silly girl! You're out of your mind. "I may be pregnant": that's what you're trying to say, isn't it? Well, that happens to women, and you're a woman. I was once pregnant with you; I was disgusted at the fact. [*A pause.*] It's not true, Silvia, you're hysterical, you're out of your senses. Oh, why are you alive, why did you ever grow up? You were so affectionate . . . why didn't you die that summer when we all expected you to? [*Controlling herself.*] Be quiet and go away. [*In a voice that gradually rises, with melancholy authority.*] There's nothing but disorder here, nothing but

chaos. I'm the only one who keeps my head and thinks. I'm
calm. I can take everything on myself. He's realised by now,
we've all realised, there's nothing more to say or do. It's
too late now. This is something that must end today.

[*A silence.*]

ANGELO [*suddenly, with unexpected calm, almost with sad-
ness*]. Agata, I want to talk to you.
AGATA [*she, too, is suddenly quiet and gentle*]. I can hear you,
Angelo. Go on.

[*A silence falls on the room.*]

ANGELO [*as before*]. Agata: must I resign myself to this?
AGATA [*as before*]. I too am resigned to it, Angelo.
ANGELO. It was you that wanted this.
AGATA. I hardly know. I seem to have been simply obeying.
ANGELO. Am I to stay down here and die?
AGATA [*lowering her voice*]. I think things cannot be altered
now, Angelo.
ANGELO. It's painful; it's terrifying to have to die down here,
here in the dark. I was still young.
AGATA. Do you think it is any less painful for me?
ANGELO. I beg you, Agata. I implore you to come and free
me. You have in your hands everything in the world that
was good and pleasant to me.
AGATA. Yes. And I would even like to set you free.
ANGELO. Then why don't you, Agata? You liked seeing me;
you liked obeying me.
AGATA. Yes. Nothing else mattered to me.
ANGELO. Without me, your life will become nothing again.
AGATA. Yes: nothing.
ANGELO. Then why don't you fetch me out of here? Why are
you doing this?
AGATA. Because . . . I was frightened, and I could bear it no
longer. I know that worse would have happened, if things
had been allowed to go on.
ANGELO. But all that could be altered.
AGATA. *I* couldn't be. Nor would I ask to be. Once a drop of
water has fallen, or a thought been thought, they remain
so throughout eternity. [*A pause.*] Angelo: one can never
turn back. I could not bear to see you go away.
ANGELO. But now you are committing the worst crime of all.
AGATA. It had to be. So that we should be at peace again.

ANGELO [*still quietly*]. You will never be at peace again! Poor
  Agata! You will be damned and cursed for all eternity!

AGATA. But that is the very thing that brings me peace: to
  receive what is due to me.

ANGELO [*his voice dying away*]. Poor Agata . . . Poor
  Agata . . .

AGATA. I do not believe in a divine mercy: I would be bewildered by it, I would be a black stain in the light. I love
  my burden. [*Meditatively.*] There is a point when we choose
  what we are to be. It is at the very beginning; when nothing
  so far exists, and everything is free for us to choose; and
  our eyes look upwards in joy and thanksgiving. Or down-
  wards . . . That is the starting point. However, there is
  always a kind of peace in being what we are, and being it
  completely: the condemned man has that blessing. I accept.
  [*A pause.*] Silvia: one day—you were only so high—the
  goat-boy brought in here a sweet little kid that he had to kill.
  [*As though she saw the scene before her.*] He slit its throat,
  just there, on the stones, sticking the knife right in. He
  skinned it, and opened it up, and fetched out its entrails;
  near by, there was a basin of steaming black blood. I
  helped him; my hands were bloody; the creature's eyes
  were still open. And suddenly I turned to the door . . .
  [AGATA *herself is terrified by what she is saying.*] . . . and
  you were there, Silvia, there, at the door; you'd been there
  for the last half-hour! You stood there stiff and white, your
  eyes wide-open, staring. You'd never seen anything of the
  kind before, you were too little. You began to cry: oh God,
  how you cried! I couldn't comfort you, I didn't know what
  to do; at first I couldn't even put my arms round you,
  because my hands were still . . . You went on crying for
  hour after hour; I begged you not to; I promised you all
  sorts of foolish things, I went down on my knees before
  you, I told you it wasn't true . . . Till at last you fell
  asleep. And then it was my turn to shake and tremble—
  my turn! my turn to weep!—in sweat and terror. I hardly
  know what it was I vowed to myself, what I cried out! But
  it was this; that you, my child, should not know this! My
  child should be clean. My child should be safe. The bloody
  hands should be mine alone, mine alone the bowl of blood,
  and the death, and the flesh, and the earth; mine alone the
  shuddering and the damnation . . . the smell of beasts . . .
  the well. And the child: away from here, safe, far away.
  Go away, Silvia. And if it's true that you are . . . [*She*

breaks off, and, going up to her daughter, caresses her tenderly.] I was rather sorry when I saw you grow up and change. We always hope our children . . . we hope everything will be better for them . . . That is what children mean. [*She breaks off.*]

[*The three of them turn towards the well. The sound of panting can be heard from it, the scratching of nails, a noise. Suddenly* PIA *screams like a madwoman:*]

PIA. He's climbing up! He's climbing up!

[*The noise is heard increasing, rising, becoming desperate, near, enormous; they all expect in a moment to see a hand grip the edge of the parapet.*

The three women stand there staring, as though turned to stone. Suddenly, there is a break in the heavy breathing. Not a cry. The noise of something falling. There is a long silence.

Loud, distinct and repeated, the sound of a motor-horn is heard. PIA *runs to the door and calls wildly:*]

PIA. Edoardo! Edoardo! Come up here! Quickly! Come up!

[*There is a prolonged pause, until the old man* EDOARDO *at last appears in the doorway.*]

EDOARDO [*coming into the room*]. What is it?

[SILVIA *breaks into sobs.*]

What's the matter?

PIA [*breathing heavily*]. Look: you're thirsty. Don't you want a drink of water? [*She repeats hysterically: it is almost a shout.*] Don't you want a drink? There. [*She points to the well.*] There. Draw yourself some water, out of there.

EDOARDO [*bewildered*]. 'Course I'm thirsty; 'course I am. [*He approaches the well, speaking in the melancholy tones of someone repeating something he has said hundreds of times before.*] I'm getting too old to go dragging that broken-down lorry all over the place in this heat. 'Course I'm thirsty. [*He has reached the well, and automatically bends over to look down it.*]

AGATA [*who has come close up to him: quietly*]. Here.

She is just behind the old man, and hands him a glass of water, which she has poured from the jug. He turns, takes it, and drinks; and asks again:]

EDOARDO. What's the matter?

AGATA. My daughter is leaving; and my sister-in-law is going with her. Will you wait for them down below? They are quite ready.

EDOARDO. What about their things?

AGATA. They're being sent on later.

EDOARDO. And what about you?

AGATA. I'm staying here.

EDOARDO. And the foreigner?

AGATA. Gone away.

EDOARDO [*moving towards the door*]. It's not only the sun, it's the air. And this wind: it burns; it burns right into you. [*To* PIA *and* SILVIA.] Then I'll wait down there for you. Don't be too long, will you? [*He goes out.*]

AGATA [*suddenly, almost fiercely, cries*]. Go away!

[PIA *rushes out after* EDOARDO.]

[*To* SILVIA.] Go away, both of you! Leave me alone.

[SILVIA *rushes out also, terrified. Her footsteps are heard receding.* AGATA *stands listening; as soon as the silence is complete, she runs to the well.*]

Angelo! Angelo! Angelo! Wait! [*She turns back frantically, seizes the rope and throws one end of it down into the well.*] Catch hold of it! Take it! Angelo! Angelo! [*Gradually her voice begins to sound as though it were coming from a long distance.*] Angelo! Angelo! Angelo! [*She straightens herself, and stands motionless; her hand lets go of the rope; she goes slowly to the window, and then to the door, bolting them both. It is dark inside the room. She seats herself calmly near the lamp, which is still burning on the table. She speaks to herself, quietly.*] Dearest Angelo, do come. Do come, even if it's only to punish me, if you want to. There's all the time in the world, now.

[*The sound of the motor-horn is heard in the very far distance. Silence again.*]

Now there are only the two of us. How simple that makes everything. You will certainly never be able to go away now; and neither shall I. We shall go on calling to each other and fighting with each other through all eternity.

END

EDUARDO DE FILIPPO

1900–

EDUARDO DE FILIPPO is the *capocomico*—actor–playwright–director–manager—of the Teatro San Ferdinando in Naples. He is a direct descendant of the *Commedia dell' Arte* troupes of the Sixteenth century and his plays are much like the *Lazzi* (a basic situation which is then improvised upon by the actors) of that tradition. For this reason, Eduardo's "scenarios" have seldom been published and hence he is largely unknown outside of Italy. There are two keys to DeFilippo's theatre: the Neapolitan family and a plebeian sense of humor. All of his plays deal with the conflicts and tribulations of family life, but they always end on a note of bittersweet reconciliation, the solidarity of the group restored. To understand the humor of his plays one needs to recall that *commedia* humor is of the painful kind that laughs at its own suffering. Eric Bentley describes it well when he writes: "There is a philosophy of the absurd, after all, in plebeian humor in general: your life is hopeless but you laugh, you are cheerful, and morally positive, against all reason." Probably no writer in the Twentieth century better exemplifies the improvisational nature and the power of the popular theatre, which undoubtedly explains why Eduardo de Filippo's work is best known in the rest of Europe and the United States through the many films which have been based on his scripts.

SON OF PULCINELLA[1]

By Eric Bentley

BOTH IN technique and in philosophy, Eduardo de Filippo is traditional. At the same time he strikes me as one of the three or four original figures in the theatre today.

When *The Big Magic* (*La Grande Magia*) was first placed before a metropolitan audience, in Rome last February, everyone cried "Pirandello!" Like the Sicilian master, Eduardo had insisted that illusions were needed because the truth was more than we could stand. Like Pirandello in *Il Piacere dell' onestà* (*The Pleasure of Honesty*) and *Ma non è una cosa seria* (*But It Isn't a Serious Matter*), Eduardo had shown an idea beginning as fiction, an escape from life, and later incorporated into life. There are even more specific resemblances to *Enrico IV*. At the beginning of each play a man retires from the bitter reality of sexual rivalry into a deliberate unreality in which time is supposed to stand still (though its not doing so is in both cases indicated by the protagonist's graying hair). At the end of each play reality irrupts into the illusion in a way calculated to shatter it; but the result is the opposite; the illusion is accepted by the protagonist in perpetuity.

Whether Eduardo was influenced by Pirandello or was simply nourished from the same sources and interested in the same problems was not discussed. Worse still: the word *Pirandello*, as such words will, prevented people from seeing things that would otherwise have been evident. For all the superficial "Pirandellism" of *La Grande Magia*, the play is really a much simpler, more commonsensical affair. Pirandello in his despair toys with a nihilistic relativism. The veiled lady at the end of *Right You Are* is one person or another as you choose; in which proposition the law of contradiction itself (that a thing cannot both be and not be) is flouted. In Eduardo, on the other hand, no such devilry is thrust upon the universe. If one man has an illusion, another sees it as such.

The next most salient feature of Neapolitan popular theatre as I have seen it is the style of acting. In Paris today you hear much about *commedia dell' arte*. What they show you is Jean-Louis Barrault and the Piccolo Teatro di Milano (the latter being more the rage in Paris than in Milan). These things are very fine, but they are art theater, and the *commedia dell' arte* was nothing if not popular theatre. You would find a much more authentic version of its famous artificial clowning in the Neapolitan comedian Totò. And for another side of the tradition—not famous at all unfortunately—you must go to Eduardo.

One of the persistent heresies about *commedia dell' arte*, often as Italian scholars denounce it as such, is the idea that the actors made up their lines as they went along. The nearest they ever got to this is probably that they sometimes wrote their lines, the script being the fruit of a collaboration between various members of the cast. At any rate, Eduardo de Filippo began his career as an actor doing this sort of writing. From reports I gather the impression that the plays he acted in must have been rather like Chaplin shorts. There would often be several to an evening, and they would represent incidents in the life of the little man, the *povero diavolo*. A play like *La Grande Magia* is of course as far from a one-act farce or melodrama in a popular Neapolitan theatre as *Monsieur Verdoux* is from a Keystone Comedy. In each case, however, the later work is made up to a surprising extent of elements from the earlier. And it is these elements that save both film and play from polemical aridity, that give them a tang and an identity, that make them dramatic art.

They would not do so if they operated as mere comic relief or melodramatic seasoning; their function is to lend definition to the author's subject. Thus in *La Grande Magia*, the idea of life as a game, the world as a show, is given body and form by, among other things, the brilliant theatre of Otto's conjuring, in which we get a back-stage glimpse of all the mechanism of magic. To be told, as my reader has been, that Otto had to convince Calogero of the reality of magic is very little compared to actually seeing Otto play his phonograph record of applause and persuade Calogero it is the sea. To be told, as my reader has been, that Matteo in *La Paura numero uno* is tricked into believing war has broken out is very little compared to actually seeing the enactment of the ruse with the microphone and the comic sequences that follow. Matteo talks at cross-purposes with the other tenants: he thinks they are talking about the war, they think he is talking about the house. Another sequence ends with Matteo's mistaking a multi-national group of pilgrims for an invading army. These two sequences lead up to a climax of laughable absurdity at the conclusion of acts one and two respectively.

For, though Eduardo's plays are chock-full of amusing and imaginative details—minor characters, bits of business, meditations as of an unsophisticated Giraudoux—they have a solid over-all structure, usually in three clearly marked phases or acts. If the sequences within the acts often derive from popular farce, the act-structure is even more often that of popular melodrama. Eduardo likes to bring the curtain down, especially the curtain of Act Two, on a terrific moment—which means "at the psychological moment," a moment when two lines of narrative suddenly intersect by amazing coincidence. Thus in *Natale in casa Cupiello*, the ugly rivalry of husband and lover reaches boiling-point just as Luca Cupiello's idyll, the adoration of the Magi, comes to actual performance—a big curtain for act two! In *La Grande Magia*, it is the denouement in act three where the arm of coincidence is longest and most active: it just happens that Marta, absent for four years, reappears one second before Calogero is to open the box. Eduardo is saying not only "such is the wonder of fairyland" but also "such is the perverseness of reality." He has not surrendered to melodrama; he has exploited it. For him it is not a jazzing-up of otherwise inert and tiresome elements. It is a legitimate accentuation of the fantastic character of life.

This purposeful manipulation of fable is nowhere more striking than in Eduardo's most popular play, *Filumena Marturano*. Since this play is also one of his most realistic works, the reader may be interested to see in more detail how the apparently curious mixture of realism and its opposite actually works out. Since, moreover, the play is Eduardo's most powerful tribute to mother love, a note on it may serve to bind together the first and second parts of this chapter and leave us with a rounded if not complete impression of Eduardo's playwriting.

The story is the unprepossessing one of the man who makes

an honest woman of a prostitute. What stands out in Eduardo's play is the prostitute herself, a heroic plebeian, a tigress of a mother. The portrait derives half its life from the language—which in translation can scarcely be shown. But, as already intimated, the mode of the narrative is a contributory factor.

Filumena comes from the lower depths of Naples. She is rescued from poverty by a prolonged liaison with a rich man, Domenico Soriano. When they are both getting along in years, and he wants to marry a younger, more beautiful, and more respectable girl, Filumena pretends to be dying and arranges a deathbed marriage. The ceremony over, she jumps light-heartedly out of bed, and Domenico realizes he has been had. It is at this point that Eduardo raises the curtain on his first act! The stormy exposition is followed by a revelation. Filumena has not been acting selfishly. Unknown to Domenico, she has three grown-up sons: they are now legitimized!

The first act ends with Domenico rushing off for a lawyer to rescind a marriage held under false pretenses. In the second, it seems that he will have his way, and Filumena, crushed for the moment, accepts the hospitality of her son Michele. As a parting shot, however, she tells Don Domenico that he is the father of one of the three sons. Another melodramatic revelation! Further: with a secrecy at once melodramatic and realistic, she will not tell him which one, because she wants no discrimination against the other two. End of the second act.

Act III is a happy epilogue. In the time between the acts Domenico has come around. The old marriage has been rescinded, but a new one is now being celebrated. He gladly accepts Filumena as wife and all three young men as sons. "I am fifty-two, you are forty-eight. We are two mature souls in duty bound to understand what they are about—ruthlessly and to the depths. We have to face it. And assume full responsibility."

The sententiousness is naïve, but the language, sunny and bland in the original, implies some unworried awareness of the fact. There is an irony about this happy ending (as there is about many others). What stays with us is the conclusion arrived at and, far more, the sense of danger and disaster this time—perhaps not next time—narrowly averted. What stays with us is Filumena's cry: *"Il tenero amor filiale lo abbiamo perduto!"*

A traditional playwright, then, in technique and philosophy. But do we understand what it means to live in a tradition—

as against merely believing in tradition, professional tradi-
tionalism? Eduardo de Filippo started with an infinitely
suggestive and dramatic milieu, Naples, and with a theatre
which, if not great, had yet a real existence—in a sense in
which our broadways and boulevards and west ends are
deserts of unreality. These circumstances conduced to a concentration of energy which stands in direct contrast to that
dissipation of energy by which talents elsewhere are frittered
away. They conduced to a growth so natural and green that
most art theatres seem hothouse products by comparison. In
short, they brought Eduardo to the threshold of great theatre;
his own gifts took him across it; and it is thus that one of
the most traditional artists of our time became one of the
most original.

FILUMENA MARTURANO

OR

A Mother's a Mother

A Comedy in Three Acts

by EDUARDO DE FILIPPO

1946

FILUMENA MARTURANO[1]

English Version by Eric Bentley

CHARACTERS

FILUMENA MARTURANO	UMBERTO
DOMENICO SORIANO	RICCARDO *Filumena's sons*
ALFREDO AMOROSO,	MICHELE
Domenico's crony	NOCELLA, *a lawyer*
ROSALIA, *Filumena's friend*	TERESINA, *a seamstress*
DIANA, *Domenico's mistress*	TWO WAITERS
LUCIA, *the maid*	

THE PLACE: *Naples*

THE TIME: *Not long ago*

[1] Copyright © 1953 by Eric Bentley. Reprinted here by permission of Eric Bentley and the Franz J. Horch Agency, the latter acting on behalf of Guilio Einaudi Editore S.P.A. All inquiries concerning performance rights to be addressed to Miss Toby Cole, 234 West 44th Street, New York, New York 10036.

ACT ONE

[*The style of* DOMENICO'S *dining room is decidedly twentieth century. The room is showily furnished in mediocre taste. Certain pictures and ornaments, carefully placed on the walls and furnishings, violently conflict with this modernism. They doubtless belonged to* DOMENICO'S *father.*

The door downstage left leads to the bedroom. Upstairs left, a large French window set across the corner of the room looks out on an ample terrace that is provided with plants and flowers and shaded by a colored, striped awning. The main door is in the back wall on the right. Upstage right there is an archway; and through partly drawn curtains one can descry what DOMENICO *dares to call his study. Here also his penchant for modernity shows itself. It is a "modern" cabinet which protects and exhibits a vast number of cups and various medals and divers forms and dimensions; these are the First Prizes his racehorses have won.*

On the opposite wall, behind a desk, two crossed banners bear witness to victories at the Festa di Montevergine. Not a book, not a journal, not even a piece of paper. The study is orderly and decent, but lifeless.

In the center of the dining room is a table laid with considerable care and taste for two. In the middle are fresh red roses.

It is the time of year when spring is turning into summer. It is the time of day when afternoon is turning into evening. The sun is shedding its last rays on the terrace.

AT RISE: *Four people are on stage—*FILUMENA, DOMENICO, ROSALIA, *and* ALFREDO.

FILUMENA *is wearing a long white nightgown. Her hair is in disorder, though a hasty attempt has been made to set it to rights. Her feet are stockingless in her old bedroom slippers. This woman's face shows signs of torment: we can see her past has been sad and stormy.* FILUMENA *doesn't look coarse, but she cannot hide her humble origin, nor would she want to. Her gestures are broad and open. Her tone of voice is candid and forceful: she is someone to reckon with, rich in instinctive intelligence and moral force. After her own fashion she knows life and its laws—and after*

*her own fashion confronts them. A strand or two of silver
on the temples announce her forty-eight years; not so her
dark eyes, which have preserved all the youthful vitality
of the dark Neapolitan type. She is pale as a corpse, partly
from the role she has just been playing (she has pretended
to be dying), partly because of the storm she knows is
coming. But she isn't afraid. On the contrary, she is waiting
like some wounded beast to leap on her adversary.*

DOMENICO SORIANO *is a strong, healthy man of about fifty.
He has lived well. Money and an easy time of it have kept
him lively in spirit and youthful in appearance. His father,
Raimondo Soriano, was one of the richest and most rascally
confectioners in Naples; he had bakeries at Vergini and
Forcella and very popular stores in Toledo and Foria. And*
DOMENICO *was the apple of his eye. The caprices of* DON
DOMENICO—*as a boy he was Signorino Don Mimi—knew
no bounds either for originality or extravagance; they were
famous and even today are the talk of Naples. A passionate
horse fancier, he can spend half the day with his cronies
going over the athletic feats of the leading champions who
have passed through his well-fed stables. And now here he
is, wearing only a pair of pants and a quickly buttoned
house jacket, pale, convulsed, facing this "thing of naught,"*
FILUMENA MARTURANO, *whom for so many years he has
treated as a slave, but who now holds him in the palm of
her hand, ready to crush him like an insect. Not that he
knows it; he sees no limits to his will. He is sure of the
triumph of his godlike reason. He is sure he can expose the
outrage, lay bare before the world the baseness which has
deceived him. He feels offended, insulted, and, in a certain
sense which he can't explain and wouldn't if he could,
desecrated. The fact that he seems publicly discomfited
turns his head; he is going berserk.*

ROSALIA *is mild and humble. She is seventy-five. Her hair
is of an uncertain color, rather more white than gray. She
is wearing a dark dress of no definite color. A little bent
but still full of life. She used to live in a* BASSO—*the name
the Neapolitans give to ground floor living quarters in the
slums. This was in San Liborio Street, right opposite where
the Marturanos lived: that's how she came to know all about
them. She has known* FILUMENA *from earliest childhood.
She was with her in her saddest moments, and did not spare
those words of comfort, understanding, and tenderness
which the common women of Italy have to offer, and which*

*are a balsam to the suffering heart. From harsh experience
she knows the effects of this man's irascibility and is petrified.*

ALFREDO *is an agreeable fellow of some seventy years,
solidly built, vigorous, muscular. He was a fine coachman,
and it was in this capacity that* DOMENICO *first took him on,
keeping him ever after at his side as handyman, scapegoat,
spy, and friend. He has come to symbolize his master's past.
You can see how loyal and devoted he is to* DOMENICO, *and
how great his self-abnegation, in the way his eyes follow
his master. He is wearing a gray jacket of perfect cut, if
a little frayed, trousers of another color, and a beret worn
jauntily on one side. On his portly belly he displays a gold
chain. He is simply waiting—perhaps the calmest of the
four people in the room, for he knows his* DOMENICO, *he
hasn't fetched and carried for him for nothing.*

As the scene opens, FILUMENA *is standing by the bedroom
door with her arms folded, a posture of defiance. Downstage
right is* DOMENICO, *facing her. Upstage left, near the terrace,
stands* ROSALIA. *Upstage right is* ALFREDO. *They are standing
in the four corners of the room as if playing a children's
game. A long pause.*]

DOMENICO [*slapping himself repeatedly, vehemently*]. Fool!
Fool! Fool!!!

ALFREDO [*intervening with a slight gesture*]. Now really, Don
Do . . .

DOMENICO. Am I a man? I should go to a mirror and spit in
my face! [*To* FILUMENA.] Married to you? I've wasted a
lifetime with you already: twenty-five years of health and
strength and youth and effort! And you want that, too?
And Don Domenico has no choice but to give it to you?
For twenty-five years you've done what you liked with me,
you've all done what you liked with me! [*To himself.*]
You thought you were Jesus Christ our Lord, and they've
all done what they liked with you! [*He turns to the three
of them one after the other.*] You, you, you—in our street
—in our precinct—in Naples—throughout the world—
you've planned my downfall! [*Now he is quiet again.*] It
won't bear thinking about. But I might have known. A
woman like you *had* to get where you've got. But don't
think you've heard the last of this. I'll murder you! And all
your accomplices, too! The doctor, the priest, and [*Pointing
at* ROSALIA *and* ALFREDO.] those two reprobates who've lived

off me and grown fat off me, I'll murder you all! [*Looks for his revolver.*] Where's my revolver? Give me my revolver.

ALFREDO [*calmly*]. It's at the gun shop. I took it to be cleaned. Like you told me.

DOMENICO. I've told you plenty in my time, haven't I? And it's beginning to look as if I was telling you what you wanted me to tell you, isn't it? Well, that's all over: My eyes have been opened! [*To* FILUMENA.] You will leave this house. And if you don't leave quietly, you'll leave dead. No law can stop me! No *God* can stop Domenico Soriano!! I'll denounce you in the streets, I'll send you to the galleys! I can pay the piper and I'll call the tune! And when I tell them who you were and where you lived when I picked you up, I'll win my case all right! I'll annihilate you!!

[*Pause.*]

FILUMENA [*not at all overwhelmed, sure of herself*]. Are you through now?

DOMENICO [*still roaring*]. And don't speak to me. I can't stand it!!!

FILUMENA [*calmly*]. When I've said my say, I'll never set eyes on you again. And you'll never hear my voice again.

DOMENICO [*still bellowing*]. A harlot: that's what you were and that's what you are!!!!

FILUMENA [*still quiet*]. Why do you shout so? It's no secret. Everyone knows who I was and where I lived. But—you—came—there. Like the others. And I treated you like the others. Why should I treat you different: aren't men created equal? What I've done . . . well, I'm sorry for it. But now I'm your wife, Domenico. The army and the navy can't change that.

DOMENICO. My—wife?

FILUMENA. Your wife.

DOMENICO. You're crazy! It was the most barefaced piece of trickery you ever heard of. You were sick, were you? You must take to your deathbed, must you? A trick: and I have witnesses! [*He indicates* ROSALIA *and* ALFREDO.]

ROSALIA [*hastily, not wanting to be dragged in*]. I know nothing. All I know is, Donna Filumena got sick, she got so bad she was going to die, but she never said nothing. I know nothing neither.

DOMENICO [*to* ALFREDO]. You know nothing either, huh? You didn't know this dying was just an act?

ALFREDO. By the Holy Virgin, Don Mimi! If Donna Filumena
wanted to tell somebody, it certainly wouldn't be me: she
can't stand the sight of me!

ROSALIA. What about the priest? Who told me to call the
priest? You did!

DOMENICO. Because she wanted him . . . I wanted to please
her . . .

FILUMENA. Oh, of course—you didn't believe I was passing
on, did you? Oh, no! You weren't thinking how nice it
would be to get rid of me, were you?

DOMENICO. Yes, I was! And you were whispering in the priest's
ear. And the priest said, "Marry her! Marry her in extremis,
poor woman! It is her one remaining wish! With the good
Lord's blessing, tie the bridal knot!!"

FILUMENA [*continuing*]. And you said to yourself, "After all,
what have I got to lose? It's only a question of hours, it
won't cost much." When the priest left, I hopped out of
bed and said, "Wish us luck, Domenico, for now—we're
husband and wife!" It must have been quite a shock.

ROSALIA [*hysterical*]. I nearly jumped out of my skin. And
laugh! I couldn't stop! [*In fact, she starts again.*] I can't
get over it, I could have sworn she was sick . . .

ALFREDO. On her deathbed in fact . . .

DOMENICO. If you two don't be quiet, *you'll* be on your deathbed!! [*Pausing.*] But I still don't get it: how could she . . .
[*He has a thought.*] What about the doctor? A qualified
doctor could come here and not notice she's in perfect
health and making a fool of him?

ALFREDO. I think . . . er . . . maybe he made a mistake.

DOMENICO [*stung*]. Shut up, Alfredo! [*Thinking hard.*] That
doctor needn't think he'll get away with it, he'll pay for
this as sure as God's in heaven! He couldn't have acted in
good faith, he was in on the deal sure as fate, *you* cut him
in on it, you *bought* him, huh?

FILUMENA. Bought! The only idea in your head: everything
you ever wanted you bought. Including me. Because you
were Don—Mimi—Soriano. You wore the best shirts, you
went to the best tailors, your race horses ran for you, and
you did quite a bit of running yourself, didn't you, after
one thing and another? And sometimes I set the pace, Don
Mimi, and you didn't know it, and you've a long way to
run yet, Don Mimi, there's blood and sweat ahead, before
—you—know—what—a—gentleman—is! [*She is quiet
again now.*] The doctor knew nothing about it, he thought

I was dying, too: why shouldn't he? [*Another change of tone.*] Any woman would be on her deathbed after twenty-five years with you. [*To* ROSALIA *and* ALFREDO.] For twenty-five years I've been his servant. You know that. He just used to go away and have a good time. In London. In Paris. Or at the race tracks. So I was his policeman. I went to the bakeries at Forcella and Vergini, I went to the stores in Toledo and Foria. If I hadn't he'd have been robbed right and left. [*She imitates his hypocritical tone.*] "I don't know what I'd do without you, Filumena, you're—a woman!" [*Shouting.*] I've kept house for him better than a . . . than a legitimate wife! [*Dropping her voice.*] I've washed his feet. Not just since I've got old. Even when I was young—I washed his feet. [*Raising her voice again.*] I might have been a housemaid he could fire from one moment to the next!

DOMENICO [*sullenly*]. You never tried to understand how things stood between us. Always mooning around the house with that sullen, resentful face. You said to yourself, "Well am *I* in the wrong? Have I done anything to him?" [*Slowly.*] I have never seen a tear in those eyes. Never. In all the years we've lived through together, I have never seen her cry!

FILUMENA. I should have cried then? For you maybe? For this fine . . .

DOMENICO. Never mind about me. You were a soul in torment that knew no peace! A woman who doesn't cry, doesn't eat, doesn't sleep—I never saw you sleep but once! A damned soul, that's you!

FILUMENA. When did you want to see me sleep? You never came home. I was always alone. Even at Easter. Even at Christmas. Like a lonely dog. Do you know when a woman cries, Don Mimi? When she catches sight of the good thing and can't have it. Filumena never caught sight of the good thing. And when all you know is the bad thing, you don't cry. It's good to cry, I know that, crying is a blessing, a blessing Filumena wasn't to know. A harlot you call me, and well you might—you always treated me as one. [*To* ROSALIA *and* ALFREDO, *sole witnesses of the sacred truth of what she is saying.*] And let's not talk of his youth and his wild oats. In those days you could say, "Well, he's rich, he's spoiled, he'll get over it." But now he's fifty-two and he still comes home with lipstick on his handkerchiefs. Pah! Where are they, Rosalia?

ROSALIA [*reassuringly*]. In the cupboard, Donna Filumena.

FILUMENA. A considerate man would say to himself, "She
mustn't find them, I must hide them someplace." What this
man thought was, "What can she do when she finds them?
Who is she, anyway? What rights has she?" And off he
goes after his little . . .

DOMENICO [*caught out and furious*]. His little—who?

FILUMENA [*not in the least intimidated, more violent than he*].
. . . after his little floozy! You think I didn't catch on?
You can't even tell good lies, that's what's wrong with you.
Fifty-two years old and he's still after girls of *twenty*-two!
He isn't ashamed of himself either. He sets her up in *my*
home. We all pretend she's a nurse. Because he believed—
oh, yes, he believed—I was dying. [*This is true but incredible.*] Not more than one hour ago, before the priest
came to marry us, they thought I was just going to give my
soul to God, and I'd lost my sense of sight, so, at the foot
of *my* bed, they started kissing and caressing! . . . [*She
can't hold her nausea back.*] Madonna, you make me feel
sick to the stomach! Why, suppose I'd *really* been dying—
with you carrying on like that at the foot of my bed!! Me
dying in there, the table laid in here. For two: him and the
corpse, I suppose!

DOMENICO. You mean, when you're dying, I'm not supposed
to eat? I had to have food, didn't I?

FILUMENA. With roses on the table?

DOMENICO [*passing it off as normal*]. With roses on the table.

FILUMENA. Red roses?

DOMENICO [*losing patience*]. Red, blue, green, good God,
can't I have roses if I want to? [*He is blustering now.*] If I
want to, can't I be glad you're dead?

FILUMENA. Only I'm not dead, Domenico. [*Defiantly.*] I
changed my mind.

DOMENICO [*to himself*]. "So put that in your pipe and smoke
it." [*Pause.*] But there's something I don't get. If you've
always treated me just like all the others, if men are all
alike, if, as you put it, they're created equal, why did you
have to marry me? And if I'm in love with this girl and
want to marry her—and I will marry Diana, mark my
words—what does it matter to you whether she's twenty or
a hundred and fifty?

FILUMENA. You're right: that girl doesn't matter. [*She buckles
down to explain.*] Did you really think I'd done it for you?
You didn't enter into my calculations at all. You never

have. A woman of my type—you've said it yourself, you've
always said it—a woman like me has it all figured. [*Under-
lining each word.*] It so happens I can use you. [*A break.*]
Or did you really believe—after the lifetime of sacrifice
I've lived—that I'd simply pick up and go?

DOMENICO [*thinking he understands, jubilant*]. Money! I knew
it! But couldn't you have had it? [*Pompously.*] You think
a son of the Sorianos would have failed to provide for you?
Failed to set you up in a home of your own? Failed to make
you a woman of independent means?

FILUMENA [*humiliated by his lack of understanding, with
scorn*]. Oh, stop! Will you men never understand anything?
As for your money, Domenico, you can keep it. Keep it.
It's something else I want of you right now. And you're
going to give it to me. [*Pause.*] I have three sons.

[DOMENICO *and* ALFREDO *are astonished.* ROSALIA *is not.*]

DOMENICO. Three sons? What are you talking about, Filumena?

FILUMENA [*repeating herself almost mechanically*]. I have
three sons.

DOMENICO [*bewildered*]. But . . . whose children are they?

FILUMENA [*what* DOMENICO *fears not having escaped her,
coldly*]. Their fathers are men like you.

DOMENICO [*gravely*]. Filumena, Filumena, you're playing with
fire. What do you mean, men like me?

FILUMENA. Men are created equal.

DOMENICO [*to* ROSALIA]. *You* knew about this?

ROSALIA [*feelingly*]. I certainly did!

DOMENICO [*to* ALFREDO]. You, too?

ALFREDO [*eager to get out of it*]. No! Donna Filumena hates
me. I told you!

DOMENICO [*not yet convinced, as if to himself*]. Three sons?

FILUMENA. The eldest is twenty-six.

DOMENICO. Twenty-six?

FILUMENA. You needn't pull such a face about it. They're not
yours.

DOMENICO [*somewhat relieved*]. Do they know you? Do they
see you? Do they know you're their mother?

FILUMENA. No, but *I* see *them.* Often. I talk to them.

DOMENICO. What do they do? Where do they live? What do
they live *on?*

FILUMENA. They live on your money.

DOMENICO [*surprised*]. They live on my money?

FILUMENA. They live on your money. I stole it from you. From your wallet when necessary. Under your very nose.

DOMENICO. So you're a thief!

FILUMENA [*boldly*]. I sold your suits, I sold your shoes, you never noticed. Remember that diamond ring? I said it was lost? Well, I'd sold it. I've raised my family on your money. I'm a thief.

DOMENICO [*appalled*]. What sort of woman *are* you?

FILUMENA [*goes on as if he hadn't spoken*]. One of them has a store in the next street. He's a plumber——

ROSALIA [*correcting her*]. An engineer: sanitary and high-droolic!

DOMENICO [*who hasn't followed this*]. What!?

ROSALIA [*pronouncing the word right this time*]. A sanitary and *hydraulic* engineer! Fixes faucets and all that. . . . The second boy, what's his name? [*Searches for the name.*] Riccardo . . . he's the handsome one, a real lady killer, lives on Via Chiaia, he has a shop too, number seventy-four, he's a shirtmaker, and what shirts, and what customers . . . Then, there's Umberto——

FILUMENA. He wants to study. He's always wanted to study. He's a thinker! Writes in the papers!

DOMENICO [*ironically*]. So we have a writer in the family——

ROSALIA. And what a mother she's made them! They've never wanted for anything. I am old and I may find myself at any moment in the presence of Him who beholdeth all things, comprehendeth all things, and forgiveth all things, so it's true, what I say, and don't you go listening to no gossip! From the time they was in their baby clothes, she's fed them on milk and honey!

DOMENICO. Paid for with Don Domenico's shirts, shoes, and diamond rings!

ROSALIA [*blurting it out*]. You threw your money to the four winds of heaven——

DOMENICO [*severely*]. And whose business was that, may I ask?

ROSALIA [*frightened, but unable not to drive her point home*]. But, saints above—you never even noticed!

FILUMENA [*with contempt*]. Take no notice of him, it's no use.

DOMENICO [*controlling himself*]. You're trying to provoke me, Filumena, you're going too far. Do you realize what you've done? You've made me look like a man of straw! Take these three young men I haven't even met, whose existence I hadn't even dreamed of, in fact—tomorrow or the next day, they can laugh in my face and say to themselves, "Fine, so that's Don Domenico. The man who foots the bill."

ROSALIA [*eagerly*]. No, no, Don Mimì, what do they know about it? Donna Filumena, she does everything the right way, she has a head on her shoulders. It was the lawyer who sent the money when Michele—he's the engineer— set up shop in the next street. He told him it came from "a lady who wishes to remain anonymous!" [*She has difficulty with the last word.*] It was the same with Riccardo, he's the shirtmaker. And the lawyer has to send Umberto his monthly allowance, so he can finish up his studies. You don't come into it at all!

DOMENICO [*bitterly*]. I only pay for it!

FILUMENA [*on a sudden impulse*]. I should have got rid of them, then? Is that what I should have done, Domenico? I should have put them out of the way, as other women do, is that what you mean? You'd admire a Filumena of that sort, wouldn't you? [*More excited.*] Answer me! Tell me I should have done what the other girls said. "What are you waiting for?" they said, "it's one worry too many!" But I'd have worried to all eternity! How could I have lived with that on my conscience? And then, when I talked with the Madonna, the little Madonna at the end of our street . . . [*Turning to* ROSALIA.] Remember?

ROSALIA [*almost insulted at the idea that she could forget*]. Do I remember? It's the Madonna of the Roses! And does she shower her favors upon us? One a day!

FILUMENA [*re-creating the scene, as if talking to herself*]. It was three o'clock in the morning. I was alone, walking down the street. Six months had passed since I left home. It was the first time. Where could I turn? Who could I confide in? I heard the other girls. "What are you waiting for?" "Just one worry too many." "I know a good one." Without knowing it, as I walked along, I'd come to "my" little street, with the little altar on the corner, the altar of the Madonna of the Roses. I went up to her. This way. [*She plants her fists on her hips and, raising her eyes to an imaginary effigy, speaks as one woman to another.*] What am I to do? Thou who knowest all things, who knowest why I have sinned, tell me: what am I to do?" But the Madonna didn't reply. She didn't say a word. "So that's it?" I said. "The more you don't talk, the more people believe in you. But I'm speaking to you. [*Arrogantly.*] Answer me!" And a voice answered me. It said: [*Now she imitates the tone of voice of someone not known to her; she hasn't been able to tell where the voice comes from.*] "A mother's a mother!" I froze. I was riveted to the spot—like this. [*She grows rigid and fixes her eyes on an imaginary effigy.*] If I'd turned around, maybe I'd have seen where the voice had come from, a house with a balcony, the next street, an open window. . . . But then I said to myself, "Why at this particular moment? What do other people know of my affairs?" [*Pause.*] Then . . . it was she, was it? It was the Madonna? I'd faced right up to her, so she agreed to talk? And of course, the Madonna makes use of *us* when she wants to talk. . . . So when they said, "One worry too many," it was the Madonna speaking, the Madonna wanted to test me? [*Slowly.*] I don't know if it was me, I don't know if it was the Madonna of the Roses, who went like this [*She nods as if to say, "I have understood."*] and said, "A mother's a mother," but I swore an oath. I swore to bring up my children. [*She turns to* DOMENICO.] And that's why I've been around you all these years! For their sake. For their sake I've put up with the way you've treated me, I've put up with . . . everything. And when that young fellow fell in love with me and wanted to marry me . . . remember? We'd been together five years then, you ànd I. At home you had your wife and out at San Potito you had me with three little rooms and a kitchen. It was the first apartment you found for me after you'd taken me out of the——that place, four years after we first met. Well, this young fellow wanted to marry me. But you acted jealous. I can hear you now, "I'm married, I can't marry you. But if this other fellow marries you, I'll . . ." And you burst out crying. *You* can cry, even if *I* can't. You can cry all right. And I said to myself, "Go slow, Filumena, it can't be helped. Domenico loves you yet, just stick to San Potito and your three little rooms . . ." Two years later your wife died. Time passed. I was still at San Potito. I said to myself, "He's still young, he wouldn't want to tie himself to another woman for life, the day will come when he'll settle down, when he'll realize what sacrifices I've made . . ." So I waited. And sometimes I'd say, "Domenico, do you know who's just got married? The girl across the way. In the house with the little windows." And you'd smile, you'd burst out laughing, just like when you came to the . . . other place with your friends. Before San Potito. The wrong

kind of laugh. I'd hear it on the stairs. It wasn't always
the same man laughing, but it was always the same laugh.
[*Bearing up.*] I waited. I waited twenty-five years. Waited
for Don Domenico's pleasure. He's an old man of fifty-two
now, but that's nothing . . . [*With a change of tone,
vehemently.*] I could die with the shame of it! This old
man of fifty-two thinks he's a schoolboy, runs after every
skirt he sets eyes on, goes around with lipstick on his
handkerchiefs, and installs in my house his latest little . . .
[*Threatening.*] Well, try it again, bring her to this house,
now I'm your wife, I'll throw you out, both of you. We're
married. Married by the holy priest. And this is my house!

[*A bell rings offstage.* ALFREDO *leaves upstage right.*]

DOMENICO. Your house! Ha! ha! ha! [*He laughs with forced
irony.*] You make me laugh!

FILIMENA [*passionately*]. All right, laugh! I don't mind hearing you laugh now. You wouldn't know how to laugh as
you did then.

[ALFREDO *returns. He gives everyone a good look. He's
bothered by what he has to say.*]

DOMENICO [*noticing him, ill-humoredly*]. What do *you* want?

ALFREDO. Me? I just wanted to say they've brought that
supper . . .

DOMENICO. Why in God's name do you all think I shouldn't
eat?

ALFREDO [*as much as to say: I wash my hands of this*]. Very
well, Don Domenico. [*Talking out through the door.*]
Come in!

[TWO WAITERS *from a restaurant come in with a wicker
hamper and other supplies for a cold supper.*]

FIRST WAITER [*rather unctuous and servile*]. Your supper,
signore! [*To his companion.*] Put it here.

[SECOND WAITER *puts the hamper down on the spot indicated.*]

FIRST WAITER. Signore, I've only brought one chicken. It's
such a big one. Enough for four, signore. All best quality
goods! [*He starts opening up the supplies.*]

DOMENICO [*stopping him with a gesture, annoyed*]. Do you
know what you can do? You can leave!

FIRST WAITER. Yes, signore, yes, indeed. [*Taking a dessert out *of the hamper and placing it on the table.*] This is the dessert the young lady is so fond of. And this is the wine . . . [*There is silence all around. To remind* DOMENICO *of a promise, he adopts a playful tone.*] You haven't forgotten, have you, signore? Our little . . .

DOMENICO. What?

FIRST WAITER. You *have* forgotten? Well, signore, when you came over to order the supper, don't you recall? I asked if you happened to have any old clothes you didn't need, and you said, "Come this evening, and if things turn out the way I'm expecting, I'll have a brand new suit. I'll make you a present of it."

[*The atmosphere is glacial. After a pause, in a tone indicating ingenuous disappointment, the waiter continues.*]

FIRST WAITER. Things did *not* turn out the way you wanted? [*He waits, but when* DOMENICO *still doesn't answer, he is impatient.*] You didn't get the good news you expected?

DOMENICO [*aggressively*]. I told you to leave!

FIRST WAITER [*amazed at his reception*]. We're going, signore. Let's go, Carlo. The good news never came. Just my luck.

[*The* TWO WAITERS *leave, upstage right.*]

FILUMENA [*after a pause, ironically*]. Eat, Don Mimì! What's the matter with you? You're not eating? Have you lost your appetite?

DOMENICO [*angry*]. Sure, I'll eat. I'll eat *and* drink—later on!

FILUMENA. When the corpse comes to keep you company!

[*Enter* DIANA *by the main door. She is a good-looking girl of twenty-two. That is, she tries to look twenty-two; actually she's twenty-seven. She dresses rather snobbishly—with affected elegance. She looks them all up and down. As she enters, she is talking to everyone in general and no one in particular. She evidently despises everybody. She doesn't even notice* FILUMENA'S *presence. She is carrying medicinal packages, which she places on the table near the door. She takes a nurse's white coat from a chair and puts it on.*]

DIANA. There was *such* a mob in the pharmacy, I just couldn't get waited on, I had to go to another one, couldn't get waited on there either, went from one pharmacy to another, must have been to *eight* in all, I'm sweating *all* over Rosalia. [*In a bossy tone.*] *Do* get my bath ready, there's a good girl.

Oh! [*Seeing the roses.*] roses, *red* roses, thank you, *thank* you, Domenico, you're a *dear*, what an *odor*. I'm working up quite an appetite, too. [*Picks up one of her packages.*] I've found the *camphor* . . . and the *adrenalin* but *oxygen* isn't to be had for a *million* lire!

[DOMENICO *is fuming.* FILUMENA *isn't batting an eyelash, she's just waiting.* ROSALIA *and* ALFREDO *seem pretty amused and happy.* DIANA *lights a cigarette and sits by the table, facing out front.*]

DIANA. I was just *thinking*, if she—heavens, how I *hate* to say the word—but, here goes, if she *dies* tonight, I'll leave, early in the morning. A girl friend of mine has room for me in her car. I'd just be in the way here, whereas at Bologna I've a *hundred and one* little things to do! I'll be back in just about ten days, and we'll be together again. Now tell me, how is she? Out of her pain yet? Has the priest come?

FILUMENA [*controlling herself, with affected courtesy, slowly approaching*]. The priest has come. [DIANA *is taken completely by surprise. She stands up and backs away several paces.*] And seeing that I was on my deathbed . . . [*Breaking off.*] Take that coat off! [*Though almost stunned* DIANA *does as she is told.*] Put it on that chair. [DIANA *does so.*] Seeing that I was in extremis, the priest advised Don Domenico Soriano to tie the bridal knot with the good Lord's blessing.

[*Not knowing what attitude to take, and trying to find something to do,* DIANA *takes one of the roses and raises it to her nose.* FILUMENA *is furious and shouts harshly.*]

PUT THAT ROSE DOWN!

[DIANA *puts the rose down like a German soldier obeying an order.* FILUMENA *is polite again.*]

Don Domenico found the priest's advice good. He said to himself, "Fair enough: the poor woman has stood by me for twenty-five years"—and lots more that we haven't time or inclination to tell you. He came to the bedside and we were married—with two witnesses and the priest's blessing. Weddings must do people a lot of good, signorina, this one certainly did me. I felt better right away. I got up and put off dying till another time. As for you, young lady, you can't be a nurse where no one needs nursing!

[FILUMENA *sticks out the index finger of her right hand and on every emphatic word strikes* DIANA *on the chin with it. Each time* DIANA *shakes her head in an involuntary "No."*]

And as for all those nasty goings-on, making love beside the deathbed and so forth, you better go and do it in someone else's house!

DIANA [*has now backed practically to the entrance with an idiotic smile on her face*]. Yes, I see. Oh, yes!

FILUMENA. And if you can't think of a good place to go, you can go . . . can go . . . where I used to live . . .

DIANA. Where's that?

FILUMENA. Ask Don Domenico. He used to frequent such places. In fact he still does.

DIANA [*dominated by* FILUMENA'S *vehement eye, almost mechanically*]. Thank you. [*And she leaves, upstage right.*]

FILUMENA. Don't mention it. [*And takes up her position again at left.*]

DOMENICO [*who has been lost in his own thoughts, snaps back again*]. So that's the way you treat her, is it?

FILUMENA. I treat her as she deserves.

DOMENICO [*taking up the thread of his previous argument*]. You're a devil, Filumena, it isn't easy to deal with you, it isn't easy to understand what you say. But now I know you: you're like some poisonous moth—that destroys whatever it lights on. A short time ago you said something I've been thinking about. You said, "It's something else I want of you, and you'll give it to me!" It can't be money, you know I'd have given you money. [*He can't bear not knowing.*] What is it then? What are you holding back? What *do* you want of me? Speak!

FILUMENA [*simply*]. A mother's a mother.

DOMENICO. What in heaven's name do you mean by that?

FILUMENA. Children should know who their mother is.

DOMENICO. So?

FILUMENA [*her heart overflowing now*]. My children must know I'm their mother. They must know what I've done for them. I want them to love me. And they mustn't feel ashamed before other men, they mustn't be made to feel bad every time they fill out a blank!

DOMENICO. But why should they?

FILUMENA. Why should they? Why should they?! Don't you see, they've never had a family. And if you don't have a family, what's your family name? You can make one up, but what does it mean, with no relations to show, not even an uncle or an aunt? You have no name! But this is going to stop for my boys, Domenico, it's going to stop. You've given your name to *me*. Now I want it for my boys.

DOMENICO. My name?

FILUMENA. Your name's Soriano. Since this afternoon, *my* name's been Soriano, too. And now my children will be called Soriano.

[*Pause.*]

DOMENICO [*swallowing the bitter pill*]. I see. In fact I saw it coming. But I had to hear you actually say it. [*Now he is in a rage.*] You snake in the grass! [*Now he is shouting his head off.*] Adder, viper, cobra, python, boa constrictor! [*Lowering his voice a little.*] And you want to bring your brood into my nest, do you? The house of the Sorianos is to be a house of another color, the son of the Sorianos'll play host to the sons of a . . .

FILUMENA [*has kept calm but has no intention of letting him say "prostitute" again*]. The sons of . . .?

DOMENICO. The sons of Filumena Marturano. The sons of Filumena Marturano and I don't know who. *You* don't know who. You thought you'd put your conscience to rest and live down your sinful past by presenting me with three strangers to live with! I'd die first! They will never set foot in this house! I swear by the sacred memory of my father . . .

FILUMENA [*with a rush of genuine feeling and deep earnestness*]. Don't swear! I swore an oath twenty-five years ago, and I've stuck to it. Don't swear an oath you wouldn't stick to. The day will come when you'll want something from me, Domenico, so don't go swearing you'll never accept it, don't swear that, Domenico, or you'll never forgive yourself!

DOMENICO [*overawed by* FILUMENA'S *words, but angry*]. What's in your mind now, you witch? I don't fear you, understand! I'm not afraid of *you!*

FILUMENA. Then why do you have to say so?

DOMENICO. Oh, be quiet! [*Taking off his house coat.*] Alfredo, bring me my coat.

[ALFREDO *goes into the study.*]

You'll leave tomorrow. This marriage is a clear case of fraud. I'll bring suit against you. I have witnesses, remember. [*He's working himself up again.*] And if I lose, I'll destroy you anyway, Filumena. I'll chop you up in little pieces!

FILUMENA [*ironically*]. May I ask where you want to send me?

DOMENICO [*very far gone, and aggressive about it*]. Back where you came from! [ALFREDO *comes back with* DOMENICO's *coat.* DOMENICO *grabs it and puts it on. To* ALFREDO.] Tomorrow morning you'll go for my lawyer: you know who that is? [ALFREDO *nods. To* FILUMENA.] Then we'll talk.

FILUMENA. Then we'll talk.

DOMENICO. And bring your secret weapon, if you have one. You'll need it.

FILUMENA. I do have a secret weapon. I'll bring it.

DOMENICO. Well, a harlot's a harlot, Filumena Marturano! [*He leaves, laughing horribly, outrageously.*]

ROSALIA. You hear that laugh, Donna Filumena, you remember that horrible laugh? And what a horrible, nasty thing to say, too! [ROSALIA *is weeping.*]

FILUMENA [*relaxing*]. Sit down, Rosalia. [*As* ROSALIA *sits at the opposite end of the table,* FILUMENA *realizes that the cold supper is before them.*] Our supper's all ready, you see. [ROSALIA *dries her tears and begins to smile.*] And that wasn't what the voice said, it said: "A mother's a mother," Rosalia Solimene! [*She is enjoying the food.*]

ACT TWO

[*The next day at nine in the morning. In order to clean the floor the maid has put all the chairs out of the way; some are on the terrace, others upside down on the table in* DON DOMENICO'S *study. The carpet, in the center of which stands the dining table, is folded back upon itself from all four sides. It is a fine, sunny morning.*

LUCIA, *the maid, is an agreeable, healthy girl of about twenty-three. She has completed the job, and is squeezing out her scrub mop in the bucket for the last time. Then she takes mop, stick, and bucket and puts them on the terrace. She starts setting the room to rights by turning down the four sides of the carpet.*]

ALFREDO [*comes in from the outer door, tired, sleepy*]. Hi, Lucia.

LUCIA [*stopping him dead with the tone she uses—and the gesture*]. Don't come walking on my floor with those feet of yours!

ALFREDO [*yawning*]. All right, I'll walk on these hands of mine.

LUCIA. So that's your tune, is it? I've been sweating blood over this floor and . . .

ALFREDO. Tune, what tune? I—am—dead. Dead! Don Domenico kept me chasing around after him the whole night. Or sitting with him on the sea wall at Mergellina—which isn't the warmest place in the world. What made the Lord God send me to *him?* But I'm not grumbling. He's not treated me bad. No, I've seen life! Madonna! The times we had together! [*Enthusiastically.*] May the Lord let him live to be a hundred, a thousand! . . . [*Misgiving strikes him.*] But—quietly, peacefully! I wasn't born yesterday. These all-night sessions are getting to be a bit much! [*He takes a chair and sits at the table—all of which is a preparation for a daring demand.*] Lucia, can I have some hot coffee?

LUCIA [*who has put the chairs back without paying attention to* ALFREDO'S *outpouring*]. No. There isn't any.

ALFREDO [*put out*]. What d'you mean, there isn't any?

LUCIA. There isn't any. There were three cups. I drank one.

Donna Rosalia didn't want the second one so I gave it to Donna Filumena. The third cup I'm keeping for Don Domenico—in case he comes back!

ALFREDO [*glaring and not convinced*]. In case he comes back!

LUCIA. In case he comes back! Donna Rosalia hasn't made any coffee today.

ALFREDO. I suppose you couldn't make any yourself?

LUCIA. No, I couldn't. I don't even know how. Coffee's none of my business.

ALFREDO. Well, why didn't Donna Rosalia make any?

LUCIA. She went out. Early. She said she had to deliver three urgent letters. For Donna Filumena.

ALFREDO [*pricking up his ears*]. Deliver three letters for Donna Filumena? [*About to repeat himself, shouting.*] Deliver three let . . .

LUCIA. Deliver three letters for Donna Filumena.

ALFREDO [*deciding to remember his state of dire exhaustion*]. Lucia, I *must* have some hot coffee!! Know what you can do, Lucia? Pour Don Domenico his cup of coffee. Pour it right now. Go on, fill the cup, fill it to the brim! Then take the cup between finger and thumb like this and—easy, easy —pour a drop, a little drop [*He makes the gesture of pouring quite a bit of coffee from one cup to another.*] into another cup that just happens to be standing by and feeling lonely! And don't you rob your master, Rosalia Solimene! Go to your kettle of lovely steaming water and fill up his cup!

LUCIA [*dryly*]. And when he notices it?

ALFREDO. But he won't! His mind is on . . . higher things. Anyway, he may not come. [*He pulls himself together heroically.*] And age before beauty, my dear! [LUCIA *doesn't get this. So* ALFREDO *tries a simpler line.*] I need it more than he does!

LUCIA [*submitting*]. Well, let me go and heat it up for you. [*She is leaving left, but seeing* ROSALIA *enter right, she stops and tells* ALFREDO.] Here's Donna Rosalia. You still want this coffee?

ALFREDO. Donna Rosalia's here? Well, good: she can make Don Domenico some fresh coffee, can't she? Anyway, bring me that half cup.

[ROSALIA *comes into the room. She sees* ALFREDO *but pretends not to. Full of her mission, she makes a beeline for* DONNA FILUMENA'S *bedroom door.*]

ALFREDO [ROSALIA'S *attitude not having escaped him, letting her get right to the door before he calls attention to himself*]. Rosalia, what is this? Have you lost your tongue?

ROSALIA [*indifferently*]. Oh, I didn't see you.

ALFREDO. I'm the invisible man.

ROSALIA. Too bad. Little boys should be seen and not heard.

ALFREDO [*grandly ignoring this last*]. You went out early this morning, didn't you?

ROSALIA [*an enigma*]. Did I?

ALFREDO. Where were you?

ROSALIA. I was at Holy Mass, if you must know, Mr. Invisible Man!

ALFREDO [*incredulous*]. At Holy Mass. [*Remembering.*] You took Donna Filumena's three letters and placed them on the holy altar, I suppose?

ROSALIA [*trapped but controlling herself*]. Why d'you ask—if you know?

ALFREDO [*also simulating indifference*]. I was just wondering. [*Pause.*] Who did you take them to?

ROSALIA. Some little boys *like* to be heard, don't they?

ALFREDO [*this being too deep for him, he starts to bluster*]. Little boys? Little . . .

ROSALIA. You talk, Alfredo Amoroso, you talk a lot. What's more, you're a spy.

ALFREDO [*huffily*]. And when did I ever spy on you, I'd like to know!

ROSALIA. Spy on me? What'd be the use of that? My record's as clear—as water from the crystal spring! What do *I* have to be ashamed of? [*She starts to reel off her life story: the singsong expression tells us she has done so very often before.*] Born in '70. Figure for yourself how many years I have to my name—of poor but honest parents, my mother Sofia Trombetta Solimene was a washerwoman, my father, Antonio Procopio Solimene was a blacksmith. Rosalia Solimene, myself in person, entered into the holy state of matrimony with Vincenzo Bagliore, who could fix anything from an umbrella to a fireplace, on the first day of April, 1887.

ALFREDO. All Fool's Day.

ROSALIA [*stopped cold, turns a little shrill*]. Did you say something?

ALFREDO [*very lah-di-dah*]. Oh, no. [*With a gesture that says, "Pray continue, my dear madam."*] Go on!

ROSALIA. Three children were born of the union, three chil-

dren came into this world, and all at the same time. When
the midwife took the news to my husband, who was at work
in the very next street to ours, she found him with his head
in a bucket . . .

ALFREDO. Full of water from the crystal spring . . .

ROSALIA [*repeating her last phrase with severity*]. With his head
in a bucket, due to a stroke—which brought him down in
sorrow to the grave. Bereft of my husband, bereft of my
parents every one . . .

ALFREDO. All three of them . . .

ROSALIA [*as before*]. My parents every one, and with three
children to raise, I came with the good Lord's help to San
Liborio Street—number eighty, and there I made my living
by selling flyswatters, alms boxes and hats for the carnival
at Piedigrotta, especially flyswatters, which I manufactured
myself, thus earning the necessary cash for the upkeep of
the family. Donna Filumena lived at number seventy-nine.
She was a little girl then, she played with my three boys,
but when they were twenty-one they went away. They
couldn't find work here. One went to Australia, two went
to America. Haven't had word of them since. So here was
I—with my flyswatters and my paper hats, and I don't wish
to talk of it, or the blood rushes to my head, and if by
good fortune Donna Filumena hadn't taken me on when
Don Domenico came into the picture, I'd have ended up on
the steps of a church, begging. [*Pause.*]

ALFREDO [*sighing ironically*]. I suppose I'll go down in sorrow
to the grave not knowing *who* you gave those letters to.

ROSALIA [*stiffly*]. The secret mission that has been entrusted to
me cannot be made public at this time.

ALFREDO [*disappointed, and with the intensity of words carefully prepared*]. You are not a nice woman, Rosalia Solimene, you aren't nice! You have a warped mind. And an
ugly, evil face.

ROSALIA [*undismayed*]. I'm not looking for a husband.

ALFREDO [*as if nothing unpleasant had been said*]. Now, how
about sewing this button on for me? [*He shows her the
place on his coat.*]

ROSALIA [*making for the bedroom, turning ever so slightly*].
Tomorrow. If I have time.

ALFREDO. And you might put some new elastic in my shorts . . .

ROSALIA. Buy the elastic, and I'll put it in. Good-bye! [*Exit
left, with dignity.*]

[LUCIA *enters upstage left. On a small plate she carries the half cup of coffee. But she is stopped in her tracks by the doorbell. She turns her back on* ALFREDO *and goes out right to answer the door. After a pause* DOMENICO *comes in, pale and sleepy,* LUCIA *behind him. He sees the coffee.*]

DOMENICO. Is that coffee?

LUCIA [*looking meaningfully at* ALFREDO, *who has got up at the first sound of* DOMENICO'S *voice*]. Yes, signore.

DOMENICO. Give it to me. [*She does so.* DOMENICO *drinks it right off.*] Just what I needed.

ALFREDO. Just what *I* needed.

DOMENICO [*to* LUCIA]. Bring him a cup of coffee.

[*He sits at the center table, covering his face in his hands, lost in his own thoughts.* LUCIA *is making signs to* ALFREDO *to tell him that the other half cup of coffee has already been diluted.*]

ALFREDO [*shouting out in impatience and anger*]. Bring it all the same!

DOMENICO. What?

ALFREDO [*with a forced smile*]. She said the coffee's cold, and I said, bring it all the same.

DOMENICO. You went to the lawyer's?

ALFREDO. Yes.

DOMENICO. When's he coming?

ALFREDO. Whenever he can fit it in. Today for sure.

[LUCIA *comes in upstage left, carrying the full cup of diluted coffee. She gives it to* ALFREDO *and enjoys herself doing so. She leaves. Suspicious,* ALFREDO *goes through the motions of drinking.*]

DOMENICO [*continuing a thought aloud, with some fearfulness*]. It's no good!

ALFREDO [*thinking he means this diluted coffee, but resigned*]. No good at all, Don Mimi, I'll have to get some at a café when we go out . . .

DOMENICO [*disoriented*]. Some what?

ALFRED [*with conviction*]. Some coffee.

DOMENICO. What's coffee got to do with it? I was just saying that if the lawyer says I don't have a case, it's no good. I'm powerless.

ALFREDO [*is not listening. He is trying a sip of the coffee. He grimaces with disgust*]. No good? It's impossible!

DOMENICO. What do *you* know about it?

ALFREDO [*a wise guy now*]. What do *I* know? I know it turns my stomach!

DOMENICO. It makes *my* stomach turn! What a mess she's always made of things! She'll never make it!

ALFREDO. She doesn't know *how* to make it!

DOMENICO. So I'll take it to court, I'll take it to one court after another, I'll take it to the Supreme Court!

ALFREDO [*astonished, wondering if* DON DOMENICO *is crazy*]. Heavens, Don Mimi, as God's above, all for one little cup of coffee?

DOMENICO. Cup of coffee? You idiot, I'm talking about Filumena . . .

ALFREDO [*groping*]. Hm . . . [*Then it dawns.*] Ah!!! [*Then he is amused.*] Ha! Ha! [*But fearing* DON DOMENICO's *anger, he suppresses his laughter and becomes a model of gravity.*] Oh, yes, of course!

DOMENICO [*realizing what has been going on in* ALFREDO's *mind, accepts his incomprehension affectionately*]. What's the use of talking about this with you? I could talk to you about the past, but this present business . . . ? [DOMENICO *looks at* ALFREDO *as if seeing him for the first time. He analyzes his present unhappy state.*] Look at him, what has he come to? White hair, drooping eyes, baggy cheeks! Alfredo Amoroso in his second childhood!

ALFREDO [*would never contradict his master, so he pleads guilty to all and resigns himself as to fate*]. Dear God!

DOMENICO [*realizing that he himself has undergone changes*]. Do you remember a certain Don Domenico Soriano, Don Mimi—do you remember him?

ALFREDO [*his mind has been wandering and maybe he wouldn't have understood anyway.*] Who's that? Who's dead? Don Domenico? . . .

DOMENICO [*swallowing the pill*]. That's it, precisely: He's dead, Don Mimi Soriano is dead!

ALFREDO [*getting it now*]. Oh, you mean . . . *you*, Don Mimi . . . you . . . good God!

DOMENICO [*seeing himself young in his mind's eye*]. With black moustaches, thin as a rail, made night into day, never slept . . .

ALFREDO [*gaping*]. You think I don't know?

DOMENICO. Remember that girl up on Capodimonte, that girl Gelsomina? She was terrific! "Let's elope, Mimi, *do* let's elope!" I can hear her voice still. Do you remember the vet's wife?

ALFREDO. Could I ever forget her? What a woman! Her sister-in-law was quite something too: what was her job? Wool carding. Ran after her a bit myself. Pity we weren't ... er ... what do you call it? Compatible? [*Enjoying the word.*] We weren't compatible!

DOMENICO. You remember the old horse trail down to the villa? And me driving the best pair in Naples?

ALFREDO. You looked like a statue!

DOMENICO. Horses! Horses, buff and gray, *my* colors, my riding cap on my head, my whip in my hand, the finest horses in ... remember Silver Eye?

ALFREDO. Unforgettable beast! [*Nostalgically.*] Silver Eye the gray mare! She had a rump like a full moon! When you looked at that rump, you kept right on looking. It was the rising of the moon, the rising of the full moon. I fell in love with that horse. That's why I had to break off with the little wool carder. And when you sold her, oh! the soul of Alfredo Amoroso was grievous sick!

DOMENICO. Paris! London! I was God Almighty! I was master of my fate, not God Himself could change my place in the world, I was monarch of all I surveyed, king of the mountains, king of the seas, king of my own life. And now? Now, I'm through. No will, no enthusiasm, no passions, and if I do try anything, it's only to prove to myself that it isn't so, that I'm still strong, that I can still get the better of other men, that I can get the better of death itself. And I do so well I believe it! I convince myself, I surprise myself, and I go on fighting! You always have to go on fighting! Domenico Soriano never gives up and never gives in! [*Coming down to earth decisively.*] Now what's been going on here? Have you found anything out?

ALFREDO [*tentatively*]. Nothing for certain. They keep me in the dark. As I told you, Donna Filumena can't stand the sight of me. I don't know what I'm supposed to have done to her. As for Rosalia, Lucia tells me—and Rosalia confirms it—she's been delivering three urgent letters from Donna Filumena.

DOMENICO [*to whom this precise number of letters seems not without significance*]. To whom?

[FILUMENA *enters in her house dress, ungirt, followed by* ROSALIA, *who is carrying sheets and clean pillowcases. She notices the two men but pretends not to. She has heard their last words but ignores them. Concentrating on her work, she calls in the direction of the main door.*]

FILUMENA. Lucia! [*To* ROSALIA.] Give me the key.

ROSALIA [*offers her a bunch of keys*]. Here you are.

FILUMENA [*pockets the keys*]. Where is that girl? [*Shouts a bit louder.*] Lucia!

LUCIA [*entering upstage left, hurriedly*]. Yes, signora?

FILUMENA [*cutting her short*]. Take these sheets. [ROSALIA *consigns the sheets and pillowcases to* LUCIA.] In the little room next to the study, there's an ottoman, make it up as a bed . . .

LUCIA. Yes, signora.

[*She starts to go.* FILUMENA *stops her.*]

FILUMENA. Wait! I need your room, too. These are the clean sheets. You'll fix up a hammock in the kitchen.

LUCIA [*dismayed*]. All right . . . but what about my things? Must I take them all out?

FILUMENA. I've told you: I need the room!

LUCIA. But where'm I to put my things?

FILUMENA. You can use the closet in the hall.

LUCIA. All right. [*She leaves upstage right.*]

FILUMENA [*pretending to be seeing* DOMENICO *for the first time*]. You're here?

DOMENICO [*coldly*]. May I ask what all these changes mean in my house?

FILUMENA. Certainly. There are no secrets between man and wife. I need two more bedrooms.

DOMENICO. You need . . . for whom?

FILUMENA [*with precision*]. For my sons. There should have been three of them, I know. But one's married, and they have four kids, so he's staying put.

DOMENICO. They have four kids, do they? And what's this tribe called, if I may ask?

FILUMENA [*still sure of her ground*]. For the time being they have my name. Later on they'll have yours.

DOMENICO. *Not* without my consent.

FILUMENA. But you'll give your consent. [*Almost vengefully.*] You'll give your consent, Domenico. [*She exits down right.*]

DOMENICO [*unable to control himself any longer*]. I'll throw them out, understand? I'll *kick* them out!

FILUMENA [*offstage*]. Close the door, will you, Rosalia?

[ROSALIA *shuts the door in* DOMENICO's *face.*]

LUCIA [*enters upstage right, turning to* DOMENICO, *quietly*]. Signore, Signorina Diana is outside . . . with a man.

DOMENICO [*interested*]. Show them in.

LUCIA [*who has obviously tried to show them in already*]. She doesn't want to come in, signore. I said she should, but she said you should come outside to her . . . [*With conviction.*] She's afraid of Donna Filumena.

DOMENICO [*put out*]. Now look, *I* wear the pants in this house! Tell them to come in, tell them I am here!

[LUCIA *leaves upstage right.*]

ALFREDO. As soon as she sees her, she'll beat her to a pulp!

DOMENICO [*shouting so as to be heard on the other side of the closed door of the bedroom*]. She will not. Alfredo, the time has come for me to make clear who is the master in this house! She is nothing: you can all put that in your pipe and smoke it.

LUCIA [*returning apologetically*]. Signore, she won't come in. She says she can't answer for her nerves if she does.

DOMENICO. Who is it that's with her?

LUCIA. Just a man. I think she called him attorney somebody. [*Giving her private opinion.*] If you ask me, he's scared, too!

DOMENICO. Ridiculous! There'll be three grown men here! . . .

ALFREDO [*earnestly*]. Don't count me! In the state you've reduced me to I'm not worth a nickel. [*Firmly.*] No, you can all have the discussion in here. I'll go wash my face in the kitchen. [*At the door.*] When you want me, don't hesitate to call! [*He exits up left.*]

LUCIA. Well, signore, what's it to be?

DOMENICO [*swallowing*]. I'll go out.

[LUCIA *exits up left,* DOMENICO *up right.* DOMENICO *returns, bringing* DIANA *and attorney* NOCELLA *with him, insisting.*]

DOMENICO. But good heavens, I tell you, this is my house and mine alone!

DIANA [*who has remained on the threshold with Attorney* NOCELLA *behind her, very excited*]. Please, Domenico! After the scene of last night, I refuse to face that woman again!

DOMENICO. But, Diana, please, you're humiliating me. Come in, there's nothing to be afraid of!

DIANA. Afraid! *Me?* Why, I don't know what fear *is!* I simply can't be a party to *disgusting* behavior!

DOMENICO. Well, you won't be: *I* am here!

DIANA. You were here last night.

DOMENICO. Well, er, that was all . . . unexpected. Today, I assure you, you have nothing to fear. Come in. Attorney Nocella, do sit down.

DIANA [*taking several paces forward*]. Where is she?

DOMENICO. I tell you again, don't worry. Just sit down, relax!

[*They sit at the center table,* DIANA *to the left, the lawyer in the middle,* DOMENICO *on the right, facing* DIANA, *who doesn't want to let the bedroom door get out of sight. She isn't at ease.*]

DOMENICO. Now!

[NOCELLA *is a man of forty, average, rather a nonentity. Dresses with a certain sober elegance. He's discussing the Soriano case because* DIANA *has dragged him in here. His tone of voice indicates a certain lack of interest.*]

NOCELLA. I live in the same *pensione* as the signorina, that's where we got acquainted some time ago . . .

DIANA. Attorney Nocella can tell who I am, what sort of life I lead.

NOCELLA [*who doesn't want to get involved*]. We see each other at table in the evening. Of course, I'm not in the *pensione* very much. I go to court, I see my clients, and then again I'm not much of a mixer . . .

DIANA. Domenico, would you mind *awfully* if we changed seats, *would* you? [*She wants a better view of the door, so they change.*] Now, last night, at table, I told this whole story of you and Filumena.

NOCELLA. That's right. We nearly laughed our heads off!

[DOMENICO *looks daggers at him.*]

DIANA. Not at all. *I,* for one, *never* laughed!

[NOCELLA *is amazed but holds his tongue.*]

DOMENICO [*indicating* DIANA]. She was here because I had her pretend to be a nurse.

DIANA [*up in arms*]. Pretend, *pretend!* But, great heavens, I *am* a nurse! With diplomas and *everything!* Didn't I ever tell you, Domenico?

DOMENICO. No! Well, I mean . . .

DIANA [*interrupts him by clearing her throat loudly*]. Well, of course, I didn't *have* to tell you, did I? The thing is, I've explained your position to Attorney Nocella, I've told him how you can't *bear* the idea of having to stay *tied* to a woman you never chose to be tied to, and Attorney Nocella has explained to me *at length* . . .

[*A bell rings offstage.*]

DOMENICO [*who hears it*]. Excuse me, but I'll have to ask you to go into my room. There's the bell.

[LUCIA *crosses from left to right upstage.*]

DIANA [*getting up*]. Yes, I suppose we should.

[*The* ATTORNEY *gets up, too.*]

DOMENICO [*shows them into the study and follows*]. Please sit down.
NOCELLA. Thank you. [*Goes out first.*]
DIANA [*following* NOCELLA, *whispers to* DOMENICO]. You're pale as a sheet!

[DIANA *and* DOMENICO *leave.*]

LUCIA [*brings* UMBERTO *in*]. Sit down, please.

[UMBERTO *is a tall, well-built young man, dressed with modest dignity, serious looking. He loves study. His way of speaking, his sharp, observant eye, inspire respect.*]

UMBERTO. Thank you. [*He opens a notebook and makes some corrections in pencil.*]
LUCIA. Won't you sit down. Donna Filumena may be a few minutes yet.
UMBERTO. I'd like to. Thanks.

[*He sits on the left, by the terrace. The bell rings again.* LUCIA *goes to answer it. Pause. Then she re-enters with* RICCARDO.]

LUCIA. Come in here, please.

[RICCARDO *is likable, lithe, lively, with very mobile black eyes. Dressed with rather showy elegance. Looks at his wrist-watch as he enters.* LUCIA *starts to go down left.*]

RICCARDO. Hey! One moment. [LUCIA *turns back.*] How long have *you* been here?

LUCIA. Eighteen months.

RICCARDO [*quite a lad*]. You're a damn goodlooking girl, you know.

LUCIA [*flattered*]. But I'll spoil with time!

RICCARDO. Why not stop by at my store some day . . .

LUCIA. You have a store?

RICCARDO. Number seventy-four, Via Chiaia, next to the porter's lodge. I'm a shirtmaker.

LUCIA. Really? And what would I do with a man's shirt? Get along with you!

RICCARDO. I take care of men *and* women. I put the men's shirts on, and I take the women's shirts off! [*With this last pronouncement he embraces her fervently.*]

LUCIA [*disentangling herself, offended*]. Hey, stop it! [*She frees herself.*] Are you crazy? What do you take me for? I'll tell the signora! [*Thinking of* UMBERTO *who, however, isn't interested.*] And with him in the room! [*The bell rings.* LUCIA *starts to go.*]

RICCARDO [*noticing* UMBERTO *for the first time, amused*]. Why, look! And I never even saw him!

LUCIA [*right back at him*]. You don't see much. Except bad women . . .

RICCARDO [*with an insinuation*]. You'll come to the store?

LUCIA [*holding her ground*]. Number seventy-four? [*Looking at him admiringly.*] Via Chiaia? [*At a sign from* RICCARDO *meaning "yes."*] I'll be there. [*Exit* LUCIA *upstage right. In the doorway she throws him a meaningful smile.*]

RICCARDO [*walks up and down a little. A couple of times his eyes meet* UMBERTO'S. *He is slightly uncomfortable.*] Nice girl. [*Pause.*] Don't you think so?

UMBERTO. It's all one to me.

RICCARDO. How's that? Studying to be a priest?

[UMBERTO *pays no attention to him. Goes on writing.*]

LUCIA [*bringing in* MICHELE]. Step this way, please.

[MICHELE *is dressed in his blue plumber's overalls. He carries a bag of tools. In good health, flourishing, rather fat. He takes off his beret as he comes in.*]

MICHELE. What goes on here, Lucia? Is it that bathroom faucet again? I thought I soldered it good.

LUCIA. No, it's working.

MICHELE. Then what is it this time?

LUCIA. Nothing, nothing at all. The faucets are fine. Just wait while I call Donna Filumena. [*Exit* LUCIA *down left.*]

MICHELE [*speaks deferentially to* RICCARDO]. Good morning, sir.

[RICCARDO *nods curtly.*]

There's nobody to mind the shop!

[RICCARDO *gives him another look.* MICHELE *consents to be more explanatory.*]

I mean, I hope she'll come soon. [*He takes a cigarette butt out of his pocket.*] Anyone got a light?

RICCARDO [*haughtily*]. Sorry, no.

MICHELE. Smoking strictly prohibited. [*Awkward pause.*] You're a relative?

RICCARDO. Is this a court of inquiry?

MICHELE. How d'you mean?

RICCARDO. My friend, I can see you're crazy about discussions. I'm not.

MICHELE. You should remember your manners, *you* should!

UMBERTO [*intervening*]. He forgot them years ago.

RICCARDO. Now look here . . .

UMBERTO. Excuse me, you come in here as if you owned the place, you throw your arms around the housemaid, while doing so you see me, and aren't in the least embarrassed, and now you spit on this poor creature.

MICHELE [*coming right back at* UMBERTO]. Poor creature, am I? If anyone spits on me, *he'll* get an eyeful! [*Turning to* RICCARDO.] You can thank your stars we're indoors.

RICCARDO. You *annoy* me, understand? Indoors or out!

MICHELE [*puts his tool bag down, turning pale*]. Let's see then! [MICHELE *comes slowly toward* RICCARDO.]

RICCARDO [*comes toward him with the same stealth*]. Sure, let's see!

[UMBERTO *now tries to intervene. He aims at stopping either of them taking the initiative.*]

MICHELE [*angry at* UMBERTO]. You little sonofa . . . [*He aims a blow at* UMBERTO, *but the latter, too quick for him, only receives half its force.*] You get out of the way!

[*Now there's a real scuffle at close quarters with many blows and kicks that miss their mark and with words, or rather half-words, spoken in rage between clenched teeth.*]

FILUMENA [*comes in from down left, her tone brisk*]. What's going on here?

[ROSALIA *follows at her heels.*]

[*The* THREE SONS *pull out of the scrimmage at the first sound of* FILUMENA'S *voice. They are now ranged in front of her trying to look as if nothing had happened.*]

FILUMENA. Now, where do you all think you are?
UMBERTO [*rubbing a sore nose*]. I was trying to keep them apart.
RICCARDO. So was I.
MICHELE. Me, too.
FILUMENA. So who was doing the fighting?
THE THREE SONS [*in unison*]. Not me!
FILUMENA. You ought to be ashamed. [*Pause. She has momentarily lost her briskness. Is at a loss.*] Boys, I, er . . . [*Trying again.*] well, how *is* everything?

[*There is another slight pause till* MICHELE *decides to be the first to speak up.*]

MICHELE. I've nothing to gripe about—thanks be to God.
FILUMENA. How are the children?
MICHELE. Pretty good. Last week the middle one had a bit of fever, now he's okay. He ate four pounds of grapes. Mamma wasn't looking, I wasn't home, his tummy was like a big drum, but you know how it is with four kids. If it isn't one, it's the other, there's always something. Take the way all of mine like castor oil. When we give it to one of them, the other three shout the house down till we give it to them too. Two hours later there they all are on their little pots—in a row!
UMBERTO [*breaking up this low conversation*]. I got your note, signora. I'm afraid your name didn't mean a thing to me. It was the address that started me thinking. I realized that this Donna Filumena was someone I see nearly every evening on my way to the newspaper office. One time I even walked her home—to this address—she had a sore foot and couldn't walk properly. It was a pleasure to help her . . . [*Drawing breath for an eloquent paragraph.*] My reconstruction of the story . . .
FILUMENA. I had a sore foot, that's right.
RICCARDO [*to bring things to a point*]. Now what's it all about?
FILUMENA [*to* RICCARDO]. How's the store doing?

RICCARDO. Fine, why shouldn't it? Though if all my customers were like you, I'd have to shut up shop in a month. Excuse my frankness, signora, but when *you* come there, I feel like running for cover. You give me such a time. You make me unpack every piece of merchandise in the place. "No, not this, I'll take that, no, not that, I must think it over!" And you leave the store in such a mess it'd take a staff of fifty to put it straight.

FILUMENA [*maternally*]. I simply mustn't trouble you in future, must I?

RICCARDO [*taken aback*]. I don't mean that, signora! The customer's the boss, after all. I just meant I can only sweat through one shirt at a time.

FILUMENA [*at ease now*]. Well, now, I've called you all together for a serious reason. If you'll step in here [*Pointing to her bedroom.*] for a moment, we can talk it over . . .

DOMENICO [*comes in from the study followed by* NOCELLA. *He again speaks in his normal tone, that of a man who is sure of himself. He turns to* FILUMENA *with good-natured energy*]. That won't be necessary, Filumena, let's not mix things up even worse than they are already. [*To the* ATTORNEY.] I'm no lawyer, but I said it would be this way. I thought of it before you did, it was plain to me as the nose on your face! [*To* FILUMENA, *who is looking doubtingly at* NOCELLA.] This is Attorney Nocella. He's going to clarify this whole situation. [*To the* THREE SONS.] The signora made a mistake. She has brought you here for nothing. You may go—we're sorry for the inconvenience.

FILUMENA. Just a moment! I made no mistake, sending for these boys, and what business is it of yours anyway?

DOMENICO [*meaningfully*]. You think we can say it all before strangers?

FILUMENA [*grasps the fact that somehow the whole course of things has changed,* DOMENICO's *tone makes this unmistakable. She turns to the* THREE BOYS.] Will you be patient for another five minutes, boys? Wait for me on the terrace, will you?

[UMBERTO *and* MICHELE *start off in that direction with a little hesitation.*]

RICCARDO [*looking at his watch*]. Listen, signora. I think you take advantage of people. I've got things to do . . .

FILUMENA [*losing her temper*]. Didn't I say there was a serious reason? [*Treating him as a little boy, in a tone that admits or no reply.*] Go out on the terrace. The others are waiting, you'll wait too!

RICCARDO [*disconcerted by her firmness*]. Well, all right. [*He will leave with the other two.*]

FILUMENA [*to* ROSALIA]. Give them some coffee, Rosalia.

ROSALIA. Yes, Donna Filumena. [*To the three of them.*] Go out on the balcony and sit down. [*Showing them where to sit.*] And I'll be right out with some lovely coffee!

[*She exits upstage left, while the* BOYS *go out on the terrace.*]

FILUMENA. Well?

DOMENICO [*loftily*]. This gentleman is a lawyer. Suppose you talk to *him*.

FILUMENA [*impatiently*]. What good ever came of the law?

[DOMENICO *clears his throat audibly.*]

Well, what is it?

NOCELLA. It's like this, signora, as I said, this . . . er . . . situation is no business of mine . . .

FILUMENA. Then what d'you want?

NOCELLA. That's just it. It's no business of mine in the sense that this gentleman isn't my client, nor has he summoned me . . .

FILUMENA. Were you sent? Or did you just come?

NOCELLA. Well, now, signora, I could *never* permit myself to be *sent* . . .

DOMENICO [*to* FILUMENA]. For God's sake, let him speak!

NOCELLA. The signorina told me about the case. [*Looking back toward the study.*] Where is she?

DOMENICO [*rather irritated, and trying to bring the discussion back on the rails*]. Attorney Nocella, I think, well, who told you is beside the point. State your conclusions.

FILUMENA [*looking toward the study*]. She's in there, is she, she just hasn't the courage to show herself! Go on, Mr. Lawyer!

NOCELLA. In the situation described by this gentleman . . . no, by the young lady . . .

[DOMENICO *coughs peremptorily.*]

. . . dealing with cases of this sort . . . well, I've found a CLAUSE. [*He is a drowning man, the CLAUSE is a straw.*] Clause Number 101! [*He takes a paper from his pocket.*] "Matrimony under imminent peril of death." [*Starting to reel it off.*] "In the case of imminent peril of death . . . "

[Another cough from DOMENICO *stops him.]*

It explains all the different possibilities. But then this was *not* a case of imminent peril of death—because your imminent peril was peril pretended or peril feigned, that comes under another heading . . .

DOMENICO. I have witnesses: Alfredo, Lucia, the janitor, Rosalia . . .

FILUMENA. The nurse.

DOMENICO. The nurse. All of them. No sooner was the priest out of the room than she bounced out of bed and shouted, "We're man and wife, Domenico Soriano!"

NOCELLA. So the clause we want is Number 122: *"Violence and error."* *[He digs another paper out of his pocket and reads.]* "The validity of a marriage may be impugned by one or other of the parties if his or her consent has been extorted by violence or granted in error." The consent of this gentleman, having been granted in error, I submit, on the basis of Clause 122, that the validity of this marriage . . .

FILUMENA. Attorney Nocella, I don't know what you're talking about.

DOMENICO *[confident that he has understood]*. Don't you see? I married you because you were about to die . . .

NOCELLA. No! Matrimony is unconditional! Clause 164. *[He recites by heart this time.]* "Should the aforesaid parties add, spend, or otherwise affix restrictions, qualifications, modifications, or other conditions, no priest of the church, no official of the state may proceed to the celebration of matrimony."

DOMENICO. But you said, if there was no imminent peril of death . . .

FILUMENA. Be quiet, you don't understand it any more than I do. Mr. Lawyer, explain it to us.

NOCELLA *[offering her the paper]*. Read it for yourself.

FILUMENA *[after a moment's hesitation, takes the paper and tears it very deliberately in two. Her voice is low]*. What use is paper to me? The likes of Filumena Marturano can't read, Mr. Lawyer!

NOCELLA *[roused]*. Signora, since you were *not* dying, your marriage is annulled, your marriage is not valid.

FILUMENA. What about the priest?

NOCELLA. The priest says it was a desecration of the Sacrament. The marriage is not valid.

FILUMENA *[livid]*. Not valid! I had to die?

NOCELLA. Exactly.

FILUMENA. If I *had* died . . .

NOCELLA. The marriage would have been valid.

FILUMENA. And he could have married again, he could have had children?

NOCELLA. Naturally. This hypothetical wife would have been marrying the deceased Signora Soriano's widower.

DOMENICO. You *would* have been Signora Soriano . . . but dead.

FILUMENA. The idea appeals to you, doesn't it? [*Changing her tone.*] All I've ever wanted is a family. I spend a lifetime at it, and now the law says "no." Is that justice, Mr. Lawyer?

NOCELLA. The law, my dear signora, cannot uphold *your* principles—however human they may be—if it thereby becomes accessory to measures operating to the detriment of a third person. Domenico Soriano has no intention of marrying you.

DOMENICO. And if you don't believe Attorney Nocella, consult any lawyer you do believe.

FILUMENA. I believe him. Not because you say the same thing —you have your own fish to fry. Not because *he's* a lawyer, I don't know lawyers. I believe him because you can look me in the face. D'you think I don't know you by this time? Why, you're your old self again, you're cocky, you're the boss, when I look at you, you look right back. That means you're telling the truth, Domenico. When you tell a lie, you don't know *where* to look, you start looking for flies on the ceiling!

DOMENICO. Attorney Nocella, proceed.

NOCELLA. As you wish, Signor Soriano.

FILUMENA [*is still pondering the lawyer's sentence, "Domenico Soriano has no intention of marrying you." Through the following speech she becomes more and more wrought up*]. Domenico Soriano has no intention of marrying me. I've no intention of marrying him either. I don't want you. Go on, Mr. Lawyer, I don't want him anymore! It's not true I was dying, I admit it, I just wanted to cheat him. I'd stolen from him before, and now I wanted to steal—a name, a family name! But, as for the law, there's the sort of law that makes people cry, isn't there, Mr. Lawyer? I want you to know there's another law—that makes people *laugh*— and that's the law for me! [*In the hard tone of Act One.*] You boys, come in now!

DOMENICO [*who'd like to smooth things over*]. Filumena, stop!

FILUMENA [*violently*]. You be quiet!

[*The* THREE SONS *come in from the balcony, rather disoriented, and take up their positions in the center of the stage.* ROSALIA *comes in upstage left with the coffee. She sees that this isn't the right moment and puts her tray on a sideboard. She listens. She gets gradually nearer* FILUMENA *down the left side of the stage. Now the stage is set.* FILUMENA *continues.*]

FILUMENA. Now listen to what I have to say. [*Indicating* DOMENICO *and the* LAWYER.] That's people, that's the world. The world with its rights of men, and laws, and clauses, the world that defends itself with pen and paper: Attorney Nocella and Don Domenico Soriano. [*Striking herself on the chest.*] And I am Filumena Marturano. A woman who doesn't know the law. A woman who wants a law of her own. A woman who can't cry. You see my eyes, how dry they are? Like tinder. [*Looking straight at the* THREE BOYS.] I am your mother.

DOMENICO. Filumena!

FILUMENA [*grimly*]. Who are you to stop me telling them? [*To* NOCELLA.] Can I tell 'em or not? What does the law say to that? [*More aggressively than emotionally.*] You are my children. I am Filumena Marturano—there's no need to explain *that* name, young fellows like you will have heard of me. [*They are petrified.*] I have nothing to say of Filumena Marturano. But I remember a girl of seventeen . . . [*Her mind fills with memories. Pause.*] Do you know the slums of Naples, Mr. Lawyer? San Giovaniello, Vergini, Forcella, Tribunale, Pallonetto. Do you know the smoke, the blackness? In summer you can't breathe for the heat, there are too many people. In winter the cold makes your teeth chatter. The narrow streets swarming with grimy children, the hovels they live in, dark even at noon. In one of those ratholes, San Liborio Street, lived the Marturanos, a mob of Marturanos. What became of them all later, what the end was, I don't know, I don't want to know. But I can see us as we were then, I can see the sullen faces, the crowded beds. We went to sleep without a good night, we got up without a good morning. I can only remember one thing my father ever said, and I wish I could forget that. I was thirteen, and he said, "You're a big girl now: do you know there's nothing to eat?" How hot it was! You could hardly breathe! I can see us sitting around the table every evening. The table had one large dish on it and forks all around, nothing but forks. There was no pleasure at those meals. If I dropped my fork, I felt I'd been caught stealing.

[*Pause.*]

I don't know when I found out that some people aren't poor. I used to stand on the corner of some big street downtown and look at all the people with good shoes on, good clothes, and the good girls on the arm of their good husbands-to-be. One evening—when I was seventeen—I saw a girl I knew. I hardly recognized her, she was so dressed up—though maybe any decent clothes seemed dressy to me at that time. She told me things. [*Pause.*] I didn't close my eyes all night. How hot it was! [*Abruptly.*] That's how I got to know you. There. Remember? Maybe you didn't think much of the place—to me it was a palace. One evening I went to see the family on Liborio Street. I was all of a tremble. I said to myself: "They won't look me in the face, they'll throw me out!" No one said a thing. Someone offered me a chair. Someone even stroked my cheek. I was a visitor from the great world, so they scraped the floor before me. Only my mother . . . well, when I went over to say good-bye, there were tears in her eyes. That was Filumena's last home-coming. [*Pause.*] Not a pretty story, is it? All I'll say for myself is this: I didn't murder my children. For twenty-five years I've thought of nothing else. My family! [*If there's a light in her eyes at this moment, she comes down to earth at once and addresses herself directly to the* THREE BOYS.] And here you are! I've raised you, I've made men of you, I've stolen from him [*Indicating* DOMENICO.] to bring you up . . .

MICHELE [*comes over to* FILUMENA, *full of emotion*]. All right, all right, that's enough . . . [*He is almost too moved to speak.*] What more could you have done?

UMBERTO [*also coming over, gravely*]. There are so many things I wish I could say. I'm not much good at talking, though. I'll write you a letter.

FILUMENA [*simply*]. I don't know how to read.

UMBERTO [*quietly*]. I'll read it to you.

[*Pause.* FILUMENA *waits for her third son to come over, but* RICCARDO *goes out through the door without a word.*]

FILUMENA [*after a pause*]. He's gone.

UMBERTO [*with sympathy*]. Oh, that's just him. He didn't understand. Tomorrow I'll stop by and talk to him.

MICHELE. You can come with me, signora. It's a small place, but there's a room. There's a terrace. [*Cheerfully.*] The kids are always asking me, "Where's granny? Where's granny?" And I always have to make something up! Now I'll go home and say, "She's here!" and it'll be like the carnival of Piedigrotta. [*Urging her.*] Let's be going!

FILUMENA [*firmly*]. Yes. I'll come.

MICHELE. Fine, let's go then.

FILUMENA. Just a moment. Wait for me at the gate [*To* UMBERTO.] You can go down together. I need ten minutes —to tell Domenico something.

MICHELE [*happily*]. Good, I'll do that. [*To* UMBERTO.] You're coming?

UMBERTO. Sure I'll come with you.

MICHELE. Good-bye, everybody! [*To* UMBERTO.] I could tell there was something, that's why I wanted to talk!

[*They leave.*]

FILUMENA. Mr. Lawyer [*She points to the study.*], give us two minutes.

NOCELLA. No, I think I'll be leaving.

FILUMENA. No, no, just two minutes, you should be here when I'm through talking to Don Domenico. Go and sit down.

[NOCELLA *reluctantly goes into the study. Without a word,* ROSALIA *exits down left.*]

FILUMENA [*after a pause, calmly*]. I'm going, Domenico. Tell the lawyer to do whatever a lawyer does. I deny nothing. I leave you free.

DOMENICO. I should think so. You could have just asked for money instead of making all this song and dance.

FILUMENA [*still very calm*]. Tomorrow I'll send for my things.

DOMENICO. You're crazy, if you ask me. What do you want to do to those three boys? Destroy their peace of mind? Who put you up to it? *Why* did you say that?

[*Pause.*]

FILUMENA [*coldly*]. Because one of those three boys is your son.

[DOMENICO *turns to stone. A long pause.*]

DOMENICO. Do you know what you're saying?

FILUMENA [*without change in manner*]. One of those three boys is your son.

DOMENICO [*not daring to shout. Intensely*]. Quiet!

FILUMENA. I could have said they were all your sons, you'd have believed it, I'd have made you believe it, but it isn't so. I know what you're thinking, you're thinking I could have told you. But I couldn't. Because you wouldn't have treated the other two right. Men are all alike, Domenico, and children are all alike. Children are created equal, too.

DOMENICO. You're lying!

FILUMENA. No, Domenico, no! Let me remind you. You can't remember because you were always going off . . . London, Paris . . . the races . . . other women . . . Let me remind you. Remember how much you paid me? You used to leave a hundred lire bill on the dressing table. Do you remember the night you said to me, "Filumena, we love each other," just before you put the light out? You didn't love me, Domenico, but I loved you. You were joking, and when you switched the light on again, you gave me the usual hundred lire bill. I put the date on it—I know numbers even if I don't know writing. Then you went on another trip. I waited. Like Our Lady of the Sorrows. You don't remember what happened, I didn't tell you, I told you my life was still the same, and it was true: when I saw you hadn't understood, I went back to—the old life.

DOMENICO [*half to himself, slightly less convinced*]. It isn't true.

FILUMENA. Domenico, I swear it by the Madonna of the Roses!

DOMENICO [*believing without hesitation*]. Ah! [*Pause.*] Which one is it, then?

FILUMENA [*firmly*]. I won't tell. [*Trying to smile it off.*] Men are created equal.

DOMENICO [*after a short pause, firmly*]. You're lying, the whole story is a lie! You'd have told me at the time, so you could keep me, so you could hold me in the hollow of your hand. You'd have told me at the time. *That* would have been a secret weapon, Filumena Marturano, and you want me to believe you wouldn't have used it?

FILUMENA. I wouldn't have used it. Because you wouldn't have let my children live. I thought that then, and I think it now. You'd have had me murder them, Domenico, so I didn't dare tell you. But for me your son would be dead.

DOMENICO. Which of them is he?

FILUMENA. Children are created equal.

DOMENICO [*at his wits' end, nasty*]. They're equal all right—
your children. I don't want to see them. Get out! I don't
know them. I don't know—my son.

FILUMENA. Yesterday I said, "The day will come when you'll
want something from me, so don't go swearing you'll never
accept it." Remember? Now you know *why* I said it.
Good-bye, Domenico. But let me promise you one thing:
If you tell my children what I've told you, I'll kill you.
And I don't just talk about killing the way you do. A
promise is a promise to Filumena Marturano. [FILUMENA
breaks off. Calls briskly in the direction of the study.] Mr.
Lawyer! Come out of hiding, I won't hurt you. You've
won your point, and I'm going. [*In the direction of the
bedroom*.] Rosalia! I'm going. Tomorrow I'll send someone
for my things.

[*The* LAWYER *comes out of the study followed by* DIANA.
From the left comes ROSALIA *and from upstage right comes*
ALFREDO.]

FILUMENA. Good luck to you all! Patience, Rosalia! Good-bye
to you, Mr. Lawyer! And no ill feelings! [*To* DOMENICO,
good-humoredly.] You've understood, haven't you, Domenico? I'll say it again in front of everyone: what I've told
you is a secret. Tell nobody nothing. [*She takes a locket
from her breast, opens it, and takes out a hundred lire
bill, folded very small. She tears a piece off and puts it
back in the locket*.] Here's a hundred lire bill. I'm tearing off
one corner, there's something written on it that I may
need one day. [*Throwing the bill in* DOMENICO's *face*.]
The hundred lire are for you, I hope you'll find it useful—
even if you can't buy a son with it, Domenico Soriano!

ACT THREE

[*Ten months later. Flowers everywhere. Many of them in beautifully arranged baskets with the donors' names sticking out on cards. The flowers are of delicate shades: not red, but not white either. The whole house breathes an atmosphere of festivity. The curtains between the dining room and the study are closed. It is almost evening.*

ROSALIA enters in her best black silks from upstage right. At the same time DOMENICO comes in from the study: he is wearing a smart blue suit. This man has undergone a complete change. There is no sign now—in gesture or tone of voice—of his old domineering nature. He has become mild and humble. His hair is a shade whiter, too. ROSALIA is moving across down left when he stops her.]

DOMENICO. You've been out already, Rosalia?

ROSALIA. I've been doing an errand for Donna Filumena.

DOMENICO. What errand's that?

ROSALIA [*with good-natured insinuation*]. Are you jealous, Don Domenico? I've been to San Liborio Street.

DOMENICO. San Liborio Street? What for?

ROSALIA [*playfully*]. Ah! So he *is* jealous!

DOMENICO [*with quiet irony*]. Terribly jealous, I've noticed it myself.

ROSALIA [*not wishing to needle him*]. Nonsense, it's just old Rosalia's little joke. [*Looking apprehensively toward FILUMENA'S room.*] I'll tell you, but you mustn't tell Donna Filumena I've told you, she doesn't want you to know . . .

DOMENICO. Then don't tell me!

ROSALIA. Silly man! I'm doing a good deed, telling you, it's something that does Donna Filumena credit. [*Then in a dramatic whisper.*] She had me carry a thousand lire and fifty candles to the Madonna of the Roses in San Liborio Street. [*Becoming more explanatory.*] You know the old crone who lives on the corner and looks after the lamp and the flowers and everything? I had to go to her and say, "Donna Filumena wants you to light these candles at six this evening—on the nose!"

DOMENICO. Six o'clock on the nose?

ROSALIA. Don't you know the time of your own wedding, Don

Domenico? At six o'clock on the nose, you and Donna
Filumena will be man and wife. Good and proper this time.
And while you're getting married in here, the candles will
be lit in San Liborio Street at the feet of the Madonna of
the Roses.

DOMENICO. I see.

ROSALIA. You're marrying an angel from heaven, Don Domè.
A young girl of an angel, too. She gets younger and lovelier
every day. I knew everything was all right. "You think
Don Domenico'll forget you?" I said to her. "Him getting
the marriage annulled, that was just one of his tantrums,
the marriage bells haven't stopped ringing for *you*, Donna
Filu . . ."

DOMENICO. That will do, Rosalia. Now suppose you go to
your mistress.

ROSALIA. I'm going, I'm going. [*But* ROSALIA *can't be hustled.*]
You're marrying an angel from heaven. If it wasn't for her,
I've have come to a bad end. She took me in, and here I
stayed, and here I am, and here I shall die. I have everything ready for the day, a lovely long white shirt with a
fine piece of lace to it, white stockings, nice underclothes,
a bonnet on my head, I have it all ready in the oak chest,
and Donna Filumena knows about it, too, she's going to
lay me out herself, she's all I have, of course my boys may
come back, where there's life there's hope . . . [*Checking
herself with a big sniff.*] You don't mind if I leave now, do
you, Don Domè? [*Exits down left.*]

[*Alone,* DOMENICO *walks around the room a little, looking at
the flowers, reading the cards. Then he involuntarily com-
pletes his thoughts aloud.*]

DOMENICO. Well, this is it!

[*From upstage right are heard the voices of the* THREE SONS.]

MICHELE. Six o'clock, the ceremony is at six o'clock.

RICCARDO. But you were supposed to be there before . . .

UMBERTO. *I* was on time anyway!

[*They enter.*]

MICHELE. I guess we said five, but I was only three quarters
of an hour late.

RICCARDO. And you didn't let us know.

MICHELE. Now look. When you say meet me at five, that

means sort of *around* five, and what's around five? Five-twenty, five-thirty, quarter of six . . .

RICCARDO. A quarter past eight the morning after, the following month, two years later . . .

MICHELE. Oh, come on. It's like this. We got a clock as a wedding present. But how long d'you suppose it lasted when the first kid started walking?

UMBERTO [*seeing* DON DOMENICO]. Hello—Don Domenico.

RICCARDO [*greeting him in the same deferential way*]. Don Domenico.

MICHELE. Don Domenico.

[*They are again ranged across the center of the stage, silent.*]

DOMENICO. Hello to you! [*Long pause.*] Well? Why've you stopped talking? You were discussing . . .

UMBERTO [*confused*]. Yes, that's right . . .

RICCARDO [*starting off confidently but collapsing*]. Why, sure, we were just saying . . . just saying . . .

MICHELE [*cheerfully*]. Well, you have to stop talking some-time!

DOMENICO. As soon as you see me, in fact. [*To* MICHELE.] You were late for your appointment?

MICHELE. Yes, sir, Don Domenico.

DOMENICO [*to* RICCARDO]. But you were on time?

RICCARDO. Yes, sir, Don Domenico.

DOMENICO [*to* UMBERTO]. How about you?

UMBERTO. Right on time, Don Domenico.

[*Pause.*]

DOMENICO. Well, sit down anyway.

[*They sit facing him.*]

The ceremony is at six. [*Pause.*] So there's time. [*Pause.*] At six the priest will be here. [*Pause.*] No guests, just our-selves, that's how Filumena wanted it. [*Pause.*] I just want to tell you . . . [*Pause.*] I think I even did tell you once before . . . [*Pause.*] This "Don Domenico" stuff isn't . . . right.

UMBERTO [*tentatively*]. No—it isn't.

MICHELE. It isn't right at all.

UMBERTO. But . . . er . . . you haven't said . . . . what you want us to call you.

DOMENICO. Well, you see, I couldn't help hoping—you'd come

to your own conclusions. This evening I'm marrying your
mother. And as for . . . the part of it that concerns you,
I've been to my lawyer about it, and by tomorrow you'll all
be called Soriano.

[*The three of them look at each other to decide who should
speak first.*]

UMBERTO [*plucking up courage*]. Well, you see . . . I know I
can answer for the three of us, we all feel the same way.
[*Bracing himself for a statement.*] We're not children, we're
men, so it isn't easy for us to . . . er . . . call you . . .
what you wish to be called, generous and fair as that wish
is. . . . There are certain things you have to feel, here.
[*He presses his hand to his heart.*]

DOMENICO [*scrutinizing* UMBERTO *intently*]. As for you, then,
you don't feel this . . . er . . . desire, this need to call
someone—me, for instance—father?

UMBERTO. I wouldn't want to lie to you, you deserve better
than that of me, so—for now at least—I'll have to say—
No!

DOMENICO [*is disappointed, and his interest shifts to* RIC-
CARDO]. What about you?

RICCARDO. The same with me.

DOMENICO [*turning his inquiring eyes on* MICHELE]. And you?

MICHELE [*coming straight out with it*]. Not me, Don Domenico.

DOMENICO. I see. [*He is discouraged.*] Such things come with
time. You get used to them gradually. [*Cheering up a bit.*]
Well, boys, it's good to be with you, you're fine fellows,
you all know how to look after yourselves. [*He is thinking
hard now.*] One in one field, another in another, fine fellows! [*Turning abruptly on* UMBERTO.] You work on a
paper, don't you? From what they tell me, you're keen
on your work, too, you take pride in it, you're a writer,
you do articles . . .

UMBERTO. Short stories, too, once in a while.

DOMENICO. Stories, too. Your ambition is to be a great writer?

UMBERTO. Oh, I wouldn't say great.

DOMENICO. Why not? It's early days yet. [*Very interested
now.*] Of course, to succeed in a field like yours, you have
to have it in you from the start, don't you? Genius has
to run in the family, so to speak.

UMBERTO. I don't know if I do have it in me. You don't

know how discouraged I get. I say to myself, "Umbè,
don't fool yourself, this isn't what you're cut out for at all."
DOMENICO [*wonders now what he is cut out for*]. Then what
is? What do you really *like* to do?
UMBERTO. Lord knows! You have dreams of all sorts—when
you're young.
RICCARDO [*rather grandly*]. It's all coincidence. For instance:
how is it I have a store in Via Chiaia? Because I made love
to a girl. Because the girl was a shirtmaker. Because . . .
DOMENICO [*jumping at this chance*]. You've made love to a lot
of girls?
RICCARDO. So so. I've not done bad.

[DOMENICO's *interest is aroused. He gets up to have a better
look at* RICCARDO. *He is on the lookout for any gestures or
inflection that he can attach to his own youth.*]

RICCARDO. Fact is, I have trouble finding the right type. I see
a girl, I like her, I say, "That's for me, I'll marry her." But
then I see another, and I seem to like her even more. I just
can't explain it, there's always this other girl—the one I
like better than the one I've got . . .
DOMENICO [*switching back to* UMBERTO]. Whereas *you* keep
calm. You don't lose your head about the girls. You think
it over.
UMBERTO. Well, yes—and no. There isn't much to think over
in the girls of today. There are good-looking girls everywhere. It's choosing that's hard. What can you do? You
have to run through quite a few—just to find the one you
really want!

[DOMENICO *concludes that there's the same tendency in* RIC-
CARDO *as in* UMBERTO, *so he turns to* MICHELE.]

DOMENICO [*to* MICHELE]. What about you? Do you go for
women?
MICHELE. I asked for trouble and I got it. I met my wife,
and . . . good-bye, Michele! So now I live with both feet
in one slipper. With my wife there's no fooling around, if
you follow me: it isn't that I don't like the other girls, I
don't like trouble, that's what . . .
DOMENICO [*discouraged*]. So you like women, too. [*Pause.
Now he's off on another tack.*] When I was a young fellow,
I used to sing. We all used to get together, seven or eight
of us. We used to go and serenade the ladies. Or we'd have

supper on the terrace in summer, and the supper would turn into a concert, we'd sing Neapolitan songs to the mandolin or the guitar. . . . Which of you can sing?

UMBERTO. I can't.

RICCARDO. Nor me neither.

DOMENICO [*happy at having eliminated two from the contest. To* MICHELE]. And you?

MICHELE. I can! I couldn't work without it. I sing all the time!

DOMENICO [*getting excited*]. Come on, then, let's hear you!

MICHELE [*already sorry he spoke up*]. What shall I sing?

DOMENICO. Anything you like, go ahead, sing!

MICHELE [*swallowing hard*]. I'm . . . er . . . ashamed!

DOMENICO. But you said you sang all the time!

MICHELE. I do. In the shop. Okay, you know "Monastery of Santa Chiara," it's good. [*He sings. His voice is negligible in volume and hideous in quality.*] "Munastero 'e Santa Chiara, tengo 'o core scuro scuro . . ."

RICCARDO [*at a certain point interrupts him*]. If that's singing, *I* can sing, too!

MICHELE [*insulted*]. What d'you mean, *if* that's singing?

UMBERTO. So can I! If that's singing, *I* can sing!

DOMENICO [*to* RICCARDO]. Let's hear you first.

RICCARDO. Naw, naw, impossible, I don't have the gall he has, of course I know the tune . . . [*He stops awkwardly.* DOMENICO *is silent, waiting for him to sing. So he strikes up.*] "Munastero 'e Santa Chiara . . ."

[*When he comes to the second line,* UMBERTO *joins in.* MICHELE *follows suit on the third. When they come to the top note of the song, loudly but not in unison and not together in rhythm,* DOMENICO *interrupts.*]

DOMENICO [*roaring the first words after which they stop*]. All right! [*Quietly.*] That will do, thank you. [*Sighing.*] Three Neapolitans, and not one of them can sing: what are we coming to?

[FILUMENA *comes in wearing lovely new clothes in comely colors. Skirt and blouse: the blouse of golden-yellow taffeta with flowers sewn into it, all this in two lighter tones, the skirt to be taffeta, too, but black. Her hair is piled high on her head in Neapolitan style. A few jewels, two ropes of pearls, a gold necklace, earrings. She looks almost youthful.*]

FILUMENA. You're just refusing to see it, Rosalia, it is wrong . . .

[TERESINA *comes in followed by* ROSALIA *and* LUCIA. *She is a dressmaker of the Neapolitan type. She is impassive, her customers' insults are just water on a duck's back, and her tranquillity irritates.*]

TERESINA. It's all your imagination, Donna Filumena, and after all the years I've worked for you . . .

FILUMENA. You have the gall to say it's right when you know very well it's all wrong?

TERESINA. I should say it's all wrong wrong just to please you, I suppose!

MICHELE [*approaching*]. Hello—Mother!

UMBERTO. Hello—and congratulations.

RICCARDO. Congratulations!

FILUMENA. You're all here already? Hello! [*To* TERESINA.] Now you know what's wrong with this skirt as well as I do: it's too tight! And why is it too tight? Because you didn't use enough silk. And why didn't you use enough silk? Because whenever you pick up a nice piece of silk, you cut a slice off for your little girl.

TERESINA [*bridling*]. I do, do I?

FILUMENA. I was in your house myself, and I saw your little girl all dressed up in the silk you'd cut out of my skirt!

TERESINA. I'll really have to get mad at you, Donna Filumena! Course, if there's some left over, I'm not saying . . . But you're right, the customer comes first, that's always been my motto!

ROSALIA. Donna Filumena, you're the loveliest bride I ever saw!

FILUMENA [*shrilly*]. I won't have you stealing from *me*, understand!

TERESINA [*imperturbable*]. Now you're going *too* far, Donna Filumena! I swear by all that's holy . . .

DOMENICO. Filumena, can I speak to you for a moment?

FILUMENA [*limping a little in her new shoes*]. Madonna, what shoes!

DOMENICO. Do they hurt? Maybe you should wear another pair.

FILUMENA. What is it you wanted to tell me?

DOMENICO [*to* TERESINA]. That'll be all for now, Teresina.

TERESINA. Yes, sir, I was just going. [*She folds the piece of cloth that she carries dresses in and puts it under her arm.*] And best wishes from your humble servant! [*Leaving*

upstage right, to LUCIA.] What was wrong with the dress,
I'd like to know, why . . .

[*Her voice trails on until she is out of hearing.* LUCIA *has gone
with her.*]

DOMENICO [*to the* THREE BOYS]. You boys go into the . . .
er . . . drawing room and entertain the guests—let the revels
commence! And you go with them, Rosalia.
ROSALIA. Yes, sir. [*To the* BOYS.] Come along! [*Exit* ROSALIA
into the study.]
MICHELE [*to the other two*]. Come on!
RICCARDO. You've missed your vocation, you should have been
a tenor at the San Carlo opera!

[*They go into the study, laughing and talking.*]

DOMENICO [*after looking* FILUMENA *over*]. You're a beautiful
woman, Filumena, and you're a *young* woman, too, a slip
of a girl. If I weren't such a confused old slob . . . I know
a man who could fall for you, hook, line, and sinker.
FILUMENA [*already has guessed what is on* DOMENICO's *mind
and doesn't want to discuss it*]. Well, everything seems to
be in order now. I never thought it would be.
DOMENICO [*not to be deflected*]. I'm not easy in my mind,
Filumena . . .
FILUMENA. How could either of us be easy in our minds with
only Lucia to depend on? Alfredo and Rosalia are old . . .
DOMENICO. Don't change the subject, Filumena, you know
perfectly well what I'm getting at. . . . You can put my
mind at rest, you can bring me peace, Filumena.
FILUMENA. Can I?
DOMENICO. I've done everything you asked. After the marriage
was annulled, I came around to the house—not once, many
times, because you always said you weren't home—I came
and I said, "Filumena Marturano, will you marry me?"
FILUMENA. And I said, "Domenico Soriano, I will."
DOMENICO. And now it's your wedding day, and you're
happy—I hope.
FILUMENA. I am happy.
DOMENICO. Then make *me* happy. Sit down, Filumena, I
have something to say. [*She sits.*] I wish you knew how
many times I've wanted to speak to you in these last
months. I couldn't, that's all, I was too shy or embarrassed
or something, I just couldn't. And for that matter I couldn't

bear to embarrass *you* and force you to talk about things that . . . aren't easy to talk about. But now we're to be man and wife. A boy and a girl think they love each other when all they feel is an emotion that can be exhausted by a single physical act, so they get married. But the two people who're coming before God this afternoon aren't children. They've *had* their lives. I am fifty-two, you are forty-eight, we should know what we're doing. [*Pause.*] Now you do know why you're marrying me. But I don't know why I'm marrying you. I only know you said one of those boys is my son.

FILUMENA. Is that your only reason for marrying me?

DOMENICO [*gently*]. No, it isn't. I'm terribly fond of you, Filumena. We've been together twenty-five years. Twenty-five years is a lifetime, a lifetime of memories, yearnings . . . I found out for myself, I couldn't just cut loose from it. Let me tell you my trouble, Filumena. [*Short pause.*] I don't sleep nights. Ten months have passed since . . . that evening. And I've had no peace. I don't sleep, I don't eat, I don't live. You know, Filumena, I don't even breathe. I go like this . . . [*He opens his mouth to take a deep breath of air*] and the air doesn't go down into my lungs, it stops here. [*Pointing to his throat.*] You can't let this happen, Filumena, you're a woman, you have a heart, you can't let this happen. I remember your saying the day would come when I'd want something from you and I mustn't swear I'd refuse it, and I didn't swear, Filumena, and the day *has* come, and I do want something from you, as you hoped I would. I am on my knees before you, Filumena, I kiss your hands, I kiss your clothes, and I implore you: which is my son, my flesh, my blood?

[*A very long pause.*]

FILUMENA [*still looking intently at her man*]. I'll tell you: it's that one. And now what happens? You'll pick "that one" out, he'll be closer to you than the others, you'll make sure he has a better future, and you'll figure out how to make him richer . . .

DOMENICO. What if I do?

FILUMENA [*with gentle cunning*]. *Take* that one, then, he certainly needs you, with his four kids . . .

DOMENICO [*very involved in this*]. It's the . . . mechanic?

FILUMENA [*nodding*]. The . . . hydraulic engineer, yes.

DOMENICO [*half to himself, getting progressively more ex-*

cited]. A good lad, well set up . . . But why did he get
married so young? With a little shop to take care of. . . .
I must take matters in hand. With a little capital he could
open a real repair shop, take on a few workers, learn to
boss the place, he needs some modern equipment . . . [*A
suspicion strikes him. Looking at* FILUMENA.] Now look,
the plumber is the poorest of the lot, he's the one with the
family, he needs help . . .

FILUMENA [*pretending to be crestfallen*]. What can a mother
do? She must help the weakest! But you didn't believe me,
you're too smart. What would you say to Riccardo?

DOMENICO. The shirtmaker?

FILUMENA [*teasing him all the time*]. No, no! It's Umberto,
the writer?

DOMENICO [*very put out and violent*]. You're at it again!
Putting me against the wall! Crucifying me!

FILUMENA [*touched by the tone of real trouble and exhaustion
in* DOMENICO'S *voice, she tries to put her innermost feelings
into words, to find the formula, the synthesis, which will
make the situation clear to him.*] Listen to me, Domenico.
And then let's never speak of this again. [*The love she has
held in so long comes welling up.*] I always loved you with
all my heart and soul. In my eyes you were a god. And you
are dear to me still—perhaps dearer than ever. [*She breaks
off, thinking of his thoughtlessness, his failure to understand.*] What have you done with your life? Did you *want*
to suffer? The Lord God gave you everything. Good looks,
good health, money . . . and me. I'd have done anything
for you. To save you the slightest pain I'd have made a
vow of perpetual silence and kept it! And if you'd been . . .
different, you'd have taken on three children and thought
nothing of it. But you were you. [*Pause.*] Never ask me
again which is your son. I won't tell. I can't tell. And you've
got to be a gentleman and not ask, or I might give way
in a moment of weakness, and that would be the end. Don't
you see? I told you it was the plumber, and within two
seconds you were talking about money, a little capital, a
real repair shop. . . . You have money, you have a right
to think of it, but what would you think of next? "Why
shouldn't I tell him he's my son?" you'd think. "And who
are these two other chaps? Intruders!" An inferno. Brother
against brother. There'd be murder in this house, Domenico.
[*Pause.*] Don't think of yourself, don't think of me,
Domenico. Think of them: it's the children that count,

Domenico. We must never forget it. When they're tiny,
we take them in our arms, we fret over them when they're
sick and can't explain what the matter is. A little later, they
come rushing at you with their arms out, shouting: Papa!
Then they come home from school in winter with their
hands freezing and their noses running and asking if you've
remembered that surprise you promised. . . . But when
they're grown up, when they're men, what are they? They're
. . . just sons. Or else enemies. I have three grown-up sons,
Domenico, decide whether you want them. You still have
time. And there'll be no ill feelings. We needn't go through
with this. If you say so, we're free to pick up and go each
his own way.

[*The organ starts to play in the study.*]

ROSALIA [*enters from the study followed by the* THREE BOYS].
He's come! The holy priest is here!

[DOMENICO *gets up and looks at them all very slowly. Provoked by* FILUMENA'S *last remark, he is trying to force himself to break with her.*]

DOMENICO. "We're free to pick up and go each his own way!"
[*To the* THREE BOYS.] I have something to say to you.
[*Suspense.*] I am a gentleman and I don't want to cheat
you. Listen.

THE THREE SONS. Yes, Father.

DOMENICO [*for this "Yes, Father" has settled it*]. Thank you,
boys. I like the sound of that expression. I like it very much.
[*Brightening up, now that this weight is off his mind.*] Now,
then, the usual thing is for the bride's father to take her
to the altar. There are no parents with us today. There are
sons, instead. Two of them will accompany the bride. The
third, the bridegroom.

MICHELE [*firmly*]. We'll go with mother. [*Inviting* RICCARDO.]

FILUMENA [*suddenly remembering*]. What time is it?

RICCARDO. Five minutes to six.

[FILUMENA *gives* ROSALIA *a meaningful look.*]

ROSALIA. Don't worry. At six o'clock on the nose those candles
will be lit!

FILUMENA [*leaning lovingly on* MICHELE *and* RICCARDO]. Let's
go in!

DOMENICO [*to* UMBERTO]. And you'll go with me.

[*Forming a procession they go into the study. We hear the "Oh!" which greets the happy pair as they enter and the handclapping of the guests.* ROSALIA *stays in the dining room, watching the ceremony through the curtains, clapping when the others clap, etc. We hear voices at first, then silence, then the wedding march. At this point* ROSALIA *weeps copiously.* ALFREDO *comes in upstage right as if looking for somebody; he sees* ROSALIA *and goes over to her.* LUCIA *comes in and joins the other two.*

Here a change of lighting indicates a passage of time.

FILUMENA *comes in from the study, followed by* UMBERTO, MICHELE, *and* ROSALIA; *goes to sit downstage left.*]

FILUMENA. Phew, I'm tired!

MICHELE. You can rest now, Mamma. We'll be going. I have to work tomorrow.

ROSALIA. It was so lovely! May you live to be a hundred, child of mine, for child of mine you are and ever will be!

RICCARDO [*comes in from the study*]. It *was* a lovely ceremony, too!

FILUMENA [*taking her shoes off and relaxing in her armchair.*] Rosalia, bring me a glass of water, will you, dear?

ROSALIA. Oh, yes, Donna Filumena. [*Exit left.*]

[DOMENICO *comes in from the study carrying a bottle of special white wine, the cork covered with sealing wax.*]

DOMENICO. No guests, no banquet, just a bottle of wine among the family. [*He takes a corkscrew and five glasses.*] The perfect nightcap. [DOMENICO *uncorks the bottle.*]

ROSALIA [*comes in with a glass of water on a plate*]. Here's the water.

DOMENICO. What do we want with *water*, for heaven's sake?

ROSALIA. It's for the signora!

DOMENICO. Tell the signora that water on an occasion of this sort is bad luck. Get two more glasses, and bring Alfredo Amoroso, jockey and coachman, connoisseur of the race-track.

ROSALIA [*calling*]. Alfredo! Alfredo! Come and have some wine with your master! You, too, Lucia! [*She brings* DOMENICO *two more glasses from a sideboard.*]

ALFREDO [*coming in, followed by* LUCIA]. Here I come!

DOMENICO [*has filled the glasses and now he is handing them around*]. Here, Filumena, drink this. [*To the others.*] Drink, everybody!

ALFREDO. Alla salute! [*He raises his glass.*]

DOMENICO. You remember the horses, don't you, Alfredo, the way they ran?

ALFREDO [*thrilled*]. Madonna!

DOMENICO. They've stopped running. They stopped some time ago. I just didn't wish to believe it. And in my mind's eye I went on seeing them. But now I realize they stopped—a long time ago. [*Indicating the* THREE BOYS.] It's their turn now. For them the race is just beginning. We'd better keep out of their way, you and I, Alfredo Amoroso, we can't compete with all this young blood.

ALFREDO [*quite overcome*]. Madonna!

DOMENICO. Drink up, Alfredo.

[*All drink.*]

I have just one thing left to say. It often happens in a family that a father with three or four children takes a special liking to one of them, maybe the ugly one, or the sick one, or the strong one, whichever it is, he's "father's boy," and the other kids don't mind. "Papa has a right to feel that way," they say. In our family this can never happen. Our family was . . . well, formed too late in the day. Maybe that's better. What I mean is, I'll still feel that special liking, but . . . I'll have to divide it among the three of you. So: alla salute!

[*They drink.*]

Now, boys, tomorrow you're coming for dinner.

THREE BOYS. Thank you, Father.

RICCARDO. But now I'll be going. It's late, and Mamma needs a rest. Good-bye—and all the best!

UMBERTO. All the best!

MICHELE. And the same from me!

[*They all kiss and embrace* FILUMENA.]

UMBERTO [*coming over to* DOMENICO, *smiling affectionately*]. Good night, Papa!

RICCARDO. G'night, Papa!

MICHELE. Sleep well, Papa!

DOMENICO [*is terribly happy. But one Italian custom remains*]. Come on, boys! [*He stretches out his arms, embraces them, one after the other, kissing them on both cheeks.*] Till tomorrow!

THREE BOYS. Till tomorrow!

[*They leave upstage right, followed by* ALFREDO, ROSALIA, *and* LUCIA.]

    DOMENICO *follows them out with his eyes, then thoughtfully returns to the table and pours himself some more wine.*]

FILUMENA [*is still sitting in the armchair, has changed her shoes*]. Madonna, how tired I am! It comes over me all at once.

DOMENICO [*understandingly, lovingly*]. You've been on your feet all day. And with all the strain of it! Now you can rest. [*He takes his glass over to the terrace.*] What a lovely evening!

[FILUMENA *has been feeling something in her throat that makes her groan slightly: at any rate a sound like sobbing comes out of her. Her eyes are staring out into nothingness. She seems to expect something. Her face is lined with tears.*]

DOMENICO [*concerned, comes over*]. What's the matter, dear?

FILUMENA [*with deep joy*]. I'm crying, Domenico, I'm crying! And, oh, how *sweet* it is to cry!

DOMENICO [*holding her lovingly to him*]. You'll be all right, Filumena, you'll be all right. *You've* done some running in your time, too, it's been a hard race, there's been a fall or two, but you always picked yourself up again somehow. And now it's time for a rest. [*He returns to the table for yet another glass of wine.*] A mother's a mother, and sons are sons, Filumena Soriano. [*He is drinking as:*]

THE CURTAIN FALLS

MARIO FRATTI

1927–

MARIO FRATTI was born in L'Aquila on July 5, 1927. He studied in Venice where he received his doctorate in languages and literature. He presently lives in New York where he covers the American theatre scene for several Italian newspapers and continues to write plays for both the stage and television. Fratti is a powerful writer, but we are not conscious of that sense of rebellion which characterizes so much of the serious contemporary theatre when we read his work. He is not even characteristically Italian; there is none of the tortured intellectuality that we associate with Pirandello, nor that quality of metaphoric explosiveness which informs Ugo Betti's plays. Fratti's plays are tight, safe, sure; they have a directness of style that precludes ambiguity and insures theatrical effectiveness. In a time when the theatre seems to be celebrating obscurity, Fratti stands firm for simplicity and the importance of immediate communication in the theatre. In a note on his work, he wrote: "I am aware. I believe in the possibility of man becoming aware. By writing plays I hope to communicate my awareness. Because I believe in man, man notwithstanding."

Almost all of Fratti's plays begin with a bizarre dramatic situation. This he then develops and exploits in innumerable ways, but his purpose is always to lead us from this distortion of reality to a fuller understanding of it. Fratti is not afraid of facing reality and he believes that one of the chief functions of the theatre is to provide a direct confrontation with it.

MY THEATRE[1]

By Mario Fratti

I DO NOT BELIEVE in composers who promise symphonies, painters who promise beautiful paintings, playwrights who promise plays. I do not believe in people who anticipate, explain, promise. I only believe in the given work which speaks for itself, explains by itself: I believe in the symphony, in the painting, in the play. Accordingly, when I am asked to explain my theatre, I immediately take a defensive attitude. It makes me nervous and upset. Nervous because I do not like to explain my plays—upset because I'm convinced they do not need any explanation.

When I am asked why I love the theatre, I have an instinctive desire to be rude. The answer seems obvious to me. Because I love life, I like people, I like "active" people. Only action is life. Theatre is and must be action. Accordingly, theatre is life. When I am asked why I insist on loving the theatre in spite of the fact that it is "dying," I smile. Theatre has supposedly been dying for centuries. It never did. It never will. As long as actors feel the need to act, to communicate their emotions to audiences and as long as audiences feel the need to live vicariously through actors' performances, theatre will be alive and needed.

There happens to be someone between the actor and the audience—the playwright. He must be clear to himself, clear to the actor, clear to the audience. The quintessence of clarity. Otherwise he is only a hysterical poet talking to himself in front of a mirror. Alone and sterile. Incapable of taking a stand in front of the actors and audiences who are waiting for his approach to life, for his clear thought. A human being

[1] Printed by permission of the author and Ninon Tallon Karlweis. All inquiries regarding rights to the works of Mario Fratti should be addressed to Robert Lantz, 111 West 57th Street, N.Y.C. 10019.

should never try to resist the temptation of communicating as clearly as possible. After all, there is a reason why playwrights choose dialogue as their working tool. Dialogue means an attempt to reach another human being. That's my purpose in the theatre. At the risk of being considered conservative and traditional, my only purpose is to "communicate" my thoughts and emotions.

Does this mean that I deny the *avant garde*? I can't of course ignore it. But let me smile when I hear the expression. Pirandello, using the traditional three acts, has put so much fire in his plays that he is to be considered the only true *avant garde* playwright of this century. Bertolt Brecht, giving us traditionally shaped fables with a beginning, a middle part and a moralistic ending is to be considered the first poet of the third millennium. The hallmark of the truly *avant garde* is not a twisted, absurd, incomprehensible pattern, nor is it some "new" form of theatre.

The contents of a play determine whether it is modern and valid. And there is nothing more revolutionary and modern than man, than the tragic reality of his life. I write about man, to be understood by men. My fundamental concern is human distress, the conflicts of every day, the reality of very day, the grotesque of human behavior in contemporary society.

A word about language. Our forefathers invented language to deceive, to conceal one's intimate sincerity, one's personal truth and belief. Must we continue on that path? Shall we go on lying? Let's at least use language to point out that man lies in order to survive (as in Pirandello). Let's point out that the future frightens every human being out of his wits. That's why he is cruel (temporarily—according to Brecht).

In all my plays there is a protagonist who seems a sly rascal or a monster of cruelty—the Professor in *The Academy*; Maso in *The Return*. They are not cruel. They are not responsible for what is happening around them. They only struggle to survive. Which is human, justifiable. They do not "see" that they spread grief around them, they do not realize that their victims are their friends: the beloved ones, the weakest, the oldest. If the protagonists of life (the characters) do not see, do not realize the harm they are doing, all the more reason why the average citizen does not see, does not realize this struggle to survive when he witnesses it in the streets around him. Cruelty and suffering do not move him. He can stop looking at them whenever he wants. He can escape. But when he becomes a member of an audience, he cannot escape. He is nailed down in his seat. He must look at the cruelty and the pain. He is moved and upset by what he sees because everything that happens on the stage is magnified and becomes important. It is like looking through a keyhole at the right moment. It is like spying from a window on the life of our neighbors. Theatre is a window open on the life of our fellow creatures—a window open on their secret, intimate behavior. Let's watch in silence from that window.

There is another important consideration. Since the playwright has such an interest for life—which is often prosaic—is he a poet in the accepted meaning of the word? At moments, unconsciously. The playwright is only a sensitive man among indifferent men. He sees, stresses, and points out what most watch with indifference. A playwright is only an "aware" man among careless people. I am aware. I believe in man's possibility of becoming aware. Writing plays, I hope to communicate my awareness because I believe in man—nothwithstanding man.

THE ACADEMY

A One Act Play

by MARIO FRATTI

1962

THE ACADEMY[1]

Translated by Raymond Rosenthal

CHARACTERS

THE PROFESSOR	*CORSO
THE SIGNORA	*DONATO
*AFRO	*ELIO
*BENITO	FORTUNATO

TIME: *The present.*

PLACE: *Venice*

[1] Printed by permission of the author and Ninon Tallon Karlweis. Copy right © 1961 by Mario Fratti. All inquiries regarding rights to the plays of Mario Fratti should be addressed to Robert Lantz, 111 West 57th Street N.Y.C. 10019.

* During Benito Mussolini's Fascist regime (1922–1945) it was common practice to give children born in that period names that glorified Mussolini dreams of conquest: Afro (Africa); Benito; Corso (Corsica); Donato (gift of providence); Elio (place in the sun).

THE SCENE: *A large, striking poster with the words: THE ACADEMY.*

A dusty classroom; stage left, a dais with two chairs, a blackboard, a map of the United States, the Italian and the American flags; stage right, some school benches.

AFRO *and* FORTUNATO *enter from left; they are two modestly dressed, virile young men; short hair, sweaters, the relaxed, easy-going attitudes of the American one sees in the movies.*

AFRO [*with a gesture, pointing to the room*]. This is the classroom. You'll be glad you came. I've already begun to work. I average three hundred dollars a month. Because I'm just a beginner, not too experienced. You know English better than I do, so he'll let you take care of more important clients. [*Pointing to the two chairs on the dais.*] "She" sits here. Still young, an attractive woman. Everything's up to the wife, remember. So give it your best, a little finesse, you understand. If she flunks you, you're finished here. You can't try again.

[BENITO *enters. A young man very much like the other two.*]

Ask him. He brought his brother. He flunked.

BENITO [*languidly*]. Ciao. A new one? [*Shakes* FORTUNATO'S *hand.*]

FORTUNATO. Yes, new.

AFRO [*to* BENITO, *insistently*]. Tell him about your brother.

BENITO [*reluctantly*]. Who knows what was going on in her head? My brother's just like me. Better perhaps. Sometimes —who knows?—it's a question of incompatibility.

[CORSO *and* DONATO *enter; two more students.* CORSO *is very tall and robust.*]

CORSO. Hi.
DONATO. Hi.

[CORSO *and* DONATO *sit down on the benches and begin talking in the background.*]

AFRO. Give her a big smile as soon as she comes in. Everything hinges on the first impression. He doesn't count at all. An ex-Fascist, they say. A sucker for American culture, now.—

"if you can't beat them, join them."—Americans are the
greatest, the best, tops in everything. They'll save us from
the Reds, etcetera. A regular ass-licker, a beaten dog who
likes to butter up his master. Unemployed, just like us.
He's satisfied with his ten per cent. He did a good job of
organizing here and that's good for us. I'll loan you the
ten thousand lire for the registration fee.

[AFRO *hands him the money; the* SIGNORA *enters; she has a
sad air.*]

CORSO *and* DONATO [*who, being the first to notice her enter,
get to their feet respectfully.*] Buon giorno, signora.

SIGNORA. *Buon giorno.*

AFRO [*apologizing for not having noticed her immediately*].
I didn't see you come in, signora. *Buon giorno.* May I
introduce a new applicant, Fortunato.

FORTUNATO [*trying to hide the money he's holding and stretching out his hand embarrassedly.*] Enchanted.

SIGNORA [*with detachment*]. Pleased to meet you. [*As* FOR-
TUNATO *is staring at her admiringly.*] Where is Elio? There's
mail for him. [*Holds up a letter.*]

CORSO. He hasn't come yet. I'll give it to him. [*He takes the
letter from her.*]

SIGNORA [*to* FORTUNATO, *making a gesture for him to follow
her.*] Come.

[*They go out together, to stage right.*]

CORSO [*looking at the envelope against the light*]. There's fifty
dollars in this. A fortune! Not a week goes by . . .

AFRO [*looking enviously at the door through which his friend
and the* SIGNORA *have gone.*] There's the fortunate one. He
was christened Fortunato and right now he's proving it.
This audition is his most beautiful moment, here . . .

[ELIO *enters. The same age as the others, but more elegant.*]

ELIO [*catching the last sentence on the fly and motioning with
his head toward the door at stage right*]. A new one?

AFRO. A new one.

ELIO [*ironically*]. Still in love with our signora?

AFRO. Frustrated, perhaps. Only once, it whets the appetite.
A woman sticks right here . . . [*Pointing to his throat.*]
if you don't have her completely.

CORSO. Mail.

ELIO [*takes letter*]. Oh, my granny!

DONATO. The usual fifty bucks.

ELIO [*kissing letter*]. *Mia divina!* If her venerable age allowed her to come back to Italy, I would treat her better. [*Ironically.*] Tell me, Afro, how would you treat our signora if she gave you another session?

AFRO. With kid gloves. So would you if given the chance. None of us have really had her.

ELIO. Could be . . . [*Reads letter that came with the fifty dollars.*] . . . She's dreaming about me, desires me . . . Hopes to come back . . . Let's hope to God she won't be able to move . . . Her pains are soothed . . . She's hungry for tenderness . . . "Hunger," they say. It's really incredible, the stamina of these American grandmas . . .

[*The* PROFESSOR *enters from stage left; he is about forty-five, lean, severe. They all rise to their feet.* ELIO *hides the letter with the money.*]

ALL. *Buon giorno*, professor.

PROFESSOR [*formally*]. Be seated. [*A moment of silence. To* ELIO, *taking him by surprise with his unexpected question.*] How much did she send you?

ELIO [*surprised*]. Fifty . . . fifty dollars.

PROFESSOR. Turn over the percentage.

[ELIO *reluctantly goes to the dais and hands over the money.*]

ELIO [*as he goes back to the seat, nastily; getting revenge for having to pay*]. There's a new applicant in the next room, with your wife.

PROFESSOR [*unconcerned, not giving it any importance*]. Let's review a few things from the preceding lesson. Donato, you. What is the capital of Maryland? [*He points with pointer to the state on the map, which does not have the names of the cities.*]

DONATO. Annapolis.

PROFESSOR. Of Alabama?

DONATO. Montgomery.

PROFESSOR. Of Kentucky?

DONATO. Frankfort.

PROFESSOR. You, Benito. Which are the thirteen states that first joined the republic?

BENITO [*slowly, counting on his fingers*]. Connecticut, Delaware, Georgia, Maryland, Massachusetts, New Hampshire, New Jersey, New York . . . Pennsylvania . . . South Carolina, North Carolina . . . Virginia . . . . . . [*He can't think of the last one.*]

PROFESSOR. You're one short.

ELIO. Rhode Island.

PROFESSOR. Right. [*To* ELIO.] When was Washington born?

ELIO. February 22, 1732.

PROFESSOR. Lincoln?

ELIO. February 12, 1809.

PROFESSOR [*to* CORSO]. How many calories does a glass of carrot juice contain?

CORSO. Fifty.

PROFESSOR. A hamburger?

CORSO. Two hundred.

PROFESSOR. A yogurt?

CORSO. One hundred and sixty-five.

PROFESSOR [*to* AFRO]. An example of high calorie food?

AFRO. Caviar, anchovies, spaghetti . . .

PROFESSOR. Low calorie?

AFRO. Celery, jello. . . .

PROFESSOR [*to* ELIO]. How many calories should a tall, raw-boned American woman ingest per day?

ELIO. Minimum, 1845. Maximum, 2580.

PROFESSOR. Good. [*Turns to* CORSO.] Vitamin A is good for . . .

CORSO. Eyesight and glandular functions.

PROFESSOR [*to* DONATO]. Vitamin C?

DONATO. Bones, teeth, gums, skin.

PROFESSOR. Good. You've not wasted your time or your money. Thanks to our Academy you are always ready to perform with eclat for our guests from across the sea. For the glory of our nation. Now . . .

[*The* SIGNORA *enters, followed by* FORTUNATO; *all eyes are on the woman who hands a test paper to the* PROFESSOR. FOR-TUNATO *sits down next to* AFRO, *who questions him in a whisper.* FORTUNATO *continues to look at the* SIGNORA, *who sits down on the dais; and he answers* AFRO'S *questions by nodding his head in a distracted manner.*]

PROFESSOR [*after a short consultation with the* SIGNORA]. My wife's report: favorable. You've passed. [*To* FORTUNATO.] Can you speak English?

FORTUNATO. Yes.

PROFESSOR. This is a bad start. When I say "can you" you

must answer "I can." If I say "do you" you must answer "I do."

PROFESSOR. Now translate: *"Le piace l' Italia?"*

FORTUNATO. Do you like Italy?

PROFESSOR. *Passeggiare.*

FORTUNATO. To walk.

PROFESSOR. *Amare.*

FORTUNATO. To love.

PROFESSOR. *Dormire.*

FORTUNATO. To sleep.

PROFESSOR. *Labbra.*

FORTUNATO. Lips.

PROFESSOR. *Carezza.*

FORTUNATO. Caress.

PROFESSOR. *Capezzolo.*

FORTUNATO. Nipple.

PROFESSOR. *Pelle liscia.*

FORTUNATO. Baby skin.

PROFESSOR. *Sangue ardente.*

FORTUNATO. Hot blood.

PROFESSOR. *Luna di miele.*

FORTUNATO. Honeymoon.

PROFESSOR. *Tenerezza.*

FORTUNATO. Tenderness.

PROFESSOR. *Desiderio.*

FORTUNATO. Desire.

PROFESSOR. *Sogno.*

FORTUNATO. Dream.

[*A pause. The* PROFESSOR *looks for other questions, reads the name on the test paper.*]

PROFESSOR. Translate: *"Mi chiamo Fortunato. Lo sono veramente, oggi. Ho incontrato lei."*

FORTUNATO [*very sure of himself, with a good accent*]. My name is Fortunato. I am really fortunate today. I met you.

PROFESSOR [*pleased*]. Good. Did you free-lance?

FORTUNATO. Yes, whenever I hit on one of them.

PROFESSOR. Do you receive money?

FORTUNATO. . . . No. . . .

PROFESSOR. You see. What you lacked is organization. The seed was there, your good will; it did not, however, bear fruit. [*He points to* ELIO.] Today he received fifty dollars. All of them receive dollars, every now and then. One of

them . . . [*Making a vague gesture.*] one whom none of you
remembers . . . once received a pair of ruby cuff links, as
a present. He resold them for two thousand five hundred
dollars. A fortune.

AFRO [*whispering to* FORTUNATO]. It's not true. He read it
in a novel by Tennessee Williams.

PROFESSOR [*taking note of the whispering*]. What's that he's
telling you? Don't listen to him. He reads too much. And
his imagination runs away with him. All right, Fortunato.
[*He looks at the* SIGNORA *who nods in agreement.*] You're
accepted. Let's have the registration fee, ten thousand lire.
[*To the* SIGNORA.] Collect the homework.

[*As* FORTUNATO *takes the ten thousand lire to the dais and
signs a paper, the* SIGNORA, *with the students staring at her
morbidly, collects the homework.*

After signing, FORTUNATO *receives a list which he takes
back to the bench and reads.*]

[*After having waited for silence, in a professorial tone,
savoring his words.*] You see, my dear Fortunato—you are
indeed fortunate to be with us—I used the word *"Organization"* not by chance. [*Scanning his words.*] This is in fact
a first-class organization, just ask. [*A vague gesture to the
other students.*] Our Academy was conceived with love,
vision, imagination. To attain—even though we suffered
and lost the war—a lofty aim. We will fortify—thanks to
our pure Latin blood—the other races. [*He takes a deep
breath.*] Which is today the race to whom the destiny of
the world is entrusted? The American race. They are the
receptacle of all culture, the refined masters of every art,
the original worshippers of *real* democracy. No civilization
can be compared to *their* civilization. No society has ever
reached such a standard of affluence. They're the most
perfect embodiment of real accomplishment, the quintessence of progress, the synthesis of the best achievements.
Their culture is on the highest level in every field. *They'll*
save Europe from the Reds. We must therefore strengthen
their race, improve it, we must contribute somehow to the
noble task of defending civilization. [*Speaking in a less
rhetorical tone.*] Therefore I am here in a school founded
with inspired insight to give you an American culture, to
put you in the position to exploit to the full your—our best
qualities. In fact the Academy develops the intensive and
rational application of our masculine, virile patrimony. The

Germans possess a splendid steel industry, the Americans have a first-class missile industry, we . . . we have created a new industry: the American woman, the American tourist . . . [*Going into details, in a less heroic tone.*] On the sheet I have just handed to you are listed our branches in other cities, the stores that give us discounts: florists, photographers, bookstores, etc. Memorize it. Now let's get to the essentials. Where do you live?

FORTUNATO. Via Garibaldi.

PROFESSOR. A working-class neighborhood, not suitable. You must move around here, to this section. [*To* ELIO.] Is the room near the square available?

ELIO. Yes.

PROFESSOR. You'll introduce him to Madame Lucia later. [*To* FORTUNATO.] A pleasant well-equipped room. A double bed, liquor, music, telephone, a good and convenient address in this section. She won't take you to her hotel. She'd be ashamed. She won't go to a place far away. Distrust. The premises have to be very nearby. And already *paid for*. In fact during the first few hours the whole subject of money must be handled with kid gloves, with tact. [*Pointing at him, imperiously.*] You must pay. At the restaurant, at the cafe, everywhere. We have the reputation of being after money. This way, you'll show that you're above all that, completely disinterested. [*Lingering over the words, understandingly.*] Certainly you're asking yourself, so where's the profit? Don't jump to conclusions. We get a daily report from the hotels. They only give us the names of the ladies who stay at least *four days*. [*Stressing.*] Four, at least. [*To* DONATO.] Why, Donato? Explain it to him.

DONATO [*standing up, repeating lesson by heart.*] The first day we pay for everything. The second day we permit a very small expenditure. The third day we tell our little story.

PROFESSOR. What little story? Explain it to him.

DONATO [*to* FORTUNATO]. The third day we will appear putting on the gloomy face, very, very sad . . . "What's the matter, darling?"—the old girl, by now head over heels in love, will ask us . . .—"My father has gone bankrupt." A disastrous crash. We've lost everything. Money, home, and honor. She will pay for lunch, then for dinner, she will reimburse us for everything we paid out before this. One ten-thousand lire note leads to another.

PROFESSOR. Be seated. [*To* FORTUNATO.] It always works. The first day you must make sure to take her address in the

States and give her yours. Desperate letters after she has left . . . I'll write or correct them for you; your English is not perfect. . . . Ingenious, isn't it? If it seems advisable, you will also follow them to the nearby cities. After the announcement of bankruptcy, they will foot all bills. For you it is an agreeable vacation. [*To* CORSO.] Telephone number in Milan?

CORSO. 482559.

PROFESSOR. In Florence?

CORSO. 53771.

PROFESSOR. In Rome?

CORSO. 815683.

PROFESSOR [*to* FORTUNATO]. Memorize these. The address of headquarters will, however, always be the most important. They will all write to you here.

AFRO. Not all of them, unfortunately.

PROFESSOR. It's your fault. [*To* FORTUNATO.] He's referring to the fact that some don't answer. That will be entirely your fault. It will mean that you haven't done your work with enough tact, sensitivity, intelligence. To conquer a human being is not easy. [*Continuing with lesson, which he knows by heart.*] Our raw material, the American Woman, can be of two types: the woman who *knows* and pays, and the woman who does *not* know and pays anyway. The first is the astute type, usually the wife of some big industrialist accustomed to buying everything. She buys the merchandise on the spot, pays, does *not* want to pay at a distance for something she no longer has in hand. Contrary to what one might think, she is actually the most difficult client. It's a matter of convincing her that she can get more and better of the same merchandise. On the last day, the demanding fiancée whom you were forced to see at brief moments, which were denied to her, will be introduced. You'll bring up the subject with regret, irritation. At that moment she will understand that you're capable of more and better services. You will also stress your revulsion at having to live here, your yearning to go to America, to accept from her *any sort* of position. Even the position of personal attendant. Only if you have been endearing, persuasive, will you get mail. An invisible thread will bind her to you, compel her to pay. [*Pointing to* BENITO.] Benito, who is so quiet, so apparently reserved, inspires a feeling of confidence and security. He is very successful with this type. We have then the type that doesn't know, the romantic type. These are the ones who produce the best results, even if, quite obviously, the initial overtures are more delicate and difficult. Donato, will you describe these initial overtures?

DONATO [*standing up*]. We get the report from the hotel, the snapshot from the photographer. Depending on how tall she is, either Corso or I go. Waiting around the hotel, shadowing, choice of the most propitious moment for the first act of politeness. Rescue from a wolf—whom we, of course pay; intervention as an interpreter when she cannot understand why she must pay that particular amount of money in a store, and so on. In desperate cases, when, for instance, we have seen one or two free-lancers firmly repulsed, we make friends with an American male, get him to approach her in some way, and to introduce us . . . We pay for a drink, then for another, and then for the dinner. Detachment, elegance, display of at least a bit of American culture, interest in and admiration for their world. Finally we ask her to come for a ride in a gondola— I'll point out to you the gondoliers who work with us—the real siege begins,—"The gondolier is blind and deaf."— This must be said jokingly, to reassure her. An arm around her shoulders, a caress. After so many courtesies and such correct behavior, she won't dare to object.

PROFESSOR. "A patronizing attitude."

DONATO. A protective, tender, still discreet attitude. Then, slowly . . .

PROFESSOR [*breaking in*]. We must trust our personal instincts, our physical appeal, the aggressiveness which is peculiar to us, us Latins. If you succeed in the gondola, all the better. Everything will become much, much easier. She will never again recover from the shock—the swift transition from thinly veiled detachment to feverish assault—she'll accept everything, your room, the night, your problems, and then your desperation when your father goes bankrupt . . . Ask my wife. [*Turning to* SIGNORA.] Isn't it true that "afterward" it is too late? That no woman has the courage to turn back, to refuse?

SIGNORA. It's true.

AFRO [*jumping at the chance*]. You, signora, are the living example of just the contrary. You never gave us a second chance. Why do you refuse?

PROFESSOR [*firmly*]. We are talking about American women, another race, another mentality. [*Changing the subject.*]

Donato has mentioned culture, before. This is why besides
English and sex psychology [*Pointing to the* SIGNORA, *as
the teacher of this subject.*] we teach history, geography,
religion, hygiene, diet, politics, sociology, et similia. To
make sure that you're up to your job, well prepared and
more interesting. Benito, tell our new student the names of
the two Presidents whom it is not advisable to praise.

BENITO [*standing up*]. Lincoln, because from the southerner's
point of view, he wronged the south, and Roosevelt, because he inflicted heavy taxes.

PROFESSOR. Elio, what question must never be put to a client
from Washington, D.C.?

ELIO [*without standing up*]. Whether it is true that in Washington they don't vote because the majority of the popula-
tion is Negro.

PROFESSOR. Who are the most famous Italians every client
will know?

AFRO. The Fontana sisters, Sophia Loren . . . Renata Tebaldi.

PROFESSOR. And who are the men?

AFRO. Pucci, Marcello Mastroianni, Volare—I mean Mo-
dugno . . . Moravia.

PROFESSOR. And Tomasi di Lampedusa: author of *The
Leopard*. It was a best-seller. [*To* CORSO.] People best to
ignore?

CORSO. Charlie Chaplin and Howard Fast.

AFRO [*correcting him*]. Howard Fast is now in the clear. He
denounced the Reds—years ago.

PROFESSOR. It would still be best to ignore him. He does have
a past. [*To* DONATO.] What poet should never be quoted
to Jewish clients because of his collaboration with the
German Reich?

DONATO [*diligently*]. Ezra Pound. Born in 1885. Still alive.
A good friend of Italy.

PROFESSOR [*to* FORTUNATO]. To appear informed on the subject of poetry *The Pocket Book of Modern Verse* will do.
It contains all the poetry of the last hundred years. The
least boring. If you go to our bookstore [*Points to list.*]
they'll charge you only four hundred lire. Learn by heart
a poem by Frost and one by Sandburg. You'll astound them.
Among the authors to be read and quoted:

Thomas Wolfe	1900	1938
William Faulkner	1897	1962
Ernest Hemingway	1898	1961
Truman Capote	1924	alive

Then there are the touchy subjects. Afro, you list them.

AFRO. Segregation, Missiles, Politics, Religion.

PROFESSOR. Ignore segregation and the south. Missiles are not so touchy now. It is again possible to speak about them. They've regained some ground. Two years ago it would have been an unforgivable faux pas.

AFRO. Politics and religion.

PROFESSOR. What's your line in politics?

AFRO. If I absolutely must talk about it—when all other subjects have been exhausted—to fill up the gaps between one session and the next, [*All laugh.*] I tell her that I had a slight interest in Socialism, which I am now losing.

PROFESSOR [*to* FORTUNATO]. Understand? You never miss. They have some vague notion what it is. If they respect it they'll try to bring you back to the "democratic variety." Otherwise, they'll be happy to help you get away from the devil. [*To* AFRO.] Be seated. Religion is another big headache. What with Baptists*, Jews, Protestants, Disciples of Christ, Catholics, Presbyterians, Episcopalians, Methodists, and Mormons, it's impossible to make head or tail of the whole thing. What is the wisest behavior, Benito?

BENITO [*standing up, recites*]. —"I am a Catholic, I'm somewhat discouraged by certain political interferences on the part of the Vatican, nevertheless I still go to church . . ."—

PROFESSOR [*to* FORTUNATO]. Do you understand? If the client isn't a Catholic, she will like your veiled reproach; if she is Catholic she will not feel too insulted, because she knows that in Italy the relationship between Church and State is completely different from theirs. [*Telephone on the dais rings. The* PROFESSOR *answers, takes notes.*]

Yes . . .

Yes . . .

Good . . .

Age?

   [*He writes.*]

Height? . . .

   [*He writes.*]

Yes . . .

A widow . . .

   [*He writes.*]

Good . . . Did you develop it? . . .

I'll send the man to get them . . .

* Substitute religions: Unitarians, Adventists, Christian Scientists, Zen-Buddhists, Evangelists, Spiritualists, Lutherans, etc.

Yes . . .

Thank you . . .

[*Puts down receiver.*]

[*Turning again to students.*] Bleached blonde, medium height, widowed eight months ago. Has inherited a number of meat-processing plants. Has taken a luxurious suite. Age fifty-seven. Who wants to go?

DONATO. I'll go.

PROFESSOR. Do you need some money in advance?

DONATO. Fifty thousand lire.

PROFESSOR [*to* SIGNORA]. Thirty thousand lire. Get them from my wife.

[*As the* SIGNORA *hands over money and makes* DONATO *sign receipt.*]

Now, don't forget. First you get the photograph—which you will carefully conceal in your wallet—then you order the flowers. Don't let her spend a single lira. In the gondola —detachment, melancholy, flashes of culture. And during the last half hour, helped by the moon, the lagoon, the night . . .

DONATO. Certainly. [*He has collected the money, goes stage left; turning to fellow students.*] Ciao. So long.

FELLOW STUDENTS *and* PROFESSOR. Good luck.

[DONATO *exits.*]

PROFESSOR [*moves, looking after him affectionately*]. One of my creations goes forth. A part of myself. As are all of you. And each of your conquests is mine. I love through you, with you. Any questions, Fortunato?

FORTUNATO [*slowly*]. If we succeed the first evening, in the gondola, why should we continue to pay the second day, too?

PROFESSOR. We know from experience that they are more generous if they are absolutely untouched by doubt. Paying for a few drinks even after having possessed and conquered is proof of impeccable morality. Anything else?

FORTUNATO. The flowers, who pays for the flowers?

PROFESSOR. I have arranged for a discount. It's up to you to pay. Don't forget that I receive only ten percent on all earnings.

[FORTUNATO *sits down again, whispers to* AFRO.]

Any more questions? [*No answer.*] Now I must make the rounds of the hotels. To get a list of arrivals. I'll leave you with my wife. For the psycho-sexual questions. [*To* BE-NITO.] You have learnt enough. Come with me. We'll be back soon.

BENITO [*to fellow students*]. Bye bye.

[PROFESSOR *and* BENITO *exit stage left. The four remaining students stare at the* SIGNORA. *A silence.*]

AFRO [*aggressively, ruthless*]. You said before that after a session with each one of us, you can't forget. This is difficult for a woman. Is it true, even now that your husband isn't here to prompt you?

SIGNORA. It is true.

AFRO. That a man *can never be forgotten?*

SIGNORA. It is true.

AFRO. . . . That no woman has the courage to say no?

SIGNORA [*a bit unsure*]. It is true.

AFRO. So where do you get the courage to reject us and to prefer that old man?

CORSO. Does our profession disgust you?

AFRO. What about the first time? You realized even then that we did it just professionally, didn't you? If we come here it's because we've accepted "the organization" and its rules . . .

CORSO. Are we any worse than your husband? After all, he is the organizer! If we were able to get jobs. . . .

FORTUNATO. And if one could survive on what they pay . . .

SIGNORA. He has taught you everything. You owe him everything.

AFRO. And what about you? What do you owe him?

[*A pause; the* SIGNORA *looks at him sternly, trying to understand the real meaning of his questions.*]

SIGNORA [*coldly*]. I owe him what every wife owes her husband. Any other questions?

ELIO [*after a short pause*]. I'm sick and tired of old women. I want something young. Do I have any hope, ever, with you? Or must I look for a sweet little fiancée?

[*The* SIGNORA *throws him a very stern look.*]

ELIO [*intimidated*]. Forget I said it.

[*Another embarrassing pause.*]

FORTUNATO [*gathering courage*]. What's your personal opinion of guys like us? That we're whores?

SIGNORA. I don't have opinions. It is a profession like any other. If each of you were given the chance to do something more respectable, you would behave better. These are the consequences of our defeat.

ELIO. That's what your husband says. [*To the others.*] She's just repeating him, like a parrot. She's in love with him.

CORSO. Incredible.

FORTUNATO. What does a woman expect from a man?

SIGNORA [*changing the subject which is too personal*]. What does an American woman expect? Perhaps a Latin Adventure. Perhaps escape. Perhaps a little companionship.

FORTUNATO. And what if the one I hit on does not belong to these categories? What if she's a good girl, like you?

SIGNORA. Don't talk so recklessly. You don't know anything about me. And you won't know anything about that client.

FORTUNATO. How can one get to know a woman well?

SIGNORA. One lets her talk and waits.

FORTUNATO. If she is the serious, clean sort—there are some— she won't feel like talking. She'll wait in silence, studying me. How should I behave?

SIGNORA. It will be up to you then to talk about yourself. At length. So she'll get to know you. And you must be patient if she is silent or sarcastic.

FORTUNATO. What do I talk about?

SIGNORA. He'll teach you. [*Points to the door through which the* PROFESSOR *left.*] Hundreds of topics, as the time goes by. For the present, with your first clients rely on inspiration. Various subjects, your life . . .

FORTUNATO [*interrupting*]. My troubles . . .

SIGNORA. You have no troubles. Don't forget you're a rich boy, with a father who can afford to go bankrupt.

[*Brief pause.*]

FORTUNATO. Is it advisable to make advances . . . the first evening?

SIGNORA. Why not? Delicately, tenderly. Women like men who are proper, tender and at the same time skillful. The man who is sure of himself, who seems detached, unconcerned about the conquest for its own sake, the sexual act in itself. You can. With discretion. Pretending to be uninterested, at the beginning. As a result, taking her by surprise.

FORTUNATO. But at a certain point she can't help but realize that that's our aim . . . that all the talk merely hides that goal.

SIGNORA. Don't give her time to think, to react. She'll immediately adapt herself, adjust to the new situation.

FORTUNATO [*after a short pause*]. Is a woman able to sense hate, irritation, revulsion? One can't like all of them. And these feelings come to the surface.

SIGNORA. Disguise them with a scene of jealousy, a fit of rage, even a promise of marriage. A lonely, tired woman responds very easily to this sort of thing. She will never forget a spontaneous proposal, a burst of tears, an avowal of love in the Latin manner . . . Even later, months later, when she'll be about to mail you the money, she'll remember that spontaneity, that violence, the flowers with which you filled her room, "afterward." She will go back to the hotel, dazed, surprised; the flowers will move her more than anything else. He knows it. [*She alludes to the* PROFESSOR.] And phone her often, with desire in your voice. And remember, you must give her your address, your telephone number, at the beginning, when you're still a "rich" man. It will burn a hole in her bag. She will *have to* call you sooner or later. Or write to you. She's lonely, don't forget. [*Caught up in what she's saying.*] To be a lonely woman is a devastating thing. You will never understand this, you men.

[*A short pause.*]

FORTUNATO. You're talking with great feeling. You're taking their side.

SIGNORA [*smiling sadly*]. Female solidarity.

AFRO. It's your fault if I have failed in some of my jobs. I was so haunted by memory of you that I let some one else steal a client right from under my nose. What's your advice on how to win back a woman?

SIGNORA. You must be a good sport, a good loser. [*Staring at him.*] No woman forgets the man who can love, wait, accept her life, her *choice*. To know how to lose enhances us in everyone's eyes. Even in the eyes of your clients: of those women.

[PROFESSOR *enters.* BENITO *isn't with him. He shows some slips of paper.*]

PROFESSOR. Benito has found his ideal. They're already at the aperitif. [*Pointing to slips.*] It isn't too bad, today. [*He hands* CORSO *descriptive note and paragraph.*] Well suited for you. Look at her front window. Some knockers! And just read what her bank account is. [*Handing slip to* AFRO.] This one is slim, hieratic. Just right for you. You have an Oedipus complex; white hair doesn't upset you. [*Handing slip to* ELIO.] Take this . . . the most difficult one. We know how good you are. She is distrustful, prejudiced. She drove one of our men in Rome crazy. If you can't do it. . . . Gentlemen, good luck. [*He dismisses them.*]

STUDENTS [*ad lib*]. Thank you, professor.
So long, professor.
Goodbye, Signora.
Until tomorrow.

[*The three "students" exit stage left.*]

PROFESSOR [*paternally to* FORTUNATO, *the last to leave*]. You take this, Fortunato. The best one . . . a thirty year old Calvinist from Illinois. . . . This is your "first." You don't yet have the stomach for the wrecks. [*Shows him photograph.*] Still young. Look what sad, beautiful eyes . . . intelligent, sensitive, majored in Fine Arts . . . You will combine business with pleasure . . . She is divorced. [*He pats him on the shoulder.*] Ciao. [*Looks after him with fondness as he starts to leave.*]

[FORTUNATO *goes out slowly, looking at the* SIGNORA *without daring to say goodbye to her.*]

Say goodbye to my wife, come on. [*Points to her.*]
FORTUNATO [*timidly*]. Goodbye, Signora.
SIGNORA. Goodbye.

[FORTUNATO *exits stage left.*]

PROFESSOR. You can see, they are all happy! Give an Italian a taste of erotic adventure and you make him feel triumphant. Italians are children. They like forbidden fruit. It's a religious complex they can never free themselves of. They are intrigued by frustrated wives, rejected wives, divorcées. As long as she belongs to someone else. To an Italian a divorcée is still somehow considered married. An ex-wife. He feels like a hero if he can invade someone else's territory.

[*A pause.* PROFESSOR *goes to window, lifts curtain, turning his back to the* SIGNORA *who gazes at him intensely.*]

[*Without turning.*] How do you like the new one, little wife? [*A silence.*] Why don't you answer, little wife?

SIGNORA. After so many . . . They are all alike.

PROFESSOR. I have the feeling that *this* one will do brilliantly and he'll bring in a good percentage. [*A pause; he studies her reaction.*] He makes a good impression. [*A slight pause.*] Even on you, little wife. I noticed it.

SIGNORA [*always sad, impenetrable*]. You're losing your intuition.

[*Another brief pause; he studies her.*]

PROFESSOR [*from his window, he can still see* FORTUNATO *walking away*]. He's built like an athlete. Strong, broad-shouldered . . . [*Brief pause.*] Do you like athletes, little wife?

SIGNORA [*after a pause; in a burst of desperation*]. "Wife, wife" . . . why do you insist on claiming for yourself a woman like me . . . a . . . a whore . . . ? I'm *not* your wife. [*Sorrowfully.*] Why do you continue to humiliate yourself? . . . You've already done too much for me by taking me off the streets . . .

PROFESSOR [*without turning around*]. It's I who's indebted to you. [*Turning around slowly to her as she stares at him with curiosity.*] The whole world is one big screwing. [*He stares at her, explains.*] They wouldn't part with the ten thousand-lire for the registration if I didn't give them something in return; something which is mine by law . . . "my wife!" [*Pointing to where* FORTUNATO *is headed.*] His gait is confident, you see. He's happy. He's had his boss's "wife." Now with some luck he'll get another. He has found a pleasant, steady profession. He goes to meet the great adventure . . . [*Ironic, loftily.*] Will he fill the great void in the life of a desperate woman? Will he change someone's fate? [*Shrugging.*] For us, what's important is the ten thousand lire of today and the percentage of tomorrow. For him, the new industry: the AMERICAN WOMAN . . .

THE CURTAIN FALLS

THE RETURN

A One Act Play

by MARIO FRATTI

1960

THE RETURN[1]

English version by Robert W. Corrigan and Mario Fratti

CHARACTERS

SYLVIA, *the fiancée; in her thirties—reserved and soft-spoken; she is resigned and gentle*

MASO, *the friend; in his late thirties—pale, sensitive; he gives the impression he is hiding from something; he has a nervous way of speaking—quickly*

THE MOTHER; *in her late fifties; thin, frail; her eyes are sad but her smile is that of a child; she moves with grace*

THE ESCORT; *same age as* MASO *but he seems at least ten years older; mature, tall, a man of integrity; reserved and dignified*

THE SISTER'S VOICE

[1] Printed by permission of the author and Ninon Tallon Karlweis. Copyright © 1961 by Mario Fratti. All inquiries regarding rights to the plays of Mario Fratti should be addressed to Robert Lantz, 111 West 57th Street, N.Y.C. 10019.

[*A dimly-lit room with a lighted hallway at the rear. There is a door Stage Right, and next to it a low window which faces a small but typical town-piazza. On the window-sill there are several flowering plants.*

One can distinguish an old cupboard, a table with freshly cut flowers, toys, and notebooks, two chairs with jackets hanging on the backs.

The fianceé, SYLVIA, *is seated at Stage Left, embroidering her wedding dress.*

After a few moments we see MASO'S *face outside, nervously looking into the room.*]

MASO [*unable to see clearly*]. Sylvia, are you there?

SYLVIA. Be careful with the flowers.

MASO. What are you doing in the dark?

SYLVIA. I'm embroidering. Be quiet. She's in the next room.

MASO. May I come in?

SYLVIA. You'd better not. You'll ruin the plants.

MASO. Just for a moment. Then we'll go.

SYLVIA. Not today. You know who's returning.

MASO. More reason to get out. There'll be tears, scenes. Let me in.

[SYLVIA *does not move.*]

If you don't open the door, I'll come through the window. [*He threatens to ruin the plants.*]

[SYLVIA *gets up wearily and opens the door,* MASO *enters the room. He is nervous and throughout the play he will smoke continually.*]

MASO [*trying to kiss her*]. Please, just one small kiss . . . [*She tries to avoid him.*] What's wrong with you?

SYLVIA [*trying to avoid him*]. Not today. Please don't insist.

MASO [*glancing around the room*]. All these flowers—this darkness . . . It's depressing. [*Indicating the lighted hallway.*] Is she in there? [SYLVIA *nods.*] I'll turn the light on. [*He turns the light on and looks around impatiently. He leafs through the notebooks, touches the toys, but avoids the two jackets with repugnance, unable to conceal his horror.*] She has dragged everything out . . . It looks like a circus. What are you doing?

SYLVIA. Can't you see?

MASO. Your wedding dress?

SYLVIA. Yes.

MASO. The—the old one?

SYLVIA. I'm fixing it. I couldn't throw it away.

MASO [*pacing nervously*]. . . . with that madwoman always in our way . . . [*He stops, looks at her with supplication; pleads.*] We have to get away from here.

SYLVIA. Not today.

MASO. Are you waiting for him here?

SYLVIA. Yes. And you should too. It would please her. [*She nods toward the hallway.*]

MASO. No, not me! Let's go away. I beg you . . . [*He succeeds in sneaking in a kiss.*]

SYLVIA. Please, Maso . . . She's in there. You know how she always watches us. Even when she pretends to ignore us.

MASO [*nervous*]. I know. That look frightens me too.

SYLVIA. Remember what she's been through, and what she's still going through. Today for instance. She was up at dawn. She arranged everything herself—the flowers, the toys, the clothes. She even dragged out the notebooks from his elementary school—God knows where she found them. Everything is in perfect order—even his suit. And you'll see—she's in her best Sunday dress . . . It frightens me too . . . And the questions she asks all the time . . .

MASO [*running his hands through his hair*]. Don't talk to me about her questions. It can drive you crazy . . .—"Did he brush his teeth?"—"Did he laugh?"—"Did he cry?"—"Did he talk about me?" Every chance she gets! If we don't leave this place she'll destroy us.

SYLVIA. Today she's going to "see him." She'll be convinced. She needs us now. If we left her, it would kill her.

MASO. Does she ask questions about us?

SYLVIA. Never.

MASO. I'm sure she knows.

SYLVIA. I'm not so sure. She deliberately ignores it. There's never a word, never a reproach.

MASO. Doesn't she suspect that we meet?

SYLVIA. She never asks. Once or twice I started to tell her but she refused to listen. She's always so lost in her own thoughts . . .

MASO. Her look is so severe, so cold . . . [*With anguish.*] I'd give anything to get away from this nightmare. We must tell her the truth.

SYLVIA. We may have our chance today. After "the return."

MASO. Just remember. We're not getting any younger. We can't let her ruin our lives . . .

[*The* MOTHER *appears silently from the hallway upstage. She is not wearing black; tragedy has not changed the gentle sweetness of her face.*]

MOTHER [*to* MASO]. Thank you for coming. Who's at the station?

MASO [*uneasy*]. Friends, banners . . .

MOTHER. How many banners?

MASO [*embarrassed*]. . . . . two.

MOTHER. And how many friends?

MASO. Many more . . . All wearing political badges . . . Even the Mayor is there. And the newspaper-boy.

[*The* MOTHER *is proud. Her eyes glitter like those of a happy child.*]

MASO. The headline of "the return" is marked in red. Everybody is buying the paper.

MOTHER [*with pride and satisfaction*]. They all love him . . . Everybody will claim him . . . [*Bitterly.*] They'll fight over him . . .

MASO. It's true. Even the priest is there. And the lawyer Lorenzo.

MOTHER. How many—would you say?

MASO. How many what?

MOTHER. Friends.

MASO [*embarrassed because they are not many*]. . . . about ten. [*Seeing that the* MOTHER *is disappointed.*] It's a bad hour. People are at work . . .

MOTHER. When will they arrive here? [*She gestures toward the window.*]

MASO [*looking at his watch*]. Any minute now. Shall I go and meet them?

MOTHER [*sharply*]. No! [*More gently.*] Stay here. Did you see all his things? [*She points to them.*] This is his best jacket . . . [*She carresses it lovingly.*] . . . the last one he bought before he went into the Army . . . his hunting-boots . . . [*She bends and picks them up.*] Did he ever tell you about the hunting he did?

MASO [*with embarrassment*]. No, he didn't . . . With all the problems we had . . . He never mentioned hunting.

MOTHER. This is his first pipe. At eighteen he was already smoking a pipe . . . He didn't have the courage to show

it to me . . . I found others later on. Did he have one in
the camp?

MASO [on guard]. He made one but he couldn't use it. It didn't
work. I told you. We gladly traded any gold we might have
for a cigarette or a leaf of tobacco. I gave them my watch
. . . I don't remember what he had. I don't think he had
any gold on him.

MOTHER. "Smoke and food together"—you said. "To keep
warm." [Pointing to SYLVIA.] Sylvia asked me about it the
other day. She did not understand what you meant. Explain it to her . . .

MASO [reluctantly]. We used to take a mouthful of smoke
and an ounce of black bread . . . We kept it in our mouth
without chewing—as long as possible—until it dissolved.
To keep our stomachs warm.

SYLVIA. Was your bread black like ours?

MASO. Yours was white by comparison.

MOTHER. These are his notebooks . . . [She picks them up,
turns the pages.] His first drawings—a ship, a mouse, an
apple . . . Did he notice the children who were at the
camp? Did he ever talk to them?

MASO. We didn't see much of them. He spoke very little. To
save his strength. He didn't look at them. It was too painful. To avoid suffering, he tried to ignore them.

SYLVIA [looking up from her work]. How old were those
children?

MASO. The youngest one I saw was twenty-six months.[2] Pregnant women were taken to the gas chamber at once.

SYLVIA. Were the children separated from their parents?

MASO. Yes. In our block alone there were four thousand
children. They were unable to work. Consequently they
were under "special treatment."

[The two WOMEN continue to look at him, waiting for details.]

MOTHER. Tell Sylvia about it.

MASO [nervously]. A nightmare . . . The parents usually gave
their children whatever jewels, rings or gold they had. When
the time of the "special treatment" came . . . I remember
a little girl—she was a skeleton covered with tears and
blood— . . . In their haste to steal her earring—the Nazis
ripped her ear open. It was bleeding like . . . [He does not
find words.]

[2] Page 231 of The Tragedy of the Deportation. Testimonies of the Survivors.
Hachette, Paris.

MOTHER [*moved*]. Did Enrico see that? What did he do?

MASO. He didn't see it. He was in another block . . .

MOTHER [*turning to* SYLVIA]. He must have talked to you about children . . .

SYLVIA [*bent over her work, with tears in her eyes*]. Yes.

MOTHER. What did he say? Did he want to have many children?

SYLVIA. . . . at least two or three. He used to tease me . . .

MOTHER [*participating, curious*]. Why?

SYLVIA. My family has only girls.

MOTHER. That's true. I remember now. He always wanted boys. What did he tell you? Did he make plans for their future?

SYLVIA [*uneasy*]. Not really . . . Only about their education. He wanted them to be good students.

MASO. And yet when you were sent to a concentration camp, only a man with a trade had some hope to survive.

[*The two* WOMEN *look at him with curiosity.*]

They were able to resist longer. Those with strong backs, accustomed to hard labor: bricklayers, ditchdiggers, peasants with strong hands. Or those who had a particular trade—like mechanics or tailors. I want my son to be a tailor. They were all able to survive. . . . almost all.

MOTHER [*severe, with authority*]. They will be no more wars! No more concentration camps!

MASO [*apologetic*]. I didn't mean that. Don't think I . . . [*He points to* SYLVIA *with the intention of bringing in their future.*] Even Sylvia wants her son to study. We'll teach him a trade just in case . . . [*There is a pause. The* MOTHER *turns to face the window, and does not listen to him.* MASO *continues.*] Sylvia wants *our* son to . . .

MOTHER. Sshhh! [*She points toward the window.*] He's coming.

[*They listen. There is no sound from outside.*]

MASO. I'll go to meet them.

MOTHER [*sharply*]. No! We'll wait in the house, *all of us.* [*She includes him in her gesture.*]

MASO [*timidly*]. I doubt if they'll stop here . . . [*He points toward the window.*] They'll just pass by on their way to the church . . .

[*Footsteps are heard approaching from the piazza—Stage
Left. The tolling of the death-knell.* SYLVIA *joins* MASO *and
reaches for his hand. They stand behind the* MOTHER, *looking beyond the window, solemn and moved.*]

MOTHER [*with anguish*]. How small—that box! My child! My
poor child! [*She leaves Stage Right, to meet "the return" of
her son: a small box containing his ashes.*]

SYLVIA [*after a silence, as she clings to* MASO]. Why is it so
small?

MASO. It's only the ashes . . . They are not even his.

SYLVIA. How do you know?

MASO. Thousands . . . all together . . .

SYLVIA. It's hard to believe . . . So young, so full of life . . .
It's terrible, Maso . . .

MASO [*almost to himself*]. The small box gave her the real
shock! I was afraid her reaction would be worse . . . She
keeps talking about him as if he were still alive . . . She even
refused his pension.

SYLVIA. But she didn't refuse the medal and the money they
give with it.

MASO [*with irony*]. How generous! Five thousand lire a year!

SYLVIA. Even heroes who survived get the same amount. The
value of a medal is symbolic . . . [*She sizes up the room
with greed.*] She *has* some money . . . She owns this house
and spends nothing on herself . . . [*Looking at* MASO.]
She said it would be mine some day. "Ours," I mean.

MASO [*with anger*]. Oh no! We must get out of here! We must
go!

SYLVIA. She won't let us.

MASO [*in an outburst of defiance*]. And who is she? Who does
she think she is?

SYLVIA [*slowly*]. The mother of the man who was my . . .

MASO. Fiancé! That's an old story, that's the past! She is not
your mother. She can't force you to wait, to die here!

SYLVIA [*staring at him*]. You're afraid of her too . . . [*Noticing the irony in* MASO's *expression.*] . . . perhaps it's pity.
You never contradicted her when she pretended that he
was still alive, when she pretended to believe that he would
return . . .

MASO [*with determination*]. But now I will. I'll talk openly.
He's really dead now. [*Pointing to the clothes.*] I've had
enough of this masquerade. I'm going to tell her right away

... [*Weakening.*] ... very soon. So we can leave this
place forever!

SYLVIA. I'm going to her now. She's waiting for me.

[*The* ESCORT *enters silently, without warning. His face cannot
be seen clearly. He could be mistaken for the dead son.
His mysterious appearance is frightening. After a moment,
the stranger steps forward, where we can see him.* SYLVIA
and MASO *realize he is not Enrico.*]

ESCORT [*to win* SYLVIA'S *confidence*]. You must be Sylvia
... I suppose ... [*He offers his hand.*]

SYLVIA [*offering her hand uncertainly*]. Yes I'm Sylvia. And
you?

ESCORT [*evading the question*]. Who is the gentleman? [*He
nods toward* MASO. *He is trying to find out how much he
can say, how freely he can speak.*]

SYLVIA. My fiancé.

[*After a moment of surprise, the two* MEN *shake hands.*]

ESCORT. How do you do?

MASO. How do you do.

ESCORT [*hesitating*]. I don't know if I can speak freely ...
[*Deciding to go ahead.*] You see ... I'm here on *his* behalf.

MASO [*astonished, frightened*]. On *whose* behalf?

ESCORT. *His.* I escorted him in the train. [*A tense pause.*]

SYLVIA. You mean—you knew him?

[*The* ESCORT *is silent. He feels that* MASO'S *presence prevents
him from speaking openly.*]

SYLVIA [*noticing his reticence*]. You speak. They were
friends. Maso knows everything.

ESCORT [*more at ease*]. May I sit down?

SYLVIA. Of course! [*When the stranger is seated.*] You say
you knew him?

ESCORT. We were in the same camp.

[SYLVIA *looks at* MASO; *she wants some confirmation.* MASO
indicates with a gesture to let the stranger continue.]

SYLVIA. What year was that?

ESCORT [*smiling at her understandable skepticism and suspicion*]. He arrived in February nineteen forty-four.

[SYLVIA *looks at* MASO *again. The date is correct. She wants*
MASO *to tell the stranger that he was in the same camp.
But* MASO *refuses. He wants to study the situation first.*]

SYLVIA [*to encourage the* ESCORT *to speak*]. Why did you say:
—"On *his* behalf?"

ESCORT. In a way. I knew him well. I even helped him.

[SYLVIA *and* MASO *stiffen, fearing some absurd blackmail.*]

[*Noticing their distrust.*] He couldn't have written about
me because we never met . . . [*He feels he has made things
worse.*]

MASO [*impatient, suspicious*]. Go on.

ESCORT [*with frankness*]. I belonged to a special Committee.
I was a "*Lagerschreiber.*" A kind of "clerk." It was our
job to save as many prisoners as possible, especially political ones . . . the so-called "red triangles." [*To* SYLVIA.]
Your . . . [*He pauses.*]

MASO [*volunteering*]. Fiancé.

ESCORT [*grateful for the help, more relieved*]. Thank you. [*To*
SYLVIA]. He belonged to a Political Party.

SYLVIA. Yes I know.

ESCORT. Antifascist of course. They were the most persecuted.
Selected for special experiments: insemination of disease,
immersion in freezing water, intravenous injections of ben-
zine . . . They were marked with two "n's"—"*Nacht und
Nebel*"—"Night and Fog." Which meant annihilation in
three months. We helped them all we could.

SYLVIA. Who is "we?"

ESCORT. We worked in the "*Schreibstube*"—the office that kept
records of the deceased. There were those among us who
knew foreign languages. Engineers, jurists, musicians. We
were the first to organize a nucleus of Resistance, and we
decided to save those who were most in danger: men in
politics—dedicated men who would be needed at the right
moment . . .

SYLVIA. And what about Enrico?

ESCORT. He was singled out the first time by Dr. Mengele—
one of the most ferocious Nazis. That was in April 1944.
We saved him. Then again in June; we hid him in the infirmary. Unfortunately he didn't live to see the Liberation.

SYLVIA. How did he die?

ESCORT. "*Sonder Behandlung.*"—"Special Treatment." The gas
chamber . . . Together with four thousand gypsies and
invalids . . . in August.

SYLVIA [*with horror*]. Is it true that . . . those ashes aren't his?

ESCORT [*without looking at her*]. It's possible. Who can tell?

SYLVIA [*accusing*]. Then what did *you* do for him? What did any of you do? [*She turns to* MASO *as well, including him in her accusation.*]

ESCORT [*apologetic, confused*]. Very little I admit. You don't know what kind of hell, you can't possibly imagine. When we could we saved the weakest from hard labor. A permit for "*Schonung*"—enforced rest—meant salvation for many . . .

SYLVIA [*with bitter accusation*]. But you, why were you privileged to stay in that office and come out of it alive?

ESCORT [*humbly*]. I was fortunate, I know. I was an interpreter. I knew a little German, some French . . . I translated Molière to an officer who loved the theatre, I even organized a gypsy orchestra for him. I'm a musician. [*Wringing his hands.*] It wasn't easy for us either . . . [*Reliving the past with anguish.*] At six in the morning we were at the gate ordered to play lively music for the prisoners on their way to work . . . They had to march with heads up. A grotesque procession. They had to walk for miles . . . We were in the "office"—counting the shoes piled up in the carrion deposit, taking inventory of eyeglasses and wedding rings. The Germans are famous for their scrupulous exactitude. . . . We also made tattoos. We saved Enrico twice by giving him a different number. We weren't supposed to go beyond 200,000. When a political prisoner was on the condemned list we waited for someone to die in the infirmary so we could send the corpse instead.

SYLVIA [*with humility, regretting her unjust accusation*]. Thank you . . .

ESCORT. Enrico had only one thing against him, poor boy . . . [*The* TWO *wait anxiously; there is a silence.*] It wasn't his fault, though . . . [*Looking at* SYLVIA.] He had three gold teeth.

SYLVIA. Yes, it's true. [*With curiosity.*] But what difference could that make?

ESCORT. No one with gold teeth could be saved. By November 1944, seventeen tons of gold had been already collected.[3]

SYLVIA [*with horror*]. How monstrous!

ESCORT. It was an inferno. Three and a half million men were killed there.

MASO. Two and a half million.

[3] *Tragedy of the Deportation*, page 442. —". . . recuperated from their victims—between the time the crematories began to function and the time they ceased to function in November, 1944—17 tons of precious gold metal."

ESCORT [*surprised at this correction; slowly*]. That was what
the Nazi Commander said in self-defense:—"ONLY two
and a half million . . ." The exact number will never be
known . . . I saw them die—by the flocks. It was endless
. . . In the beginning of 1943 I was forced to help build
the Bunker twins: crematories two and three. They were
inaugurated by burning eight thousand Jews from Poland.
Forty-six ovens could liquidate twenty-five thousand people
a day.

MASO [*correcting the* ESCORT *again*]. Twelve thousand people
a day—in that block.

[*The* ESCORT *looks at him suspiciously, wondering how he
would know so many details.*]

ESCORT. How do you . . . ?

SYLVIA [*intervening at last*]. He was there.

ESCORT. At Auschwitz–Birkenau?

MASO. Yes, I was at Auschwitz–Birkenau. The man who organized that gypsy orchestra was Captain Broad.

ESCORT. Broad, yes . . . [*With a mixture of diffidence and
suspicion.*] Why didn't you say so before?

MASO. I like to listen. I was reliving that nightmare . . .

ESCORT. Where did they capture you?

MASO [*evasively*]. I worked for some time in D.A.W. Siemens,
then at Buna for I.G. Farben. One day I spilled some paint
by mistake. They made the usual accusation: sabotage!

ESCORT. What was your job at the camp?

MASO. "*Sonderkommando*" of the Crematories. Under orders
of the top murderer: Mohl.

ESCORT [*with disgust*] The "Blood-Thirsty Baby." I never
saw him, but his very name brought terror to everyone.
You're probably one of the few who saw him and can
give an account of his crimes.

MASO [*to* SYLVIA]. He was blond, handsome. He had a baby
face. The two things he loved most were: his family and
flowers.

ESCORT. What unit were you in?

MASO. The barbers'. We sent the hair to the mills for weaving.

ESCORT [*trying to remember*]. With Supervisor Klein. I can
still see him. [*He taps his forehead.*] He used to bring
large cartons of Zyklon B[4] and went back with carloads
of hair.

[4] The gas used to eliminate deportees who were unable to work. Made at
Dessau.

MASO. He was Pierre's protector. Did you know him?

ESCORT. I knew him.

MASO [to SYLVIA]. This Supervisor Klein saved Pierre, a French boy, only because he had an obscene tattoo on his back.

ESCORT. Our lives hung by a thread. If they liked the color of your eyes . . . If you knew a foreign language . . .

MASO. As in your case.

SYLVIA [horrified]. I'm going to Church now. They're waiting for me.

[SYLVIA leaves with relief. There is a pause. The TWO MEN stare at each other in silence.]

ESCORT. You were fortunate. There were nine hundred of you in the *Sonderkommando*. Two hundred were sent to the gas chamber on the seventh of September. Five hundred were shot on the seventh of October. The rest left November 27 for an unknown destination.

MASO. You really know every detail—even the dates. I was among them. I managed to escape.

ESCORT [slowly]. Those dates are unforgettable. Especially in the last months . . .

[They look at each other with caution and suspicion.]

MASO. What about you? How did you get away?

ESCORT. I helped them burn the records, the photographs. Then I went to the K.B., the Hospital.[5] They gave precedence to the Crematories—wanting to destroy every last trace. There was no time left to assassinate us.

MASO. They were nightmarish hours. I had almost forgotten . . . [Confidentially, looking around.] Even though the torture hasn't ended for me in this house.

ESCORT [looking at him with surprise and curiosity]. What do you mean?

MASO. I knew Enrico since we were children. His mother gives me no peace. Questions, questions . . . She persecutes us both, me and Sylvia, with endless questions. Not out of jealousy, no! [Trying to explain.] We became engaged only recently, living a hell with those questions from his mother . . .

ESCORT [trying to justify her]. She's a mother . . .

MASO. She'll do the same with you; you'll see. She'll ask you a thousand different questions.

[5] K.B.—*Kranken Bau* (Ersatz for a dirty infirmary).

ESCORT. But I didn't know him personally.

MASO. She'll ask you all the same . . . Why are you here? [*He looks questioningly, with renewed distrust.*]

ESCORT. I kept putting it off. When it was all over and I returned I couldn't believe I had friends again, a bed, all the bread I wanted, all the cigarettes . . .

MASO. We traded our last potato for a cigarette—only to die a little later of starvation. It was terrible. No one can believe it. [*He lights another cigarette from the butt of the one he has been smoking. He is very nervous.*]

ESCORT. I don't quite dare return to normality. When I wake up in the morning—even now—I kiss the pillow, the clean sheet . . . And I think of those we left there . . . Poor Enrico—I can still see him—those sad eyes . . . His was a very tragic case. Almost unique . . .

MASO. Why?

ESCORT. If only he hadn't had those gold teeth . . .

MASO [*impudently*]. There were many who had gold teeth.

ESCORT. Yes, but . . .

MASO [*with curiosity*]. What?

ESCORT [*slowly*]. Not everybody knew who had them. There were some who pulled out their own . . . And no one had confidants or close friends who might inform . . .

MASO. That's true.

ESCORT. None trusted anybody. Even the existence of our Committee was known only to a very few. Perhaps not even you . . .

MASO [*confirming this*]. I was told about it later.

ESCORT. When some fortunate individual was taken off the death list, he thought it was Providence, or some miracle.

MASO. No one could guess that some of you had the courage to organize . . . No one shared secrets, exchanged opinions. We hardly spoke to one another. We watched every word, we saved every sigh . . .

ESCORT. And we're alive, now. What's your name?

MASO. Maso Cimmi. I was born in 1923.

ESCORT. And I in 1922. I look much older.

MASO. With all we went through . . .

[*A* WOMAN'S VOICE *is heard calling from outside, with insistence.*]

SISTER'S VOICE. Tommi! . . . Tommi! . . . TOMMI! . . .

[*The* ESCORT *leaps to his feet. His face takes on a menacing terrible expression. Surprise and hatred transform the lines of his face.* MASO *who was about to answer the call, is terrified by this sudden transformation and is almost speechless.*]

MASO [*disturbed, in a low voice*]. It's my sister.

[*The* ESCORT *seizes him by the neck.*]

ESCORT. That's who you are! *You're* "Tommi the Jackal!"

SISTER'S VOICE [*nearer the window*]. Tommi! They're all waiting in the Church! Come, Tommi!

ESCORT. Tell her you're going. [*Commanding.*] Answer her!

MASO [*to his sister, in a half-suffocated voice*]. I'm coming . . . right away.

[*The* SISTER *leaves. The* ESCORT *forces* MASO *to his knees, and holds him there, by the neck.*]

ESCORT. Maso, Tommaso, Tommi . . . I hadn't thought of that. *You* are "Tommi the Jackal!" [*With slow emphasis.*] *I came for you!* We knew he had been betrayed by someone from his town . . . [*Unable to convince himself.*] You the "Jackal" . . . [*With fury, as he realizes.*] And you visit his mother . . . You caress his fiancée . . .

MASO [*almost choking*]. No . . . No . . . I—I assure you that . . .

ESCORT. "Tommi" . . . That was all we knew. I could have believed anything but that you would be living in his house. Doesn't it haunt you? *It was YOU who killed him!*

MASO [*struggling*]. It's not true, no . . . You know it isn't true . . . You—you're the only one who can understand. You know what it was like! It was hell!

ESCORT. Dirty traitors like you made it even worse.

MASO. Let me explain, I beg you . . .

[*The* ESCORT *releases his grip, but forces* MASO *to remain on his knees.*]

You know, you saw what they gave him the last day: fifteen blows with the whip. He was in the "Himmelfahrt Block"[6]—which meant sure death. There was *no* hope! They would have sent him to the gas chamber in any case.

[6] "*Himmelfahrt* Block" means: "group of prisoners ready for a trip to Heaven."

His body—you must have seen it—it was an open wound . . .

ESCORT. It was *you* who knew about his gold teeth: it was *you* who informed! A friend of the family, from the same town . . .

MASO. It wasn't only me! I wasn't the only one who knew . . .

ESCORT. But you didn't hesitate to go *first*. And you sold him for three cigarettes.

MASO [*with difficulty*]. You're right. I did go first . . . You know how a cigarette can help when you're bleeding, exhausted . . . It was like a transfusion of energy, of strength for our bodies . . .

ESCORT. For three R.6 cigarettes.

MASO. You know the brand too. You know everything. I remember—the Commander letting them fall out of his cigarette case . . . It was the end for Enrico. He couldn't have survived. I shortened his agony.

ESCORT. And as a reward you're taking his fiancée.

MASO [*ignoring*]. . . . . In my case—it could have been that cigarette which saved me . . . [*With desperation, as he relives the past.*] Somebody else would have spoken, if I hadn't . . . Why should someone else get those cigarettes? A stranger—someone who meant nothing to him?

[*The* ESCORT *slaps his face.*]

I—I swear to you . . . You're the only one who can understand . . . Only you! I always did the best I could—for all of them . . . You know what fear and terror held us— you know how they degraded us, dehumanized us . . . Yet I tried . . . I really did . . . [MASO *regains some courage, determined to defend himself at all cost.*] For instance— when the Jews hid their babies under their clothes—the clothes that were seized as they entered the gas chambers, it was I who consoled them and helped them! Yes, me! I even went *inside* to reassure them—at my own risk! They could have locked me in there, forgetting me . . .

ESCORT [*pulls* MASO *to his feet and looks straight at him with contempt and disgust*]. You must leave this house forever.

MASO [*relieved, with sincerity*]. I promise! Yes, forever!

ESCORT. Your presence here is an insult. You must leave at once, disappear!

MASO [*with relief, not daring to believe his ears*]. You're right! Of course!

[*The* MOTHER *enters quietly, unnoticed. They see her. They freeze immediately. There is a silence. The* ESCORT *is embarrassed and tries to find a way to explain the dispute, the position in which she found them.*]

ESCORT. I am . . .

MOTHER [*cordially*]. Sylvia told me. You're most welcome here. [*A silence.*]

ESCORT [*confused and embarrassed, alluding to* MASO]. We were having a—an argument. He made a remark in defense of the Nazis. Imagine, we were in the same concentration camp . . .

MOTHER [*to* MASO]. I want you to go to Church now. They're waiting for you.

[MASO *sneaks out of the room quickly, relieved to get away. The* MOTHER'S *face is now relaxed, softer.*]

Sylvia knows nothing.

[*The* ESCORT *looks at her, not understanding. He is waiting for an explanation.*]

I was outside . . . I overheard . . . [*She looks at him maternally, serenely; then she says—clearly and slowly—*] I always knew.

ESCORT [*stunned*]. You always *knew*? Knew *what*?

MOTHER [*without hatred, resigned*]. Everything . . . That it was he who betrayed Enrico.

[*The* ESCORT *is speechless. His face shows both shock and remorse for having disturbed the tragic equilibrium of this family. The* MOTHER *speaks very gently, slowly.*]

But I need him anyway. He and Sylvia are the only ones who shared with Enrico hours and days that weren't mine. They are the only ones who can tell me about him . . . I see him in their eyes when they talk about him . . . I see him living . . . I feel he's alive . . . Those moments are the most beautiful in my life . . . I might even give Sylvia to him . . . perhaps . . . [*With a tired gesture.*] And this house of mine . . . later . . .

CURTAIN

All the remarks concerning the camp of Auschwitz–Birkenau are taken from testimonies that correspond to absolute fact.

THE WRITERS AND THEIR PLAYS

PIRANDELLO, LUIGI—1867–1936 (publication dates).
Scamandra, 1910; The Vise, 1913; Sicilian Limes, 1913; If Not
Thus, 1915; Liola, 1916; Think It Over, Jimmy, 1916; Right
You Are (If You Think So), 1916; At the Gate, 1916; The
Pleasure of Honesty, 1917; Cap and Bells, 1917; Grafting, 1917;
The Game as He Played It, 1918; He Didn't Mean It, 1918;
Man, Beast, and Virtue, 1919; All for the Best, 1920; Floriani's
Wife, 1920; Signora Morli, 1920; One and Two, 1920; By
Judgment of the Court, 1920; The Other's Reason, 1921; Six
Characters in Search of an Author, 1921; The Mock Emperor
(Enrico IV), 1922; Naked, 1922; The Life I Gave You, 1923;
The Man with the Flower in His Mouth, 1923; Each in His
Own Way, 1924; Our Lord of the Ship, 1925; The House with
the Column, 1925; The Jar, 1925; Diana and Tuda, 1926;
Friendship of Women, 1927; The New Colony, 1928; Lazarus,
1929; One's or Nobody's, 1929; As You Desire Me, 1930; To-
night We Improvise, 1930; The Phantoms, 1931; Finding One-
self, 1932; One Knows Not How, 1935; The Mountain Giants,
1958. (In addition, these undated but post-1913 plays: The
Doctor's Duty, Chee-chee, The Imbecile.)

BETTI, UGO—1892–1953 (publication dates).
The Mistress, 1927; La Donna sullo Scudo, 1927; The House on
the Water, 1929; L'Isola Meravigliosa, 1930; A Hotel on the
Waterfront, 1933; Landslide at North Station, 1936; The Duck
Hunter, 1937; A Beautiful Day in September, 1937; I Nostri
Sogni, 1937; Summertime, 1942; Night in the House of a Rich
Man, 1942; The Deluge, 1943; Night Wind, 1945; Inspection,
1947; Husband and Wife, 1947; Favola di Natale, 1948; Cor-
ruption in the Palace of Justice, 1949; Struggle Until Dawn,
1949; Irene the Innocent, 1950; Spiritism in the Old House,
1950; Crime on Goat Island, 1950; The Queen and the Rebels,
1951; The Gambler, 1951; The Inquisition, 1952; The Burnt
Flowerbed, 1953; The Fugitives, 1953.

DE FILIPPO, EDUARDO—1900–   (publication dates).
Chi è cchiú felice 'e me? 1932; Ditegli sempre si, 1932; Sik,
Sik, l'artifice magico, 1932; L'abito nuovo (with Luigi Piran-

dello), 1936; Uno coi capelli bianchi, 1938; Non ti pago! 1941; Io, l'erede, 1942; Natalie in casa Cupiello, 1943; Questi fantasmi, 1946; Le bugie con le gambe lunghe, 1948; Le voci di dentro, 1949; Napoli milionaria! 1950; Le grande magia, 1950; La paura numero uno, 1951; Amicizia, 1956; Mia famiglia, 1956; Bene mio e core mio, 1956; Filumena Marturano, A Mother's a Mother, 1964; Oh, These Ghosts! 1964.

FRATTI, MARIO—1927—   (completion dates).
The Doorbell, 1957; A, 1957; The Lie, 1958; The Coffin, 1958; Waiting, 1958; The Third Daughter, 1959; The Refusal, 1959; The Match, 1959; The Suicide, 1959; The Moroccan Dagger, 1960; The Return, 1960; The Cage, 1961; White Cat, 1961; The Academy, 1962; The Spies, 1962; Mafia, 1963; The Gift, 1963; The Refrigerators, 1964; The Seducers, 1964; The Wish, 1965; Treasons, 1965; Rescues, 1966; The Bridge, 1966; The Victim, 1966; The Roman Quest, 1967; Eleonora Duse, 1967.

SELECTED BIBLIOGRAPHY

General

BENTLEY, ERIC (Editor), *The Genius of the Italian Theater*, New York, 1964.
MACCLINTOCK, LANDER, *The Age of Pirandello*, Bloomington, Indiana, 1951.
Tulane Drama Review, "Post-War Italian Theatre" Issue, Vol. 8, No. 3, 1964.

Pirandello

BENTLEY, ERIC, *In Search of Theater*, New York, 1953.
BRUSTEIN, ROBERT, *The Theatre of Revolt*, Boston, 1964.
FERGUSSON, FRANCIS, *The Idea of a Theater*, Princeton, 1949.
KRUTCH, J. W., *"Modernism" in Modern Drama*, Ithaca, N. Y., 1953.
VITTORINI, DOMENICO, *The Drama of Luigi Pirandello*, New York, 1957.

Betti

CORRIGAN, ROBERT W., "Five Dramas of Selfhood," *New Theatre of Europe I*, New York, 1962.
MCWILLIAM, G. H., "Introduction" to *Crime on Goat Island*, San Francisco, 1961.
———, "Introduction" to *Three Plays on Justice*, San Francisco, 1964.
RIZZO, GINO, "Regression–Progression In Ugo Betti's Drama," *Tulane Drama Review*, Vol. 8, No. 1, 1963.
Tulane Drama Review, "Betti Issue," Vol. 5, No. 2, 1960.

De Filippo

ACTON, HAROLD, "Eduardo De Filippo," *The London Magazine*, June, 1962.
BENTLEY, ERIC, *In Search of Theater*, New York, 1953.

Fratti

CORRIGAN, ROBERT W., "The Disavowal of Identity in the Contemporary Theatre," *New Theatre of Europe II*, New York, 1964.
Italian Theatre Review, "Fratti Issue," Rome, March, 1964.